£20-00

CW00801347

£20-00

The Ottoman Steam Navy

Orhaniye
1897.
Güleryüz

The
Ottoman Steam Navy
1828 – 1923

Bernd Langensiepen
&
Ahmet Güleryüz

Edited & Translated by
James Cooper

CONWAY
MARITIME PRESS

First published in Great Britain in 1995 by
Conway Maritime Press,
an imprint of Brassey's (UK) Ltd,
33 John Street,
London WC1N 2AT

British Library Cataloguing in Publication data
Langensiepen, Bernd
Ottoman Steam Navy: 1828-1923
I. Title II. Güleryüz, Ahmet
III. Cooper, James
359.00956

ISBN 0-85177-610-8

Designed and typeset by Trevor Ridley
Printed and bound in Great Britain by
The Bath Press, Bath

CONTENTS

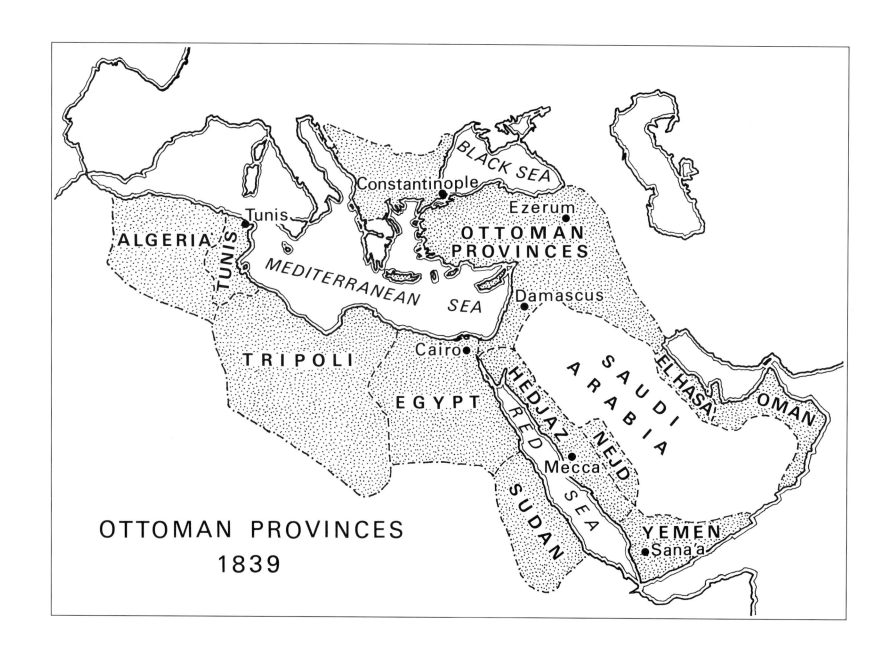

BLACK SEA

Constantinople

Tunis

Ezerum

ALGERIA

TUNIS

OTTOMAN
PROVINCES

MEDITERRANEAN

SEA

Damascus

TRIPOLI

Cairo

EGYPT

HEDJAZ

RED

SAUDI

ARABIA

ELHASA

OMAN

NEJD

SEA

Mecca

SUDAN

YEMEN

Sana'a

OTTOMAN PROVINCES
1839

The Ottoman Navy
1828 – 1923

The Ottoman Navy, 1828–1870

In the sixteenth century Ottoman shipbuilders had enjoyed a fine reputation, but the navy like the Empire had failed to keep up with the latest technology. Towards the end of the eighteenth century, foreign engineers and constructors began to take over the management of the İstanbul yards, and some improvement was soon apparent. Among these foreign technicians were the Swede Klensburg and the Frenchmen le Brun and Benois, who designed modern ships of the line which were then constructed in large numbers.

In 1805 work began on a major new dockyard on the Haliç in the Aynalikavak district; earlier, in 1792, Klensburg had constructed a drydock further up the Haliç, near the present Atatürk Bridge. A second drydock, large enough for the navy's biggest ships, was built in 1825, and in the succeeding years the space between these facilities and Aynalikavak was filled with new buildings for the navy's bureaucracy and the Divanhane, the Ottoman naval ministry.

The head of the navy was the Derya Kaptan, a position which combined the role of navy minister and fleet commander. Senior positions in the Ottoman state at this time were rarely secured by merit, bribery and personal contacts being more effective. Thus the Derya Kaptan at the time, Popuccu Ahmet Paşa, was a former shoemaker, who made little or no attempt to pretend he was carrying out his duties competently. He had as an adviser a British naval officer, Adolphus Slade, who managed to hold down the position for forty years, so he evidently came to terms with the limitations of Ottoman administration.

Traditionally, the best seamen had been drawn from the subject Greeks, but the War of Independence cut off this source of supply. The 1820s were thus a period of decline and contraction in the Ottoman navy, the officer corps being subject to the same corrupt methods of appointment as the administrators, while the conscript crews were treated with almost medieval brutality and given very little sea training. The intervention of the Great Powers in the Greek struggle ended for the Ottomans in the disastrous Battle of Navarino in 1827, when nearly all the major operational warships were lost.

Mahmut II ordered a new construction programme to rebuild the navy, and between 1827 and 1834 warships were laid down at Gemlik, İzmit and Sinop, as well as İstanbul. Skilled workmen were in short supply and foreigners had to be employed in senior positions in the new yards, while the workforce was made up of Albanians, Greeks and even ex-galley slaves. Of the imported specialists, a trio of Americans was to exert the greatest influence in the 1830s. The famous New York shipbuilder Henry Eckford came to İstanbul in 1831 to try to recoup his fortune after a financial débâcle at home. He brought one of his new 1,000-ton corvette-type ships, the *United States*, which he successfully sold to the Turkish navy as the *Mesir-i Ferah*. On the invitation of the Ottoman authorities, he then built a dispatch schooner, and began a 74-gun ship and a frigate for the navy before an illness caused his untimely death in November 1832. At the same time a second American, Charles Ross, was running the Aynalikavak yards, but the most influential of the three was Forster Rhodes.

Rhodes arrived in İstanbul in 1831 and quickly impressed the Derya Kaptan, who appointed him chief of construction at the navy yards, and under his direction a number of excellent warships were completed. He installed the first steam engines in the Ottoman Empire, at Aynalikavak in 1835, and as a next step planned to build steam-powered ships for the navy. However, this needed the express permission of the Sultan, and although Rhodes was supported by the Derya Kaptan, when he was approached about the scheme on 26 May 1836 at the launch of Rhodes's frigate *Nusretiye*, Mahmut II made it clear that he regarded steamships as little more than amusing toys. This was to change in the following year, with an unexpected turn of events. The Sultan was returning to İstanbul on the new frigate *Fevziye*, having been to İzmit to witness the launch, when the ship ran into a violent storm and would have been driven ashore if a British and an Austrian steamer had not been on hand to take the frigate in tow. With such potent firsthand evidence of the efficacy of steam, the Sultan was quick to give permission for a series of naval steamships. It is reasonable to assume that the design of these ships was attributable to Rhodes and Ross, although the latter is rarely mentioned in Ottoman records. Engines and boilers for these ships had to be imported from Great Britain, beginning a long commercial association between that country and the Ottoman navy.

The first steamship built within the Ottoman Empire was the *Eser-i Hayir*, launched at Aynalikavak on 24 November 1837. It was followed by *Mesir-i Bahri* and *Tahir-i Bahri,* which entered service in 1838–1839. The latter two were both listed officially as yachts for the new Sultan, Abdul Mecid, but although they were fitted with a saloon for the exclusive use of the Sultan, they were more commonly employed by senior government officials. Like so many early steamers, *Mesir-i Bahri*'s boilers had a short life and by 1841 the ship was laid up, and seldom went to sea thereafter.

The next step was to construct genuine warships powered by steam, and in 1846–1847 two pairs of steam frigates were laid down

The Ottoman screw ship of the line Mahmudiye, *taken from a postcard reproduction of an original illustration.* İstanbul Navy Museum

at İstanbul. *Taif, Saik-i Sadi* and *Feyza-i Bahri* were sister-ships, but *Mecidiye* was fitted as another yacht for the Sultan during the early stages of construction. The guns were of British manufacture, a sad reflection on the once-renowned Ottoman cannon foundries that could no longer keep up with the new technological standards. There was also a shortage of local experience with steam machinery, and so four engineers were engaged for each ship under a contract that required them to train Ottoman engineers and stokers.

After operating alongside British screw ships of the line during the Crimean War, the Ottoman navy was inspired to consider the conversion of the *Mahmudiye*, built in 1829 and still the largest sailing warship in the world. Engines and boilers were ordered from Britain, but on closer inspection it was discovered that the *Mahmudiye*'s wooden hull was rotten and not worth reconstruction. Instead the machinery replaced the worn out engines of the *Mubir-i Sürur*.

In 1856 the line of battle ships *Peyk-i Zafer* and *Kervan-i Bahri* were sent to Britain to have screw machinery installed, followed two years later by the *Şadiye* and *Fethiye*. There may have been some rationale for the money spent on these ships, but it is more difficult to justify the conversion of the final group, *Kosovo, Ertuğrul* and *Hüdavandigar*, which were sent to Britain for similar treatment in 1864. By that date the armoured ship was well established in the major navies of the world, and the Ottoman Empire had begun work on the ironclad frigates of the *Osmaniye* class, although a programme of wooden steam frigates was carried on in parallel.

Ottoman industrial development had been slow. In 1855 a factory at Zeytinburnu constructed the country's first steam boiler and a firm of British engineers set up an engine works at Aynalikavak. Both were fully employed during the Crimean War with repair and maintenance work on allied ships, and the workforce was steadily increased to cope with the flow of work. However, it was not until 1863 that the Aynalikavak works felt able to offer to design and construct a complete set of engines and boilers for a new warship. Even this was over-ambitious: the wooden screw frigate ordered for this machinery, the *Selimiye*, was not ready until 1870, and the machinery was always unreliable and prone to breakdown. This inglorious episode brought to an end the once-great tradition of Ottoman wooden shipbuilding.

Merchant shipping progressed no faster. The autocratic nature of the Ottoman state did not encourage individual enterprise, and centuries of commercial concessions to foreign firms left

the Empire's external trade in the hands of other nationalities. The coastal trade in Ottoman sailing craft survived, but the coming of the steamship, with the larger capital investment that these vessels implied, strengthened the position of foreign companies. There were no domestic shipping companies to call on, even for essential state requirements like troop transportation, and warships had to fill the role.

This task grew with the increasing logistical support required by modern armies and it occurred to some in authority that naval steamers might carry civilian passengers as well as military stores. In 1839 the *Sürat, Sagir, Peyk-i Şevket, Tahir-i Bahri* and *Mesir-i Bahri* were turned over to a new state concern called Tersane-i Amire, but since the ships were still officially warships, they only went to sea on the orders of the Derya Kaptan. As a result most voyages were on official business for senior government officials. Attempts were made to bring in commercial expertise, such as the franchise granted to the British sea captain John Count to run a service from İstanbul to İzmir using the *Peyk-i Şevket*, but prejudice ran high against Ottoman steamers and foreign competitors took most of the trade. Even a law compelling subjects of the Empire to use the new line failed, since most of the traffic consisted of foreign businessmen. Ottoman vessels had a poor reputation; for example, the famous Prussian soldier Von Moltke, then in Ottoman service, recorded a disastrous voyage on the *Sagir* in 1836, when the ship ran aground and was then subject to an explosion, caused by the inexperienced engineers over-pressurising the boiler.

The state company underwent a number of status changes, being removed from navy control and renamed successively Şirket-i Osmaniye and Şirket-i Mecidiye, but continued to make large losses. In 1843 the navy regained control, but a formal division between navy and merchant service was ordered by the Derya Kaptan, the state company being renamed yet again; its new title, Fevaidi Osmaniye, could be freely translated as 'bringer of Ottoman success'. Initially the company ran ferry services along the Bosporus with the occasional foray into the Black Sea, using the steamers *Eser-i Hayir, Seyf-i Bahri, Hümapervaz* and *Tahir-i Bahri*. These were under navy administration until the early death of the Derya Kaptan, when a Frenchman named Bonal was brought in as manager. He achieved little, except to make French the official language of the company, so that Ottoman captains needed a translator even to deal with their own officers; he was replaced by the far more effective Greek, John Avramidis. Once a corps of trained cabin staff had been introduced in 1847, services from İstanbul to Trabzon (Trebizond) and Selanik (Salonica) became very popular, to the point where in 1848 the steam frigates *Mecidiye* and *Taif* had to be drafted in to help out on the Samsun run. In 1854 the Bosporus ferry services were turned over to a new commercial concern, Şirket-i Hayriye, but the state shipping company remained under navy control until 1910.

For the navy, the succession of Abdul Aziz to the Ottoman throne on 20 April 1861 was potentially beneficial since he had been interested in naval affairs since his youth; he was also a frequent traveller on the yacht *Saik-i Sadi*, whose commander Binbaşı Vesim had convinced him of the value of a strong navy. However, as a second son, Abdul Aziz had not been prepared for the Sultanate (indeed, he was lucky to escape the usual fate of brothers of the Sultan-designate in the House of Osman – strangulation with a silken cord). As a result, on tasting power he rapidly fell into extravagant ways, including spending large sums on the armed forces. Unfortunately, although he was intrigued by new technology, he was not sufficiently educated to discriminate between a practical invention and a visionary scheme, and so was prey to every projector and salesman. This weakness extended to warship procurement, and the Sultan's whims burdened the navy with warships it did not need and could not effectively use.

The Sultan was also unfortunate in his technical advisers, most of whom were recruited in Britain. With the exception of the long-serving Slade, who was mainly employed on naval staff work and Henry J Wood, who took over command of the naval school at Heybeliada, they were generally adventurers who were ill-equipped, or ill-disposed, to deal with the obstructionism of the navy ministry. A prime example was Captain Augustus Charles Hobart, who arrived in İstanbul during the fighting in Crete with a reputation made as a blockade-runner during the American Civil War. By February 1868 he had manoeuvred himself into a five-year contract that included the reform of officer training as well as command at sea. He was successful in operations off Crete, but proved a reluctant and intolerant administrator. Training was confined to the translation of British shiphandling manuals, with no practical dimension to the instruction. Indeed, it was not until January 1871, when naval officers were seconded to the newly reorganised state shipping company, that many of them obtained any sea experience and navigational training.

Abdul Aziz's extravagances far exceeded tax revenues and led the country into increasing foreign debt, and further dependence on imported capital and expertise. For the navy a particularly sensitive issue was the British ownership of the Black Sea coal mines, which was its main supply of bunker fuel. For obvious strategic reasons the navy wished to control this source, but all attempts were foiled by a reluctance to enter into conflict with the British government.

Egypt's ambitions for independence continued to trouble the Sublime Porte in the 1860s. The new Vali, Ismail Paşa, was presented with a powerful bargaining chip in the form of the Suez Canal, but made a major strategic mistake in omitting to invite the Sultan to the opening ceremony. The Sultan was stirred to exert his authority and a Ferman of 5 June 1867 insisted that Egypt hand over the ironclads building in France and Austria and reduce its army to 30,000. Negotiations dragged on, and it was not until 29 August 1869 that the warships were formally handed over to the Ottoman navy. Egypt remained a nominal province of the Ottoman Empire, but British occupation of the country in 1882 ended Ottoman influence forever.

The Russian War, 1828–1829

20 May 1828: In the middle of the Russian war the British *Swift* is the first steamer to arrive at İstanbul. Sold by its owner, Captain Kelly, to a group of Armenian merchants, the ship is renamed *Sürat*, painted white and presented as a gift to the Sultan. However, it is not until February 1829 that the steamer is used for short excursions into the Sea of Marmara.

Impressed by the potential of steam, the Derya Kaptan purchases a second vessel direct from Britain. The *Hilton Joliffe* is renamed *Sagir*, and Captain Hanchet and the ship's engineer take up commissions in the Ottoman navy, as had Captain Kelly. Their principal task is to train personnel in the operation and maintenance of the machinery, but with no support facilities and considerable opposition on social and even religious grounds to the introduction of steam, this is fraught with difficulty. The local population, on the other hand, merely find the steamers amusing, and nickname

Sürat simply *buğ* ('steam').

15 February 1829: During the war with Russia, the Ottoman navy plays no active role in the fighting, and seldom leaves the Bosporus. On 15 February, however, the Russian fleet begins landing troops at Süzebolu. This is well behind Turkish lines and the Sultan orders the navy into action.

19 May 1829: The Ottoman fleet finally leaves the Bosporus. It has taken three months to prepare the line of battle ships *Selimiye*, *Mukaddeme-i Hayir* and *Büruç-u Zafer*, the frigates *Bad-i Nusret*, *Küsad-i Zafer* and *Muin-i Zafer* and the corvettes *Medar-i Zafer*, *Hilal-i Zafer*, *Fevz-i Bahri*, *Fevz-i Mabur* and *Fazlullah*.

20/21 May 1829: During the night the Russian frigate *Rafael* and sloop *Merkur* sailed among the Ottoman fleet by mistake. On discovering the error, the *Rafael* surrenders, but the dismal standard of Ottoman gunnery and shiphandling allow the *Merkur* to escape with only minor damage. The fleet returns in triumph to İstanbul with its prize, which is renamed *Nimetulla*.

15 June 1829: A Turkish fleet of five ships of the line, three frigates, five corvettes and three brigs encounters a small and very inferior Russian squadron off Süzebolu, but without firing a shot sets course for home.

May–September 1829: An effective Russian blockade of the Narrows prevents any Ottoman ship making the passage until the end of the war on 19 September.

The Egyptian Crisis, 1831–1840

November 1831: Palestine is invaded by the troops of Ibrahim Paşa, the adopted son of Mehmet Ali, the Vali of Egypt, who is attempting to establish his independence from the Ottoman Empire.

July–August 1831: The Great Powers decide to resist any weakening of the Ottoman Empire and a British fleet co-operates with the Ottoman navy off İskenderun, the Egyptian fleet's base.

18 August 1831: The Ottoman fleet makes a demonstration off İskenderun, but action is confined to a long-range cannonade.

February–March 1833: Responding to the Sultan's request for help after the Egyptian army reaches as far inland as Konya, the Russians land 5,000 troops at Üsküdar, but they are not committed to battle. Diplomatic pressure effects the withdrawal of Mehmet Ali's army, but the Russians exact their reward at the Treaty of Hünkar Iskelesi (8 July 1833), which guarantees that the Dardanelles will be closed to the Tsar's enemies in any future conflict.

1834–1839: Further intriguing by Mehmet Ali, including support for an anti-Ottoman revolt in Albania. French support is switched to Egypt, but Britain, Russia and Austria are prepared to oppose French influence in the Levant.

30 June 1839: The death of Mahmut II sparks off a series of intrigues and internal power struggles in the Ottoman establishment. A principal player in this drama is the Sadrazam (Grand Vizir) Hüsrev Paşa, who is known to be pro-Russian, and is a rival of the Derya Kaptan. His influence with the new Sultan, Abdul Mecid, provokes the Derya Kaptan to consider going over to the Egyptians.

4 July 1839: The fleet, consisting of eight ships of the line, twelve frigates, a corvette, two schooners, three fireships and a steamer sails for Besike Bay, where naval squadrons of the Great Powers are anchored. Keeping his intentions secret from his commanders, whose loyalty is suspect, but with the connivance of the French, the Derya Kaptan then arranges the transfer of the fleet to Kos (although a brig and the steamer *Peyk-i Şevket* manage to detach themselves and return to İstanbul).

14 July 1839: After opening communication with the Egyptians from Kos, the Ottoman fleet sails into İskenderun and places itself under the protection of the Egyptians. Its British adviser, Captain Walker, remains loyal and returns to İstanbul. Great Power interest in the issue remains high.

July 1840: Hüsrev Paşa resigns as Sadrazam, and Mehmet Ali as a bargaining ploy takes the opportunity to offer the return of the Ottoman fleet. Mehmet Ali uses his Ottoman/Egyptian squadron to put down unrest in and around Beyrut, ostensibly in support of the Sultan's authority; but the British deliver an ultimatum to the Egyptian viceroy to evacuate Syria and Palestine.

August 1840: When the Egyptians fail to comply, a thirty-strong fleet is dispatched to enforce the ultimatum. This includes an Ottoman squadron under Captain Walker (known as Yaver Paşa), who has been promoted to fleet commander. Numerous actions against coastal positions occur in the ensuing weeks.

1 November 1840: By October only Acre still holds out; on 1 November a combined land and sea assault is launched, with the Ottoman battleship *Mukaddeme-i Hayir* taking part.

3 November 1840: Acre capitulates and with this the Egyptian cause collapses. Mehmet Ali agrees to the removal of all of his troops from Syria and on 27 November acquiesces in the return of the Ottoman fleet to İstanbul.

The Crimean War, 1853–1856

March 1853: Russian imperial designs on Turkish territory are renewed in the guise of a dispute about the rights of Orthodox Christians within the Ottoman Empire. When Russian demands are finally rejected in March 1853, an invasion of the Empire's Danube principalities follows in July.

31 May 1853: The Tsar decides to occupy principalities of Moldavia and Wallachia. As a deterrent, the British and French governments agree to send their squadrons to Besike Bay near the Dardanelles.

2 July 1853: Russian Forces invade the principalities. The European powers protest, but restrain the Ottoman government in its desire to declare war.

8 July 1853: Ottoman sailing ships are sent to patrol the Black Sea. Following the reported sighting of a Russian steamer off the Bosporus the Derya Kaptan orders the patrols to avoid action.

July–August 1853: The Vali of Egypt begins mobilisation of his army; the fleet, comprising the ships of the line *Benhauf, Halep* and *Mefta Cihat*, the frigates *Bahri, Dimyad, Resid* and *Zir-i Cihat*, the corvettes *Cihat Bekker, Cena Bahri* and *Samrah Bahri* and auxiliary vessels are sent to İstanbul.

23 September 1853: Following demonstrations and disorder in İstanbul the British fleet is sent to the city at the Sultan's request.

29 September 1853: Three squadrons of Ottoman and Egyptian warships are formed. Kayserili Ahmet Paşa takes command of an eighteen-ship squadron which is to patrol the Black Sea and protect troop transports to Eastern Anatolia. Mustafa Paşa's squadron of four steam frigates is to be employed on trooping between Batumii and İstanbul. The third squadron under Osman Paşa consists of seven frigates, three corvettes and auxiliaries and is to be stationed at Sinop throughout the winter.

4 October 1853: The Ottoman Empire declares war on Russia. Kayserili Ahmet Paşa's squadron, with Musari Paşa, the high command's adviser, on board *Nusretiye*, sails from the Bosporus

to patrol the Black Sea.

23 October 1853: The Ottoman army under Omer Paşa crosses the Danube and in a number of engagements holds its own against the Russians.

15 November 1853: Osman Paşa's squadron, badly delayed by severe weather conditions, finally arrives in position off Sinop.

16 November 1853: The Russian paddle frigate *Bessarabia* captures the armed steamer *Madr-i Ticaret* off Sinop.

18 November 1853: The Russian steamer *Kolchida* attacks shore batteries near Batumi before running aground. Stranded, *Kolchida* is hit repeatedly by field artillery and suffers casualties on board.

The Egyptian steamship *Pervaz-i Bahri*, en route from Ereğli to Benderaki, is stopped by the paddle frigate *Vladimir*. Fifty-eight of the crew are killed during an exchange of gunfire before the Egyptian steamer is forced to surrender.

19 November 1853: A Russian squadron appears off Sinop but does not attack Osman Paşa's winter squadron anchored near the lightly defended harbour. During the same night Mustafa Paşa's steam frigate squadron encounters the Russian frigate *Flora,* but fail to inflict serious damage. Mustafa Paşa then sails on to Sinop. Here he tries to persuade Osman Paşa to return with him to İstanbul but the latter insists on resting his still untrained and inexperienced crews.

22 November 1853: Mustafa Paşa's squadron departs Sinop for İstanbul. Here he attempts to dispatch the remaining ships of the line as quickly as possible to reinforce Osman Paşa's fleet at Sinop.

30 November 1853: The Russian fleet, under the command of Vice-Admiral Pavel Nachimov and comprising six ships of the line, attacks Sinop. In the early hours of the morning, in rain and mist, the Russians open fire on the unprepared Ottoman fleet. Within a few hours the entire Ottoman fleet and the auxiliaries are sunk, the coastal batteries and emplacements destroyed and the town set ablaze. The Russians lose only forty men, the Ottomans over 3,000 killed, wounded or taken prisoner, including Osman Paşa and three of his captains. Only *Taif* escapes the disaster and manages to reach İstanbul with the news of the destruction of the fleet.

Ottoman losses comprise the steamer *Ereğli*, the frigates *Avnullah* and *Nizammiye*, the corvettes *Nesim-i Zafer, Fazlullah, Navek-i Bahri, Kadi-i Zafer, Necm-Efsan, Feyz-i Mabud* and *Gul-i Sefid*. Egyptian losses comprise the frigates *Dimyad* and *Pervaz-i Bahri*.

3 January 1854: The British and French fleets enter the Black Sea to protect the Ottoman coast and transports. Although the Ottoman fleet was not completely destroyed at Sinop, the battle marks the end of the Ottoman fleet as a first class navy. For the remainder of the Crimean war the Ottoman warships play a minor supporting role in Black Sea operations and during the bombardment of Sebastopol in October 1854 and April–June 1855.

17 March 1854: Alliance of Great Britain and France with the Ottoman Empire.

28 March 1854: Great Britain and France declare war on Russia.

14 September 1854: Allied troops land at Yevpatoriya. The British are commanded by Lord Raglan, the French by Marshal St. Arnaud. The allied objective is the strongly-defended fortress at Sebastopol.

17–19 October 1854: First bombardment of Sebastopol.

25 October 1854: Battle of Balaclava – a cavalry engagement noteworthy for the charge of the Light Brigade, and an allied victory.

8 September 1855: French forces capture the Malakoff Fort, the key Russian position. This action effectively ends the war.

11 September 1855: The Russians abandon Sebastopol, scuttling their ships and destroying the forts.

1 February 1856: Peace talks begin in Vienna.

30 March 1856: Treaty of Paris. The European powers promise integrity of the Ottoman Empire. Russia agrees to the neutralisation of the Black Sea and to give up its claim to a protectorate over Christians in the Ottoman Empire. The Ottoman Empire had previously (18 February 1856) issued the Hat-i Humayan edict guaranteeing the Christians security of life, honour and property. Full liberty of conscience is granted and all civil offices made open to all subjects of the Sultan.

The Cretan Crisis, 1866–1869

Spring 1866: The outbreak of an uprising among the majority Greek population of Crete, aspiring to union with Greece.

April 1866: The Vali of Crete, Heliomoghi Ismail Paşa, requests naval assistance to intercept the steady flow of arms from the mainland to the insurgents. There are no naval forces on station and Ottoman naval facilities on the island are minimal: a harbour and small maintenance depot at Khania, and anchorages at Suda, Rethimnon and Iraklion. As a result two squadrons are formed from forces in the Aegean, off the Ionian coast, and from İstanbul. They are known as the Rumeli (European) and Anadolu (Asian) Squadrons, under Ethem Paşa and Ibraheim Paşa respectively.

Autumn 1866: İstanbul sends reinforcements for the 40,000 troops under Osman Paşa plus an Egyptian brigade under Şahin Paşa already on the island.

October 1866: Ships of the line *Şadiye* and *Fethiye* ready to replace the sloops *Medar-i Zafer* and *Talia* off Crete. Gun-running continues unabated despite the naval patrols.

November 1866: Ottoman forces are reckoned to have regained control of the island, but renewed fighting is expected in the spring. *Feyz-i Bahri* and *Molakov* are sent to Crete with more troops, escorted by the sloop *Ismail* in case of attack by the Greek navy.

5 April 1867: The new navy minister (Bahriye Nazaret), Haci Mustafa Paşa, sails for Crete aboard the *Kervan-i Bahri.* Known as Ingiliz Mustafa because of his British training and anglophile leanings, he is the first to hold the new title, which replaces the old Derya Kaptan. This initiative in going to see for himself the situation on Crete results in a conference on 20 April in which it is decided to increase the Anadolu Squadron to four battleships, five frigates, fourteen corvettes and twenty-five armed steamers. The squadron, under Ethan Paşa, is based at Preveze and charged with patrolling the eastern coast of Crete, but is not large enough to keep an eye on the Greek coast. It experiences considerable problems with the quantity and quality of its coal supplies.

August 1867: A barrage of thirty mines is laid off Siros in the Cyclades in an attempt to close off one of the Greek supply routes, and the corvettes *Meriç* and *İskenderiye* are sent to patrol the area.

20 August 1867: The particularly troublesome fast Greek blockade-runner *Arkadion* is driven ashore by the sloop *İzzeddin,* sent from İstanbul specifically for this task. The *Arkadion* is later refloated and incorporated into the Ottoman navy as the *Arkadi.* Hobart Paşa, *Izzeddin*'s commander, is promoted and takes over the Anadolu Squadron's Second Group.

Spring 1863: The Cretan uprising flares up once again, but apart from the capture of a few small sailing vessels by *Şadiye* and *Eser-i Hayir* in August and September, naval successes are scarce.

January 1869: The Treaty of Paris, brought about by Great

Power pressure, confirms the status quo in Crete, but in anticipation of further disturbances on the island, a large part of the Ottoman navy remains stationed at Suda.

13 March 1869: Hobart Paşa, now a Tümamiral, turns over command to Albay Mehmet and returns to İstanbul to begin the task of reorganising the Ottoman navy. On his recommendation the new armoured vessels built in Britain and France are sent to Crete on completion.

The Russo-Ottoman War, 1877–1878

Political background

31 October 1870: Russia repudiates the Black Sea clauses of the Treaty of Paris, taking advantage of the confused situation in Europe caused by the Franco-Prussian War. Great Britain and Austria protest but Russia is supported by Prussia.

13 March 1871: A conference at London finally accepts the Russian action while declaring against unilateral breaches of international agreements. Russia is sufficiently encouraged to continue imperial expansion in the Caucasus and the Balkans.

July 1875: Insurrection in Herzegovina and Bosnia.

10 May 1876: Midhat Paşa (1822–1884) dominant figure of a new administration.

29 May 1876: Midhat Paşa, the war minister Huseyin Paşa and their associates instigate a coup d'etat and depose the Sultan. A few days later he is dead, probably murdered, and is succeeded by the weak-minded Murad V.

2 July 1876: Serbia declares war on the Ottoman Empire.

31 August 1876: Murad V deposed. Abdul Hamid II becomes Sultan.

31 October 1876: Armistice signed between Serbia and the Ottoman Empire, Great Britain acting as mediator.

5 February 1877: Midhat Paşa dismissed and sent into exile.

24 April 1877: Russia declares war on the Ottoman Empire.

6 May 1877: British note to Russia, warning against an attempted blockade of the Suez Canal or occupation of Egypt. The note also reaffirms Britain's traditional stand with regard to İstanbul and the Straits.

10 December 1877: Fall of Plevne and the resumption of the Russian advance.

12 December 1877: The Ottoman government appeals to the European powers for mediation; the appeal is rejected by Germany and later by Britain.

9 January 1878: The Ottoman government appeals to Russia for an armistice.

31 January 1878: Armistice concluded.

3 March 1878: Treaty of Yeşilköy (San Stefano).

Black Sea operations

September 1876: Black Sea Squadron assembles in the Bay of Büyükdere. Ferik Riza replaces Ferik Mustafa as commander. An intensive training programme modelled on British lines is initiated. *Mesudiye*, recently refitted at İstanbul, becomes flagship.

December 1876: The armoured corvettes *Avnillah* and *Muin-i Zafer* are ordered to Batumi following reports of increased Russian naval activity, and the steamer *Sehber* is ordered to load a cargo of sea mines. Due to bureaucratic incompetence the steamer and its cargo are not ready to sail until mid-April 1877. The ships arrive at Batumi as war breaks out.

24 April 1877: Russia declares war. Ottoman war plans are immediately changed. Two squadrons are formed under the command of Musir Bozcaadali Hasan Husn, and an eastern squadron under Ferik Mustafa.

5 May 1877: The area from Killi to Cürüksu is declared a prohibited zone and neutrals given three days to clear the ports and sea area.

May 1877: The Black Sea Wooden Ship Squadron is sent to Batumii. The corvettes *Mubir-i Sürur* and *Asar-i Şevket,* the steamers *Taif, Asır, İsmaıl, Resmo* and *Mecidiye* arrive at Batumi under Ferik Hasan's command.

12 May 1877: The armed Russian steamer *Velikit Knjaz Konstantin* leads a torpedo attack on the harbour at Batumi. The torpedo launcher *Cesma* successfully passes the mine barrage and torpedoes the yacht *Sultaniye,* but the torpedo fails to detonate and the alarm is raised. The Russian ships return to Poti safely.

14 May 1877: Ferik Hasan's squadron, comprising *Muin-i Zafer, Necm-i Şevket, Feth-i Bülend, Mukaddeme-i Hayir, Avnillah* and *İclaliye* sail to Sochum and shell Russian artillery positions near the town.

16 May 1877: Sochum falls to the Ottoman marine forces.

5 July 1877: Following the sinking of merchant ships near Aydos the approaches to the Bosporus are given increased protection.

Summer 1877: The Ottoman naval squadrons are redeployed, Musir Boszcaadali Hasan Husn's being based at Sünne, while Ferik Ahmet's remains at Batumi.

July 1877: The Ottoman squadrons are moved to Varna in anticipation of a Russian advance across the Danube.

23 July 1877: The *Feth-i Bülend* is engaged in a short engagement with the armed Russian steamer *Vesta* near Sünne. Both vessels are damaged but casualties are light; the engagement is broken off due to poor visibility because of smoke and escaping steam.

31 July 1877: *Feth-i Bülend, Mubir-i Sürur, Mukaddeme-i Hayir, Asir, Süreyya* and *Talia* depart Sochum for Trabzon to transport troops to Varna. Ferik Ahmet's squadron is employed carrying troops and refugees from Sochum to Batumi, Trabzon and other places on the Black Sea. The old screw ships of the line *Mahmudiye* and *Selimiye* prove to be highly suitable as transports and are able to carry large numbers of troops. The Sultan's yacht *Sultaniye* and ten steamers of the Idare-i Mahsusa perform sterling service as transports during this period.

3 August 1877: A Russian raiding party from the *Velikit Knjaz Konstantin* captures three small sailing vessels in the Bay of Kilyoz, only a half-hour sailing from the Bosporus. The vessels are set on fire and sunk. The *Velikit Knjaz Konstantin* and its torpedo launchers remain a threat, eluding extensive Ottoman patrols.

Autumn 1877: The fleet remains inactive off Batumi.

23 August 1877: The Russian torpedo launchers *Miner, Navarin* and *Sinop* attack the anchored *Asar-i Tevfik* off the roads at Sochum. One torpedo explodes below the waterline, but damage is slight and the warship is later repaired at Batumi. The Russian vessels return safely.

25 August 1877: *Feth-i Bülend* again encounters an enemy vessel, but the Russian yacht *Livadia* turns away and no action takes place.

27 December 1877: The torpedo-launchers *Cesma* and *Sinop,* armed with Whitehead torpedoes, and *Navarin* and *Suchum-Kale,* with outdated spar torpedoes, attack the *Asar-i Tevfik* and *Mahmudiye* at Batumi. The torpedoes miss. Although the alarm is raised immediately, the Russian raiders are able to escape back to the mothership.

26 January 1878: Another attack by *Cesma* and *Sinop*. In the darkness the Russians miss the armoured corvettes but succeeded in sink-

ing the *İntibah* with the loss of twenty-three lives.

31 January 1878: Armistice in force. The Ottoman Empire surrenders Batumi to the Russians.

Danube operations

24 April 1877: A Cossack regiment seizes the strategic railway bridge over the river Seret at Barbus. A demolition party on board *Hifz-ur Rahman,* lying near the river mouth, was unaware that war had been declared.

30 March 1877: The Russians mine the Danube near Kalas and Reni, cutting off the Ottoman river fleet's escape route to the Black Sea.

3 May 1877: *Semendire* and *Feth-ül İslam* attack the Russian batteries at Ismail but cause no serious damage.

4 May 1877: *Hifz-ül İslam* attempts to break through to Reni but is shelled by Russian artillery and retreats back to Maçin.

11 May 1877: Russian artillery hits the *Lütf-ü Celil* near Ismail. *Feth-ül İslam* rescues twenty crew but more than 160 men are lost in the explosion that sinks the Ottoman vessel.

13 May 1877: Russian troops cross the Danube at Putbas and ransack the coaling station there while the Ottoman army is unable to intervene.

25 May 1877: Russian river forces comprising *Careva, Cesparevic, Dzigit* and *Xenia* (all armed with spar torpedoes) attack Ottoman vessels at Maçin at midnight. *Cesparevic* and *Xenia* torpedo the *Seyfi,* which sinks in fifteen minutes. Casualties are slight, the survivors managing to reach land.

5 June 1877: An extremely low tide makes a clearance of two Russian mine barrages possible.

8 June 1877: *Akka, Arkadi, Feth-ül İslam, Kiliç Alı* and *Semendire* break out from Maçin for Hirsova.

June 1877: Russian mine-laying operations increase along the Danube. Ottoman river craft are unable to stop these operations.

28 June 1877: Russian artillery shells Rusçuk, destroying the naval arsenal and damaging the *Hizber* and *Semendire*.

27–29 June 1877: The Russian army crosses the Danube at Zisteri and advances towards the Balkan mountains. Only a few sections of the river now remain in Ottoman hands.

16 July 1877: *Podgorice* and *İskodra* are captured when Niğbolu is occupied by the Russians. Both vessels are repaired and enter the Russian fleet.

8 October 1877: The gunboat *Sünne* is mined and sunk on newly-laid mine barrages off Sünne. The paddle steamer *Kartal* picks up the survivors, but twenty-seven crew lose their lives. Russian forces then shell the remaining Ottoman ships off Sünne but no hits are recorded; this action marks the end of naval action on the Danube.

Mediterranean and Sea of Marmara operations

During the course of the war the Ottoman navy made no contact with the enemy. The Russian forces in the Black Sea were small and the naval authorities in İstanbul saw no need to move the squadron from the Mediterranean to the Black Sea.

18 April 1877: Ferik Giritli Huseyin Paşa is ordered to prepare his squadron for action. The ironclads remain at Suda Bay but the wooden-hulled warships patrol the Albanian coast. When it becomes clear that no Russian warships are in the Mediterranean the ships are withdrawn and put on escort duties accompanying Egyptian troops from Alexandria to Gelibolu (Gallipoli) and İstanbul.

July–December 1877: Naval activities limited to patrols between Bar and Kilik by the corvettes *İzmir, Mansure* and *Muzaffer*.

A group of 'Germania' and Schichau-built torpedo-boats at İstanbul in 1888. In the background is Ceylan-i Bahri (left) and the bow of the ship of the line Fethiye (right).
Güleryüz

January 1878: The Russian army crosses the Balkan mountain range. The 35,000-man Ottoman reserve army under Suleman Paşa at Dedeağa is transported to Gelibolu by the steamers *Selanik* and *Malakof* and the frigate *Selimiye*.

31 January 1878: The *Osmaniye* and the yacht *Sultaniye* complete this operation, the entire army being transported without incident.

February 1878: A squadron comprising the *Asar-i Nusret*, *Fethiye*, *Hanya*, *Kandıya*, *Medar-i Zafer*, *İzzeddin* and *Zafer* is set up in the Sea of Marmara, in anticipation of a Russian advance in the area. The squadron is never used and remains at anchor off Büyükdere until the end of the war.

The Greco-Ottoman War, 1897

February 1896: Outbreak of insurrection on Crete, fomented by the Greeks who are intent on the annexation of the island.

8 July 1896: Under pressure from the European powers, the Sultan agrees to the restoration of the pact made in 1878. This introduced a large measure of self-government to Crete, but this had been suppressed after the rising in 1889. Greek support for the insurgents continues.

25 July 1896: The Austrian government proposes a blockade of Crete, rejected a few days later by Great Britain.

28 August 1896: The Sultan accepts a new package of reforms for Crete drawn up in İstanbul by the ambassadors of the European powers.

12 September 1896: The insurgents on Crete accept the reforms.

2 February 1897: Cretan insurrection resumes, supported by movements in Greece and in Macedonia.

10 February 1897: The Greek government, under pressure of public opinion, sends ships and troops to Crete. This follows the proclamation of Cretan unity with Greece on the 6th.

15 February 1897: At the suggestion of the Russian foreign minister Muraviev, the European powers land troops in Crete. A Russian/Austrian proposal to blockade Piraeus is rejected.

2 March 1897: The European powers hand diplomatic notes to Greece and the Ottoman Empire promising autonomy for Crete and demanding the withdrawal of the troops. The Greek government rejects the note.

The corvette Heybetnüma; a photograph taken in Crete sometime during the Greco-Ottoman War of 1896–97.
Güleryüz

(Below) Şemşir-i Hücum in the Haliç in about 1895.
Güleryüz

Berkefşan: *the
ship's officers posed
around a torpedo
tube in 1897.*
Güleryüz

(Below)
Asar-i Tevfik:
*reproduction of a
hand-coloured post-
card showing a
deck view of the
armoured corvette
in about 1896.*
Güleryüz

(Lower)
Hifz-ur Rahman
(left) and Asar-i
Şevket *in the
Dardanelles during
the Greco-Ottoman
War of 1897.*
Güleryüz

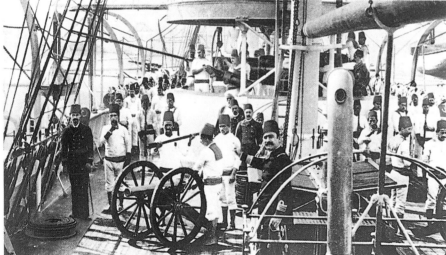

January 1897: The Ottoman fleet commander, Müsiramiral Hasan Rami, is ordered to form two squadrons of armoured warships and torpedo-boats. The squadrons is to take up station in the Dardanelles. The First Squadron under Admiral Hayri is to be based at Selanik (Saloniki) to protect the Narrows and prevent Greek naval operations in the area. Admiral Mehmet Resit's Second Squadron is to have responsibility for troop transport from İzmir to Selanik and the area around the islands. On paper these plans are impressive, in reality it is soon seen that the navy is in no position to carry out the orders. After being laid up in the Haliç for over nineteen years, the fleet has deteriorated seriously; the ships are rotten and the crews untrained.

18 March 1897: A blockade of Crete is proclaimed by the European powers, but fighting continues unabated.

19 March 1897: The *Mesudiye, Hamidiye, Aziziye, Necm-i Şevket* and *Hizber,* escorted by three torpedo-boats, leave the Haliç.

20 March 1897: The squadron of armoured warships sails, dressed overall, for the Dardanelles. Although conditions on board the warships are chaotic, the vessels present a magnificent picture to the civilian population. The escorting torpedo boats soon prove to be unseaworthy and have to be taken in tow by *Peleng-i Derya.*

22 March 1897: The squadron anchors off Lapseki. *Hamidiye,* making its very first voyage, has serious boiler trouble. *Mesudiye* is also found to be unfit for sea duty.

15 April 1897: The German Vice-Admiral von Hofe and his British colleague Admiral Henry Wood arrive at Çanakkale to inspect the Ottoman warships. Together with Admiral Hayri they proposed an intensive programme of battle manoeuvres and gunnery practice. The programme is given a good chance of success now that the navy is away from the negative influence of İstanbul, with its indifference, incompetence and corruption at court, in the government and at navy headquarters. The foreign admirals' report on the Ottoman

A photograph taken at Nara in the Dardanelles during the Greco-Ottoman War of 1897, showing (foreground) the torpedo-boats Burhaneddin *and* Gilyum, *and (background, left to right)* Aziziye, Orhaniye *and* Osmaniye.
Güleryüz

fleet is devastating: the guns on all the ships of the *Osmaniye* class are useless, with runners on the Armstrong guns immovable, and hydraulic pistons on the Krupp quick-firing guns bent. On some of the class the complete armament had not been installed, and it comes as no great surprise when the inspection finds that the breaches for the 240mm guns on the *Aziziye* are still lying at the Arsenal in İstanbul. Generally, the engines and boilers are found to be in reasonable working order, although engine failure and boiler and condenser problems are regular occurrences.

The reports consider only *Mesudiye, Necm-i Şevket* and the modern torpedo-boats *Berkefşan* and *Peleng-i Derya* fit for service. The report closes with the comments that 'normal' condition on some of the torpedo-boats encompasses regular boiler trouble, engine failure and unavailable spare parts, and that even if the fleet was in better condition it would still be inferior to that of Greece since the Ottoman armour and armament are completely out of date. Von Hofe states that since it takes the crews over two hours to load and train the Armstrong guns, it would be better to leave the fleet under the protection of the strong forts at the Dardanelles.

The fleet's passage from İstanbul takes place in full view of foreign observers, so that the true weakness of the Ottoman fleet is soon known internationally.

April–May 1897: The navy makes a number of sorties into the Aegean Sea. Müsiramiral Hasan Rami, on board the corvette *Mansure* and with an escort of three torpedo-boats, conducts these operations more to raise the morale of the crews than to threaten the Greek navy. All plans to activate the fleet have by now been completely abandoned by the Ottoman government.

Fatih and *Ejder* are stationed as advance patrol boats near Kepez and *Hizber* and *Hifz-ur Rahman* at Morto Bay. The armoured warships remain anchored at Naga, the narrowest point of the Dardanelles.

Fewer troops are required than originally planned on the Greek front, so plans for using naval vessels to transport troops by sea are not put into effect. Troops from West-Anatolia are brought to Lapseki and ferried to Gelibolu on the chartered ferries of the Şirket-i Hayriye. *Azizye, Hizber* and *Necm-i Şevket* act as escorts, but this is more to impress the ordinary soldiers with the might of the Ottoman navy than to protect the ferries. During this time the opportunity is taken to carry out gunnery exercises off the Dardanelles.

15 May 1897: *Azizye, Hamidiye, Mesudiye, Osmaniye, Seham, Sihan, Burhaneddin, Necm-i Şevket, Peleng-i Derya* and *Tir-i Zafer* put to sea on exercise. These are observed by von Hofe, and he notes that few of the warships are able to train their guns properly and that the time required to load and train the guns would be ample

Heybetnüma at İstanbul in 1897, after the Greco-Ottoman War.
Güleryüz

to allow any enemy to approach the Ottoman fleet without difficulty or danger. After this miserable showing the fleet returns to the safety of the Dardanelles.

Plans to attach the steamers *İzmir, Mekke, Marmara, Hüdeyde* and *Dolmabahçe* to the fleet as auxiliary cruisers come to nothing.

Following a Greek appeal to the European powers, an armistice is arranged. The fleet, with the exception of the ships of the *Osmaniye* class which remain at Çanakkale for some years, return to İstanbul.

18 September 1897: A peace settlement is reached between Greece and the Ottoman Empire.

The Reorganisation of the Fleet, 1897–1906

The complete failure of the fleet during the Greco-Ottoman War confirmed the worst fears of the Sultan's critics. Abdul Hamid was forced by mounting criticism to change his negative attitude towards the navy. Realising that there was no alternative to a naval modernisation programme he instructed the navy minister, Hasan Rami Paşa, to set up a naval commission.

May 1897: The commission presents its report and recommends that the old armoured warships be modernised and that six warships be built abroad. After the report has been presented to the Sultan, there follows a round of diplomatic intrigues and industrial

A general view of the naval dockyard (Tersane-i Amire) and the Navy Ministry at İstanbul in about 1885.
Langensiepen

double-dealing, with Abdul Hamid playing off one one potential supplier of warships against another. During May the Thames Iron Works is discreetly informed of the commission's plans. The British shipbuilder then offers to take over the Tersane-i Amire at İstanbul on lease for 5m gold lira for a period of five years and to modernise the yard. They will then build three 10,000-ton battleships and three cruisers of 6,000 tons, and also put through the modernisation programme on the old warships. The builders insist, however, that all material should be imported duty-free from Britain, and since this is unacceptable to Abdul Hamid because of Russia's purported veto, the negotiations come to nothing.

June–July 1897: Negotiations begin with the Krupp Works, who are owed vast sums for guns delivered to the Ottoman army. Krupp is asked to co-operate with the Schichau Werft at Elbing in plans for the fleet modernisation and the proposed new construction. The German tender is then leaked by İstanbul to Krupp's competitor, Armstrong of Elswick (Armstrong had been discreetly promised the contract as compensation for the Krupp artillery orders). With the Ottoman navy minister on its side, Armstrong is able to tender 2m gold lira, some thirty percent under Krupp's offer. It is generally accepted in İstanbul and abroad that Armstrong cannot refit eight armoured warships and build two battleships and two cruisers for this sum, but the British yard is almost certainly assuming that the programme will not be completed, and that only the two cruisers will ultimately be required.

October 1897: Kaiser Wilhelm II succeeds in convincing Krupp and Schichau that they should rebid for the contract and bring the Vulkan Werft at Stettin into the consortium. German complaints of bribery and corruption force the Sultan to dismiss the navy minister, and Hasan Rami Paşa is replaced on the procurement commission by admirals from the Tersane-i Amire.

4 December 1897: A modified programme is submitted by the newly formed commission and approved by the Sultan. The modified plan still includes reconstruction of the old warships, but new construction is to consist of two battleships of 10,000 tons, two armoured cruisers of 6,000 tons, two protected cruisers of 5,000 tons and two light cruisers of 2,500 tons. The programme is so unrealistic that Krupp withdraws from further negotiations. The German companies have already surveyed the old warships and had found the vessels in such poor condition that reconstruction is neither practicable, financially possible nor profitable.

January 1898: Armstrong is informed that it can expect an order

for a cruiser and two large torpedo-boats, and that the modernisation programme will be put through at İstanbul.

Spring 1898: The British yard is considered by its competitors to have won the construction contract.

July–August 1898: Tümamiral Ahmet Paşa arrives in London to close negotiations with Armstrong. On the Sultan's order he then proceeds to Essen to attempt pacification of Krupp. Discussions on armament for the old warships are broken off after a few days when Ahmet Paşa is recalled and Krupp loses all interest in a project perceived as unrealistic.

October 1898: The Italian ambassador has an audience with the Sultan. During the Armenian massacres of 1895 and 1896 a great amount of foreign-owned property and holdings had been destroyed and the foreign states had submitted compensation claims. The Sultan hoped to settle these considerable claims by placing armament orders with the various states involved. As a claimant, Italy is requested to submit proposals from suitable yards for the reconstruction of the *Mesudiye* and *Asar-i Tevfik*.

November 1898: Ansaldo submits a tender and intimates that it wishes to survey the two warships as soon as possible. The new guns are to be supplied by Armstrong, Krupp having refused to have anything to do with the Italian contract.

28 January 1899: The two warships arrive at Genoa. Ansaldo has arranged for the ships to be brought to its yard without waiting for the contract. The negotiations concerning the extent of the reconstruction and the armament to be installed dragon and it is not until autumn that an agreement is reached. The *Mesudiye* will be rebuilt at Genoa and *Asar-i Tevfik* at the Germania Werft at Kiel.

11 August 1900: Krupp receives the contract to rearm the armoured warships *Orhaniye*, *Aziziye*, *Mahmudiye*, *Osmaniye*, *Muin-i Zafer*, *Feth-i Bülend* and *Mukaddeme-i Hayir*. Krupp's price for the work is 648,000 gold lira, Armstrong-Ansaldo's price for their contract is 550,000 gold lira.

29 May 1901: The Ottoman warships arrive at Kiel. The voyage from Genoa under the command of Admiral von Hofe Paşa has been delayed for months due to Ottoman debts at Genoa. Only when Krupp agrees to settle for İstanbul is it possible to bunker the warships for the voyage to Germany.

The following chronology details reconstruction and orders from 1900 onwards.

Mecidiye

The US government submitted claims for compensation for losses incurred by American citizens during the Armenian disturbances. The total amount was only 22,000 gold lira but the Sultan was not prepared to pay even this relatively small sum. When the Americans threatened to send a squadron to İstanbul to enforce their claims the Sultan decided to order a cruiser in the United States to offset the compensation claims.

November 1899: Representatives of William Cramp & Sons, Philadelphia, meet Admiral von Hofe Paşa in İstanbul and agreement is quickly reached to build a protected cruiser. Building costs remain a problem, however.

April 1900: General Ahmet Paşa goes to America to negotiate with the US government. The Ottoman government suggests that Cramp should reduce its price from 585,000 to 300,000 gold lira and in addition pay 100,000 gold lira compensation to settle the Ottoman debt. The US government officially refuses the suggestion, but lets it be known that compensation claims will be waived if and when the contract is signed with Cramp.

May 1900: The contract signed, the price being 355,000 gold lira.

December 1903: *Mecidiye* delivered to the Ottoman navy. *Mecidiye* proves to be a failure in service. Construction supervision, under Yüzbaşı Sabri and Yüzbaşı Ali, was totally inadequate and the navy receives a cruiser that is plagued with stability problems; until World War I the ship can be handled only with great care and with continuous trim adjustments.

October 1914: A German inspection finds that the boilers are wrongly sited on board. Some of the coal bunkers are moved but the cruiser remains troublesome and seldom puts to sea.

Hamidiye

1897: Initial construction plans approved. These are to be subjected to considerable change over the next three years.

Spring 1900: Ordered from Armstrong. Contract price 456,000 gold lira. Supervision is under the control of Binbaşı Tefik and Binbaşı Aziz.

December 1903: Completed. *Hamidiye*, although nearly identical to *Mecidiye*, proves to be one of the best warships built for the Ottoman navy and serves for forty years, taking part in more operations than any other warship.

Mesudiye, *Drama*, torpedo-boats

Although all the contracts for new constructions were signed with Ansaldo it was Armstrong, the Italian company's main partner, which received the greater part of the work.

January 1900: Ansaldo quotes a final price of 12m Italian lire to refit the ironclads, an amount the Ottoman government cannot pay. There then follows a round of talks on financing, refinancing and alterations and modification of the building contract. The first two instalments are made for *Mesudiye*'s rebuild and there is a good chance that work will be finished by the end of 1901. The cruiser is cut down fore and aft and a new built-up superstructure is fitted amidships. Turrets are fitted for Vickers single 9in (25cm) guns. Ansaldo in the meantime recalculates its contract price, and when no further instalments are received from İstanbul all work stops on the *Mesudiye,* and the warship is laid up.

March 1901: The Ottoman government agrees to settle with Ansaldo if the Italians will build two torpedo-boats of the *Hamidiye* class. At the same time İstanbul asks for a moratorium on the payments. Abdul Hamid actually pays for the boats with surprising promptness, although he takes his time in settling for *Mesudiye* and for the modernisation of the other ironclads.

December 1902: Armstrong-Ansaldo conclude a further agreement with the Ottoman navy. Now, only *Muin-i Zafer* and *Feth-i Bülend* are to be reconstructed. İstanbul is now prepared to lease part of the Tersane-i Amire to the shipbuilders, and their staff will be allowed to work on these premises. Payments are to be settled by 1904 and two torpedo-boats of the *Akhisar* class are contracted.

15 March 1904: *Mesudiye* completes sea trials. The opportunity is used to begin talks on a repeat of the *Hamidiye*. The Ottoman government is naturally interested in the proposal but cannot

Muin-i Zafer (left) and Avnillah *(right) undergoing engine trials at Istanbul in 1905, overseen by Ansaldo personnel.*
Ansaldo Archive

Alpagot at İstanbul, shortly after arriving from the builders.
Güleryüz

finance it. It is also considered that British influence in the navy has become too obvious and that consideration should be given to offers from other countries.

August 1907: Ansaldo receives the contract to build a modified version of the *Hamidiye,* to be named *Drama.* In the event the nearly-completed cruiser is pledged by the Italians shortly before the outbreak of the Italo-Ottoman war in compensation for non-payment, and seized by the Italian government at the outbreak of hostilities.

25 March 1913: *Drama* is completed as the Italian *Libia*.

Asar-i Tevfik, Peyk-i Şevket class

29 May 1900: *Asar-i Tevfik* arrives at Krupp's Germania Werft at Kiel accompanied by the transport *İzmir*. With the total Ottoman debt to the Essen armaments company now standing at 648,000 gold lira, Krupp is naturally doubtful that the rebuilding programme can be completed in a reasonable time. The ironclad is moored at the fitting-out berth and the crew transferred to *İzmir* ready for the voyage to İstanbul. Germania Werft strips the *Asar-i Tevfik* down and then awaits instructions from İstanbul. From May 1900 until the end of the year nothing is heard from the Ottoman government. The five hundred Ottoman crew members receive no pay, and those officers and ratings whose commissions and service have now ended are left penniless. It appears that the Sultan and his embassy have forgotten the warship and its crew. By the summer of 1901, after nearly 13 months of waiting, the situation for the Ottoman seamen is critical. It is impossible for them to get credit in Kiel and even Admiral von Hofe Paşa's appeals for assistance have met with no response. Even the Kaiser, hearing of the whole unfortunate matter during Kiel Week, is unable to make the Sultan take any action to settle the mounting debt of his destitute seamen. On the contrary, the Sultan now demands that Krupp advance 6,000 gold lira to make *İzmir* ready for sea and pay the salaries of the four Ottoman supervisors on the *Asar-i Tevfik*. Krupp now find themselves in a nearly hopeless situation: refusal to meet the Sultan's outrageous demands could endanger negotiations for a large contract for the Ottoman army.

Autumn 1901: With payment from İstanbul and an advance from Krupp the debts in Kiel are settled and *İzmir* finally sails for home.

18 January 1904: After endless waiting, broken promises, misunderstandings and silence, a new round of negotiations begins. İstanbul now proposes that Krupp reduce the cost of the reconstruction of the ironclad from 282,000 to 65,000 gold lira, an amount that will not even cover the preparatory work already carried out. In addition, the amount of material to be sent to İstanbul for the modernisation of the ironclads there is to be considerably reduced. As a consolation, Germania Werft receives the contract to build two torpedo-cruisers.

These demands, amounting to little less than diplomatic blackmail, mean financial disaster for Krupp. But now that the large armaments orders for field artillery and for naval guns for the Dardanelles and the Bosporus seem secure, Krupp has no choice but to concede to pressure.

April 1904: Krupp receives a highly profitable order from the Ottoman army and, although no payment has been received to date for reconstruction or new building for the Ottoman navy, two slipways are kept free for the planned torpedo-cruisers. Work also proceeds slowly on the *Asar-i Tevfik*.

19 November 1906: After lying at the Germania yard for over six years, the refitted *Asar-i Tevfik* finally sails for İstanbul. The Germania Werft association with the Ottoman navy ends when the two torpedo-cruisers, *Peyk-i Şevket* and *Berk-i Satvet,* are delivered. The Ottoman navy obtains two torpedo-cruisers at a ridiculously low price and is satisfied with the reconstruction, even if *Asar-i Tevfik*'s value as a fighting ship is limited.

French-built destroyers and gunboats

French shipbuilders had wisely kept out of the negotiations for warships for the Ottoman navy, and French armaments manufacturers had concentrated on the sales of artillery, equipment and munitions for the Ottoman army. When in 1904 Krupp received the large artillery order noted above, the Ottoman government felt compelled to keep the diplomatic and financial balance by placing further orders in France. A rough balance was achieved through the order of four torpedo-boats of the *Sivrihisar* class from the Schneider-Creusot concern. This small order was not enough

Two views of Ayintab-*class gunboats under construction at Schneider et Cie, Châlons-s-Saone, reproduced from French postcards.* Güleryüz

to satisfy France, and Schneider-Creusot received instructions to design a gunboat of 200 tons, the later *Refahiye* class, and the larger 420-ton *Marmaris*. The design was based on a class of 200-ton gunboats in service in the Ottoman navy. Those boats had been inexpensive to build, easy to maintain and their sea-speed, armament and sea-keeping qualities had made them ideal boats for coastal duties and combating smuggling and piracy.

22 January 1906: Contract signed. Four boats are built by Ateliers de la Loire at Nantes and four by Schneider et Cie; all prove to be good boats in service. While the negotiations are in progress the French succeed in convincing İstanbul of the necessity of ordering destroyers as well. Four boats of the *Durandal* class of 280 tons are constructed by Ateliers de la Garonde (three) and Schneider et Cie (one) and are built 1907–1908. During World War I these boats carry the main burden of convoy escort duties and anti-submarine warfare and prove to be first-rate in service. Three remain in the fleet until 1932 and are not stricken until after World War II.

During the period 1896–1914 a number of smaller craft, gunboats, tugs and naval auxiliaries were built at the Tersane-i Amire and abroad. As these vessels were of lower prestige, the Sultan took little interest in their construction and negotiations, and ordering and payment proceeded quickly, at least by Ottoman standards.

The British Naval Mission, 1907–1910

The period from 1896 to 1908 saw the emergence of the Young Turk Movement in the Ottoman Empire. The Young Turks, mostly exiles living in France, England and Switzerland, hoped to capitalise on the discredit of the Sultan. The chief aim was to prevent the disruption of the Ottoman Empire and to reconstitute it on a liberal, national basis. The movement was seriously hampered by factional disputes between the powerful İttihat ve Terakki (Committee for Union and Progress) and the western-liberal orientated İttihat ve Hurriyet (Committee for Union and Freedom). These disputes were played on by the Sultan and severe repres-

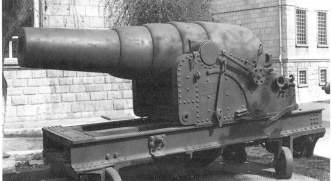

sive measures taken against the movement made all Young Turk activity within the Empire impossible.

December 1907: A meeting takes place in Paris of various Young Turks and revolutionary groups. Plans are concerted for action and contacts established with groups of discontented officers in the I and II Army Corps.

5 July 1908: Niazi Bey, chief organiser of the revolutionary movement, raises the standard of revolt in Macedonia. An insurrection among the troops stationed in the province breaks out and the Sultan is forced to reenact the constitution of 1876 after gov-

Ottoman merchant vessels laid up at İstanbul in 1908.
Güleryüz

ary *İhsaniye,* which, with a crew of thirty-five men, had thirteen officers on the ship's list, most of whom had never seen their ship but drew naval pay, demonstrates why Gamble's proposals were doomed to failure. The work of the mission was further complicated by rivalry between the navy minister and the Ottoman Foreign Office, with each side often opposed to each other's politics.

In March 1909 the officer corps of 5,000 was reduced with some moderate success.

May 1909: As part of Admiral Gamble's reform programme the first manoeuvre of the active fleet takes place in the Sea of Marmara. The flagship *Mesudiye,* with *Asar-i Tevfik* and *Mecidiye,* takes up station between Büyükada and Maltepe. The passage between the other Marmara Islands is protected by *Peyk-i Şevket, Berk-i Satvet, Samsun* and *Yarhisar.* The exercises includes a torpedo attack on the larger units, and *Musul, Kütahya, Draç, Alpagot, Hamidiye, Demirhisar* and *Sultanhisar* sail from Sivriada to join the fleet. The British mission is on board the *Tirimüjgan* as observers. Although the exercises are not particularly realistic and could not be compared with those of other navies, they are at least a start for a navy which has not held a naval exercise of any description for over twenty years. At the conclusion the fleet steams in review past the Sultan's yacht *Ertuğrul* off Sarayburnu. Admiral Gamble takes the opportunity to address a group of visiting parliamentarians. He points out that reviews, gun salutes and a sea of flags and banners are no substitute for ample funds for new construction and for dockyard facilities to handle a modern fighting fleet. His powerful speech has, however, little effect. The treasury simply has no finances available for the fleet.

At this stage the German military attache, Major von Stremple, enters the picture. Proposals had been made for a national subscription to raise funds for warship construction. Von Stremple had close contacts with the İttihat ve Terakki, and he suggested that the government encourage the foundation of an organisation similar to the German *Flottenverein* (Naval Society). The Donanma-i Milliye Cemiyetti (national help fund for the fleet) was founded in İstanbul on 19 July 1910. Its main object was to help maintain the naval balance of power in the Aegean.

From the beginning of 1910 Admiral Gamble had a series of clashes with various Ottoman ministers regarding warship orders and finances. Gamble proposed that all decisions in these matters should be left to himself and the navy minister, with other ministers merely to be informed of decisions made. Gamble's outspoken remarks cost the navy minister, Ali Paşa, his post and his successor, Tümamiral Halil Paşa, joined the ranks of Gamble's opponents. Gamble prepared a programme of new construction which was to include two capital ships, three cruisers and ten destroyers. Halil Paşa used this programme during his negotiations with Armstrong and was prepared to pay the shipbuilders 5m gold lira for two battleships and an armoured cruiser. This was an amount which the country could not afford to pay, and when the government learned of these unauthorised dealings the navy minister was dismissed on 3 May 1910. Gamble was succeeded as mission chief by Admiral Williams, whose career at İstanbul was dogged by misfortune. Albay Mehmet Muktar, the navy minister, refused to work with the British and did everything possible to sabotage the policy of co-operation. The Ottoman navy ministers' deep distrust of Gamble's mission lay in their annoyance that the work of modernising and enlarging the fleet lay in the hands of foreigners. Under these circumstances the mission achieved little. When the British departed in the autumn of 1914 they left behind an incomplete construction programme, but also many trained and quali-

ernment troops sent to quell the revolt desert to the rebels.

24 July 1908: Restoration of the constitution. Several weeks of celebration throughout the Empire follow.

17 December 1908: First meeting of parliament. The Young Turks have a large majority. Factional differences continue to grow, the main issue being that of decentralisation in favour of the nationalities.

13 February 1909: Fall of the Sadrazan (Grand Vizir) Kamil Paşa, a liberal, who is replaced by Hilmi Paşa, a committee sympathiser.

13 April 1909: The I Army Corps mutinies at İstanbul.

18 April 1909: A number of army officers are hanged for treason, prompting intervention by the army; 30,000 soldiers under Mahmut Şevket Paşa occupy İstanbul on the 24th.

26 April 1909: Abdul Hamid deposed by the unanimous vote of parliament. He goes into exile and dies in 1918. He is succeeded by his brother Mehmet Reşad V, a weak ruler. The country is now under the firm control of the İttihat ve Terakki Cemiyetti, and nascent liberal hopes are crushed. A new, dynamic Ottoman nationalism appears, with the Ottoman-Islamic religious state replaced by the concepts of nation and fatherland.

Against this background Admiral Sir Douglas Gamble arrived on 18 September 1908 to take over command of the British Naval Mission at İstanbul. For over a hundred years British officers had served with the Ottoman navy, either as instructors or in command, but their influence had mostly been slight. This changed with Gamble's arrival, although his proved a thankless task as the mission became more and more involved in the internal difficulties of the Ottoman Empire.

Between 1908 and 1911 the navy minister was changed nine times; since each minister had a different personal relationship with and appreciation of the British, the work of the mission proved to be nearly impossible to fulfil. Gamble's instructions were to continue the training programme for Ottoman naval officers, obtain orders for the British shipbuilding industry and to protect British interests in the empire.

Gamble started his mission well enough by proposing that the overmanned and overage naval officer corps be much reduced in size and rejuvenated by the promotion of younger, British-trained officers. These proposals proved to be impossible to carry through, as a naval rank was considered by many to be no more than an additional source of income, and promotion was dependent on the benevolence of influential contacts. The example of the station-

fied officers who had gratefully attended their school and were to remain staunch anglophiles throughout the war, much to the consternation of the Germans who filled the void left by the British mission's departure.

The Italo-Ottoman War, 1911–1912

By agreements with Germany and Austria in 1887, Great Britain in 1890, France in 1900 and Russia in 1909, Italy had secured approval for eventual action to acquire Tripolitania. The second Moroccan crisis, the Agadir crisis of June-November 1911, and the prospects of a French protectorate in Morocco induced the Italian government to act before it was too late. Its decision was influenced by pressure exerted by the revived Italian nationalist movement. The pretext used was Ottoman obstruction of peaceful Italian penetration of the province of Libya.

27 September 1911: Italian ultimatum issued: Italy will take over the province, by force if necessary, in order to reestablish law and order. The Ottoman government is sure that the European powers will not permit Italy to invade Libya and therefore orders only a slow mobilisation.

28 September 1911: The Italian ultimatum is rejected by the Ottoman government.

29 September 1911: The ultimatum expires at 1430hrs and a state of war now exists between the two powers. The stationary *Seyyar-i Derya* is scuttled at Tripoli, after the arrival of the Italian fleet.

1 October 1911: The Ottoman fleet, comprising *Torgud Reis*, *Barbaros Hayreddin*, *Mesudiye*, the destroyers *Basra*, *Samsun*, *Taşoz* and *Yarhisar* and the torpedo-boat *Demirhisar* are at anchor at Nara. The fleet had carried out exercises and manoeuvres since July and despite the worsening political climate had undertaken the traditional summer cruise which ended at Beyrut (Beirut).

2 October 1911: The fleet returns to İstanbul to repair and refit for war.

6 October 1911: The Italians land a force at Tripoli and occupy the town. The other coastal towns are taken in rapid succession.

12 October 1911: The refitted Ottoman fleet returns to Nara ready to defend the Dardanelles against Italian action.

29 October 1911: The torpedo-boats *Antalya* and *Tokad*, en route to Singin (Shengjin/Albania), are attacked off Kalamic (Kanalion/Greece) by Italian destroyers. *Tokad* flees north and is followed and shelled by Italian warships with the loss of nine men. *Antalya*, pursued by two Italian ships, manages to reach base at Preveze with slight damage.

1 October 1911: The torpedo-boats *Hamidiye* and *Alpagot* are sunk by enemy gunfire at Reşadiye (Igoumenitsa/Greece). The yacht *Trablus*, undergoing boiler repairs, is scuttled in the harbour, but an Italian boarding party manages to close the sea-cocks.

October 1911: Under pressure from Austria-Hungary the Italian blockade squadron is removed from the Ionian coast. Operations on this and the Aegean coast are forbidden under the Triple Alliance and other agreements. The Ottoman government nevertheless considerably strengthens the defences at Selanik and İzmir. In addition, the approaches to Yenikale (Gulf of İzmir) are blocked by scuttling the old steamers *Adana* and *Saadet* of the Osmanli S.S.I. The Sultan's yacht *Sultaniye* and the transport *İzmir* are also released by the navy for scuttling. Later a further mine barrage is laid to protect Yenikale.

5 November 1911: The Italian government proclaims the annex-

Ordu, *photographed in 1911 in Arabian waters.*
Güleryüz

An Italian photograph of the wreck of Gökçedağ, *sunk in 1911.*
Güleryüz

ation of Tripoli, though the country is far from being conquered.

December 1911: Italian forces in the Red Sea are considerably strengthened by the arrival of the protected cruisers *Piemonte*, *Puglia* and *Calabria* and the destroyers *Artigliere* and *Garibaldino*.

5 December 1911: *Puglia* damages the Ottoman gunboat *Haliç* off Akkaba by gunfire; the boat is later scuttled.

16 December 1911: *Puglia* stops the *Kayseri* on passage Suez to Kunfuda with bunker coal.

7 January 1912: *Piemonte*, *Artigliere* and *Garibaldino* shell the harbour at Kunfuda and sink the gunboats *Kastamonu*, *Ayintab*,

The sunken Avnillah *at Beyrut, photographed on 16 May 1915.*
Langensiepen

(Top)
Another view of the sunken Avnillah, *taken early in 1914.*
Langensiepen

(Above)
The sunken torpedo-boat Ankara *at Beyrut, reproduced from a contemporary magazine.*
Güleryüz

The port of Vathi on the island of Simis (Samos) during the Italo-Ottoman War of 1911.
Güleryüz

Ordu, Bafra, Refahiye, Gökçedağ, the armed tug *Muha* and the yacht *Şipka.* The *Şipka* is later salvaged and towed to Italy.

24 January 1912: The Italian armoured cruisers *Giuseppe Garibaldi* and *Francesco Ferruccio* shell the port and town of Beyrut after an ultimatum to the Vali goes unanswered. The *Avnillah* is hit and set ablaze. At 0930hrs the Ottoman guns stop firing and at 1100hrs the *Giuseppe Garibaldi* enters the harbour and torpedoes the *Avnillah.* Two officers and forty-nine men are killed in the explosion. The *Ankara* is scuttled by its crew, the Italian cruiser firing at the torpedo-boat as it sinks. Over 140 civilians are killed and two hundred injured during the bombardment.

Italian civilians in the Şam (Damascus), Beyrut and Halep (Aleppo) areas, who up till now have lived peacefully within the Ottoman Empire suffer retaliation for the Italian naval raid; over 55,000 are compelled to leave.

18 April 1912: The battleship *Emanuele Filiberto* sinks the yacht *İhsaniye* at Vathi on Simis (Samos). The yacht, which had lain in the harbour since September 1911, is the only warship in the area.

On the same day *Giuseppe Garibaldi* and *Varese* shell the Dardanelles forts, bombarding Seddülbahir and Kumkale and inflicting heavy damage.

20 April 1912: The Ottoman government retaliates by closing the Straits with mine barrages at Çanakkale. Over 170 merchant vessels are now trapped in the Sea of Marmara.

29 April 1912: The Ottoman steamer *Texas* (480gt/1888), sailing under the American flag on passage İzmir to Mersin hits one of the newly laid mines off Yenikale and sinks with the loss of ten crew members.

1 May 1912: Following pressure on the Italians by the European powers to lift their blockade the Ottomans are forced to clear the minefields. While work is in progress the naval tug *Semender* hits a mine and sinks with all hands (twenty-two).

4–16 May 1912: The Italians occupy Rhodes and the other Dodecanese Islands.

24 May 1912: The *Nevada* (507gt/1878), an Ottoman steamer under American flag, on passage from İstanbul, hits a mine while entering the İzmir harbour and sinks.

July 1912: Peace negotiations open, but neither side is ready to yield on any of its claims. Only the impending threat of the Balkan War finally induces the Ottoman Empire to concede to Italian demands.

18 October 1912: Treaty of Lausanne. The Ottoman Empire is forced to abandon its sovereignty over Tripoli. The Italians are to recognise a representative of the Sultan as Caliph, the Ottoman religious authority. The Dodecanese Islands are to be returned to Ottoman rule as soon as Tripoli is evacuated by Ottoman forces.

The German Warship Purchase, 1910–1914

The most spectacular purchase made by the Ottoman navy was that of two battleships of the *Brandenburg* class. It was less the warships themselves than the political exploitation surrounding their acquisition which made the transaction so significant.

On 10 December 1909 a conversation took place in İstanbul between the German military attache, Major von Stremple, and Sadrazan (Grand Vizir) Osman Paşa. He told the attache that the Ottoman navy was anxious to obtain an armoured cruiser and a number of destroyers to counterbalance Greek naval strength. Enquiries in Britain had come to nothing, Osman reported, so that if Germany was prepared to transfer one of the armoured cruisers now building, this would be much appreciated by the Ottoman Empire.

Before reporting this conversation to Berlin, von Stremple talked to Admiral Gamble. Both agreed that the Ottoman navy was not capable of handling large warships. When he reported to his superiors, von Stremple added that supply of a new warship to İstanbul would merely give the British naval mission the opportunity to study the latest German naval construction methods.

The question of the three destroyers was quickly answered. On 30 January 1910 Admiral von Tirpitz agreed to the sale of S 165–S 167, then under construction by Schichau at Elbing. The shipbuilders were to settle the price themselves.

The purchase of an armoured cruiser or even a battlecruiser was more complicated. On 24 March the Secretary of State at the Foreign Ministry von Schoen unwisely told the Ottoman ambassador that it was probable that the *Blücher* would be transferred to his country. Von Schoen had acted without instructions and his remarks caused consternation amongst high-ranking naval officers. General opinion was that if the brand-new *Blücher* was to be transferred then the price would have to be 44m marks, the cost of a replacement. It would also be expected that all future Ottoman orders for warships of all types would be placed in Germany. Krupp promptly pointed to the futility of these expectations. The precarious state of the Ottoman finances would prohibit payment of the proposed amount, and the deal would almost certainly be used as international political blackmail against Germany.

After Krupp's warning, a revised proposal was to sell the larger *Von der Tann*, then nearing completion at Blohm & Voss in Hamburg, for the same price. This deal had the advantage that a replacement could be built without permission from the Reichstag at Berlin.

The decision now lay with the Kaiser, and on 8 April he announced that the *Blücher* was for sale for 44m marks, and that it was to be manned by German officers. At about the same time the Ottoman government informed Germany that it still wished to purchase the *Blücher,* but at a reduced price, and that the obligation to place all future naval construction work in Germany was unacceptable.

It was left to the German ambassador in İstanbul to inform the government of the Kaiser's decision. A meeting was held on 21 June to discuss other alternatives. The Ottoman government badly wanted a warship to match the Greek armoured cruiser *Georgios Averoff* which was completing at Livorno. In desperation, İstanbul now contacted Krupp and Blohm & Voss directly. Blohm & Voss offered the *Moltke*, still fitting out at Hamburg, for sale. Although Y and Z gun turrets had still to be installed, the battlecruiser, even incomplete, would nevertheless be a more than adequate opponent for the Greek cruiser, mounting a main armament of six 280mm guns to the *Averoff*'s four 240mm, and a sea speed of 25 knots to the Greek ship's 22 knots design speed. The shipbuilders were to fit the remaining guns at İstanbul after delivery of the ship. The other possibility considered was to transfer instead a battlecruiser only just laid down at Hamburg and still designated 'H'. All these negotiations led nowhere, and nobody could have foreseen that four years later İstanbul would receive 'H', as *Goeben*, for nothing.

On 15 July Admiral von Tirpitz stopped all further discussion on the sale of the new battlecruisers, but announced that four battleships of the *Brandenburg* class were available for purchase at 10m marks each. On 25 July the German ambassador reported that İstanbul had selected the *Kurfürst Friedrich Wilhelm* and *Weissenburg,* which were armoured with Krupp nickel steel (the other two, *Brandenburg* and *Wörth*, had compound armour).

5 August 1910: Contract signed. The two German warships, with twenty-four officers and thirty-eight crew of the Ottoman navy as a study group on board, leave Wilhelmshaven on 14 August. They arrive at Çanakkale on 29 August and are welcomed on arrival by the *Hamidiye*.

1 September 1910: the two warships are officially transferred to the Ottoman navy and renamed *Barbaros Hayreddin* and *Torgud Reis*. The German crews return to Wilhelmshaven and the newly commissioned Ottoman battleships sail for the capital, escorted by the Schichau destroyers, commissioned two weeks before.

Payment for the two battleships and the destroyers amounted to 25m marks. Questions were soon raised as to how the Ottoman government proposed to settle payment. It was pointed out that the Naval Society had bought the ships, and the Society proceeded to raise the money by public subscription. In addition the Deutsche Bank held some 13 million marks on account for the deposed Abdul Hamid. Although any such transaction was officially denied, this money was used to settle with Germany and by mid-summer 1911 the Naval Society had cleared the remaining debt.

Opposition parties in İstanbul protested that the price paid for the two warships was too high. Although they had been built in 1891, both warships had been reboilered and modernised in 1902–1904 and had come straight from active service and were therefore in good condition. Despite being comparatively simple warships to man and maintain, they initially proved too much for the Ottoman navy and were plagued by condenser troubles which reduced their speed to 8–10 knots. It was to take some considerable time before both ships were ready for action with the Ottoman fleet.

After the initial uproar over the purchase of the ex-German warships had settled, the Ottoman government began discussions with Great Britain in the autumn of 1911 on purchase of the *Minas Gerais* and the *Rio de Janeiro*. The former had been completed in 1910 and the latter was under construction at Elswick. When it became obvious that finances were not available the talks with Armstrong were terminated. Vickers was more successful. Sir Douglas Gamble had prepared plans for two capital ships, and thanks to the intervention of Cemal Paşa an order was placed with Vickers for a battleship, the *Mehmed Reşad V*, at a cost of 1.5m gold lira. Work, however, was suspended in 1912 owing to the Balkan War and only resumed in 1913. The *Reşadiye,* ex *Mehmet Reşad V*, was completed in 1914 and seized by the British government in August for service in the Royal Navy as HMS *Erin*.

Due to the Balkan War no negotiations took place in 1912, but realistic plans were drawn up for new fleet construction. Initially two light cruisers of 5,500 tons, four destroyers of 1,000 tons, two submarines and a minelayer were proposed, and financing appeared possible. By April 1913, however, the Ottoman government knew that there was no hope of reconquering the Greek-held islands without the backing of a powerful naval force. Some members of the government wished to obtain the two remaining units of the *Brandenburg* class as well as additional destroyers, and Berlin intimated that the battleships remained available for sale. The navy, however, sought new, not reconditioned battleships. The Dresdner Bank was approached by the Ottoman government with a request to provide funds to purchase the *Rio de Janeiro,* under construction for Brazil by Armstrong. The Brazilian government, shaken by a mutiny on the *Minas Gerais* in 1910 and a dramatic slump in the economy, now wished to dispose of the battleship. Top level talks were held at Berlin between the Dresdner and Deutsche Banks, Krupp and the Foreign Office and agreement was reached that no financial assistance would be given to İstanbul to facilitate warship purchases abroad.

Reports were received in İstanbul that Greece and Italy were both interested in buying the *Rio de Janeiro,* but the Ottoman Empire had the advantage that it had already assured Armstrong of its intention to place further orders for naval construction at Elswick. The value of this assurance was weakened, however, by İstanbul's usual difficulty in obtaining the necessary finance. Italy tried to stop the sale of the Brazilian battleship by offering to exchange two armoured cruisers of the *Pisa* class, the model for the Greek *Georgios Averoff* for the Elswick contract and also offered to sell the Ottoman government two submarines for 68,000 gold lira each. On 1 December 1913 the İzmit Arrangement came into force. This gave Armstrong the authority to erect a navy yard at Gölçük, and guaranteed the Armstrong group all further building contracts for the navy. The British company also took over an interest in the Tersane-i Amire, and this yard as well as the new yard at Gölçük were named Doklar, Tersaneler ve Insaat Bahriye Sirketi (Naval Shipbuilding and Drydock Company). Little more than the initial planning for these yards had been completed before the war broke out.

The *Rio de Janeiro* was renamed *Sultan Osman-i Evvel* and construction proceeded for the Ottoman Empire's account. A 500-man crew arrived at Newcastle on 27 July 1914. The official handing over and voyage home was planned for 3 August. The warship was seized by the Royal Navy on 2 August and commissioned as HMS *Agincourt*.

In May 1914 orders were placed with Armstrong for two scout cruisers and two submarines. Four 1,100 ton destroyers from Armstrong were subcontracted to Hawthorn, Leslie and it was planned to have two of the same type built at İstanbul. Six destroyers were ordered from France, with six more planned for 1917. A further four destroyers of 700 tons were ordered from Italy. When war broke out all the contracts were annulled and construction stopped. Considering the precarious state of the Empire's finances it is doubtful that this ambitious programme could ever have been paid for.

The Balkan Wars, 1912–1913

Outline of the campaigns

18 October 1912: Outbreak of the First Balkan War between Bulgaria, Serbia and Greece on the one side and the Ottoman Empire on the other. The Bulgarian army crosses the Ottoman border.

22 October 1912: Bulgarian victory at Kirk Kilini in Thrace.

23 October 1912: Edirne encircled and the Ottoman army beaten back to the Çatalca (Chatalya) Line. Parallel to the main Bulgarian army small forces advance along the Black Sea coast and cavalry reaches Tekirdağ and Gelibolu on the Sea of Marmara. Greek forces occupy the islands in the Aegean without meeting opposition from the Ottoman navy. Serbia and Montenegro, acting independently, begin the occupation of the region around İskodra (Scutari), a region also claimed by Austria-Hungary. The region declares its independence and the European powers prompt-

ly dispatched warships to assist the newly-created Albania. They remained in Albanian waters until 1914.

24–26 October 1912: Serbian victory at Knaanovo.

28 October–3 November 1912: Bulgarian victory at Lüleburgaz. The victorious army advances to the Çatalca Line, the last Ottoman line of defence before İstanbul.

4 November 1912: The Russian government warns the Bulgarians against occupation of İstanbul, which Russia would resist by the use of its fleet.

10 November 1912: Serbian forces reach the Adriatic after overrunning the northern part of Albania.

15–18 November 1912: Serbian victory at Monastir. Bulgarian forces attack the Çatalca Line but are driven back.

24 November 1912: The Austro-Hungarian government announces its implacable opposition to Serbian access to the Adriatic, and reiterates its support for an independent Albania. An acute international crisis quickly develops. The Serbian government remains steadfast, backed by Russia's assurances of support, which are themselves backed by French assurances of assistance to Russia in the event of war with Germany. Austria-Hungary is supported by Italy, a partner in the Tripartite Agreement, which also opposes the appearance of Serbian forces in the Adriatic. Germany, after initial hesitation promises to support Austria-Hungary if the Hapsburg Empire is attacked while defending its interests. Great Britain, sympathetic to the Austro-Hungarian position, tries to work with Germany for a settlement while simultaneously preserving good relations with France and Russia.

Late November 1912: The international crisis reaches its most acute stage, with both Russia and Austria-Hungary beginning mobilisation. War is only avoided when Russia, unprepared for war, abandons the Serbian territorial claims.

3 December 1912: An armistice between the Ottoman Empire, Bulgaria and Serbia. Greece refuses to accept the armistice, despite strong international pressure, and the fighting continues.

17 December 1912: Opening of the London Peace Conference. At the same time an ambassadorial meeting takes place in London to discuss the status and boundaries of Albania, the fate of the Aegean islands and territorial claims by Bulgaria.

6 January 1913: Breakdown of the London talks. The Ottoman Empire refuses to give up Edirne, the Aegean Islands and Crete.

22 January 1913: Under pressure from the European powers, the Ottoman government agrees to relinquish Edirne.

23 January 1913: Coup d'etat in İstanbul by the Committee for Unity and Progress, which now seizes control of the Empire.

3 February 1913: Resumption of hostilities. The Ottoman army holds the Çatalca Line while Greek forces make considerable territorial gains.

5 March 1913: The Greeks occupy Janina.

26 March 1913: The Bulgarians occupy Edirne.

16 April 1913: Bulgaria and the Ottoman Empire conclude another armistice, also accepted by the other belligerents.

22 April 1913: Montenegrin forces take İskodra despite strong protests by the European powers who have already assigned the region to Albania.

3–5 May 1913: Montenegro abandons İşkodra after Austria-Hungary threatens war. Serbia evacuates Draç (Durazzo).

20 May 1913: Reopening of the London Peace Conference. The victorious allies are obliged by an ultimatum from Great Britain to accept the settlement agreed by the Great Powers.

30 May 1913: Treaty of London, ending the Balkan War. The Ottoman Empire cedes all territory west of a line between Enez (Enos) and Meriç (Midia) and abandons all claims to Crete. The

A 1915 photograph of the wreck of the transport Babıl, *run aground in April 1912 off Tekirdağ.*
Langensiepen

future status of Albania and the Aegean islands is left to the decision of the Great Powers.

1 June 1913: Treaty of alliance between Serbia and Greece against Bulgaria. This is the result of Serbia's failed claims on the Adriatic and Bulgaria's unwillingness to grant Serbia more territory in Macedonia.

29 June–30 July 1913: Second Balkan War. The Bulgarian army attacks Serbian-Greek positions without government authority. Although the Bulgarian government quickly disavows the action, the Serbian-Greek alliance takes advantage of the provocation to carry out a long-planned attack. Romania and the Ottoman Empire enter the war against Bulgaria, which is rapidly defeated.

20 July 1913: Ottoman forces retake Edirne.

10 August 1913: Treaty of Bucharest. Romania receives the northern Dobrudja. Serbia and Greece retain those parts of Macedonia already occupied. Bulgaria, the loser, retains only a small part of Macedonia and a small stretch of coastline on the Aegean.

29 October 1913: Treaty of İstanbul between Bulgaria and the Ottoman Empire, the latter recovering Edirne.

Aegean operations

When the Greek navy mobilised on 1 October 1913 the Ottoman government clung to the slender hope that Greece might still remain neutral.

6 October 1912: The chartered steamer *Florida* is sent by the naval command at Kusadası to Sisan to take off the island's military personnel. With the completion of this operation all Ottoman troops are evacuated from the Aegean.

13 October 1912: Fifty-five embargoed Greek merchant vessels, anchored in the Sea of Marmara, are released as a gesture of goodwill.

16 October 1912: The Ottoman navy sequesters over thirty-three freighters, thirty-eight tugs and steamboats and a number of sailing vessels in İstanbul harbour.

As in the Italo-Ottoman War, supplies for the Ottoman war effort could be imported only through Rumania. Ammunition and coal were in short supply and many badly-run Ottoman industries collapsed under the pressure of war. Hunger, disease and epidemics spread rapidly throughout the population.

The Ottoman navy was withdrawn to the Sea of Marmara. Here the fleet was kept ready for war. Although supplies, ammunition and fuel were scarce, morale remained high at first, but army losses on the battlefield and political upheavals within the Empire did much to weaken initial enthusiasm.

Since the Italian conflict the Ottoman navy had not ventured into Aegean waters. Only small garrisons of the Jandarma now remained on Midilli and Sakiz. Without opposition, the Greeks rapidly occupied the remaining islands. Imroz and Bozca Ada became Greek naval bases and were well situated to blockade the Dardanelles.

At the outbreak of war there were Ottoman naval bases on the European Aegean coast at Selanik and Preveze. In addition a naval detachment was stationed on the İskodra Sea, half of which formed the border with Montenegro. Selanik was protected by four 210mm gun emplacements and two twenty-four-mine barrages which had been laid before the war with Italy. The naval garrison commander was Binbaşı Aziz Mahmut Bey, who was also commander of the *Feth-i Bülend*. This old corvette had been disarmed at the start of the Italian war and its four 150mm, four 75mm and the four 57mm guns mounted in the Selanik fortifications as additional batteries. The *Feth-i Bülend* was reduced to an accommodation hulk and ninety of the crew landed to man the shore guns. Aziz

The steamer Akdeniz, *which served as a troop transport in the Black Sea in 1913 and again in 1914, photographed in 1924.*
Güleryüz

Mahmut Bey also had the tugs *Sürat*, *Teshilat*, *Katerin* and *Selanik* at his disposal. *Selanik* was fitted out as a minelayer and all the tugs were armed with a 37mm gun.

31 October 1912: The Greek torpedo-boat *No 11* departs Leftehois for Selanik. At 2220hrs it slips passed the searchlight batteries at Vardar and Karaburnu and the mine barrages. At 2330hrs three torpedoes are fired at the *Feth-i Bülend;* one runs wide and hits the coaling pier, causing serious damage, but the other two hit the target between the foremast and the funnel. The hulk capsizes and sinks with the loss of seven crew, including the ship's imam. *No 11* makes its escape by the same route.

31 October 1912: The naval base at Preveze, near the Greek border, surrenders to superior enemy troops. The torpedo-boats *Antalya*, the burnt-out *Tokad* and the motor gunboats *No 9* and *No 10* are scuttled on the order of the garrison commander, Binbaşı Hüsameddin, before the surrender. The Greeks later salvage the two torpedo-boats.

Ottoman forces at İşkodra comprised the steamer *Güre*, an old ex-Bosporus ferry; the lake steamers *İşkodra* and *Kiyoncya;* two motorboats, *Filiyo* and *Kilsnya*, purchased in 1912; and the steam pinnaces from the *Mesudiye* and *Asar-i Tevfik;* also a large number of sailing craft and barges.

On the Montenegrin side was a small naval force of three steamers and two steam launches.

15 October 1912: Serbian forces encircle İşkodra. Montenegro in turn attempts to stop further Serbian advances to ensure its own territorial claims.

7 November 1912: Greek troops surround Selanik. The foreign consuls there are approached with the request to assist in convincing the Ottoman forces to surrender. The Greeks occupy the town the same day.

9 November 1912: Two Greek auxiliaries sail into the bay and fire on the *Teshilat*. The *Teshilat*, with the *Sürat* and *Selanik,* were hastily disarmed and transferred to the French register just before the garrison surrendered. The Greek attack on a French ship leads to an immediate protest from the French naval commanders present.

9 November 1912: The armed steamer *Trabzon*, underway from Ayvalik to Midilli, is stopped, torpedoed and sunk by the Greek torpedo-boat *No 14;* both captain and engineer are killed in the torpedo explosion. *Trabzon*, a fifty-year-old wooden vessel, is the only merchant ship lost to the enemy.

15 November 1912: The Greeks seize the yacht *Fuad* which they refuse to recognise as a hospital ship under the Red Crescent at Selanik.

27 November 1912: *Selanik*, *Sürat* and *Teşhilat* leave port under the French *tricolore* and, although the Greeks try to stop the group off Limni, the tugs reach the Dardanelles.

28 November 1912: The three vessels change register again and the Ottoman flag is raised.

17 January 1913: Montenegro attacks İşkodra again.

23 April 1913: İşkodra falls, but is not granted to Montenegro. Under Esad Paşa's leadership, the whole region is granted to Albania.

İzmir, the Anatolian naval base, received only sporadic attention from the Greeks. Greek warships always remained far out in the bay and no action took place. During the course of the war the Ottoman forces at İzmir comprised only the demobilised armoured corvette *Muin-i Zafer*, the destroyer *Yunus*, laid up with damaged boilers, the yacht *İzzeddin*, *Timsah* and the steamer *Arşipel*, and the chartered Golden Horn ferry *No 8*.

Black Sea operations

With the Italian war confined to the African continent, the Ottoman fleet was left on station in home waters. It was intended that the fleet be prepared for the expected conflict with the Balkan countries but despite a stream of correspondence between the fleet command and the navy ministry from May 1912 onwards nothing was done to allow the necessary repairs to begin.

Summer 1912: *Torgud Reis*, *Barbaros Hayreddin* and the Schichau-built destroyers *Demirhisar* and *Hamidabad* are considered ready for service, although the warships are not up to European fleet standards. On the battleships the rangefinders and the ammunition hoists have been removed. Telephones are out of order and the pump piping corroded. Finally, most of the watertight doors cannot be closed. After only two years under the Ottoman flag the ex-German battleships are in fact in poor condition. The blame lies equally with the ministry and the fleet, responsibility being continually shunted back and forth. Problems with condensers on the old armoured warships and the modern cruisers were a regular feature of the maintenance reports.

2 October 1912: *Nevşehir* takes station at Trabzon, and *Zuhaf* off the Bosporus.

7 October 1912: The fleet, comprising *Torgud Reis*, *Barbaros Hayreddin*, *Hamidiye*, *Mecidiye*, the *Schichau* and *Samsun* class destroyers, lies at anchor off Haydarpaşa, outwardly the picture of a fully prepared and well-maintained navy. At the same time the *Mesudiye*, *Hamidabad* and *Kütahya* are at anchor off Büyükdere as guardships.

17 October 1912: *Barbaros Hayreddin*, with fleet commander Miralay Tahir Bey on board, leaves Büyükdere in company with *Torgud Reis*, *Muavent-i Milliye* and *Taşoz* for İğneada.

19 October 1912: The Ottoman battleships shell Bulgarian artillery emplacements at Galata Burnu, near Varna, the two destroyers on patrol in attendance. The fleet returns to Büyükdere, the two battleships still plagued by boiler trouble and clearly unsuitable for this type of operation.

21–31 October 1912: The cruisers *Hamidiye* and *Mecidiye*, assisted by *Yadigar-i Millet* and the *Nümune-i Hamiyet*, make a number of raids along the coast, shelling artillery positions at Varna and the batteries at Galata Burnu and scouting as far as Constanza. Plans to sent the torpedo-boats *Sivrihisar* and *Musul* are abandoned due to storms on the Black Sea.

29 October 1912: *Mecidiye* and *Yarhisar* anchor off Midye, where the transport *Marmara* (2472gt/1872) from Trabzon has transported the last remaining Ottoman troops. *Mecidiye* is detailed to protect further transports against possible torpedo-boat attacks from Varna.

30 October 1912: *Mecidiye* and *Yarhisar* leave for Varna. *Barbaros Hayreddin* and *Nümune-i Hamiyet* take over guard duties.

1 November 1912: *Bezm-i Alem* (4084gt/1889) arrives with over 2,500 troops, *Akdeniz* (5062gt/1890) with 2,000 infantry and 400 pack animals.

2 November 1912: The Bulgarians occupied Midye. *Resid Paşa* (4458gt/1901) disembarks five further battalions. *Barbaros Hayreddin* and *Nümune-i Hamiyet* take no part in the fighting for fear of hitting their own soldiers in the confusion around Midye.

3–10 November 1912: A steady flow of Ottoman warships reaches Midye to shell the Bulgarian troop concentrations. Even the ancient armoured corvettes *İclaliye* and *Necm-i Şevket* are pressed into service. They have to be towed to position and remain there only for a short time.

3 November 1912: The battleships carry out firing practice in the Sea of Marmara. These exercises are halted after only a few salvos when gun mountings begin to give trouble and threaten to break down completely. *Hamidiye* makes only half speed due to boiler trouble and *Mecidiye* reports condenser problems.

November 1912: Ottoman convoys to and from Rumania increase steadily and reach a peak with *Marmara*, *Güzel Girit* (1232gt/1891), *Kızılırmak* (1945gt/1890), *Akdeniz* and *Mithat Paşa* (4455gt/1900) all underway to İstanbul with cargoes of arms and ammunition.

19 November 1912: *Berk-i Satvet* ordered into Bulgarian/ Rumanian coastal waters to give the transports additional protection against possible enemy torpedo-boat attacks. *Hamidiye*, *Berkefşan* and *Yarhisar* are to station off Varna as scouts for the *Mecidiye*.

21 November 1912: *Mecidiye* departs the Bosporus, followed later by *Hamidiye* and *Yarhisar*. *Berkefşan's* sailing is delayed by some four hours due to engine trouble. The squadron sails under the command of the *Hamidiye*'s captain, Yüzbaşı Rauf Bey. *Yarhisar*'s orders are to patrol the coastal waters inside the Varna mine barrage from Kanci to Balçik, with the *Berkefşan* as escort as far as Varna.

21 November 1912: *Hamidiye* and *Berkefşan* ordered to search the sea off Varna for a Russian and a French steamer reported there. At midnight *Hamidiye*, steaming just outside the mine barrier, is attacked by the Bulgarian torpedo-boats *Drski*, *Lettasci*, *Smeli* and *Stogi*.

22 November 1912: At 0004hrs in position 43° 9' 45' N, 28° 21' 5' E, *Hamidiye* is hit by a torpedo from the *Stogi*. The explosion blows a hole 6ft square below the waterline. The outer hull is ripped open for a length of 40ft by 20ft on the starboard side between the forward boiler room and the 150mm magazine. The crew is well trained and damage control functions quickly and efficiently. All the pumps work without trouble (unusual by the normal standards of an Ottoman warship), and a dangerous list to starboard is corrected by counter-flooding, though the bow remains submerged as far aft as the forward gun. Speed drops to five knots. There are no casualties. At 0230hrs the cruiser is trimmed nearer an even keel, and with the enemy boats now out of range the guns stop firing.

Yarhisar and *Berkefşan* hunt the Bulgarian ships, the former towards Varna while the latter sights *Drski* and *Smeli* and successfully beats off their attacks. Once it has been ascertained that the cruiser is not in danger of sinking, the *Yarhisar* and *Berkefşan* remain inside the mine barrage until daybreak. *Berk-i Satvet* is ordered by wireless during the night to send the escorted steamers back to Constanza and to proceed along the coast to Varna.

At 1130hrs *Torgud Reis* meets up with the damaged cruiser off Karaburnu to assist if necessary. The minelayer *İntibah* takes up the tow off the Bosporus. *Mecidiye* replaces *Hamidiye* at Varna.

23 November 1912: At 0100hrs *Hamidiye* arrives to dock in the Haliç for repairs.

Plans to operate the destroyers as escorts for the transports and for sorties in the area off Varna came to nothing and the warships remained in the Bosporus. The Bulgarians now expected a ceasefire and left the Ottoman transports alone.

3 December 1912: Armistice is signed by the belligerents.

7 February 1913: The Ottoman army plans a raid near Podima. *Asar-i Tevfik* is ordered to proceed at 1800hrs to Podima to make contact with the army. It is planned to give further destroyer cover to the landings, but only *Basra* and *Taşoz* are in service, and both departed the Bosporus at 0600hrs in company with the steamer *Bezmialem* to escort the *Kızılırmak*, loaded with arms and ammunition, from Constanza to İstanbul.

8 February 1913: The small raiding force lands at Podima and immediately meets strong Bulgarian resistance; the operation is abandoned and the raiders return to their Greek prize transports.

12.45 pm: *Asar-i Tevfik* runs aground on an uncharted sandbank while approaching Podima to bombard the town. Despite immediate attempts to free the ship by use of the engines, the corvette remains fast and begins to sink deeper into the sand. The warship is not equipped with radio, so a small party is sent ashore to make contact with İstanbul.

10 February 1913: The transport *Giresun* departs İstanbul with a salvage team in the morning, followed by *Basra* and *Taşoz* at noon and *Berkefşan* later in the afternoon. The salvage group arrives later in the day and work begins transferring all serviceable equipment and fittings.

11 February 1913: The Greek prize *Nicolaos* (870gt/1885) comes alongside the stranded corvette and off-loads ammunition and guns. *Giresun* takes off the bulk of the coal.

12 February 1913: The task of stripping and disarming the corvette is completed, the exhausted crew boards the *Giresun* and the salvage fleet returns to İstanbul. The Bulgarians later destroy the wreck by gunfire.

April–May 1913: The steamer *Kızılırmak*, with *Taşoz* and *Berkefşan* as escorts, continues to make a weekly run to Constanza, the only Ottoman merchant ship keeping the lines of supply to and from Rumania open.

Dardanelles operations

There were considerable differences of opinion in the naval officer corps over the Dardanelles operations. This was due in part to the army command's concept of the military operations and in part to party politics and political loyalties.

7 December 1912: Tahir Bey is replaced as commander-in-chief by Ramiz Naman Bey, the leader of the pro-war faction of the officer corps. New operational plans are quickly drawn up. These foresee attacks on the Greek fleet whenever it is known that the cruiser *Georgios Averoff* is out of range.

The Ottoman fleet was reorganised into an armoured ship division, two destroyer divisions and an operations group acting independently. Energetic and competent officers were given command over the groups. The crews responded with enthusiasm to the new requirements, but the concept was soon seen to be impracticable. Machinery and equipment on board were in a poor state of repair and maintenance. No arrangements had been made for bunkering and for adequate supplies of fuel, ammunition and stores.

12 December 1912: *Basra* and *Taşoz* are ordered to patrol off the Dardanelles and lure the Greek destroyers into the sights of the waiting *Yadigar-i Millet* and *Muavent-i Milliye*. The operation, under the command of Yüzbaşı Rauf Bey, has to be cancelled due to boiler trouble on the *Basra*-class boats.

14 December 1912: Reports are received that the *Georgios Averoff* is grounded off Imroz and out of action. *Sultanhisar* is to proceed towards Bozca Ada and draw the enemy destroyers to the *Mecidiye,* lying in wait between Imroz and Seddülbahir. At 0420hrs *Basra* leaves the Narrows and proceeds along the Anatolian coast as far as Kumkale on patrol, then turns back toward the fleet. At 0645hrs *Basra* stops close to the fleet at Nara and reports sighting Greek warships.

At 1145hrs *Sultanhisar* makes contact with the enemy and is soon under fire from the destroyers *Sphendoni* and *Lonchi*. *Sultanhisar* makes for the Dardanelles and *Mecidiye* alters course towards the Greek destroyers. At 1330hrs *Mecidiye* opens fire on the *Sphendoni* and *Lonchi,* and also on the newly-arrived *Thylla* and *Nafkratoussa*. The destroyers *Doxa*, *Neagenea* and *Venos* are also sighted approaching the cruiser from Bozca Ada. The engagement lasts over an hour without serious damage to either side. At 1420hrs *Nümune-i Hamiyet* sends a radio report of the action to Nara, the cruiser's radio equipment being out of action, and at 1500hrs the Ottoman warships meet up and proceed home. At 1645hrs they join the fleet at Nara, fears of attack by the Greek submarine *Delfin* during the run home having proved groundless.

16 December 1912: An operation is planned against Imroz. The Battleship and Second Divisions are to steam out of the Dardanelles in line ahead, with the Third Division, comprising the fleet auxiliaries, taking up station off Kumkale to offer towing assistance if necessary. The battleships are to sail from the Narrows for Imroz while remaining under the protection of the fortress guns at Kumkale; the First Division is to cover the battleships from the starboard against an expected destroyer attack from the northeast, and the Second Division has a similar assignment to port. The warships leave their anchorages between Nara and Çanakkale between 0700 and 0800hrs.

At 0800hrs *Sivrihisar, Barbaros Hayreddin, Torgud Reis, Mesudiye* and *Asar-i Tevfik* take up station off Seddülbahir. The First Division steams ahead of the battleships and alters course near Hellas to proceed north. The Greek fleet is soon sighted, and *Mecidiye* joins the Second Division to reinforce its capability against the submarine *Delfin*. *Samsun* and *Akhisar* steam ahead as scouts but, lacking radio equipment, can only communicate with the main fleet by semaphore via *Tirimüjgan*. The battle fleet sails towards the approaching Greek fleet, consisting of the *Georgios Averoff, Spetsai, Hydra* and *Psara*.

The Ottoman warships open fire at 0940hrs, at 9,000 metres. At 0945hrs *Georgios Averoff* crosses the bows of the fleet, and the Ottoman battleships are soon being fired on from both sides. The Ottoman commander has no alternative but to break off the engagement and make for the Dardanelles. The First Division passes up the chance to attack the Greek cruiser, now separated from the rest of the enemy fleet. The Greeks also fail to send their destroyers after the retreating Ottoman ships.

At 0950hrs the *Barbaros Hayreddin* begins the turning manoeuvre, and the squadron follows round. The manoeuvre is poorly executed, and rapidly degenerates into chaos. In the confusion the ships block each other's gun arcs and speed drops to ten knots. At 0955hrs *Barbaros Hayreddin* receives a hit on the afterdeck and five men from a damage control party are killed. Shortly afterwards the after turret is hit and jammed out of action. Shrapnel pierces the unarmoured hull, damaging a number of boilers and starting a bunker fire. *Torgud Reis* and *Mesudiye* also receive hits, but casualties are light and only slight damage is done to the upperworks and guns.

Firing ceases at 1017hrs and the squadron makes for Hellas, *Mesudiye* and *Asar-i Tevfik* going on ahead and circling off the Dardanelles to cover the rear of the slower battleships and to relieve the Second Division of its flanking role. The squadron reaches Seddülbahir at 1200hrs, and Çanakkale at 1300hrs, where the eighteen dead and forty wounded were landed and transferred to the hospital ship *Resit Paşa*. The First Division then sails for Bozca Ada and sights a group of Greek destroyers making for the Dardanelles. At 1545hrs both sides fire a few rounds before separating.

The results of the day's fighting are disappointing, but the navy has at least set an example of courage and determination in a time of few successes and considerable tension within the government. This is also the first time that the navy had seen action since 1877.

19 December 1912: The steamer *Nilüfer* brings a group of top-ranking army officers and the navy minister from İstanbul to Maydos and anchors near the *Barbaros Hayreddin*. At a top-level conference on board the army proposes combined action to recapture some of the enemy-held islands. This is rejected by the navy, which considered itself unable either to support logistically or protect adequately such an undertaking. The navy does, however, agree to seize every opportunity to harass the enemy. At the conference no decision is reached on withdrawal from service of the *Asar-i Tevfik* and the *Mesudiye*, both continually plagued by boiler problems. The navy seeks approval to lay up the *Asar-i Tevfik* at the Dardanelles but to refit the *Mesudiye*.

20 December 1912: The fleet divisions are regrouped, and the energetic leader of the First Division, Yüzbaşı Rauf Bey, is given a free hand in meeting enemy attacks on the Dardanelles. At the same time he is warned against unnecessarily endangering his command and wasting fuel and ammunition.

22 December 1912: *Mecidiye, Berk-i Satvet* and the First Division leave Çanakkale for Imroz, the Second Division for a holding position in the Narrows. Rauf Bey hopes to trap the Greek destroyers, which were active off the Anatolian coast, between his two divisions. The Greek *Niki* and *Doxa* are sighted by *Mecidiye* and *Berk-i Satvet* and pursued, but the Greeks are soon out of range.

Off Imroz *Muavent-i Milliye* stops and searches the Rumanian steamers *Elma* and *Kalafat;* they are allowed to proceed after the ships' papers are found to be correct.

At 0955hrs *Mecidiye* and *Berk-i Satvet* engage a force of six Greek destroyers, which breaks off action after a few minutes and makes off at high speed. Off Bozca Ada at 1040hrs the cruisers sight the *Aspis* and begin closing the range. *Aspis* quickly makes for the coast and the cruisers alter course to bring their guns to bear. While altering position the *Mecidiye* comes dangerously close to the *Delfin*. The submarine attacks at a range of some 800 metres, but the torpedo breaks surface and passes the cruiser; this is the first submarine torpedo attack in naval history.

At 1100hrs *Mecidiye* and *Berk-i Satvet* are ordered back to Çanakkale, the Ottoman destroyers remaining on patrol. The destroyers leave the Bozca Ada area at 1300hrs and return to base. The army remained determined to attempt a landing on Bozca Ada, convinced that the island could be occupied and held by a light military presence, and began planning the landing of an infantry regiment. The navy could cover the landings with its cruisers and destroyers. The navy again protested that it could not prevent Greek countermeasures, but plans went ahead. The *Plevne* (1845gt/1892) was made ready to embark the 'Yenihan' regiment. The Battleship and the Second Divisions received orders to prepare for escorting the transports. *Hamidiye, Mecidiye* and *Berk-i Satvet* were to cover the actual landings.

4 January 1913: The weather for the landing is ideal, with poor visibility and an overcast sky. *Plevne* is ready for sea but the troops have not arrived. The naval command decides to make use of the opportunity and orders the waiting squadron into the waters around Bozca Ada. The cruisers, accompanied by *Berk-i Satvet* raise anchor off Çanakkale at 0600hrs. At 0715 the cruisers and escorts pass Hellas, followed by the destroyer squadron, under Rauf Bey. The Second Division is now also off the Narrows.

At 0730hrs the cruisers sight a Greek squadron near Imroz. The Ottoman destroyers alter course towards the *Hamidiye*. Both sides open fire at 0740hrs, but the shots fall short and no attempt is made to close the range. The Ottoman fleet then divides, the destroyers making for Tarsan Ada. *Mecidiye* and *Berk-i Satvet* cover against an attack from Bozca Ada.

At 1000hrs the battleships clear the Narrows and are joined by

Kütahya *in the Dardanelles during the Balkan War of 1913.* Hamidiye *is visible in the background.*
Güleryüz

the cruisers and destroyers. *Hamidiye*, *Mecidiye* and *Berk-i Satvet* take up station astern of the battleships with the First Division to port and the second Division to starboard of the main fleet. By 1130hrs the fleet has reached a position where it is in danger of being cut off from the Dardanelles by the Greek fleet. The battleships and their escorting destroyers alter course for the Dardanelles and the cruisers are ordered to make for the enemy.

The cruisers open fire on the retreating Greeks at 1150hrs, but firing ceases at 1230hrs without any hits being recorded. The Greek formation splits up and disappears to the south. The Ottoman cruisers rejoin the main fleet. By 1530hrs the fleet is anchored off Çanakkale; the *Plevne* has not even begun embarking troops for the landing, and the operation is cancelled.

10 January 1913: *Hamidiye*, *Mecidiye* and *Berk-i Satvet* put to sea to hunt the destroyer *Doxa*, sighted near the Anatolian coast. The cruisers pass the Narrows at 1400hrs, and on sighting the *Doxa* give chase. By the time the destroyer reaches Bozca Ada it is out of range, and after firing a few rounds the Ottoman cruisers return to base.

The action of 10 January was just one of many cat-and-mouse games played between the two sides. The Greek destroyers always managed to remain outside the Ottoman warships' range, and each time the cruisers fired a few rounds before breaking off the chase.

In this incident the navy minister wanted to know why the two cruisers did not close with the enemy. The fleet command answered that it was not prepared to risk the cruisers for a few enemy destroyers, and that shortage of coal made it necessary to send the modern destroyers back to base early in the engagement.

The commander-in-chief Albay Ramiz now proposed shelling Imroz to draw out the enemy warships. With the exception of *Nümune-i Hamiyet* (laid up with turbine problems) the entire squadron received orders to prepare for sea. The battleships, cruisers and destroyers were to attack Imroz. *Asar-i Tevfik*, *İntibah* and four torpedoboats were to patrol the sea area off the Dardanelles. The hospital ship *Reşit Paşa* would remain at Çanakkale and *Tirimüjgan* was to act as a floating signal station between the squadron and the patrols, and would be positioned near Kumkale.

10 January 1913: At 0825hrs the flagship *Barbaros Hayreddin*, leading *Torgud Reis*, *Mesudiye* and *Asar-i Tevfik*, passes Hellas; *Mecidiye* and *Hamidiye* are a few miles ahead and the main fleet follows, on a general course of 250° at 12.5 knots. The destroyers of the Second Division steam in echelon with the battleships. The First Division takes up position north of the main force but still close to the Anatolian coast. *Asar-i Tevfik* is now detached to patrol the area between Hellas and Kumkale.

The cruisers sight two enemy destroyers at 0833hrs and, increasing speed, give chase. The Greeks turn away when the cruisers close to 1800 metres. The cruisers reduce speed and wait until the ships of the Second Division come up. At 0840hrs *Tirimüjgan* picks up a signal from *Asar-i Tevfik* reporting enemy warships in its area. Albay Ramiz receives the information at 1005hrs, and orders the squadron to turn around. Picking up the cruisers and the escorting destroyers, the fleet sets course for the Dardanelles.

At 1130hrs the squadron again turns on to a northerly course towards Imroz and divides, with the First and Second Division taking up station to starboard of the main fleet. In this formation the fleet advances on a course parallel to Kephalo Burnu. *Asar-i Tevfik* reports three more enemy destroyers east of the fleet.

The battleships open fire at 1215hrs, and the Greeks turn away. At 1225hrs the Greek ships return and are soon in range of *Asar-i Tevfik*'s guns; a few rounds are fired but no hits recorded, and the destroyers turn away again. *Hamidiye* and *Mecidiye* alter course towards the gun flashes. At 1245hrs the battleships alter course to the south.

Hamidiye fires on two enemy destroyers off Kephalo Burnu at 1250hrs, but no attempt is made to follow the fleeing enemy. At 1350hrs the battleships pick up the cruisers and head west, the whole fleet setting course for the Dardanelles at 1415hrs.

18 January 1913: A further action is planned by Albay Ramiz. *Hamidiye*, in the Aegean Sea since 13 January, is signalled to return from patrol to join the fleet, but the signal is not received; the operation goes ahead without the cruiser. The plan is to advance towards Limanli and seek contact with the Greek ships, on the assumption that the *Georgios Averoff* will be with the enemy fleet and not at sea hunting the *Hamidiye*.

The fleet leaves the Dardanelles at 0820hrs on course 253 degrees, at a speed of only eleven knots. The flagship *Barbaros Hayreddin* leads the main force, with *Mecidiye* forging ahead and *Berk-i Satvet*, *Basra* and *Yarhisar* to port and starboard. The fleet auxiliaries are in position in the Narrows and the tugs *Samsun* and *İntibah* have steam up, reading for salvage operations if necessary.

The Greek destroyer *Leon*, accompanied by the torpedo-boat *Aspis*, is waiting off the Dardanelles and signals the Ottoman sortie. The *Georgios Averoff*, *Hydra*, *Psara* and five destroyers immediately steam to meet the Ottoman force.

At 1055hrs *Mecidiye* sights the approaching Greeks, reports to the flagship and then speeds back to the fleet with *Basra* and *Yarhisar*. Albay Ramiz orders a course alteration to the south and the fleet begins to close the enemy. 1155hrs: *Barbaros Hayreddin* opens fire on the *Georgios Averoff* at 1155hrs, at a range of 8,000 metres. The other warships also begin concentrating their gunfire on the enemy cruiser. At 1200hrs the Greeks return fire. They make use of their superior sea speed (the Ottoman battleships could only make about sixteen knots) to try to steam round the enemy.

Albay Ramiz orders *Mecidiye* and the destroyer escort to withdraw and continues the engagement with his major warships. At 1250hrs Greek attempts to 'cross the T' are foiled when the Ottoman fleet, *Barbaros Hayreddin* leading, alters course to the north. *Mesudiye* is hit on the 150mm battery at 1255hrs and three guns are put out of action, though there are no casualties. Already seriously hampered by boiler problems, *Mesudiye* is ordered to withdraw and returned to base. *Barbaros Hayreddin* is hit on the centre 280mm turret and the entire gun crew is killed; further hits on the superstructure cause only slight damage but smoke and escaping steam and fumes are sucked into the engine and boiler rooms. The crews are forced to abandon their stations, and speed falls off to five knots. *Torgud Reis* takes over as leader.

At 1255hrs the damaged flagship passes *Torgud Reis* and is covered by the latter. The enemy are kept at a distance, and finding themselves close to the Ottoman batteries of Kumkale, the Greek ships break off the engagement and turn away. The action ends at 1400hrs as both sides return to base.

February 1913: The Bulgarian High Command charters five merchant ships at Fiume. They load food supplies and are prepared to leave for Dedegaz.

16 February 1913: İstanbul receives word of the convoy, and *Hamidiye*, at sea in the Mediterranean, is ordered to capture the Bulgarian ships.

20 February 1913: Yüzbası Rifat is ordered to prepare a light task force. This force is to operate off the Dardanelles and intercept any Greek ship sent to hunt the *Hamidiye*. However, due to typical lack of co-ordination and co-operation between the departments at the navy ministry and naval command, the *Hamidiye* receives no orders for action and continues to patrol off Haifa.

22 February 1913: The task force, the sole purpose of which is to distract the enemy while *Hamidiye* hunts down the chartered Bulgarian cargo vessels, puts to sea. *Mecidiye*, *Muavent-i Milliye*, *Gayret-i Vataniye*, *Yarhisar*, *Demirhisar* and *Hamidabad* pass Hellas at 0830hrs. *Muavent-i Milliye* is detached for the Gulf of Saros to cover the flank and the remaining ships proceed towards Imroz. A light sea fog reduces visibility, and speed is reduced. Two enemy destroyers are sighted, but no action is taken. Both sides turned away as the range closes, and the Ottoman ships, still proceeding at reduced speed, make for base. At 1200hrs the force passes Çanakkale, and the operation ends.

Meanwhile, reports reach the navy ministry at İstanbul that the *Georgios Averoff* is damaged and out of service. The army command uses this unconfirmed information to justify landings on Midilli and Sakiz. Orders are given to prepare seven steamers to act as troop transports and have them ready for embarkation at the Dardanelles. The naval command doubts the validity of the reports, and treats the proposed landings with scepticism. However, in order to confirm the reports, the fleet is ordered to put to sea and proceed to Imroz. Here it is hoped to meet the Greeks, with or without the *Georgios Averoff*. The naval command believes that the Greek cruiser is at sea hunting the *Hamidiye*.

3 March 1913: *Demirhisar* and *Sultanhisar* leave the Dardanelles and sail along the Anatolian coast to hunt the submarine *Delfin*, believed to be patrolling in the area. The destroyers *Muavent-i Milliye*, *Gayret-i Vataniye* and *Yarhisar* are detached from the main fleet, the former to the Gulf of Saros and the others going on towards Tarsan Ada with orders to watch for the enemy near Bozca Ada.

A Greek squadron is sighted at 0934hrs coming from Imroz and

the Ottoman flotilla leader, Binbasi Muzaffer Ali, on board the *Mecidiye,* is certain that he has the *Georgios Averoff*, two armoured cruisers and six destroyers ahead. By 0955hrs *Berk-i Satvet* is in torpedo range of the enemy, but neither side takes action and the Greeks, apparently unwilling to risk action, turn away towards Bozca Ada. This unwillingness is hard to understand since the superior Greek force could have cut off the Ottoman ships from the Dardanelles; instead, they reach the Narrows safely, and the proposed landings are cancelled.

9 March 1913: Another operation is planned against Imroz. *Mecidiye* sails from the Dardanelles in company with *Berk-i Satvet* and *Yarhisar*. *Demirhisar* and *Hamidabad* patrol off the Dardanelles. After passing the Narrows the ships split up. *Berk-i Satvet* turns north for the Gulf of Saros and *Yarhisar* makes for Bozca Ada.

At 1045hrs Greek destroyers are sighted by *Yarhisar*, which makes for *Mecidiye* to report. At 1230hrs *Berk-i Satvet* radios sighting two destroyers and a steamer near Imroz. *Mecidiye* orders the torpedo-boats to return to Çanakkale. The remaining Ottoman warships then head towards the enemy and open fire. The Greek ships return fire briefly, then make off. *Berk-i Satvet* stops the steamer, which is sailing under the name *Hanri* (or, more probably, *Henri*) under the French flag, and carrying foodstuffs. *Mecidiye*'s captain suspects that the owners are in fact Bulgarians and that the steamer is en route to Dedeağa. A prize crew from *Yarhisar* goes on board and the steamer, with destroyer escort, is taken to Çanakkale. At 1600hrs *Mecidiye*'s patrol ends, and the cruiser returns to the Narrows.

March 1913: *Torgud Reis* and *Mesudiye* are out of action with damaged guns, and the repairs are considerably delayed due to a shortage of materials. During the month no task forces leave the Narrows, although the opportunity is taken to carry out battle manoeuvres and gunnery practice in the Sea of Marmara.

April 1913: The customs post at Urla reports sighting a cruiser and four destroyers. It is obvious that the Greeks are going to attempt to blockade the Gulf of İzmir.

8 April 1913: *Mecidiye* and a destroyer flotilla comprising *Gayret-i Vataniye*, *Muavent-i Milliye* and *Nümune-i Hamiyet* depart the Narrows to investigate the reported sightings. *Gayret-i Vataniye* proceeds as far as the Gulf of Saros, and the cruiser and its escorts go to Tarsan Ada. Three enemy destroyers are sighted maintaining their long-range blockade of the Dardanelles, but since they are too far away no action is taken. At 1720hrs *Gayret-i Vataniye* rejoins the group, which then returns to Çanakkale.

10 April 1913: *Georgios Averoff* sighted off Bozca Ada. The fleet commander orders his squadron to move from Nara to Çanakkale to coal and replenish ammunition and stores.

11 April 1913: *Gayret-i Vataniye* and *Yadigar-i Millet* depart the Dardanelles at 0930hrs and, steaming southeast, soon sight two enemy destroyers near Bozca Ada. The sightings are immediately reported to base, and fleet command orders the boats to shadow the enemy ships. At 1140hrs two further Greek destroyers join up, and close the torpedo-boats. After firing a few rounds they make off for base.

At 1217hrs *Barbaros Hayreddin* (with the fleet commander on board), *Torgud Reis*, *Berk-i Satvet*, *Nümune-i Hamiyet* and *Hamidabad* anchor off Çanakkale. *Asar-i Tevfik* joins shortly afterwards and the squadron is ready for action. Meanwhile, *Mecidiye* sails at 1220hrs to join the two destroyers off the Dardanelles, reaching Kumkale by 1300hrs. The destroyers reach Kumkale at 1350hrs, and the Greeks now approach at high speed.

At 1335hrs, steaming parallel courses, both sides open fire. At

1400hrs the Ottoman warships break off the action and made for home, while the Greeks make for Imroz. No hits on either side are reported. As usual, the range was great enough to ensure that there was little chance of a serious damage.

Sea of Marmara operations

30 October 1912: Bulgarian cavalry reaches Tekirdağ. Patrols are soon seen in the Gelibolu area. Ottoman troops are withdrawn behind the Çatalca Line, and the navy is ordered to support the Line from the Sea of Marmara. The old gunboats stationed there however are not suitable for the task, and İstanbul orders the two old armoured corvettes *İclaliye* and *Necm-i Şevket,* laid-up out of service, fitted out and made ready for sea. Both warships could reach their designated firing stations only under tow.

6 November 1912: *Hamidiye* relieves the battleships, and *Asar-i Tevfik*, following another round of boiler repairs, takes up station off Tekirdağ.

7 November 1912: The Bulgarians occupy Tekirdağ. *Asar-i Tevfik* shells the beach, but the bombardment has little impact on the enemy. *Torgud Reis* and *Basra*, sent to assist, are withdrawn after a day's bombardment.

13–14 November 1912: *Hamidiye* and *Mecidiye* bombard Bulgarian troops at Çatalca. The action has to be curtailed due to a shortage of ammunition.

15 November 1912: *Hamidiye* brings the navy minister Salih Paşa from İstanbul to Büyükçekmece.

15–20 November 1912: *Torgud Reis*, *Barbaros Hayreddin*, *Mesudiye*, *Asar-i Tevfik*, *Necm-i Şevket* and *İclaliye* are on station at Büyükçekmece, but make little contact with the enemy.

3 December 1912: The commander of the Black Sea Fleet requests additional ships to strengthen his command. Accordingly *Bezm-i Alem*, *Berk-i Satvet* and *Berkefşan* are sent from Marmara to the Black Sea. The Marmara force, under Albay Tekirdağ Kadi, is now left with few serviceable ships. These comprise the *İclaliye* at anchor off Büyükçekmece, the corvette *Zuhaf* at Çanakkale and the gunboat *Nevşehir* off the Marmara Islands. The gunboat *Nur-ül Bahir,* actually an armed steamer, is in dock at İstanbul undergoing boiler repairs but is expected back shortly.

14 December 1912: The destroyers *Akhisar*, *Musul* and *Yarhisar* are sent on rotation to supplement the Marmara force.

January 1913: The gunboats are reassigned to duties as tugs for sailing ships in the Marmara.

January–February 1913: The X Army Corps is set up at İzmir and Bandırma. The troops are briefed to occupy the Bulgarian-held positions once the ceasefire is signed, as part of the government's plan to retake Edirne.

4 February 1913: Special forces from the Jandarma land from the *Zuhaf* near Mürefte to test the enemy's strength, but are repulsed by the waiting Bulgarians. Eight members of the landing force are killed. On the same day at 0900hrs, *Berk-i Satvet* and *Nur-ül Bahir* bombard Şarköy and later Mürefte.

5 February 1913: *Mesudiye* arrives off Şarköy with the other units and the town is bombarded from 0930hrs to 1830hrs. More damage is inflicted on the civilian population than on the Bulgarian troops.

Light attacks by Ottoman forces on Bulgarian-held positions on the Çatalca front had little effect on the enemy. İstanbul, despite serious doubts on the part of commander-in-chief, General Ahmet İzzet, decided to go ahead with a full-scale landing at Şarköy. Two divisions of the X Army Corps began embarkation at İzmit and Bandırma at the beginning of February. In order to speed up the operation, the government chartered twelve of the fast Bosporus

ferries as transports.

5–7 February 1913: All troops are embarked for the landing, which is openly reported in the İstanbul newspapers.

8 February 1913: At 0500hrs the transports from İstanbul, İzmit, Bandırma and Erdek are in position in a line Şarköy-Inceburnu. Due to a lack of co-ordination the covering warships fail to arrive on time. The liaison officer on the transport *Nilüfer* and the divisional staffs on the steamer *Baslangic* are compelled to postpone the landing and await the arrival of the naval force. At 0900hrs *Barbaros Hayreddin*, *Torgud Reis*, *Mecidiye* and *Berk-i Satvet*, which have only begun weighing anchor at Nara at 0550hrs, arrive and commence firing on the Bulgarian entrenchments on both sides of Şarköy. After the bombardment ends, the transports move in and the troops are landed over pontoons; they meet only light resistance.

9 February 1913: Additional battalions are landed, but the Bulgarians now counter-attack in strength, and by the afternoon the landing troops are being driven steadily back.

10 February 1913: The situation is now becoming critical for the Ottoman army, and, although the transports still have large numbers of fresh troops on board and more are on their way from İstanbul, orders are given to abandon the landings. The situation around Gelibolu has also worsened, and the troops at Şarköy are needed to prop up the Gelibolu front. At 1620hrs evacuation of the landing forces commences and the embarkation is speedily completed without serious interference from the Bulgarians.

11 February 1913: The last remaining troops are embarked from the beaches by four of the chartered Bosporus ferries.

18 February 1913: Another landing at Şarköy is ordered by Enver Paşa. The landings are a complete failure and the troops are quickly reembarked on the transports *Akdeniz* and *Karadeniz,* which then return to İstanbul. the army command had failed to inform the navy of these plans, so that no warships were present at this fiasco.

Until the final armistice in April, naval activity was restricted to patrols by *Musul* and *Draç* to Tekirdağ and Silivri, though the two torpedo-boats made no attempt to fire on the enemy. During this last phase of the war the *İclaliye* remained inactive off Büyükhekmece.

The cruise of the *Hamidiye*

This undertaking, actually three separate sorties, is perhaps the best known of all exploits of the Ottoman navy, with the *Hamidiye* and its commanding officer Yüzbaşı Hüseyin Rauf (1881–1964) achieving a certain celebrity throughout the world.

Hüseyin Rauf, who changed his family name to Rauf Orbay in 1930, joined the İttihat ve Terakki movement as a young naval lieutenant. While captain of the torpedo cruiser *Peyk-i Şevket,* which he commanded from 1908 until 1911, Hüseyin Rauf took an active role during the abdication crisis of Sultan Abdül Hamid II. When the *Peyk-i Şevket* was interned at Suez at the outbreak of the Italian war, Hüseyin Rauf made his way back to İstanbul to take command of the *Hamidiye*. He always considered himself to be a political officer, so that when the Balkan wars were over it was natural that he should be posted to the navy ministry. Here he directed the planning department responsible for the new capital ships under construction in Britain. He was also designated to command the *Sultan Osman I*.

During World War I he was employed for much of the duration on political missions. He visited Baghdad and made contact with high ranking Persian officers in an attempt to bring that country into the war on the Ottoman side against Britain, and as navy minister (14 September–23 November 1918) was signatory to the ceasefire agreement at Mudros on 30 October 1918.

Although politically active on behalf of Enver Paşa and also an activist in the İttihat ve Terakki, Hüseyin Rauf went over to Kemal Paşa (Atatürk) at the end of 1918. He became chief minister (12 July 1922–14 August 1923) of the Republic. As a diplomat he represented the Republic at the London conference in 1922. He went into exile following disagreements with Atatürk, remaining abroad until July 1935. He was elected to parliament in October 1939. Rauf Orbay remained politically active until his death on 16 September 1964. This, then, was the energetic officer entrusted in early 1913 with a mission which few observers considered the Ottoman navy capable of carrying out.

All previous encounters had demonstrated clearly that as long as the *Georgios Averoff* was present there was little chance of the Ottoman navy sinking or even seriously damaging the lighter units of the Greek navy. It was therefore proposed that a cruiser should be sent into the Aegean to attack the smaller Greek ports and coastal towns and capture or sink enemy merchant vessels. It was assumed that the Greeks would then withdraw the *Georgios Averoff* from the Dardanelles area to hunt down and destroy the marauder.

The cruiser selected was *Hamidiye* which, unlike the very similar *Mecidiye*, had no stability problems. Torpedo damage from November 1912 had now been repaired and the cruiser was ready for sea. One flaw in these preparations was that the radio equipment continued to give trouble. Hüseyin Rauf was ordered to sail from the Dardanelles to raid the port at Ernupolis on Syros, then return to Çanakkale. At the same time the fleet would sail from the Narrows and seek action with the enemy.

13 January 1913: *Hamidiye* anchors off Küsetabya, a small Dardanelles village near Nara.

14 January 1913: At 0900hrs the *Hamidiye* departs Kephez, while *Mecidiye*, escorted by the destroyers *Basra* and *Yarhisar*, patrols the entrance to the Dardanelles. The patrol returns to base without sighting enemy ships. *Hamidiye*, steaming at only fifteen knots, leaves home waters at about 1800hrs and, sailing through rough seas and in overcast weather passes Semendirek and Limnos.

15 January 1913: *Hamidiye* is off Sira before noon and finds the British merchant vessel *Alexandra* and the Greek auxiliary *Makedonia* in port. Both ships are signalled to leave the port. *Makedonia* (5033gt/1912) is quickly abandoned by its crew, and is shelled, set on fire and sunk. *Hamidiye* also bombards the town, damaging the power station. At 1300hrs Hüseyin Rauf ends the bombardment and the cruiser makes for the open sea. The Greeks later raise the *Makedonia* and it is repaired and returned to service. Although this action is only a limited success, the propaganda effect within the Empire is considerable. At last the navy appeared to be actively pursuing the *Georgios Averoff*. Unfortunately for the Empire, the Greek commander, Admiral Londuriotis, refuses to fall into the trap and the cruiser remained on station in the Aegean.

16 January 1913: Aware of the danger of meeting the enemy en route to the Dardanelles and without radio contact to the fleet, Hüseyin Rauf sets course for Crete on his own authority.

18 January 1913: *Hamidiye* anchors off Beirut. Here the cruiser quickly takes on coal and provisions and sets course for Egypt.

19 January 1913: *Hamidiye* arrives at Port Said at 0130hrs. Although Egypt is nominally still under Ottoman rule, the influence of the British authorities is sufficient to ensure that only 150 tons of coal are made available and minor boiler repairs carried out.

21 January 1913: After remaining in neutral waters for over thirty hours *Hamidiye* departs Port Said and passes through the Suez Canal and into the Red Sea. On the way the cruiser stops at every Ottoman outpost for news and instructions from İstanbul. At Cidde repairs to the condensers are made and a small quantity of coal bunkered.

5 February 1913: The navy minister decides that it would still be unwise for the cruiser to attempt the break through to the Dardanelles. *Hamidiye* is ordered to proceed to the Adriatic and operate along the Albanian coast.

6 February 1913: *Hamidiye* anchors off Port Said at 0300hrs. The Ottoman embassy in Vienna has chartered the Italian steamer *Alba* to take 450 tons of bunker coal to Malta, and *Hamidiye* is ordered to proceed there.

13 January 1913: Bad weather and rough seas make the transfer of the coal in international waters off Malta impossible. *Alba* is ordered to make for La Valetta.

14 February 1913: On arrival at La Valetta, *Hamidiye* finds that the *Alba* has departed for Beirut, and bunker coal has to be obtained from Maltese suppliers.

17 February 1913: Bunkering is completed by midnight, but the limited supplies of fuel now on board make operations along the Albanian coast out of the question.

23 February 1913: *Hamidiye* arrives at Haifa and takes on 350 tons of coal, supplied by the Hejaz Railway. Declining to contact the navy ministry, Hüseyin Rauf decides to make for the Anatolian coast.

25 February 1913: *Hamidiye* arrives at Kekava and receives news from İstanbul. Following minor boiler repairs the cruiser proceeds to Antalya, where 10,000 gold lira and fifty tons of ammunition are to be loaded for the Northern Army and the intention is to make for the Albanian coast as originally planned. Owing to the general inefficiency of the Ottoman administration these essential supplies fail to arrive on time (the roads and the railways to Antalya are unable to cope with this amount of freight).

29 February 1913: *Hamidiye* proceeds to Beirut to bunker from the *Alba,* then sails for Avrat Island to load ammunition.

6 March 1913: The cruiser arrives at Avrat and the ammunition is taken on board from small sailing boats, which have collected the ammunition from Mersin and other small ports and brought it to the island. Once loading has been completed it is discovered that the fuses are missing, and *Hamidiye* is ordered to İskenderun to pick these up.

8 March 1913: *Hamidiye* departs at 0500hrs, with orders to make for Semeni River on the Albanian coast.

12 March 1913: The cruiser appears off Draç (Durazzo) and shells a Greek military camp before making off at high speed. Later *Hamidiye* arrives at Singin (S. Giovanni di Medua), where seven Greek and one Austrian steamer lie at anchor. These are the *Harisonalis Sifneos* (in ballast), *Trifilya* (troops and twelve field guns), *Elpis* (1,116 troops, seventy-five pack animals, ammunition), *Zanof Sifneos* (troops, pack animals), *Marika* (1,250 troops, three aircraft), *Zeva* (200 troops, 288 pack animals, nine field guns), *N. Verveniotis* (1,250 troops, twenty-three pack animals, twenty-nine guns) and the Austrian *Scutari*. *Hamidiye* orders the latter to beach itself and opens fire on the Greek steamers – all transports for the Serbian army – and heavily damages six vessels. More than 120 Serbians lose their lives in the attack. At 1245hrs *Hamidiye* departs Singin.

15 March 1913: The Greek gunboats *Acheloos*, *Alpheos*, *Eurotas* and *Peneos* hunt the Ottoman cruiser in the Straits of Otranto. Off Cape Rodni *Acheloos* sights *Hamidiye,* which opens fire and hits the gunboat before making its escape. With fuel supplies running low and all the ports along the Aegean coast and the waters off Anatolia blockaded by the Greeks, Hüseyin Rauf decides to return to Egypt.

16 March 1913: *Hamidiye* arrives at Alexandria. Here again difficulty is experienced in obtaining coal and an attempt to purchase a cargo of coal from a British collier fails. Without exact information from the naval command on the whereabouts and strength of the enemy fleet, Hüseyin Rauf is compelled to keep moving from port to port, and any instructions he receives from İstanbul are usually too late to be of any practical value.

22 March 1913: *Hamidiye* arrives at Beyrut. Here word is waiting from the navy ministry that attempts are to be made to refit and supply the cruiser at Antalya, and that small sailing craft are already on their way with cargoes of coal and ammunition.

23–28 March 1913: *Hamidiye* puts to sea and cruises between Gaza and Haifa.

29 March 1913: *Hamidiye* sails for Antalya. West of Crete the Greek sailing vessel *Ispandis* is stopped and a prize crew takes the boat with its cargo of bricks to Antalya.

2 April 1913: The cruiser returns to Beirut. Hüseyin Rauf suspects that the Greek navy now knows of his plans and when he arrives in port his suspicions are confirmed. After bunkering the *Hamidiye* sails for the Red Sea to await further instructions.

6 April 1913: *Hamidiye* arrives at Cidde, and proceeds to show the flag round Yemen. Hüseyin Rauf had been there in 1911 with the *Peyk-i Şevket* and knew the area and the local dignitaries well. During this visit, lasting some weeks, many of the local sheiks are welcomed on board and a number of agreements are reached.

30 May 1913: The ceasefire comes into force.

15 June 1913: *Hamidiye* bunkers at Kameron (Red Sea) and after repairs have been made to the boilers and condensers the cruiser sets course for home.

21 August 1913: The cruiser arrives at Suez and bunkers coal without difficulty.

23 August 1913: *Hamidiye* bunkers at Gaza and then sails at eleven knots for home.

5 September 1913: *Hamidiye* arrives at Çanakkale and remained overnight while preparations are made for an official welcome.

7 September 1913: The *Hamidiye* receives a tumultuous welcome from the population of İstanbul. The cruiser is later moored off the Dolmabahçe Palace, and here the eight-month cruise ends.

The Ottoman Empire and World War I, 1914

The Ottoman Empire's entry into World War I in 1914 is still surrounded by the legend that the *Goeben* played the decisive part in bringing the Empire in on the side of the Central Powers. At the outbreak of the war, the policy of the Empire was determined primarily by Enver Paşa, the minister of war, whose pro-German inclinations were well known internationally. Nevertheless İstanbul was not prepared to go to war, with all its incalculable risks, simply through the presence of a battlecruiser in the Dardanelles. Propaganda from all sides gave the *Goeben* and the *Breslau* a more important role in the dramatic days leading up to the declaration of war than they actually earned; the roots of the Ottoman decision were to be found in the pro-German leanings of the government.

At the end of 1913 İstanbul convinced the German government to send a military mission to the Dardanelles. Berlin agreed, but was soon in conflict with the other European powers who wished to maintain their existing influence without interference from Germany.

Berlin's decision to become involved in Ottoman internal affairs is all the more surprising when one considers that France had already over-committed itself financially in the Near East. The French government knew that there was little chance of recovering its considerable investments. The French financial difficulty was, of course, well recognised in finance and banking circles in Berlin and in German industry. Heavy industry companies, while interested in receiving orders from İstanbul, cautioned Berlin to approach the Ottoman proposals with reserve and suggested that Berlin should encourage the exploitation of the İskenderun region along both sides of the Baghdad Railway. Industry also suggested that foreign assistance should be invited to support any Ottoman projects, thereby reducing Germany's own financial risks and at the same time helping to reduce the considerable international ill-feeling over Germany's favoured status.

Industry was dismayed at the idea that Germany should send a military mission to İstanbul, and no company honestly believed that larger orders for arms would result. The problems experienced by Krupp over the past decades were, of course, widely known.

Imperial Germany's long-term goals were more than simply investment in the Ottoman Empire. Through deliveries of arms and political support in international affairs Berlin hoped to keep the Ottoman Empire intact as a functional state until the expected final collapse occurred at which point Germany would be in a strong position to make justifiable claims for compensation.

Germany's main sphere of influence was in the region from İskenderun to Diyarbakir. In 1913–1914 the *Goeben* visited İskenderun and the harbour was surveyed as a possible naval base. Russia was conducting similar surveys along the Black Sea at the time.

Nevertheless it is hard to understand why Berlin assumed that Britain would allow Germany to set up a naval base in the Mediterranean. Naturally, İstanbul was aware of all these problems but continued to hope that envy and distrust amongst the European powers would be sufficient to hold them back from making any aggressive moves against the Ottoman state. Until July 1914 İstanbul's hopes appeared to be justified; then the country was caught in a chain of events that lead to the declaration of war.

Russia was exerting considerable pressure on the Empire to remain neutral in the event of hostilities, but refused to give any guarantee to respect the Ottoman borders. Following the visit of the Tsar to Constanza and Bucharest in June Russia and Rumania agreed to co-operate in the event of the closure of the Straits. Russia also encouraged Rumania and Bulgaria to take action 'to disturb the Turks' although this was not specified.

15 June 1914: Anglo-German agreement signed. This settles the Baghdad Railway problem, the Germans now promising not to extend the line further south of Basra. Berlin also agrees to recognise Britain's interests in shipping on the Euphrates. The agreement reflects real desire on both sides to remove outstanding colonial difficulties in this area.

24 June 1914: Austrian memorandum to Berlin. Vienna favours an alliance with Bulgaria and the Ottoman Empire to make a reconstitution of the Balkan League under Russian and French auspices impossible. Berlin urges Austria-Hungary to reach an agreement with Serbia, Rumania and Greece.

28 June 1914: Assassination of the Archduke Franz Ferdinand at Sarajevo.

June 1914: The chief of the German military mission Liman von Sanders sends a favourable report on the strength and fighting condition of the Ottoman army. Sanders' positive judgement did much to influence Berlin.

22 July 1914: Enver Paşa asks the German ambassador Von Wangenheim to report to Berlin that the Ottoman government wishes to discuss the possibility of an agreement between the two countries. This alliance is to be directed against Russia only. Germany accepts without detailed consideration of the scope of a military alliance with the Ottoman Empire.

1–2 August 1914: The treaty between Imperial Germany and the Ottoman Empire is signed at Yeşilköy, the residence of the Grand Vizier, its contents known only to a few ministers of the government. İstanbul would enter the war as soon as hostilities are opened by Russia against Germany or Austria-Hungary (also a signatory).

It soon becomes clear that both sides have different ideas as to the actual meaning of mutual support. Germany insists on an immediate Ottoman attack on Russia. Only after considerable discussion do the other signatories assent to İstanbul's request for time and neutrality in order to complete the necessary military preparations.

İstanbul seeks specialist assistance in mine and torpedo warfare and gunnery exports for the forts and gun emplacements on the Bosporus and the Dardanelles. Berlin complies, and by the middle of August over six hundred specialists, travelling as traders, merchants, fitters and engineers, have been sent to İstanbul. These men were placed under the command of Admiral von Usedom.

3 August 1914: *Barbaros Hayreddin, Mecidiye* and *Peyk-i Şevket* arrive at the naval shipyard at İstanbul to begin refits. *Mesudiye* follows shortly afterwards. German engineers begin their inspections of the ships and find them in a poor state of repair and maintenance. However, in the short time available, only the very worst deficiencies can be corrected, the ships painted and ammunition, fuel and stores loaded.

At this very early stage of the war the serious shortage of fuel, coal and ammunition is already apparent, with the country dependent on Russia and Rumania for its oil supplies.

İstanbul and the Bosporus, 1914–1918

4 August 1914: Mine barrages are laid by the tugs *İstinye* and *Bospordok* in the Bosporus, the work continuing during the following days. A channel close to the European coast is kept free for the fleet.

6 August 1914: The torpedo-boats of the *Sultanhisar* class are moved from the Bosporus into the Narrows as advance scouts. *Zuhaf* reports sighting Russian cruisers but no action is taken.

11 August 1914: *Goeben* and *Breslau* arrive at the Dardanelles. German experts now present their list of defects on the Ottoman warships. With the exception of *Hamidiye*, well-maintained and ready for sea, and *Mecidiye*, ready for action if not employed in rough seas, all the ships are unfit for service.

Most have boiler problems, leaking condensers and piping. The engines are in a poor state with valves missing. Watertight doors and hatches are missing and the hulls are rusting and leaking. Most of the sights had been removed from the guns. The living quarters and sanitation are in such a desperate state that German seamen refuse to use them.

This poor state of maintenance is used as propaganda by the Germans against the British mission. It was, however, not the purpose of the mission to maintain the Ottoman fleet, but rather to represent British interests in the Middle East and to ensure that British yards received important orders from the Ottoman navy. Any attempt by the mission to encourage reform had already met with the opposition of the officer corps, so that Britain had conceded to Ottoman interest, a policy which worked well enough. As a result the British mission and its work were looked upon favourably and the staff with respect throughout the war.

August–September 1914: German gun crews begin manning the coastal batteries along the Bosporus. This marks the beginning of the Empire's loss of authority in the area.

21 September 1914: *Yavuz Sultan Selim,* escorted by *Taşoz* and *Basra,* steams into the Black Sea on patrol. It is not Admiral Souchon's intention to seek out the enemy, but action is to be joined if the opportunity arises. No enemy sighted.

15 October 1914: Shortage of destroyers forces the navy ministry to reduce the number on patrol off the Bosporus to two, and to restrict the main fleet to the Sea of Marmara.

20 October 1914: The Persian steamer *Shiraz* (785gt/1867) hits a mine near the second barrage in the Bosporus and sinks near Rumelihisari

10 January 1915: The gunboat *Hizir Reis* hits a mine near the third barrage while returning from patrol. The boat is seriously damaged forward and is towed to İstinye for docking and inspection. Repairs prove difficult and the boat is not returned to service until the middle of the year.

Following the *Hizir Reis* incident the fleet commander orders that the minefields be relaid and the channels be swept clear.

30 January 1915: *Nevşehir* and the auxiliary motor minesweeper *No. 3* begin work on the second barrage. While the first mine is being raised the crane on *No. 3* snaps and the mine drifts off towards Büyükdere. During recovery the mine drifts under the bows of both boats and explodes. Both vessels sink with light casualties.

February 1915: *Castor, Pollux, İstinye* and *Bospordok* take over the work and the four mine barrages are relaid by midsummer. They remain in place until the end of the war, deterring any enemy attempt to force the Bosporus.

February 1916: Visit of the German Vice-Admiral Hofman to İstanbul. He meets senior army commanders and the navy minister at 0700hrs to discuss the future role of the Ottoman navy. The result of the meeting is a memorandum which proposes the build up of a powerful fleet within ten years, a navy superior to those of Russia and Greece. Destroyers and submarines would be built at İstanbul under the supervision of Blohm & Voss, Hamburg.

Since the yard at Haliç is found to be unsuitable for this work, the foreign-owned yard at İstinye is to be used. However, this proposal has to be abandoned due to the lack of suitable land for expansion. Further sites are examined, but other than Blohm & Voss's yard plans nothing further is done and the project is abandoned.

10 April 1916: The navy ministry draws up plans for the proposed fleet of six battleships, six light cruisers, twenty-four destroyers, thirty-six submarines, thirty-four gunboats plus auxiliary vessels and fifty aircraft for an enlarged fleet aid arm. The total cost of this programme is estimated at over £36m. The programme is modified after the purchase of the *Goeben, Breslau* and a number of destroyers.

25 August 1917: Cemal Paşa, accompanied by a number of ministers, makes an official visit to Germany and Austria. Berlin

The corvette Zuhaf, *photographed at İstanbul in March 1914.*
Langensiepen

Midilli *and* Torgud Reis *(background) photographed in October 1914 in the Sea of Marmara.*
Güleryüz

was informed in advance that the Ottoman navy wished to purchase a number of warships for delivery after the war. A meeting takes place with Admiral von Capelle and officials from the finance ministry and an agreement is reached. For 95m gold marks the Ottoman navy will receive the *Goeben*, *Breslau*, the destroyers S 56, 60–62, V 77–80, G 89–90, 92–93 and the U-boats U 82, 84, 86, UB 62, 63 and UC 63–65. With the defeat of both partners in 1918 these extensive and very expensive plans come to nothing.

As a result of the 1914/17 meetings hundreds of young Ottoman apprentices were sent to Germany for training. Although many of them had not finished their practical apprenticeship by the end of the war, the knowledge they gained was to prove of immense value to the young post-war republic, and these men formed the nucleus of future generations of technicians in Turkey.

The Dardanelles, 1914–1918

May 1914: The Ottoman navy begins preparing for the arrival of the battleships *Sultan Osman-i Evvel* and *Reşadiye* from the British builders.
25 May 1914: İstanbul fears a Greek attempt to stop the two super-dreadnoughts from reaching İstanbul. All serviceable destroyers and torpedo-boats leave the Haliç for stations in the Sea of Marmara.
11 June 1914: Çanakkale reports Greek warships and *Taşoz* is sent to patrol off Sakiz and Midilli islands.
13 June 1914: A state of emergency is declared in the Gulf of İzmit and the Dardanelles and remains in force for over three weeks.
21 July 1914: Delivery of the two battleships is postponed. During a meeting with government officials in Paris, Cemal Paşa, the navy minister, appeals to the French to intervene with London to release the warships.
4 August 1914: *Resit Paşa* (4458 gt/1900) departs İstanbul for London with crew for the new warships.
7 August 1914: The transport is stopped at Lisbon and ordered to return home, the Ottoman government now hearing that it will not now receive the two finest warships ordered for the navy.

Nevşehir: *the mast and funnel visible above water a few days after the vessel was mined in the Bosporus.*
Güleryüz

July–August 1914: 1st Torpedo Boat Flotilla transferred to the Dardanelles. *Draç, Musul, Kütahya* and *Akhisar* rotate patrol duties in the Narrows, on occasion patrolling as far as İmroz.
3 August 1914: The gunboat *Durak Reis* arrives at Çanakkale from İzmit to strengthen the flotilla.
14–16 August 1914: *Selanik* and *Giresun* lay mine barrages from Çanakkale. *Nümune-i Hamiyet* and *Gayret-i Vataniye* join the flotilla from İzmit. British warships are sighted patrolling the seas off the Narrows entrance and further mine barrages are laid.

İntibah arrives from the Bosporus with further mines and components. *Berk-i Satvet* and *Taşoz* join the patrols off the Narrows.

Muaventi-i Milliye *arriving at İstanbul on 15 May 1915 after sinking the pre-dreadnought battleship* HMS Goliath. *Güleryüz*

Kaptl Müller and the crew from the light cruiser Emden *leaving* Yadigar-i Millet *on 23 May 1915 at İstanbul. The destroyer had ferried the Germans across the Bosporus on their epic journey back to Germany from the Pacific after the loss of the Emden. Langensiepen*

18 August 1914: The German steamer *Lilly Rickmers* (4081gt/1910) slips past the British warships to reach Çanakkale safely.

30 August 1914: Admiral von Usedom and a 140-man group of naval gunners, mining experts and specialists arrive at Çanakkale. All the old British mission mining plans are replaced and all remaining Entente officers are ordered to leave the Dardanelles.

6 September 1914: *Mesudiye*, intended for service as a floating battery, anchors off Nara and *İntibah* and *Nusret* are detailed to provide protection.

10 September 1914: An Ottoman seaplane makes a forced landing off Imroz and is taken in tow to Çanakkale by *Draç*. On arrival *Draç*'s captain reports that a British destroyer had come close to observe the salvage.

29 September 1914: *Akhisar* departs on a reconnaissance voyage to Imroz. On board is the German Oblt z S. Frige, intending to gather information on the British blockade force. Shortly after the torpedo-boat leaves the Narrows it is stopped. The British hand over a declaration of intent to the effect that no further Ottoman or enemy merchant ship or warship will be permitted to leave the Dardanelles.

30 September 1914: Admiral von Usedom orders the mine barrages to be strengthened and increased in number.

1 October 1914: The steamer *Mersin* (361gt/1883) hits one of the newly laid mines off Çanakkale and has to be beached.

27 October 1914: Despite their declaration, the British allow the gunboats *Nevşehir, Yozgat* and *Malatya* to transit the Dardanelles, the last Ottoman warship to pass through. By the end of the month all the ships required to maintain patrols from Çanakkale had arrived on station.

1 November 1914: The British *Wolverine* and *Scorpion* enter the

Gulf of İzmit and sink the survey vessel *Beyrut* off Urla and the steamer *Kinaliada* (297gt/1883). The crews of both ships are given time to abandon before the vessels are sunk by gunfire.

5 November 1914: Britain and France declare war. British warships shell the gun batteries at Seddülbahir and Ertuğrul and French forces fired on those at Kumkale and Orhaniye. Casualties are slight but the arsenal at Seddülbahir is badly damaged by a direct hit.

30 December 1914: The old imperial yacht *İstanbul* and another yacht, *Galata,* are transferred from the Marmara Ada to İmrali Ada as the first units of a submarine observation force. The *Zuhaf* patrols the water between Marmara Ada and the European coast. The confiscated British tug *Maggie Grech* is stationed at Çanakkale for possible anti-submarine duties.

19 February 1915: British warships begin their naval action against the Dardanelles.

25 February 1915: British forces land on Lemnos. Several companies of marines are landed without any difficulty, the forts silenced and the island quickly occupied. This suggests that a more extensive military operation at this time on the peninsula would have been relatively easy.

1 March 1915: British minesweepers make repeated sweeps into the Narrows. British warships continue their bombardment of the forts and shore installations. All available artillery in İstanbul is rushed to the threatened front.

2 March 1915: *İntibah* arrives at Çanakkale with the last twenty-five mines from the arsenal's reserve in İstanbul; additional mines from Germany are still awaited.

8 March 1915: The *Nusret* leaves Nara at 0500hrs for the Bay of Erenköy. The bay is in use as an enemy anchorage, and during the next two hours a twenty-six mine barrage is laid across the bay. The *Nusret* returns to Çanakkale at 0800hrs without sighting the enemy.

18 March 1915: A combined Allied naval force under Admiral de Robeck tries to force the Narrows. The battleships *Irresistible*, *Ocean* and *Bouvet* strike mines laid by the *Nusret*, undetected despite continuous sweeping of the area, and there are heavy casualties. De Robeck gives up the attempt to force the Narrows, prematurely.

10–11 March 1915: The *Demirhisar*, with an Ottoman crew under the command of the German Kptl Freiherr von Fricks, departs Çesme for İzmit, with orders to attack any warships at anchor in the area. Off Baba Burnu the torpedo-boat sights a cruiser and a seaplane carrier and prepares to launch a torpedo attack. Just as the torpedoes are ready, a steamer appears out of the darkness. This proves to be the captured German freighter *Aenne Rickmers* (4083gt/1898). A torpedo is fired at a range of some 300 metres, and explodes in the freighter's cargo of timber. The cargo effectively dampens the explosion and the ship is only slightly damaged.

15 April 1915: Following lengthy repairs at İzmit, *Demirhisar* again departs on patrol. At about 1000hrs the British transport *Manitou* (6894gt/1898), en route from Skyros to Gallipoli, is stopped. Orders are given to abandon the ship and when, after ten minutes, no action has been taken *Demirhisar* fires two torpedoes. Both fail to explode, but panic breaks out among the troops on board and a number of hastily overloaded lifeboats capsize. Over a hundred soldiers, many without lifejackets, are drowned. *Manitou* is able to proceed with its voyage.

Enemy warships are now sighted approaching at high speed, and *Demirhisar* makes off towards Sakiz. By noon the enemy ships have closed to 3,000 metres, and all heavy equipment is thrown overboard in an attempt to lighten the torpedo-boat and increase speed. By 1500hrs speed is down to 12 knots.

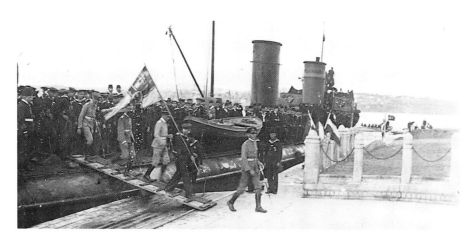

Further destroyers are sighted approaching from Çesme, and when the engines failed the *Demirhisar* was sailed into Greek territorial waters and abandoned. The allied warships fire on the grounded torpedo-boat until the crew has left. A British destroyer then comes alongside and a demolition party sets charges. The stern is blown up, making salvage impossible. The crew of one German and twenty-three Ottomans is interned by the Greeks, but later released to return to İstanbul. Infringement of Greek territorial waters does not appear to trouble the British.

During March and April 1915 the Ottoman defences were considerably strengthened and the army, under Liman von Sanders, was increased to about 100,000 men. The British assembled an expeditionary force of about 75,000 men, under the command of General Sir Ian Hamilton.

25 April 1915: British forces land at several places on the tip of the Gallipoli peninsula, while Australian and New Zealand troops land further north and the French land on the Asiatic shore. Poor co-ordination between the different forces and heroic resistance on the part of the Ottoman troops characterise the opening stages of the battle.

5 May 1915: Admiral von Usedom plans a torpedo-boat attack against the enemy warships at Morto Liman. The battleships *Canopus* and *Goliath's* gunfire was inflicting heavy casualties on the Ottoman forces.

10 May 1915: *Muavent-i Milliye* arrives at Çanakkale. During the next two days the boat is prepared for action and three Mark A/08 Schwarzkopf torpedoes are fitted.

12 May 1915: At 1800hrs *Muavent-i Milliye*, under the command of the German Kaptl Firle, departs Çanakkale. At 1940hrs the boat anchors in Soghandere Bay and waits for nightfall.

13 May 1915: Just after midnight the anchor is raised and the boat moves along the coast at a speed of some 8 knots, passing unnoticed a group of patrolling British destroyers at close range. Eski Hisarlik was reached at 0100hrs, and the battleships *Canopus* and *Goliath* sighted at anchor at Morto Liman. At close range and under cover of gunfire from ashore the three torpedoes are fired and det-

onate successfully. *Goliath* immediately begins to list to starboard. By the time the second torpedo has exploded *Muavent-i Milliye* has turned away and made for the protection of the coast at top speed. The torpedo-boat reaches Soghandere Bay by 0200hrs and is safely back at Çanakkale by 0500hrs. After *Muavent-i Milliye*'s

success, no further Ottoman ventures into the Mediterranean are made.

Reinforced by additional troops from Britain and elsewhere, the Allies made further landings at Suvla Bay in August. Four days of heavy fighting followed at the battle of Sari Bahir. Allied leadership was indecisive and the Ottoman defenders fought with considerable courage despite heavy losses, and were able to retain the heights. For the most part the British naval squadron was withdrawn to Mudros after its battleship losses, and used only as support for the landings. This second land failure turned opinion in Britain against the entire Gallipoli project. Hamilton was

One of a series of rare action photographs showing Basra *escorting the German UB8 from Çanakkale to İstanbul on 3 June 1915. Other photographs from the same series are included in the main photographs section.*
Langensiepen

The barracks vessel Olga *(the Turkish name* Urla *was simply a transliteration of the German original) at İstinye in 1917.*
Langensiepen

S. S. Olga.

Yavuz aground at Nara in the Dardanelles after the action on 20 January 1918. The steamer on the left is the transport Kerkyra.
Güleryüz

replaced by Sir Charles Munro, who began preparations to evacuate the land forces.

19–20 December 1915: The Allies evacuate their Gallipoli positions.

9 January 1916: The evacuation is completed without loss, much to the astonishment of the British command. With the failure of the Dardanelles effort, the straits remain closed and Russia is effectively cut off from supplies from the western Allies.

In December 1917 plans were drawn up to send the *Yavuz* and *Midilli* to operate off the Dardanelles. At this time the Ottoman position in Palestine was steadily worsening, and İstanbul requested Berlin to send U-boats to harass the enemy troop transports. This request was rejected by Berlin, but the new fleet commander, Admiral von Rehbeur-Paschwitz, felt he could safely order *Yavuz* and *Midilli* out to Imroz as a morale booster for the Ottoman Empire. Although the navy was under little illusion about the effectiveness of such a sortie, plans were drawn up for an attack on the suspected concentration of enemy warships there.

19 January 1918: A decoy operation using destroyers and the U-boats UB 66 and UC 23 takes place in the Sea of Marmara. By this time the destroyers have been fitted with depth charges.

20 January 1918: *Yavuz* and *Midilli* reach a position off Seddülbahir. Here the escorts *Muavent-i Milliye, Nümune-i Hamiyet, Samsun* and *Basra* are detached. At 0600hrs *Yavuz* hits a mine, which slightly damages X and XI compartments. *Yavuz* sails on to shell the radio station at Kaphalo. *Midilli* continues to İmroz and sights *Lizard* and *Tigress,* though no action occurs. *Yavuz* and *Midilli* arrive at Kusu Bay and sink the monitors M 28 and *Raglan.* Due to compass problems, a planned action at Mudros Bay is abandoned. At 0800hrs *Lizard, Tigress* and enemy aircraft are sighted. *Midilli* is ordered ahead of *Yavuz* to enable to cruiser's anti-aircraft guns a better field of fire. *Midilli* has hardly taken up

Turkish destroyers of the Samsun *and* Muavent-i Milliye *classes at İstinye in 1916.*
Langensiepen

station when the first bombs fall close to *Yavuz;* shortly afterwards, *Midilli* is mined. The cruiser immediately loses way and fails to answer the helm. *Yavuz* makes ready to tow, but a second explosion close by causes the operation to be abandoned. Both warships have run into an enemy minefield.

At 0855hrs *Yavuz* hits another mine on the port side. Five minutes later, while moving slowly astern, *Midilli* hits another two mines, which wreck the after boiler room and the port engines. The cruiser begins to list, and strikes yet another mine.

At 0955hrs *Midilli* hits a fifth mine, capsizes to port and sinks. An hour later, 162 of the crew are picked up by British destroy-

ers. In the meantime, *Basra, Muavent-i Milliye,* and the other two destroyers have been signalled to come to *Midilli*'s assistance. While closing the cruiser's last position, *Basra* is fired on by *Lizard* and *Tigress* and damaged aft.

The pumps are quickly connected up and manage to check the flooding in the first two compartments. *Basra* makes smoke and then heads for home, the enemy destroyers being held off by gunfire from the nearby coastal batteries.

At 0950hrs *Yavuz* had struck another mine, flooding III and IV compartments. An attack by British aircraft on the battlecruiser is beaten off, and the ship makes for the Dardanelles, passing Seddülbahir at 1030hrs. Just after the pilot has come aboard at 1230hrs, *Yavuz* runs on to the Nara Bank and remains fast. The British make many attempts to sink the stranded warship, dropping hundreds of light bombs.

22 January 1918: *Yavuz* is hit twice, on the after funnel and on the port net locker. During the course of the salvage operation *Samsun* and *Muavent-i Milliye* close on the *Yavuz* while *Nümune-i Hamiyet, Taşoz* and *Akhisar* stand ready at Çanakkale for action against enemy submarines. All available artillery is lined up along the Gallipoli coast and on *Yavuz* all the heavy guns are prepared for action.

22–26 January 1918: *Torgud Reis, İntibah,* the tug *Alemdar* and the transports *Giresun* and *Kerkyra* arrive from İstanbul and attempts are made to free the battlecruiser using turbulence from the combined force of the ships' propellers to clear the sand. At 0745hrs on the 26th the *Yavuz* comes free and is escorted to İstanbul by the *Torgud Reis.* The minelayer group remains at Çanakkale.

28 January 1918: The British submarine E 14 (Lt Cdr White) penetrates the Narrows and makes for Nara. With *Yavuz* now gone, the E 14 attacks *İntibah.* The torpedo misses and hits the wreck of *Grap* nearby. Alerted by the explosion, *Nusret, İntibah* and the gunboat *Kemal Reis* pursue the half-submerged submarine. E 14 is shelled by coastal guns and sunk of Çanakkale. Nine of the crew are rescued.

From late January until the end of the war the Dardanelles remained quiet apart from occasional dogfights between the British and Ottoman air forces.

Torgud Reis and *Barbaros Hayreddin* in the Dardanelles

Autumn 1914: Both battleships are laid up at Haliç in a poor state of repair. Admiral von Usedom orders them to move to Nara to act as floating batteries.

14 December 1914: Escorted by *Peleng-i Derya,* the battleships take up station off Kilya. Here they remain for five days before returning to base for repairs and gunnery practice.

18 February 1915: Arif Bey, the fleet's second-in-command, is on board when the two battleships head for the Dardanelles. Here the warships anchored off the coast and observation posts are set up on land to aid sighting. The ships are anchored well apart to reduce the danger from enemy action. Normally the engines were stopped during firing but later steam is kept up as the danger from submarines increases. As an additional protection, a steamer is moved nearby as a floating barrage. *Üsküdar* (2900gt/1907) takes up this duty at the beginning of March and remains on station until sunk by a shell from the battleship *Queen Elizabeth*.

11 March 1915: *Barbaros Hayreddin* returns to İstanbul, the naval command having decided that there is little to be achieved by keeping both warships on station.

18 March 1915: *Torgud Reis* is alone off Maydos when the Allies attempt to force the Narrows. No action is taken, since the ship's orders are to seek action only once the barrages at Çanakkale have been breached.

Since ammunition was always in short supply, very little firing, as little as eight shots per day, took place. The two battleships alternated on station, with one returning to İstanbul to bunker, store and load ammunition for the Fifth Army every five days. During the return passage a stop was often made at Gelibolu to unload deck

cargo. There was usually an overlap of two days in which both battleships were on station together.

25 April 1915: Both warships shell the British landings. The fifteenth shell fired by *Barbaros Hayreddin* detonates prematurely and destroys the starboard barrel of the midships gun turret. Casualties are light. The battleship remains on station and *Torgud Reis* returns to İstanbul as planned.

5 June 1915: A shell explodes in the forward turret of *Torgud Reis*, killing four gunners and injuring thirty-two. The battleship returns immediately to İstanbul, and the naval command uses the opportunity to suspend further operations. The reasons given are that all important targets are now out of range of the battleships' 280mm guns, and that ammunition is running low. The army wants the battleships to remain on station, since although the average thirty shells per day have little effect on the Allied forces, the presence of the warships helps lift morale amongst the Ottoman soldiers, fighting courageously without adequate artillery support.

7 August 1915: Additional British forces land at Anafarta (Suvla Bay) and Admiral Souchon reluctantly agrees to release *Barbaros Hayreddin* for action. The battleship leaves the Haliç with only the slow torpedo-boat *Sivrihisar* as escort. The *Mahmut Şevket Paşa* (24,490gt/1898) follows as an additional screening escort. No further escorts are available, all the destroyers and the other torpedo-boats being at action stations. Normally the battleship would have been off Gelibolu by dawn, but is slowed by *Sivrihisar*'s low sea speed.

8 August 1915: While off Bulayir, *Barbaros Hayreddin* is torpedoed at 0500hrs by E 11. The torpedo explodes in way of the forward funnel and the battleship capsizes about seven minutes later, floating bottom-up for a few more minutes before sinking. Twenty-one officers and 237 crew lose their lives. All the German naval personnel, fifty-one Ottoman officers and 347 crew are rescued by *Sivrihisar* and *Basra*, on patrol in the area, or manage to reach the nearby coast. The Fifth Army loses a large quantity of ammunition, including 10,000 hand grenades, in the sinking.

A few hours later E 14 torpedoes the *Mahmut Şevket Paşa* off Doğan Aslan. The steamer is beached.

12 August 1915: Two planes take off from the British aircraft carrier *Ben-My-Chree* and launch a torpedo attack on the stranded vessel. Although the pilot, Fl Lt Edmonds, reports hitting the ship, the torpedo fails to explode. The steamer is refloated some weeks later and towed to İstanbul.

Torgud Reis was laid up at the Haliç until February 1918, when it assisted in *Yavuz*'s salvage at Nara.

Allied Submarines in the Sea of Marmara, 1915

As the roads and railways along the coasts had not been developed by 1914, all passenger and goods traffic still went by sea. Only İstanbul and İzmit had the facilities to handle cargo and deal with passengers. Cargo could be landed at Çanakkale, Gelibolu, Bandırma and Mudanya, where the piers were equipped with cranes. All the other ports on the Sea of Marmara and the Dardanelles were open roads, so shallow that they could only be served by small craft. Akbaş, the main transfer base throughout the Dardanelles campaign, was only a small village with a short wooden jetty out from the shore. Here oxen, camels and bearers took over the carrying.

Yunus coming alongside the battleship Törgud Reis *in March 1915.*
Langensiepen

Two views of the battleship Barbaros Hayreddin, *torpedoed and sunk at 0500hrs on 8 August 1915 by the Royal Navy submarine E 11.*
Güleryüz

A rare photograph
of Akbas, the main
disembarkation
point in the
Dardanelles for
Ottoman troops for
the Gallipoli front,
taken in May 1915.
The large steamer is
the Plevne.
Langensiepen

The Bosporus ferry
Sükran, *one of
many used as transports in the Black
Sea and the Sea of
Marmara during
World War I. In the
background (right)
is the Galata tower.*
Güleryüz

(Above right)
Aydin Reis *photographed at the
naval dockyard at
İstanbul in the
1930s.*
Güleryüz

By the time the Anglo-French landings began in 1915 five Ottoman divisions of over fifty thousand men were already in position on both sides of the Narrows. They had been brought into position without difficulty. The *Schichau* class destroyers were used as escorts for the transports between İstanbul and Gelibolu. Boats of the *Samsun* class then took over for the voyage to Çanakkale. Boats of the *Draç* class covered the ports on the European side of the Sea of Marmara.

27 April 1915: The First Torpedo-boat Flotilla takes over responsibility for coastal patrols. The Gelibolu patrols come under the responsibility of the First Destroyer Flotilla. The Second Destroyer Flotilla is employed in the Dardanelles on anti-submarine duties.
3 June 1915: Admiral Souchon reorganises the flotilla duties. The destroyers are withdrawn to the Bosporus and the torpedo-boats take over all escort work.

Attempts to introduce convoys between İstanbul and the Dardanelles front were soon abandoned due to congestion at the open roads. After large convoys were stopped a 'Night Express' was introduced. Five tugs, each towing five barges, made the run between Haydarpaşa and Gallipoli, with torpedo-boats as escorts. This service was the main supply line from midsummer onwards. During this time single steamers carried ammunition and supplies through the Sea of Marmara to the Dardanelles, the fast ferries of the Şirket-i Hayriye proving to be particularly suitable for this purpose.

Admiral von Usedom took command of all anti-submarine forces in the Sea of Marmara in April 1915. Observation posts were set up on the Marmara Islands and the motor gunboat *No 13*, the steamers *Aydin* (75gt/1898), *Bahrisafit* (210gt/–) and *İskenderun* (142gt/1894) formed the units of the anti-submarine force and were based at Paşalı. *Aydin Reis* and a number of motor boats later strengthened the small fleet. The patrols were later supported by German and Ottoman spotter planes which arrived between July and October 1915.

In August 1915 decoy ships ('Q' ships) were introduced. As these were little more than lightly armed sailing vessels, they were unable to inflict serious damage on enemy submarines, and the project was soon abandoned.

The loss of the *Mesudiye*

September 1914: The submarines B 9–11 join the British blockade fleet.
13 December 1914: B 11, under the command of Lt Cdr N Hochrook, leaves Tenedos to attempt to force the Narrows. The submarine, fitted with new batteries, reaches a position a mile off Hellas Burnu. Here it dives and proceeds for over five hours along the European coast, passing under five mine barrages on the way.

At about 1130hrs a large warship, the *Mesudiye*, is sighted at anchor off the Hauslar estuary on the Asiatic side of the Narrows. A torpedo is fired at a range of 750 metres, and explodes against the ship's stern. The ship's guns, firing at the submarine's periscope, stop and the warship starts to capsize. The *Mesudiye* sinks in shallow water. Casualties are slight. The six 150mm and 75mm guns are later salvaged.

B 11 returns to base after a difficult voyage, nine hours submerged through mined waters with all enemy warships on the surface on the alert.

Saphir

17 December 1914: The French submarine *Saphir* arrives at Tenedos to reinforce the Dardanelles blockade. An agreement had been reached between the Allies that no submarine would sail on patrol without the express permission of the senior officer, Admiral Sackville Carden, but *Saphir* failed to obtain such permission before setting out for the Sea of Marmara.
15 January 1915: *Saphir* leaves base at 0600hrs to attempt a breakthrough to the Sea of Marmara. The submarine passes under the mine barrages without incident and surfaces to periscope depth off Nara. Here it is sighted by the motorboat *Çanakkale,* gunboat *İsa Reis* and minelayer *Nusret*. The boats open fire on the diving submarine. While taking avoiding action, *Saphir* hits the bottom and the glands and riveting, hastily repaired at Malta some weeks previously, open up. Although the submarine comes free, the flooding cannot be stopped and it sinks again to the bottom at some sixty-six metres.

With the batteries now leaking badly and poisonous gasses

spreading rapidly, the captain has no alternative but to surface and surrender. *Nusret* comes alongside and rescues thirteen of the twenty-seven crew members before the submarine sinks again. Lying 300 metres off the coast at a depth of over thirty metres and in a strong current, the submarine proves impossible to salvage.

E 15

17 April 1915: At 0600hrs E 15 is just off the battery at Dardanelles when caught by the strong current and driven on to the sandbanks. The shore batteries immediately open fire, and the first shell hits the conning tower, killing the commanding officer (Lt Cdr T S Brodie). After a second shell kills a further three members of the crew E 15 is abandoned. In the afternoon the tugs *Maltepe* and *Sana* arrive from Çanakkale to begin salvage. British spotter planes have already reported the stranding, and the Allied command orders that E 15 be destroyed.

18 April 1915: B 6 makes an attempt to do so during the night, but the torpedo attack fails to destroy the stranded submarine. An attempt by *Scorpion* and *Grampus* fails as the destroyers are unable to locate the target at night.

Over the next few days further torpedo attacks by the submarines B 6 and B 11 are also unsuccessful and long-range gunfire from the battleships *Majestic* and *Triumph* succeed only in interrupting salvage operations.

23 April 1915: Two pinnaces from the battleships, each armed with torpedoes, are sent in during the night. The gun batteries succeed in destroying *Triumph*'s boat but the *Majestic*'s gets close enough to fire, and the torpedo hits E 15 midships, causing serious damage. The stripped-down wreck lies on the beach until broken up in 1920.

AE 2

24 April 1915: AE 2, under the command of Lt Cdr H G Stoker, leaves Tenedos on patrol but is forced to return to base with periscope problems.

25 April 1915: The Australian submarine sails again at 0130hrs. At 0730hrs the battleship *Torgud Reis* is sighted at anchor off Kilya. AE 2 fires all torpedoes without success, and is spotted by the gunboat *Aydin Reis* and forced to crash dive. the submarine remains under water for over fourteen hours, during which time the motor gunboats *No 18* and *No 20* continue patrolling the area. At 2200hrs AE 2 surfaces at the entrance to the Sea of Marmara.

26 April 1915: At dawn the *Barbaros Hayreddin*, escorted by the torpedo-boat *Kütahya* is sighted near the Doğan Aslan Bank. Near the Yapildak lighthouse, AE 2 fires a torpedo which again misses the battleship. Sighted by *Kütahya*, AE 2 dives to thirty metres and slips out of the Narrows.

27 April 1915: An attack on the destroyer *Yarhisar* also fails, and AE 2 leaves the waters off Gallipoli for the Marmara Islands.

The Royal Navy submarine E 15 on the day it was captured by the Ottoman navy.
German private collection

The Royal Navy submarine E 15 photographed on 18 May 1915 with a German-Ottoman salvage team aboard. Alongside is the salvage tug Kurt.
Güleryüz

28 April 1915: AE 2 remains in the Dardanelles without encountering enemy ships, then heads into Gallipoli to find that the harbour is empty of transports. Back off the islands AE 2 sights a four-ship convoy escorted by *Muavent-i Milliye*. Again the torpedo goes wide and AE 2 is forced to dive after being spotted by the escort.

29 April 1915: AE 2 remains in the area and spends the night submerged near the Asiatic coast.

30 April 1915: At 0800hrs the *Sultanhisar* is sighted through the early morning fog in the Gulf of Erdek at the end of a patrol. AE 2's periscope is sighted, and *Sultanhisar*'s starboard guns open fire. *Zuhaf* joins the scene from a patrol of Gelibolu and prepares to ram the surfaced submarine. Just as the torpedo-boat is about to hit the submarine a white flag appears and *Zuhaf* turns sharply away to avoid the collision. *Sultanhisar* picks up the crew of three officers and twenty-nine men before AE 2 sinks, at 27° 25' E, 40° 35' N. The captured crew are taken to Gallipoli.

E 14: first cruise

27 April 1915: At 0240hrs E 14 (Lt Cdr C Boyle) departs Tenedos on its first mission to the Sea of Marmara. Off Soghandere the submarine is picked out by the searchlight and fired on by the battery at Mecidye. After passing through the mine barrages E 14 sights the *Barbaros Hayreddin* near Maydos at 0600hrs. The torpedo fired misses, and E 14 is forced to dive and remain submerged until 1400hrs. The submarine then proceeds along the European coast without being observed by coastal forces. Off Şarköy *Aydin Reis* and the torpedo-boat *Yunus* are waiting for E 14 to surface. Both boats open fire and E 14 dives and remains under water for over fifty hours.

29 April 1915: At 1400hrs an attack on *Muavent-i Milliye*, escorting the steamer *İttihat* (921gt/1883) near the Marmara Islands, fails. Later that afternoon E 14 meets up with AE 2, and the two submarines remain together, surfaced, overnight.

30 April 1915: E 14 stops a three-barge tow off Şarköy, but no action is taken. The night is spent submerged off Karabiga.

1 May 1915: E 14 torpedoes the gunboat *Nur-ül Bahir* near Mürefte. The gunboat sinks with the loss of four officers and thirty-two crew. Twenty-nine men are rescued by *Zuhaf* which comes quickly to the scene.

2–3 May 1915: E 14 is hunted by Ottoman destroyers and torpedo-boats.

4–7 May 1915: E 14 cruises between Şarköy and the Marmara Islands without action.

8 May 1915: The steamers *Tecilli* (275gt/–) and *Hayrullah* (139gt/1895) on voyage Tekirdağ to Bandırma with expelled Greeks on board are stopped near the Marmara Islands but after being searched are allowed to proceed.

10 May 1915: At 1900hrs the transports *Patmos* and *Gülcemal* and

the escort *Gayret-i Vataniye* are sighted near İmali Ada. A torpedo fired at *Patmos* at 2030hrs hours misses the stern, but a second hits *Gülcemal* on the bow. Damage is not serious. The escort remains with the damaged transport, which has over 1,600 men on board, while *Patmos* carries on alone. The Bosporus ferries *No 26* and *No 46* arrive later and take the *Gülcemal* in tow to İstanbul. Here it is found that the bow has broken completely through.

11–12 May 1915: E 14 cruises east of the Marmara Islands without sighting any targets.

13 May 1915: The steamer *Doğan* is chased and forced aground near Tekirdağ. E 14 shells the nearby gun battery before breaking off the attack. There are now no further torpedoes left on board. The remaining days of the patrol are bitter for Lt Cdr Boyle: without torpedoes he watches helplessly as *Şam* and *Halep*, escorted by *Muavent-i Milliye*, sail close by his periscope.

17 May 1915: Boyle notes in the log 'no torpedo'.

18 May 1915: Another day spent in the Sea of Marmara before entering the Dardanelles. It is disappointing and frustrating for Boyle and his crew to sail past *Barbaros Hayreddin* and a line of valuable transports off Akbaş and not be able to attack the enemy.

19 May 1915: During the night E 14 passes through the barrages and surfaces at about 0440hrs near one of the French battleships of the blockade fleet. A destroyer then escorts the submarine into Tenedos.

E 11: first cruise

19 May 1915: E 11 (Lt Cdr M E Nasmith) leaves Kephalo at 0100hrs on its first mission through the Dardanelles. Gallipoli is passed at 0900hrs, and E 11 surfaces close to the European shore. After signalling its arrival in the Sea of Marmara, the submarine submerges and remains overnight on the bottom.

20–21 May 1915: E 11 patrols the seas between the Marmara Islands and KoCaburnu. Course is then altered for the Bosporus.

23 May 1915: E 11 torpedoes and sinks the gunboat *Peleng-i Derya* at 0600hrs, at a range of 300 metres. The boat goes down by the bows, then capsizes; two crew lose their lives in the quick sinking. E 11's periscope is damaged by a shot from the gunboat, and the submarine remains underwater until 1030hrs, while repairs are completed.

24 May 1915: The *Naga* (474gt/1879) is stopped west of Tekirdağ. The crew are ordered to abandon ship and a boarding party searches the ship. In the forward hold they discover a 150mm gun barrel, gun mountings and 250 shells. The after hold contains 350 88mm shells as well as fuses and shells for field artillery. The guns and ammunition have been removed from the *Yavuz* and are destined for the Dardanelles front; *Naga*'s hold was strengthened the previous day for this voyage. Charges are placed on board and the steamer, with its valuable cargo is sunk off Koçaburnu. It is difficult to understand why the German/Ottoman naval command selected an old and slow steamer for this transport.

E 11 then makes for Tekirdağ and torpedoes the ferry *Hünkar İskelesı* moored at the pier. An immense explosion from rifle ammunition on board follows the hit and the ferry sinks at its berth with two crew killed.

E 11 then heads for Ereğli. The paddle tug *Kismet* is sighted, and tries to outrun the half-submerged submarine. When this fails *Kismet* is run aground on a soft, sandy beach near Tekirdağ. E 11 surfaces close by but attempts to board and destroy the tug are foiled by the appearance of cavalry on the beach. E 11 makes a quick dive and departs at about 1525hrs. The *Kismet* is refloated on the following day, and proceeds to Tekirdağ.

E 11 reaches the Bosporus that evening, the first time that a sub-

The 5017gt Gülcemal, photographed in 1923. The ship was damaged but not sunk by British torpedoes during the war, despite Allied claims to the contrary. Güleryuz

marine has sailed so far into enemy waters. At 2220hrs E 11 dives to 15 metres for the night.

25 May 1915: E 11 starts the passage to İstanbul at 0300hrs. By midday the submarine is near the Galata pier. Assembled here are eight merchant ships which, with a further six at Sirkeci, are to transport the First Division to the Dardanelles front. Two torpedoes are fired at the *İstanbul* (3559gt/1904), one of which explodes on the pier. The second wrecks a steel barge and rips a 6 metre by 4 metre hole in the *İstanbul*'s hull between the engine room and the No 4 hold. The transport remains afloat and is soon repaired and returned to service. The pier explosions cause panic among the civilian population and rumours that the Allied fleet is attacking the city. Reports of the event and the reaction of the foreign and non-Islamic population are, however, greatly exaggerated.

The troop embarkation at Galata is halted and the army sent overland, the army command realising that it is now no longer possible to send troop transports through the submarine-infested waters of the Sea of Marmara. Admiral Souchon had already decided that troop transportation should be halted because of the submarine threat, but this does not detract from Nasmith's achievement in bringing E 11 so far and boldly attacking the Galata transports. Following the action E 11 makes for the Sea of Marmara, surfacing at 1530hrs.

26 May 1915: The day is spent at sea overhauling the torpedoes, and as no enemy shipping is sighted, in rest and relaxation.

27 May 1915: A clear, moonlit night spoils any chance of a successful, undetected, attack on *Barbaros Hayreddin* which, escorted by *Draç* and *Yarhisar*, steams past E 11's periscope at 0200hrs en route for Gelibolu. Later that afternoon an attack on *İskenderun* near the Marmara Islands is equally unsuccessful when the patrol boat opens fire and the submarine has to crash dive to escape.

28 May 1915: At 0630hrs E 11 is on course for the Gulf of İzmit when large clouds of smoke are sighted near the European coast. At 0715hrs E 11 is submerged ahead of a convoy of three Bosporus ferries, the transport *Bandırma* and the torpedo-boat *Akhisar*. E 11 torpedoes the *Bandırma* (474gt/1879) on the port side, and the transport sinks within a minute with the loss of 250 lives. Only a few survivors are picked up by the *Akhisar*. *Bandırma*'s sinking represents the greatest loss suffered by the Ottoman army at sea in the entire war. In addition a large quantity of auxiliary ammunition is lost.

E 11 dives and remains under water until 1000hrs before making for Sivri Ada. The steamer *Doğan*, unarmed and with over 500 civilians on board, is sighted on passage from İstanbul to Bandırma. E 11 fires a torpedo at 1345hrs which hits the steamer but fails to explode. Undamaged, *Doğan* proceeds towards Bandırma, and E 11 later surfaces to recover the floating torpedo.

29–30 May 1915: E 11 cruises off the Marmara Islands without sighting any shipping.

31 May 1915: E 11 torpedoes the steamer *Madeleine Rickmers* (3431 gt/1913) at Bandırma pier. The steamer is hit near the engine room and begins listing to port. A tug succeeds in towing the sinking freighter away from its berth and beaching it. The *Madeleine Rickmers* is later salvaged and taken to İstanbul for repairs.

1 June 1915: E 11 enters the Gulf of İzmit and patrols near Yalova, but no shipping is sighted.

2 June 1915: A convoy of *Tecilli* (390gt/–), *Baslangic* (381gt/1854) and the destroyer *Samsun* is sighted near Tekirdağ. E 11 waits until *Samsun* is some 10 miles ahead, then moves in and torpedoes *Tecilli,* which sinks in three minutes with the loss of the entire crew of eighteen. *Baslangic* is also attacked, and though the torpedo misses, the crew run the steamer aground and aban-

don it. Gunfire from the nearby shore battery forces E 11 to break off the action.

5 June 1915: The crankshaft of the main engine breaks down and E 11 reports the damage and requests permission to leave the Dardanelles and return to base. No further shipping is sighted, the transports now being in harbour at either İstanbul or Akbaş.

7 May 1915: E 11 dives at 0340hrs to begin the passage through the Narrows. While passing Mousşa Bay at noon, E 11 sights *Ceyhan* (3509gt/1890) acting as a guardship to the anchored battleships. Nasmith fires one of the last two torpedoes on board; it hits the *Ceyhan* amidships, and the steamer sinks immediately in shallow water.

E 11 passes under the mine barrages without incident and surfaces at 1600hrs near Seddülbahir, then proceeds to base.

E 14: second cruise

10 June 1915: E 14 (Lt Cdr E C Boyle), refitted with a new deck gun, leaves base for the Dardanelles, proceeding on the surface to Dardanos before diving. Nara is passed at 0630hrs, Gelibolu at 1130hrs and the submarine surfaces off Doğan Aslan at 1350hrs. E 14 continues along the European coast to Şarköy and remains there for the night.

11 June 1915: A brigantine with a cargo of timber is stopped off Karaburnu at about 1000hrs and sunk by incendiaries.

(Top)
The German transport Keryra *embarking Ottoman troops for the Dardanelles in March 1915. The ship is shown at the İstanbul-Galata pier, which was shortly afterwards struck by a torpedo from the British submarine E 11.*
Güleryüz

The port of Gelibolu (Gallipoli) in the Dardanelles, showing two ferries of the Şirket-i Hayriye unloading troops and munitions for the front.
Langensiepen

12 June 1915: E 14 spends the morning west of the Erdek peninsula before altering course towards Bandırma. An attack on *İttihat* and four dhows at the pier fails when two torpedoes, fired at 1400hrs, miss the targets and explode on the jetty.

13–17 June 1915: E 14 patrols the waters round the Marmara Islands without sighting any enemy shipping. Near the Bosporus on the 17th the submarine is chased off by *Samsun* and *Yarhisar* but manages to escape without difficulty.

18 June 1915: A torpedo fired at *Kütahya* passes close to the stern, but Boyle is unable to bring E 14 into a better firing position.

19 June 1915: E 14 visits Silivri and Bandırma, but both ports are empty.

20 June 1915: Three small sailing vessels are stopped and later destroyed by incendiaries and explosive charges.

21 June 1915: E 14 meets up with E 12, and a rendezvous is arranged for the 25th west of the Marmara Islands.

21–26 June 1915: E 14 sights no enemy shipping and proceeds to the meeting point as arranged; Boyle waits until the morning of the 26th before E 12 eventually turns up.

27 June–2 July 1915: A torpedo fired at *Kütahya* off Erdek on the 29th misses, as does one fired at *Yadigar-i Millet* west of Marmara Ada on 1 July. Boyle allows the hospital ships *Gülnihal* and *Rember* (287gt/1890), en route to Gelibolu, to pass on 1 July. Boyle is also confused by an unusual combination of signal flags flown on the *İntizam* (244gt/1894) and, uncertain that the Bosporus ferry is not also a hospital ship, decides to break off the attack.

3 July 1915: E 14 begins the passage of the Dardanelles at 0430hrs, and by midday has passed Seddülbahir without incident. Off Kumkale the submarine is fired on by the shore batteries without suffering any damage, and E 14 reaches base without any further difficulty.

E 12: first cruise

19 June 1915: E 12 (Lt Cdr K Bruce) leaves base late in the afternoon and passes under the mine barrages without incident.

20 June 1915: E 12 is off Gelibolu by 1015hrs. By this time the electric motors are beginning to make trouble and by the time E 12 reaches the Sea of Marmara the motors are so hot that Bruce has to surface and run on diesels. At 1830hrs E 12 and E 14 meet up and remain together for over an hour while plans for combined operations are worked out. E 12 continues on patrol, plagued by motor trouble.

22 June 1915: *Peyk-i Şevket* is sighted at 1500hrs off Tekirdağ. The torpedo cruiser is loaded with ammunition for the front and on its way to Çanakkale. E 12 is forced to dive when the Ottoman warship alters course to Ardautepe, and the overheated motors make quick underwater manoeuvres impossible. From 1730hrs the submarine lies on the sea bed off Adadutepe while repairs are made to the motors.

23 June 1915: Repair work continues throughout the day but despite all efforts the starboard motor remains defective.

24 June 1915: E 12 and E 14 meet briefly at 0900hrs, then part, E 12 carrying on slowly into the eastern Sea of Marmara. A sailing vessel loaded with sulphur is stopped in the afternoon and sunk.

25 June 1915: At 1045hrs E 12 sights *Haliç* (144gt/1910) *1* towing two sailing vessels and, slightly further off, *Haliç 3* (141gt/1910) with three boats. E 12 surfaces ahead and orders *Haliç 1* to stop. E 12 comes alongside and an officer goes on board to find the crew ready with their lifejackets on. An object is suddenly dropped into the submarine and Bruce, suspecting a bomb attack, backs off and opens fire. *Haliç 1* is hit several times and sinks quickly, taking the sailing boats under, too. Only two of the crew are saved.

E 12 now turns to *Haliç 3* and opens fire. Alerted by the gunfire, the coastal guns on İmrali Ada open fire, and E 12 makes off. Before leaving, E 12 succeeds in hitting the steamer three times. *Haliç 3* is beached, slightly damaged, and later salvaged.

26 June 1915: The ferry *İntizam* is stopped off Paşa İskelesı while on service as a transport. It is forced aground, but Bruce refrains from firing on the stranded boat for fear of setting the wooded coastline on fire. E 12 and E 14 meet up as arranged, then Bruce set course for base.

28 June 1915: E 12 passes the Dardanelles on the surface to avoid further damaging the motors, reaching Gelibolu at 0640hrs, then dives under the barrages. E 12 surfaces again off Çanakkale at 1400hrs and returns to base.

E 7: first cruise

30 June 1915: E 7 (Lt Cdr Cochrane) leaves base early, passes Hellas Burnu at 0350hrs and submerges to pass the patrols at Çanakkale and reach Nara at 0720hrs. Here E 7 touches bottom and one of the motors fails. Despite this, E 7 makes good time and surfaces near Gelibolu at noon. Although sighted by *Aydin Reis*, E 7 dives to safety and the gunboat, after searching the area for some time, turns away towards İstanbul.

1 July 1915: E 7 remains on patrol off the Dardanelles but sights only the hospital ship *Gülnihal* coming from Gelibolu. The deck gun is now mounted and trimming trials carried out before E 7 and E 14 meet.

2 July 1915: E 7 reaches Tekirdağ mid-morning and sinks the tug *Bülbül* (93gt/–), the brig *Ceylanibahri* and some small sailing boats by gunfire. The hospital ship *Gülnihal*, also at Tekirdağ, is unharmed. *Aydin Reis* quickly appears on the spot and E 7 makes a quick dive to escape.

3 July 1915: E 7 sinks a small brigantine by gunfire before increased enemy patrols near the Marmara Islands force the submarine to submerge.

4–5 July 1915: Further problems with the electric motors keep E 7 out of action while repairs are effected.

6 July 1915: E 7 sinks a large dhow by gunfire before noon and then proceeds to Mudanya. A torpedo fired at the berthed ferry *Biga* (784gt/1894) hits the pier when the steamer unexpectedly changes berth. In the evening a large brigantine is stopped of Mudanya and sunk by explosive charges.

7 July 1915: E 7 stops the ferry *Nusret* (230gt/1873) off Marmara Ereğli. The ferry and its tug-tow are forced ashore and shelled before E 7 returns to the waters off Tekirdağ. E 7 reaches the Gulf of Erdek in the afternoon and forces the *İntizim* (244gt/1894) aground near Karaburnu. Cochrane fires a few rounds into the hull before making off.

It was usually possible to salvage these small steamers and ferries within a few days, and to repair them and return them to sevice.

8–10 July 1915: The continuous presence of patrol boats hampers E 7's attempts to attack enemy shipping along the coast towards İstanbul.

10 July 1915: E 7 again attacks the *Biga* at Mudanya. A torpedo hit amidships sinks the ferry in shallow water.

11 July 1915: Two sailing vessels are sunk by gunfire, but further engine trouble and then problems with the torpedoes brings several days of inactivity and frustration. Targets are missed in the Bay of Karabiga and in Karabiga harbour.

15 July 1915: Cochrane takes E 7 to İstanbul but finds Galata pier empty. He later shells the munitions factories at Zeytinburnu and the railway lines from İstanbul to İzmit without causing serious damage.

16–24 July 1915: E 7 continues to patrol in the Gulf of İzmit, off İstanbul and the Marmara Islands, but only succeeds in sinking a few small brigantines and dhows before returning, without incident, to Morto Liman to meet up with a British destroyer for the last part of the passage back to base.

E 14: third cruise

21–22 July 1915: E 14 (Lt Cdr E C Boyle) leaves Tenedos during the night and sails unobserved through the Dardanelles to the Sea of Marmara. After meeting up with E 7 Boyle proceeds to Mudanya and Gemlik, but finds both harbours empty. The patrol continues along the European coast but the only ships sighted are the hospital ships *Gülnihal* and *Ziya* near Sirivli and Yeşilköy.

22–26 July 1915: E 14 sinks a small sailing vessel off Yeşilköy and a brigantine and five dhows off Bozburnu.

27 July 1915: E 14 torpedoes the transport *Hayrullah* (139 gt/1895) at the pier of Şarköy.

29 July–4 August 1915: E 14 sinks a number of small sailing vessels in the Gulf of İzmit, off the European coast of the Sea of Marmara, and near Marmara Ada and Bandırma. An attack on a small convoy near Tekirdağ, comprising *Tenedos* (3564 gt/1889), *Bandırma* (474gt/1879) and the destroyer *Samsun* fails when the torpedoes pass under *Tenedos*.

5 August 1915: E 14 and *Aydin Reis* meet at sea but no action is taken by either side.

6 August 1915: E 14 and E 11 meet up and later jointly attack the torpedo cruiser *Peyk-i Şevket*, E 11 sinking it. E 14 patrols along the coast and shells roads and railways near the shore without causing serious damage.

8 August 1915: E 14 sights the *Mahmut Şevket Paşa* between Doğan Aslan and Ince Burnu. The steamer is en route to take up duty as a guardship for the battleship *Barbaros Hayreddin*. The steamer is hit amidships and beached, and E 11, which has just sunk *Barbaros Hayreddin* itself, joins E 14 in shelling the stranded steamer. Later E 14 destroys another sailing vessel off Tekirdağ with explosives.

9 August 1915: E 14 and E 11 meet at sea and E 14 transfers two torpedoes before sailing for base. Although fired on by coastal batteries the submarine makes the passage through the Dardanelles without difficulty.

E 11: second cruise

5 August 1915: E 11 (Lt Cdr M E Nasmith), fitted with a deck gun, departs Kephalo at 0130hrs and reaches Akbaş Liman at 0700. Here Nasmith sights the hospital ship *Ziya*, the transport *Halep* (3648 gt/1881) and a number of sailing ships. A torpedo hits the transport forward on the starboard side, and it sinks up to the upperworks in shallow waters. *Halep* is raised on the 8th and towed to İstanbul for repairs. E 11 submerges when enemy patrol boats appear, and makes for Gelibolu. Finding the harbour empty, E 11 makes for the Dardanelles and after an eight-hour passage surfaces near Doğan Aslan. In the early evening E 11 sights *Aydin Reis* approaching from İstanbul. On board is Admiral von Usedom's staff. After a brief exchange of gunfire, E 11 dives but, since the batteries are not completely recharged, Nasmith could not attack the gunboat with torpedoes. E 11 spends the night in the Dardanelles.

6 August 1915: E 11 and E 14 meet up and joint operations are planned. Hardly have the boats parted company when E 11 is attacked and bombed by a single-seater Gotha aircraft . The bombs miss the target but the pilot reports the submarine's position in Map Square 43 after he lands at Çanakkale. At 1500hrs the two submarines stalk the *Peyk-i Şevket*, and E 11's torpedo hits the torpedo cruiser, which

sinks in shallow water, with the loss of four crew members.

7 August 1915: *Gayret-i Vataniye*, *Yarhisar* and *Musul* arrive from İstanbul and began patrolling the waters near the wreck. Salvage parties are sent on board and the radio equipment, ammunition and the guns are removed. At 1830hrs *Sultanhisar* arrives with a diving barge in tow and a salvage team from the *Midilli*. At 1930hrs the pumping tug *Liverpool* arrives.

8 August 1915: After the pumping tug *Kurt* has also joined, work begins and by 1900hrs the *Peyk-i Şevket* has been raised; with *Liverpool* and *Kurt* in attendance, the salvage vessels make for İstanbul with the cruiser.

9 August 1915: At 0900hrs the damaged torpedo cruiser is docked at the No 2 Dock in İstanbul. The German flotilla commander, Oblt z S Lehelin, who was on board during the sinking, writes a report of the incident and praises both German and Ottoman crew members for their courage, enthusiasm and willingness to tackle any task ordered. Lehelin had previously been highly critical of his flotilla's Ottoman crews.

8 August 1915: E 11 torpedoes the battleship *Barbaros Hayreddin* at 0500hrs near Bolayir. The battleship immediately begins to list, then capsizes and sinks within a short time. The destroyer *Basra* picks up the survivors and while engaged in the rescue work narrowly misses being sunk by E 11, a torpedo passing close to the destroyer's stern. The guardship *Mahmut Şevket Paşa* is attacked near Doğan Aslan at 1245hrs and hit several times while making for the shore. E 14 later joins the action, but despite the damage caused by the submarines' gunfire it proves possible to salvage the steamer some days later.

8–10 August 1915: Two small sailing vessels are sunk and the hospital ship *Ziya* stopped and searched before being allowed to proceed.

11 August 1915: *Sivrihisar* sights E 11 and fires on the submarine, causing it to crash dive to avoid being hit. E 11 makes no attempt to torpedo the *Sivrihisar*. which makes off towards İstanbul. E 11 sinks two more sailing boats off Yeşilköy before leaving the European coast.

13 August 1915: E 11 visits Erdek, but finds the harbour empty. Nasmith then proceeds to İstanbul and torpedoes the *İsfahan* (843gt/1886) unloading coal for the Baghdad railway at the pier at Haydarpasa. The steamer is hit forward and sinks near the berth. *İsfahan* is later raised and then laid up at Kadıköy.

13–21 August 1915: E 11 patrols the western waters of the Sea of Marmara without encountering any enemy shipping.

22 August 1915: E 11 surfaces between Hora and Marmara Ada in the morning and sights *Yarhisar* escorting the tug *Dofen* (124 gt/1895) and four sailing barges. E 11 exchanges fire with *Yarhisar* before the destroyer turns away; abandoning its charges. E 11 sinks the tug and one of the barges by gunfire then takes twenty of the survivors on board. Nasmith later stops a small sailing vessel and the prisoners are handed over.

22 August 1915: After meeting up with E 2 at sea, E 11 proceeds to Mudanya and bombards the railway station, but most of the shells hit the surrounding houses.

23 August 1915: E 11 pays an unsuccessful visit to İstanbul, finding no enemy shipping, and Nasmith decides to return to the Dardanelles.

25 August 1915: At 0720hrs, off Akbaş, E 11 sights a line of transports at anchor in the roads. A torpedo fired at *Durak Reis* misses the target but hits the steamer *Kios* (3304gt/1893). *Kios* had been bombed by a British aircraft on the 17th and grounded, but quickly salvaged; E 11's torpedo sinks the steamer permanently. At 1025hrs E 11 torpedoes the *Halep* (3648gt/1884); hit amidships, the ship capsizes and sinks. The wreck was later broken up in situ in 1919.

A few minutes later E 11 torpedoes the *Tenedos* (3564 gt/1889), which sinks quickly in deep water. E 11 then leaves Akbaş and makes for Gelibolu. In the afternoon the submarine attacks *Şam* (3662 gt/1884) but the torpedo misses and the steamer escapes to Çardak. Here *Şam* anchors and the cargo is unloaded. E 11 again attacks but, although the torpedo hits, damage is slight and the steamer is later towed to İstanbul for repairs. Later that afternoon E 11 torpedoes the *Lilly Rickmers* (4081gt/1910), but again damage is slight and the steamer is able to return to the Bosporus unaied.

E 11 now departs the area and makes for Doğan Aslan, where E 1 is again encountered, before going on to Tekirdağ. Nasmith finds no suitable targets and is reduced to shelling the railway station at Mudanya.

3 September 1915: Leaving the Sea of Marmara, E 11 sinks a number of small sailing vessels by gunfire before passing under the mine barrages. The submarine reaches İmroz without incident at 1030hrs and returns to base.

E 2: first cruise

13 August 1915: E 2 (Lt Cdr D Stocks) departs Suvla at 0115hrs with a destroyer escort, proceeds on the surface to Seddülbahir, then runs underwater through the Narrows to Naga. In the afternoon radio contact is made with base while the submarine is off Doğan Aslan.

14 August 1915: E 2 sights the minelayer *Samsun*, a converted tug, at about 0300hrs. The minelayer escorted a group of sailing vessels to Gelibolu the previous day and is now returning to İstanbul. *Samsun* spots E 2's periscope and Stocks breaks off the attack, but returns and torpedoes *Samsun* at about 0500hrs. The torpedo strikes the engine room on the starboard side and the boat sinks within five minutes with the loss of two officers and eight crew.

15 August 1915: E 2 meets up with E 14 off İmrali Ada at noon and ammunition is transferred between the two submarines, then E 2 continues on patrol. At 1700hrs E 2 is involved in an exchange of fire with *İskenderun* which ends abruptly when the submarine's deck gun pivot snaps after the sixth shot. E 2 submerges before *İskenderun* can take any further action.

16 August 1915: Two large dhows are sunk by incendiaries off the Gulf of İzmit. E 2 enters the Gulf and finds the waters empty, but the opportunity is taken to repair the deck gun. E 2 now proceeds to the Gulf of Erdek, also empty of shipping, and further repairs are made to the gun off Büyükçekmece.

19 August 1915: E 2 torpedoes the patrol vessel *Sakiz* alongside the pier at Erdek at about 1415hrs. The torpedo hits amidships and *Sakiz* breaks apart and sinks in shallow water. There are no casualties.

21 August 1915: E 2 attacks *Gelibolu* (282gt/1867) off Tekirdağ, but the torpedo misses the target which is partly masked by the wreck of the *Bülbül*.

22 August 1915: Attacks on *Edremit* (414gt/1887) and *Armagan* (– /–) at Mudanya fail when the torpedoes miss the targets.

24 August 1915: A small dhow, loaded with a cargo of melons, is stopped off Tekirdağ and sunk by incendiaries.

25 August–14 September 1915: E 2 sinks a number of dhows and small sailing vessels in the waters of the Gulf of Mudanya, this period of the patrol being plagued by continuous trouble with the deck gun and a lack of larger targets in likely harbours and roads. While passing through the Dardanelles E 2 attacks *Aydin Reis* near Gelibolu, but again the torpedo misses the target. E 2 passes under

the barrage without incident and returns to base.

E 7: second cruise

4 September 1915: E 7 (Lt Cdr Cochrane) departs Kephalo Bay at 0200hrs and reaches the Dardanelles without difficulty. Although sighted by the coastal batteries, the submarine makes Çanakkale without interference. The motor gunboats *No 18* and *No 20* and the patrol boat *No 32* are on guard duty near the mine barrage between Nara and Bulayir. E 7 becomes entangled in the nets between No 13 and No 14 buoys, at a depth of 35 metres, and at 0700hrs the patrol boats notice that the buoys are being dragged under water; this is reported to the naval base at Çanakkale.

On board E 7 everything is tried to free the boat, but by the afternoon the batteries are running low. During the day the submarine touched off two mines without causing damage, but the explosions have also alerted the Ottoman patrols to the submarine's position.

The German submarine UB 14, under Oblt z S Hugo von Heimburg, is lying at Çanakkale, and Heimburg and one of his crew go out by launch to Bulayir. Explosives are dropped at the reported site of the enemy submarine, and at 1930hrs *No 32* drops further explosives, detonating at 35 metres. E 7 surfaces at 1945hrs, and the crew begin to abandon ship. Cochrane and his crew are picked up by *No 18* and E 7 is scuttled. As the submarine sinks it takes the nets and the net buoys with it.

E 12: second cruise

16 September 1915: E 12 (Lt Cdr K Bruce) leaves base early, clears all the barrages and is off Nara by 0700hrs. The submarine then proceeds along the Asiatic coast. At 0900hrs E 12 torpedoes the Austrian steamer *Bitinia* (3125gt/1900) at anchor in the Saltik Liman roads. The steamer sinks quickly by the bows and takes two sailing vessels, moored alongside as protection, with it. *Bitinia* lies half-submerged for weeks before being eventually salvaged and towed to İstanbul. E 12 continues on patrol and surfaces at 1400hrs near Gelibolu to radio back to base.

17 September 1915: Bad weather and rough seas hamper any action and E 12 makes its way along the European coast, past the empty harbour at Tekirdağ, to İmrali Ada. *Sivrihisar* is sighted near the island and both vessels open fire, at 2,500 metres. No hits are recorded and both sides break off the action after a few rounds.

19 September 1915: E 12 shells the railway station and the harbour tug *Eftimos* (– /–) at Mudanya without causing serious damage, then makes a hasty retreat when the coastal batteries open fire.

20–21 September 1915: Bad weather, with fog and heavy rain, force Bruce to move to the waters round the Marmara Islands. Experience has shown that the transports use this route on their way to Gelibolu, unlike the tug and barge convoys which normally pass between the islands.

In the afternoon E 12 stops the steamer *Kesendire* (438gt/1902) by gunfire between Kursurle and Muhaliç. The crew are given time to abandon the ship with its cargo of provisions and livestock, then the submarine sinks the ship by gunfire. Six small dhows are sunk off Bandırma later in the day.

22–29 September 1915: Bad weather and near empty seas reduce sinkings to three sailing boats in the Gulf of İzmit on the 28th and five boats sunk between Tekirdağ and Sarköy on the 29th. Just before sunset on the 29th E 12 is attacked by a German spotter plane and the bomb misses the stern by only 10 metres.

30 September–7 October 1915: Bad weather, with fog lasting for days, hamper patrols between the European and the Asiatic coasts and no ships are sunk during this time. E 12 meets up with H 1 on

The damaged transport Bitinia *(left) and the German transport* Stambul *at İstanbul-Haliç in late 1915 or early 1916.*

German official photograph

the 4th and again on the 7th, when both boats remain together, at rest, for the whole day.

8 October 1915: Both boats made for Yeşilköy, then part, and E 12 makes for Bandırma and the Bosporus.

17 October 1915: E 12 joins up with H 1 to patrol the Gulf of İzmit. Here both submarines attack the gunboat *Taşköprü* with torpedoes and gunfire. E 12 succeeds in hitting the gunboat, but *Taşköprü* reaches the safety of Bandırma at 1430hrs.

18 October 1915: E 12 patrols the waters off Bandırma and is forced to dive when *Yarhisar* and *Basra* appear suddenly. No action is taken.

19 October 1915: E 12 attempts to shell the munition factories at Bakırköy, but the coastal batteries open fire. An attack on a berthed steamer and sailing vessels at Mudanya also fails when the torpedo misses the target and detonates on the pier.

22 October 1915: E 12 meets up with H 1 and the French submarine *Turquoise*, and with E 20 on the following day.

24 October 1915: Preparations are made for the return passage, but E 12 is sighted by *Akhisar* off Gelibolu and forced to dive prematurely. After passing the first net barrage the submarine suddenly sinks to 74 metres. Bruce is eventually able to bring the boat up to 36 metres, and E 12 passes the remaining barrages without further incident. Off Çanakkale the bow and conning tower suddenly break the surface for some minutes and the coastal batteries open fire, but without hitting the submarine. In addition the battery at Kilitbahir launches two torpedoes, which also miss the half-surfaced boat. E 12 leaves the Narrows at 1730hrs and is picked up by a destroyer and escorted back to base.

H 1

2 October 1915: H 1 (Lt W B Pirie) departs Kephalo at 0245hrs, passes under a newly laid forty-seven mine field between Dardanos and Soğanlı, and passes Kilya at 0830hrs. Coastal batteries open fire on H 1's periscope about a half hour later without success, and the submarine reaches Gelibolu at 1325hrs without further difficulty. Finding the harbour empty, Pirie carries on into the Sea of Marmara and surfaces. The submarine is immediately sighted by *Aydin Reis* and *Nusret,* and crash dives, remaining under water until 2100hrs. H 1 then surfaces, recharges the batteries and contacts base.

3–4 October 1915: E 12 fails to rendezvous as planned and H 1

spends two days patrolling in Bandırma Bay. E 12 eventually makes contact on the 4th and plans for joint operations are discussed, then the boats separate.

5 October 1915: H 1 sinks three small sailing vessels by gunfire in the waters between Karaburnu and Surluköy, and torpedoes the *Edremit* (287gt/1887) at Mudanya. *Edremit* sinks up to the superstructure and the explosion damages the nearby *Rehber* (287 gt/1890). Both vessels are repaired and returned to service at the end of October. H 1 is forced to break off the attack when, first, the coastal artillery opens fire and, second, *Yarhisar* appears at 1500hrs. H 1 makes a quick escape and no further action takes place.

7 October 1915: H 1 and E 12 meet up again for a day of rest and repair at sea.

8 October 1915: Both boats proceed to Mudanya Bay and then part, E 12 making for Bakirköy and the Bosporus and H 1 heading in the opposite direction towards Küçükçekmece.

9–17 October 1915: H 1 patrols the waters around Mudanya without sighting enemy shipping. The boat develops trouble with a battery leak and contaminated fresh water supplies, rudder and steering difficulties and bad weather throughout the week-long patrol. On the 17th E 12 and H 1 begin a joint patrol in the Gulf of İzmit. In the early hours of daylight the gunboat *Taşköprü* is sighted near İmrali Ada. H 1 launches a torpedo which misses the target, and the gunboat flees towards Bandırma, shadowed by the two submarines. At 0950hrs E 12 opens fire and *Taşköprü* replies, firing over 200 rounds during the next two hours. Nearly half the ammunition fails to explode and at noon *Taşköprü* makes off towards İmrali Ada and the protection of the coastal gun batteries. During the fight E 12 scores one hit which kills one crew member and causes light casualties from the splinters. At 1430hrs the gunboat reaches the safety of Bandırma, the submarines having successfully blocked off the escape route to Mudanya. A later attack on *Taşköprü* and the steamer *Hüdavandigar* (818gt/1877) is foiled by heavy rain showers and poor visibility.

18–19 October 1915: The two submarines operate together off the Marmara Islands and towards İstanbul, but without success.

20 October 1915: At 0900hrs H 1 is off the Şarköy roads. Here *Plevne* (1154 gt/1892), *Gelibolu* (282gt/1867) and *Hanefiye* (506gt/1879) are at anchor, unloading their cargoes of provisions for the Fifth Army into barges alongside. The minelayer

İntibah lies anchored nearby.

The steamer presents an easy target, and H 1 sinks the *Plevne* and the *Hanefiye*, both ships sinking immediately. A torpedo fired at *Gelibolu* misses the target. During the one-hour action *İntibah* remains at anchor with unlit boilers and takes no part in the fight.

21–24 October 1915: H 1 continues on patrol, seeing no action in the waters between Karabiga and Türkeli Ada. The submarine meets up with E 12, E 20 and the French submarine *Turquoise* during this period.

27 October 1915: An attack on the old torpedo-boat *Berkefşan* and the steamer *Hüdavandigar* off the Marmara Islands fails.

28 October 1915: H 1 again attacks *Hüdavandigar* off Bandırma, and again the attack fails.

29 October 1915: H 1 meets up with E 20, then proceeds to Bandırma, and this time succeeds in hitting *Hüdavandigar*. The attack causes slight damage to the steamer's bow, which is soon repaired.

30 October 1915: H 1 sinks a small sailing vessel near Mudanya Island, meets up with E 20 again, then sets course for the Dardanelles. The deck gun is dismounted and anti-fouling cables set up over the tower and deck to give an easier passage under the net barrages.

31 October 1915: During the morning *Aydin Reis* is sighted near Gelibolu, and the gunboat alerts the coastal batteries and the anti-submarine force. However, H 1 proceeds through the straits without difficulty, passing Seddülbahir at 1300hrs, and then makes for home.

Turquoise

The *Turquoise* was the only French submarine to penetrate into the Sea of Marmara.

19 October 1915: *Turquoise* leaves Mudros at dusk and anchors off the Dardanelles.

20 October 1915: At 0300hrs the submarine dives and begins the passage under the barrages at a depth of 25 metres. At 0700hrs the submarine grounds off Çanakkale and, on surfacing, is fired on by the motorboats *No 19* and *No 20*. No hits are recorded, and the *Turquoise* dives and continues the passage without further incident. An attack on two anchored steamers near Gelibolu has to be abandoned due to problems with the day periscope and here the first problems with the electric motors occur.

20–22 October 1915: Owing to motor trouble, *Turquoise* is forced to cross the Sea of Marmara on the surface, but makes the passage without incident to meet up with E 12 and E 20 on the 20th

The submarine Müstecıp Onbaşı, *commissioned 5 November 1915, at İstanbul. In the background (behind the submarine's conning tower) is the aviso* İsmail. *German official photograph*

as planned. A short-circuit starts a fire on board which is quickly extinguished, but motor failures continue to plague the boat for the remainder of the patrol.

22–30 October 1915: Little contact is made with enemy shipping and two sailing vessels stopped are able to escape unharmed due to *Turquoise*'s inaccurate gunfire. *Turquoise* meets up with E 20 on the 25th as planned, then proceeds on patrol. At 1600hrs the patrol boat *Bahr-i Sefid* is sighted, and immediately opens fire; the submarine breaks off the attack and makes off. A torpedo attack on a small sailing vessel near Tekirdağ on the 26th fails when both torpedoes miss. *Turquoise* surfaces to find that the boat is filled with Greek refugees. It is allowed to proceed unharmed.

30 October 1915: *Turquoise* begins the return passage to base and by 0900hrs has passed Gelibolu and submerged to begin the passage through the mine and net barrages. The periscope is run up as the boat approaches the nets off Akbaş and it is spotted by the coastal batteries and field artillery, which promptly open fire. While manoeuvring, the submarine hits the bottom and then surfaces. The conning tower is immediately fired on by 75mm field gun batteries and, after hoisting a white flag, the crew abandons ship. *Turquoise* is captured after the crew has been picked up by launch, and when a German staff officer boards he finds that no attempt has been made by the French crew to destroy the submarine's logs and code books before abandoning ship.

2 November 1915: The submarine, lying in water only four metres deep with most of the hull above the surface, is easily salvaged by the tug *Sana* and the pumping tug *Kurt*.

3 November 1915: *Turquoise* is towed to İstanbul by the minelayer *Nusret*. *Aydin Reis* joins the tow off the Dardanelles and is then relieved by *Samsun* off the Marmara Islands at 1800hrs. The convoy, with *Samsun* leading, passes blacked-out through waters in which Allied submarines are active. During the night a rapid alteration of course causes *Samsun* to collide with the fast-moving *Nusret*. *Samsun* is damaged forward and begins to fill quickly, and it is only with great difficulty that Palatya on Marmara Ada is reached. The tug *Paris* tows *Samsun* for the last part of the voyage. *Nusret* is also damaged in the collision but makes Palatya without assistance. During the collision the tow parts but it proves possible to start the motors on the *Turquoise,* and the submarine also makes Palatya.

4 November 1915: *Gayret-i Vataniye* arrives from İstanbul and takes the submarine in tow, to dock at İstanbul on the 5th.

7 November 1915: *Samsun* is towed into İstinye by the salvage tugs *France* and *Paris*. The destroyer is to remain out of service until the spring of 1916.

11 November 1915: *Turquoise* is transferred to the Ottoman navy and renamed *Müstecip Onbaşı* after the artillery commander whose quick action led to the submarine's capture on the 30th.

The transfer, in the presence of Enver Paşa, was put to good propaganda use and the newly-acquired addition to the fleet was sent on a number of short passages along the Bosporus to demonstrate that it was fit for service. However, the equipment on board the ex-*Turquoise* was outdated and spares and replacements were unobtainable. The boat remained officially on active service, with a listed commander, but was actually laid up and acted as a battery charging station for the German submarines.

E 20

As a result of the submarine's loss it is difficult to retrace E 20's movements. Reports that the submarine torpedoed two steamers off Saltik Liman appear to be incorrect. It is possible that the torpedoes hit sunken wrecks or exploded on beaches. Certainly there is no record of any sinkings in the official Ottoman documents for this period. From the secret documents found on the *Turquoise* on 30 October, the German/Ottoman naval command had learned of the rendezvous position of the enemy submarines.

21 October 1915: E 20 (Lt Cdr Warren) leaves base for another patrol in the Sea of Marmara.

27 October 1915: *Taşoz* reports sighting torpedo tracks near Marmara Ada.

27 October 1915: *Durak Reis* makes a similar report. Since the other British submarines can be ruled out, it can be assumed that the torpedoes fired were from E 20.

5 November 1915: UB 14 (Oblt z S Hugo von Heimburg) departs İstanbul and arrives at the meeting point, 28° 10' E, 40° 45' N, and waits there between 0900 and 1000hrs, and again from 1545hrs. Heimburg expects E 11, E 12 and H 1 to meet here at the scheduled times. The German/Ottoman high command is unaware that only E 20 is operating in the Sea of Marmara. At 1600hrs UB 14 sights a coming tower five miles to the north. Course is altered by 90° and the German boat closes the enemy by two miles. At 1625hrs UB 14 approaches the stopped E 20 out of the setting sun and submerges to periscope depth. The sea is an oily calm, so the Germans use the periscope with caution. Bearings are checked at 2,000 then 1,200 metres, and at 500 metres a torpedo is fired.

An explosion is heard and felt at 1716hrs, and E 20 disappears in a cloud of smoke and water. When this disperses, E 20 is gone. At 1720hrs UB 14 surfaces and the captain, two officers and six ratings of E 20's crew are rescued. No wreckage is sighted, and UB 14 returns on the surface to base.

E 11: third cruise

6 November 1915: E 11 (Lt Cdr M E Nasmith) departs Kephalo at 0400hrs on its last mission in the Sea of Marmara. E 11 dives off Sarlayandere at 0635hrs, and passes under the mine and net barrages to surface off Gelibolu at noon.

7 November 1915: The sailing vessel *Evliyadifis* is sunk by gunfire near Kara Burnu. E 11 then proceeds to Bandırma, where a Greek agent is to be landed. Bad weather and rough seas cause the plan to be abandoned. The bad weather continues all the next day, and E 11 stays close to land near Kara Burnu.

9 November 1915: An attack on two Bosporus ferries fails when the torpedoes miss. Later the sailing vessel *Hildon*, with a cargo of oil in drums, is stopped and sunk by explosives. At midnight the Greek agent is put ashore at Edincik.

10–11 November 1915: Two sailing vessels are sunk near Türkeli Ada and Tekirdağ.

12 November 1915: E 11 arrives off Haydarpaşa, but an attack on the torpedo-boats in their berths is impossible. E 11 dives and, after observing the normal ferry traffic and the anchored hospital ship *Gülnihal* for some time, makes for the European coast at Sivriada. Here a number of small sailing boats are sunk on the 13th.

15 November 1915: E 11 returns to Akbaş and in the Kemikilialan Bay torpedoes the Austrian steamer *Arimatea* (3891gt/1912). The steamer sinks by the bow in shallow water but is raised some weeks later and repaired. A second torpedo hits the *Lilly Rickmers,* but torpedo nets help to reduce the force of the explosion and the steamer is repaired at İstanbul. At Çardak the *Despina* (774gt/1866) is torpedoed and sunk with a cargo of wheat. Three crew members lose their lives in the sinking.

16–25 November 1915: Bad weather with heavy rain showers and rough seas reduces sinkings to two sailing vessels, one on the 16th and one on the 25th, both near Tekirdağ.

26 November 1915: E 11 arrives at Erdek in the morning to find *Gelibolu* (284gt/1867), *Edremit* (414gt/1887) and the naval tug *Sana* in port. At noon E 11 surfaces and shells the ships before being driven off by shore guns. At 1600hrs E 11 again surfaces and resumes firing until smoke, flames and the approaching dusk make sighting impossible. *Gelibolu* is sunk, *Edremit* damaged and *Sana* unharmed by the attack.

27 November–2 December 1915: Bad weather hampers operations and no shipping is sighted.

3 December 1915: E 11 torpedoes the destroyer *Yarhisar* off Yalova at 1230hrs. The torpedo hits the after boiler room and the explosion tears the boat apart. Both ends rise briefly before *Yarhisar* sinks. E 11 surfaces and picks up the survivors, and they are later transferred to a passing sailing boat and taken to Heybeliada.

4 December 1915: The steamer *Bosporus* (2995gt/1911) is sighted under escort to Bandırma by the *Berkefşan*. When the torpedo-boat disappears into a fog bank, E 11 quickly surfaces and opens fire. By the time the escort has returned the *Bosporus* is ablaze, listing heavily and being abandoned by its German crew. *Bosporus* sinks before help can be brought from Bandırma.

5 December 1915: E 11 sinks the bark *Elenora* near Kemer Liman, and fires on the ferry *Rehber* (287gt/1890) at 2020hrs near Yurmuta Ada on its return passage from Gelibolu. E 11 comes alongside the burning *Rehber* and takes off five of the crew. From the captain Nasmith learns that another ferry will be leaving Erdek the following day.

6 December 1915: E 11 sinks the berthed *Eser-i Merhamet* (230 gt/1892) by gunfire at Erdek. The ferry is raised in 1916 and returned to service.

7 December 1915: E 11 rams and sinks a small sailing boat near Erdek, then proceeds to the east of Gelibolu. At 2000hrs the submarine opens fire on the *İntibah* near Şarköy. The minelayer returns fire and E 11 dives. *İntibah* reports slight damage and one killed on arrival at Palanya.

8 December 1915: During the morning E 11 and *İntibah* are in action again off Palanya, without damage to either side.

9–10 December 1915: E 11 and E 7 meet at sea to transfer stores and ammunition.

12 December 1915: E 11 sinks the tug *Meno* and the bark *Cezlani Bahri* by gunfire in the Gulf of İzmit.

14 December 1915: E 11 torpedoes the *Leros* (247gt/1915), berthed at Haydarpaşa. The steamer, just arrived from Karaköy, is being docked by tug when the torpedo strikes the bows. Barges and tugs are quickly brought alongside and managed to keep *Leros* afloat. E 11 makes a quick exit from Haydarpaşa, and hits the base of the sea wall, though without serious damage. The submarine leaves İstanbul and makes for the Gulf of İzmit.

South of Tuzla E 11 surfaces and shells the nearby main İstanbul-İzmit railway. A shell hits the İstanbul express train service 1678, a regular passenger train to İzmit and not a troop train as supposed by the British.

19 December 1915: E 11 is signalled to return to base and departs the area, now empty of enemy shipping.

23 December 1915: E 11 passes through the Dardanelles without difficulty, passes the last mine and net barrages at midnight and arrives at Mudros in the early hours of the morning of Christmas Eve.

E 2: second cruise

It was clear to the Allied naval command that submarine warfare in the Sea of Marmara was nearing its end by December. There were now only a few steamers operating as transports in these waters, so the chances of sinkings were small. The battle front on the Gallipoli peninsula was being successfully held by the Ottoman army, and reports indicated that the rail link between the war zone and İstanbul would be opened within the next few days.

9 December 1915: E 2 (Lt Cdr A C M Bennet) leaves base on patrol, passing the net barrages during the early hours of the morning, and is sighted by the coast guards. They alert the anti-submarine force, and a Gotha spotter plane sights E 2 off Gelibolu at 1345hrs. Patrol boats make for the reported position, but E 2 has dived by the time the boats arrive. At 1600hrs E 2 surfaces after a ten-hour passage and is now well out into the Sea of Marmara.

10 December 1915: During the morning E 2 sinks a large dhow, with a cargo of salt and olive oil, off Şarköy. At noon an air attack by planes of the Ottoman Air Corps force E 2 to dive quickly off Tekirdağ, but the submarine is able to surface later in the afternoon to rendezvous with E 11 and transfer stores and ammunition and plan further operations.

12 December 1915: E 2 visits Erdek to find the harbour and bay empty of shipping; this situation is repeated on the following day between the Marmara islands and Mudanya. Ottoman spotter planes are now flying regular patrols over the Sea of Marmara, and E 2 is forced to remain under water for a greater part of the patrol, according to the submarine's log book.

14 December 1915: An attempt is made to destroy the submarine cable between Bandırma and İstanbul with explosives, but with no success.

15–16 December 1915: Bad weather and very rough seas hamper the patrol and no shipping is sighted.

17 December 1915: E 2 sinks two dhows and the schooner *Emanetullah* off Mora, and is forced to break off further action by the sudden appearance of *Akhisar*.

18 December 1915: E 2 encounters thick fog until midday, then sinks a dhow by explosives in the waters between Şarköy and

Turkish gunboats and destroyers in the Sea of Marmara in 1928. The same vessels hunted British submarines in the same area in 1915.
Güleryüz

Tekirdağ. Later the submarine meets up with E 11, and both boats conduct a vain search for a German U-boat which E 11 sighted earlier.

19 December 1915: The armed tug *Tarik*, with barges in tow, is sighted off Mora and E 2 opens fire, but breaks off the action when *Tarik* returns the fire with its 57mm gun.

20–21 December 1915: Thick fog continues to hamper operations in the Bay of Mudanya and off the Marmara Islands.

22 December 1915: E 2 stops the regular İstanbul/Mudanya ferry, but allows it to proceed after a search.

22–28 December 1915: E 2 cruises the entire Sea of Marmara without sighting any enemy shipping. Before finally departing the area, E 2 succeeds in sinking only a small sailing vessel off Bandırma and three dhows off Yalova.

31 December 1915: E 2 shells Mudanya, but causes little damage in the port and the town. The shore guns do not return fire as their ammunition supplies are now running low. E 2 then proceeds on to Yeşilköy, sinking three more sailing vessels with cargoes of foodstuffs for İstanbul, en route.

1 January 1916: E 2 arrives at İstanbul but is too late to sight the last Ottoman transport convoy to the front. The submarine remains off Büyükçekmece throughout the night.

2 January 1916: E 2 proceeds along the northern coast as far as Gelibolu, dives and passes under the mine and net barrages to reach Kumkale on the afternoon of 3 January. Here the submarine surfaces and proceeds to base without incident.

The Black Sea, 1914–1918

26 October 1914: 'Preparations for a reconnaissance exercise', is the explanation issued by naval command to account for the hectic activity; the officers, however, are issued with sealed instructions, unnecessary for training off the Bosporus.

27 October 1914: The greater part of the fleet leaves the anchorages off Haydarpasa, Büyükdere and İstinye and assembles within the protected waters. At 1700hrs *Yavuz* signals three times 'Do the utmost for the future of Turkey', then 'To all ships: all naval actions are secret. This also applies after any action.' Secret orders are opened on board; the German officers are not surprised by the contents, the Ottoman officers generally indifferent.

28 October 1914: *Yavuz,* with *Taşoz* and *Samsun* as escorts, leaves base and steams along the Anatolian coast as far as Amasra.

29 October 1914: At 0500hrs the destroyers, with minesweeping gear out, take up position ahead of *Yavuz*. At 0630hrs *Yavuz,* seven miles away from Sebastopol, opens fire on the shore batteries. The batteries immediately return fire, *Yavuz* is hit three times near the funnel and the action is broken off. The destroyers bring in their sweeping gear and make off at high speed, zig-zagging, with *Yavuz* following. The three warships unwittingly pass through a Russian minefield.

Shortly afterwards *Yavuz* meets the Russian minelayer *Prut,* which is scuttled by its crew to avoid capture. *Yavuz* fires on the escorting destroyer, *Leytenant Pushchin,* which, though damaged, manages to reach port. Later *Yavuz* captures the steamer *Ida* (1708gt/1889), and a prize crew brings it into İstanbul. *Yavuz* arrives back at base at 1200hrs on the 30th.

29 October 1914: The passenger liner *Nilüfer* was selected for conversion to a minelayer and the work completed in August. Disguised as a Russian steamboat with a black hull and yellow funnel, *Nilüfer* lays a sixty-mine barrage off Sebastopol, then makes for base. Near the middle of the Black Sea the minelayer sights and stops the Russian steamer *Velikiy Knyaz Aleksandr* (1852gt/–). Once the crew has taken to the boats, the steamer is sunk by gunfire. *Nilüfer*'s German captain, Kaptl D R Leverhorn, is later severely criticised for not bringing the Russian steamer to İstanbul.

29 October 1914: *Hamidiye* arrives off Feodosia at 0630hrs, and an Ottoman and a German officer are sent ashore by steam pinnace to inform the local authorities that hostilities will begin in two hours' time.

Chivalrously, *Hamidiye* waits until 0900hrs before opening fire on the harbour installations, then shells the port for over an hour before proceeding to Yalta. Here *Hamidiye* sinks the steamer *Sura* (1113gt/–) and the sailing vessel *Svyatoy Nikolay* (300gt/–) by gunfire before returning to İstanbul via the Snake Islands. The cruiser is back at base by the 31st.

29 October 1914: *Gayret-i Vataniye* and *Muavent-i Milliye* arrive off Odessa at 0230hrs. A small convoy is making its way through the southern entrance into the harbour. *Gayret-i Vataniye* torpedoes the gunboat *Donets,* which sinks immediately. *Muavent-i Milliye* fires on the gunboat *Kuranets,* sinks a motorboat by ramming and then shells the oil tank terminal and a berthed merchant ship. A landing to destroy the grain port installations was abandoned due to artillery fire, and the two destroyers make for the Snake Islands and then on to the Bosporus, meeting up with *Yavuz* and the escorts en route.

29 October 1914: *Midilli* and *Berk-i Satvet* arrive off Novorossiysk after a rough passage during which most of the Ottoman crew are seasick. An officer from *Berk-i Satvet* is sent ashore to warn the authorities of the intended attack. However, the Russians refuse to recognise the officer's authority and he is promptly arrested. *Berk-i Satvet* then steams into the harbour and signals that firing will commence if the emissary is not freed. Once this is done, the torpedo cruiser waits until 1050hrs before opening fire on the shore artillery positions. *Midilli* completes laying a sixty-mine barrage in the Straits of Kerch, then joins *Berk-i Satvet* in the bombardment. The oil tanks are soon ablaze, so the Ottoman ships concentrate on the merchant vessels in port. Seven ships are damaged, and the *Nikolai* (1085gt/–) sunk. At 1300hrs *Midilli* departs Odessa for Varna to destroy the telegraph to Sebastopol. Both ships then return to the Bosporus, and *Midilli* joins *Barbaros Hayreddin* and *Torgud Reis* and the destroyers *Yarhisar* and *Basra* on duty in the forward defence line.

29 October 1914: Great Britain and the Allies sever relations and send an ultimatum to the Ottoman Empire.

1 November 1914: A conference is held at İstanbul to review the operations carried out against Sebastopol, Feodosia and Odessa. None of the operations has been a success, and Russian losses, two warships and six merchant vessels, are slight. The German officers are particularly critical of the operations, and voice a low opinion of the Ottoman navy in general, although they praise the Ottoman seamen for their bravery and hard work during the action, especially since the crews had little sea training.

The German crews, however, have their own problems, and Admiral Souchon's order of the day states 'that feigned illness is cowardice in the face of the enemy' – and this order is addressed only to the German crews.

2 November 1914: Russia declares war on the Ottoman Empire.

5 November 1914: Great Britain and France declare war.

5 November 1914: The Russian destroyers *Gnevniy, Pronzitel'niy* and *Derzkiy* mine the entrance to the Bosporus.

6 November 1914: The battleship *Rostislav*, the cruiser *Kagul* and six destroyers shell Zonguldak, damaging the steamer *Beyköz* (1188gt/1882) and the tugs *Dauphin* and *Eole*. On their way back to base the Russians sink the *Nikna* (905gt/1889) off Kandilli and the transports *Bahriye Amer* (3603gt/1893), *Bezm-i Alem* (4527 gt/1889) and *Mithat Paşa* (4455gt/1900), steaming unescorted in convoy.

During the first two months of the war the X Army Corps was transported from Ordu and Samsun to Trabzon and its equip-

ment was shipped from İstanbul to the Caucasus front. The navy provided the escorts but the transports were placed under army command. At first Admiral Souchon refused to seek action with the Russians, but eventually he gave in to pressure and released *Midilli* and *Hamidiye* for escort duties. Army command did not keep to the sailing schedule and sent the three transports off to Giresun, only to have them sunk off Kandilli.

5–6 November 1914: *Hamidiye* arrives at Giresun to find only the *Akdeniz* (5062gt/1890). After 3,000 troops have been embarked, *Hamidiye* escorts the transport to Trabzon. By now the alarm has been raised because of the long overdue transports and the *Hamidiye* and *Midilli* search the area for the missing ships.

6 November 1914: *Yavuz* and *Berk-i Satvet* leave İstanbul to attack Sebastopol. At sea they are ordered to make for Ereğli and Zonguldak, where enemy warships have been sighted. A search of the area proves fruitless, and *Yavuz* is hampered by *Berk-i Satvet*'s 18-knot maximum sea speed. The torpedo cruiser is in fact at sea with *Yavuz* only to train the crew.

7 November 1914: *Midilli* shells the port and installations at Poti. A conference is held at İstanbul of the army and navy commands. Again the army, represented by Enver Paşa, insists that the navy make all serviceable vessels available for escort duties. Admiral Souchon, while regretting the loss of the three transports, protests that the navy is not ready for sea and that the crews are untrained. Souchon's protests are brushed aside by Enver.

9 November 1914: The Port Authority at İstanbul informs the navy that the transports *Ceyhun* (3509gt/1890), *Mahmut Şevket Paşa* (2690gt/1886) and *Şam* (3662gt/1884) are being loaded with troops and will be sailing the same day for Trabzon. Souchon has no choice but to send *Yavuz* to sea until the 12th. In the event the transports never sail, and the only result of *Yavuz*'s excursion into the Black Sea is the cutting of the Varna sea cable.

14 November 1914: Word reaches İstanbul that a Russian submarine shelled Trabzon on the 7th, and *Yavuz* and *Midilli* depart at 1530hrs for the Crimea. In addition *Hamidiye* is ordered to proceed the following day to Tuapse and the *Gayret-i Vataniye, Muavent-i Milliye, Peyk-i Şevket* and *Samsun* also to prepare for sea.

18 November 1914: At noon *Midilli* sights enemy warships off the Crimea, and *Yavuz* joins the cruiser just as a Russian squadron appears through the haze. Both sides immediately open fire. *Yavuz* is hit on port casemate III and sixteen crew are killed. The Russian battleship *Evstafiy* is hit four times and as a result is out of commission undergoing repairs for a long time. After about fif-

Akdeniz as a hospital ship bunkering coal at İstanbul in summer 1915. This is the only known photograph of the ship during World War I.
Güleryüz

teen minutes the Russians break off the action and retire behind a fog bank. *Yavuz* and *Midilli*, which is undamaged, make for home.

18 November 1914: During the night the Russian minelayers *Konstantin* and *Kseniya* lay a 123-mine barrage off Trabzon. This minefield claims a small sailing vessel the following day, thereby revealing its existence; the field and those off Samsun and Ünye are swept during the following days, before the transports can again use the ports.

19 November 1914: The *Nilüfer* leaves the Bosporus for the mouth of the Danube. A signal from Admiral Souchon countermanding the sailing order is not received, and *Nilüfer* heads for Varna. Nothing further is head of of the minelayer. Some days later the bodies of two German sailors and wreckage are found drifting off Kilyos. As nothing is known of any action off the Bulgarian coast it can be safely assumed that *Nilüfer* was mined near Kilyos and sank with the loss of the entire crew of eight Germans and fifty-five Ottomans, on the 19th.

19 November 1914: *Mecidiye* reenters service and joins *Midilli* and *Hamidiye* on transport escort duties.

20 November 1914: *Hamidiye* shells the harbour installations at Tuapse and returns to base, meeting up with *Midilli* en route. *Yavuz* and *Peyk-i Şevket* remain off the Bosporus on patrol.

Berk-i Satvet: *two views in January 1915 in the drydock at İstinye, showing damage caused near the stern by a mine on 2 January.*
Ackermann collection

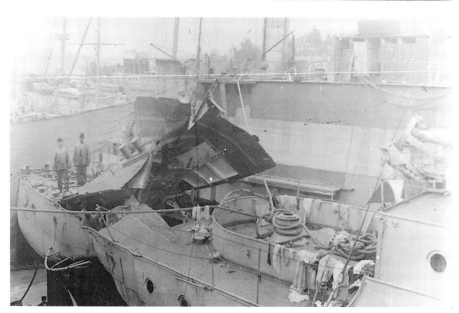

20 November 1914: The transports *Akdeniz* and *Zonguldak* (1545 gt/1884) leave İstanbul for Trabzon, escorted by *Midilli* and *Hamidiye*. *Midilli* remains at Trabzon until the 28th, while *Hamidiye* continues escort duties. The second echelon of transports, *Ceyhun* and *Mahmut Şevket Paşa,* arrive at Trabzon on the 26th.

5 December 1914: *Midilli* and the steamer *Zafer* (332gt/1905) leave the Bosporus for the Snake Islands. Here the vessels part, and *Zafer* proceeds to Akkerman and lands a raiding party whose task is to destroy railway installations. *Zafer* returns to İstanbul safely and *Midilli* goes on to shell Sebastopol, damaging a number of anchored minesweepers, then returns to base. The raid on Akkerman is a failure and all the soldiers are captured.

5 December 1914: The transports *Akdeniz, Derince* (3337gt/1912), *Mahmut Şevket Paşa* and *Şam* load two battalions of infantry and equipment at İstanbul-Karaköy and sail for Rize, escorted by *Midilli. Yavuz, Peyk-i Şevket* and *Berk-i Satvet* are sent as additional cover because the enemy are now aware of all troop transport movements from İstanbul. Enver Paşa is on board *Yavuz* for the voyage to Rize, where he is to take over command of the Third Army.

10 December 1914: After the landings the transports return home and *Yavuz* proceeds to shell Batumi before meeting up with *Mecidiye* and *Berk-i Satvet* at sea.

14 December 1914: *Derince* is sunk by destroyer gunfire off Tirebolu while en route Trabzon to İstanbul. The crew are able to reach the coast by boat.

17 December 1914: The Ottoman army begins its offensive against Kars.

21 December 1914: The transports *Akdeniz, Mahmut Şevket Paşa* and *Şam* leave the Bosporus, with *Yavuz* and *Hamidiye* providing cover.

23 December 1914: *Midilli* joins up with *Yavuz* off the Anatolian coast. It is assumed that the Russians will take some form of naval action over the Christmas period.

25 December 1914: *Hamidiye* shells Batumi.

On the 20th a Russian fleet left Sebastopol for the Bosporus. The minelayers *Kseniya, Konstantin, Aleksey* and *Georgiy* and four blockships were escorted by the entire Russian squadron. Two large minefields were laid. Near Zonguldak the battleship *Rostislav* sighted *Midilli* but the cruiser was able to escape and later sank the blockship *Athos* (1891gt/–) by gunfire. Two other blockships, *Erne* and *Istok,* had to be scuttled by the Russians at sea, coastal artillery making it impossible to sink the ships off Kandilli and Zonguldak as planned.

26 December 1914: *Yavuz* hits two of the newly laid Russian mines while approaching the Bosporus. Although over six hundred tons of water enter the battlecruiser forward, the trim is unaffected and the ship makes the Bosporus safely. However, since there are no docking facilities at İstanbul, *Yavuz* is out of action for some considerable time for the repairs. *Hamidiye* and *Midilli* are warned by radio of the minefield and reach the Bosporus safely by another route.

30 December 1914: The minesweeper *Ron* is sunk while clearing the minefield with the loss of the crew.

2 January 1915: *Midilli, Hamidiye* and *Berk-i Satvet* leave the Bosporus at 1500hrs, escorting the steamer *Yeşilirmak* (85gt/–) to Zonguldak. The escorts are instructed to leave the transports at Zonguldak and patrol the war zone.

At 1800hrs the sweep gear detonates a mine and, while taking action to avoid *Yeşilirmak, Berk-i Satvet* leaves the channel in the darkness and hits another mine. The explosion wrecks the propellers and starts flooding aft. Two tugs tow the damaged warship back to İstinye, and *Hamidiye* and *Yeşilirmak* also returned to port. *Midilli* carries on to Zonguldak and Trabzon.

2–4 January 1915: *Midilli* operates along the coastal war zone, shelling port installations and army positions before making for Novorossiysk. Russian naval command intercepts Ottoman radio signals and conclude that *Midilli* is escorting seven transports. A fleet of five battleships, two cruisers and ten destroyers leaves Sebastopol on the 3rd to intercept the convoy.

4 January 1915: The cruiser *Pamyat Merkuriya* and an escorting destroyer sight *Hamidiye* steaming west to meet *Midilli* off the Crimea. In the ensuing action *Hamidiye* is hit by gunfire but escapes in a rain squall towards the Crimea. The Russians later capture the Italian steamer *Marie Rosette* (759gt/1885) off Sinop. The Italian ship was en route to İstanbul with a cargo of oil in barrels.

6 January 1915: The Russian squadron again steams to intercept *Midilli* and *Hamidiye*. At 1830hrs both sides open fire, and hits are registered on the *Evstafiy* and *Hamidiye* although no serious damage is done. The Russians fail to follow up the action; instead, they make for the Anatolian coast and sink over fifty small sailing vessels before returning to Sebastopol.

10 January 1915: *Hamidiye* begins refitting at İstanbul. The armoured decks are strengthened, additional bunker space installed, the stability problems reduced and the fore and aft bridges removed to give a more 'warlike' appearance. Searchlights are repositioned and the guns overhauled. The work is completed by 21 January.

11 January 1915: Russian warships now operate continually along the Anatolian coast and all available Ottoman cruisers are detailed for transport escort duties.

8 February 1915: The Russian cruisers *Kagul* and *Pamyat Merkuriya* sink the Ottoman steamer *Vaştinton* (1043gt/1869) at Trabzon. The ship was sailing under the American flag, transporting medical supplies for the American Red Cross.

9 February 1915: All Ottoman warships return from the Crimea area to base. *Yavuz* goes into dock for repairs and is out of commission for some considerable time.

1 March 1915: Russian warships begin a blockade of the coal ports on the Anatolian coast.

7 March 1915: The cruisers *Kagul* and *Pamyat Merkuriya* shell the port and coal loading piers at Zonguldak. Russian destroyers enter the harbour and sink the *Taksiyarhi* (885gt/1887) and damage the *Hilal* (1502gt/1887). The Russians then move on to Ereğli and destroy the *Principessa Giovanna* (904gt/–), *Persiya* (740gt/1889), *Neva* (549gt/1872), *Heybeliada* (927gt/1873), *On Temmuz* (2165gt/1892), *Kesan* (156gt/–) and the bark *Barbaros*. The town is seriously damaged but the coal mines and loading stages remain intact.

17 March 1915: *Midilli* shells Feodosia without causing serious damage before proceeding to Constanza.

20 March 1915: *Midilli* sights Russian units off the Narrows but takes no action and makes off at high speed to reach İstinye safely.

27 March 1915: The Russian fleet steams from Sebastopol for the Bosporus. An attack on the gun batteries is planned to relieve pressure on the Allied front at the Dardanelles. The cruisers *Kagul* and *Pamyat Merkuriya* take up station off the Bulgarian/Rumanian coasts.

28 March 1915: By the early hours of the morning the Russian fleet is some 25 miles from the Narrows and the *Tri Svyateliya* and *Rostislav*, accompanied by the two aircraft tenders, proceed towards the coast. Six aircraft fly off to bomb the lighthouses at Rumelifenerlı and Anadolufenerlı, coastal installations and gun batteries before returning to the tenders.

29 March 1915: *Kagul* and *Pamyat Merkuriya* shell the coal ports and sink the *Sadiç* (765 gt/1872) at Zonguldak and the *Dafni* (1321

gt/1889) at Kozlu, and attack Ereğli and Kandilli.

31 March 1915: The Russian fleet returns to Sebastopol.

1 April 1915: The refitted *Yavuz* and the *Midilli* sail for Sebastopol. Destroyer escorts join up during the night.

2 April 1915: *Hamidiye*, *Mecidiye* and a destroyer escort sail for Odessa.

3 April 1915: At 0600hrs Odessa is sighted and at 0630hrs *Mecidiye* hits a mine while some fifteen miles away from the Odessa lighthouse. The mine detonates on the port side, flooding the boiler rooms and the cruiser begins to sink. *Mecidiye* sinks, partly submerged in shallow water, with a loss of twenty-six crew killed. All logs and ciphers, radio equipment and sighting gear are destroyed before the cruiser goes down, and at 0720hrs *Yadigar-i Millet* torpedoes the wreck. *Hamidiye* picks up the survivors and *Yavuz* orders the squadron to return to base. At noon *Hamidiye* receives a signal that the Russians are again at sea. *Samsun* and *Taşoz* set off along the coast to intercept, but sea speed cannot be maintained and the destroyer returns to the Bosporus.

4 April 1915: The warships meet up, all operations off Odessa are halted, and the fleet makes for base, *Yavuz* sinking the freighters *Vostochnaia* (944gt/–) and *Providence* (748gt/–). At about 1500hrs *Yavuz* sights the *Pamyat Merkuriya,* and gunfire is exchanged until contact is lost in the approaching darkness. On arrival at İstinye *Yavuz* goes into dock until 1 May.

Even with the addition of *Yavuz* to the fleet, the Ottoman navy was unable to hit the enemy hard and Souchon's entire operation in the Black Sea was considered a farce. Even the attempt to sink *Mecidiye* failed and the Russians raised the cruiser, repaired it and had it commissioned as *Prut*.

15 April 1915: The Russian destroyers *Derzkiy*, *Gnevniy* and *Pronzitel'niy* attack Ereğli early in the morning and sink the sailing vessel *Avni Rabani* and six smaller sailing boats. The destroyers then go on to Kozin to sink the *Dafni* (1321gt/1899) and damage *Despina* (714gt/1864) which is beached and later refloated.

1 May 1915: Russian battleships shell the Bosporus forts, spotter planes being used to register and report the shots. *Yavuz* is moved from İstinye to the Bay of Beyboz. *Kagul* and *Pamyat Merkuriya* are detached from the main fleet and sent to attack Zonguldak. They shell the *Necat* (1523gt/1870) and sank it at İlliksu, near Kozlu.

2 May 1915: The Russians again bombard the Bosporus forts without causing serious damage. The fleet then retires to Bulgarian coastal waters. *Kagul* captures the Italian steamer *Amalia* (413 gt/1881) with a cargo of flour and oil in drums. A prize crew takes the steamer, on charter to the Ottoman Empire, to Sebastopol. *Pamyat Merkuriya* also sinks a fully-loaded 950-ton bark off Kozlu.

5 May 1915: The destroyers *Gnevniy* and *Pronzitel'niy* sink the steamer *Yeşilirmak* (865gt/–) and hit the *Güzel Girit* (1232 gt/1891). The latter steamer is set on fire, drifts out to sea and sinks the following day. Later the destroyers sink the *Morna* (1495 gt/1891) by gunfire off Kandilli. The Russian units meet up again off the Bosporus and return to Sebastopol. The operation is well planned and carried out and brings the Ottoman coal transport to a complete halt.

7–8 May 1915: *Yavuz*, *Midilli* and *Hamidiye* put to sea. *Yavuz* visits Sebastopol, but takes no action against the port due to a now chronic shortage of heavy ammunition. *Midilli* heads for Constanza and *Hamidiye* to Zonguldak.

9 May 1915: The Russian destroyers *Derzkiy* and *Bespokoyniy* enter the harbour at Kozlu at 0545hrs and shell the mining installations and coaling stages, and sink the collier *Selanik* (1127gt/1873). After an hour the destroyers leave, without the shore batteries taking any

an hour the destroyers leave, without the shore batteries taking any action. At sea they meet up with the cruisers to sail on to Ereğli. At 0830hrs they sink the *Millet* (817gt/1892), just arrived from İstanbul, and the *Sadiç* (817gt/1871). At 1000hrs a signal is sent from Ereğli to İstanbul reporting the attack, but falsely stating that a landing has taken place. *Yavuz* immediately puts to sea, but fails to find the enemy.

10 May 1915: *Nümune-i Hamiyet* joins the *Yavuz*. At 0540hrs the destroyer sights smoke. *Yavuz* sends the destroyer to shadow the enemy squadron, and the battlecruiser starts to close. *Nümune-i Hamiyet* attacks the minesweeper escort, but breaks off the action when the battleships *Tri Svyatiteliya* and *Panteleimon* appears. At 0715hrs *Yavuz* opens fire on the enemy ships, which return fire immediately. Within ten minutes *Yavuz* is hit twice above the waterline. Although not seriously damaged, *Yavuz* increases speed and turns away from the enemy. Lighter units of both sides continue to shadow the opposing capital ships as they steam away from the Straits.

At 1215hrs the Russians turn away to starboard and make off.

This engagement was humiliating for the captain and crew of the *Yavuz* for, despite superior speed and heavier guns, the battlecruiser registered no hits and allowed the enemy to escape. Souchon stated later that it had been the *Yavuz*'s intention to draw the enemy towards the Bosporus. The problem remained that it was impossible to engage the enemy and at the same time avoid damage to the battlecruiser on which Ottoman hopes of matching Russian naval strength rested.

15 May 1915: Russian destroyers shell Ereğli and sink the patrol boat *Rüsumet No 5* and the steamers *Hellesponte* (1985gt/1883) and *Hilal* (1502gt/1877).

20 May 1915: A Russian raiding party lands at Çamli and destroys the coal mines, loading equipment and the power house. By now all regular coal supplies to İstanbul have ended.

27 May 1915: *Midilli* escorts the steamers *Seyhun* and *Tevfikiye*, loaded with coal, from Zonguldak to İstanbul.

7 June 1915: A Russian force of five battleships, three cruisers and fourteen destroyers shells Zonguldak and then Ereğli, where they sink the *Progress* (408gt/1884). Near Karasu they capture the *Edincik* (786gt/–) and recover logbooks giving all information on collier movements, and the date of arrival of the German U-boat UB 8 at İstanbul.

10 June 1915: *Midilli* encounters the destroyers *Derzkiy* and *Gnevniy* off Zonguldak at about 2000hrs. During the short engagement *Derzkiy* is hit and loses all power. *Midilli* is hit seven times, with slight damage and light casualties. No attempt is made to sink the crippled Russian destroyer, and *Midilli* breaks off the action and makes off. *Gnevniy* takes the *Derzkiy* in tow and both ships reach Sebastopol safely the next day.

14 June 1915: The Russians sink the tug *Leon* off the Anatolian coast.

16 June 1915: *Derzkiy* and *Gnevniy* fire on the steamer *Edirne* (646 gt/1863) near Karasu. The steamer is beached, then torpedoed and

25 June 1915: *Pronzitel'niy* and *Bespokoyniy* appear off Zonguldak and fire on the numerous half-submerged wrecks. *Erdek* (600gt/1878) is damaged at the loading berth.

3 July 1915: Collier convoys are reintroduced. *Gayret-i Vataniye* and *Nümune-i Hamiyet* escort the steamer *Seyhun* (3013gt/1896) and *Eresos* (3022gt/1893) from İstanbul to Zonguldak. Russian destroyers appear off the port on the 4th but withdraw when the Ottoman destroyers return fire.

10 July 1915: The Russian submarine *Kars* lays a 58-mine barrage off the Bosporus. *İsa Reis* hits a mine just outside the partially swept channel the following day. The gunboat is heavily damaged and towed in a sinking condition to İstinye and laid up.

11 July 1915: The steamer *Ugurola* (964gt/1875) is mined off Galataburnu, a mine laid by *Kars*.

11 July 1915: The destroyers escort another collier convoy to Zonguldak.

15 July 1915: *Yadigar-i Millet* arrives at Zonguldak with fuel oil for the German submarines. In the afternoon the *Bespokoyniy, Derzkiy* and *Pronzitel'niy* shell the port. *Seyhun* is hit and sunk in shallow water, but is raised some days later and repaired. The destroyer and *Eresos* receive only slight damage. The Russians withdraw after an hour's action.

18 July 1915: The convoy departs for İstanbul; though it scatters after an enemy sighting, it reassembles to reach port safely.

18 July 1915: *Midilli* departs the Bosporus for Karaburnu to meet the steamer *Kesan*, loaded with petrol, and escort it through the minefields into İstanbul. After only a half-hour's steaming the cruiser hits a mine, which explodes under the No 4 boiler room. Though flooded with over six hundred tons of sea water, the cruiser manages to reach İstinye. Eight of the crew are killed. *Midilli* is dry-docked and the inspection reveals only slight damage. Due to a shortage of materials and qualified personnel the repairs are not completed until February 1916.

25 July 1915: The Russian destroyers *Schastliviy* and *Bystriy* venture as far as Kefken Ada and sink the *Erdek* (660gt/1879). A further attack at Şile destroys the *Skiros* (2634gt/1896). The wreck is beached and abandoned.

29 July 1915: The Russian destroyers sink a dredger off the River Sakarya.

Throughout July the Russian destroyer division based at Batumi steadily increased operations off the Anatolian coast and, in addition to the larger vessels noted above, over 150 small sailing vessels were destroyed.

3 August 1915: The destroyers *Muavent-i Milliye, Numune-i Hamiyet,* and *Taşoz* and the cruiser *Hamidiye* escort the *Zonguldak, Eresos, Illiria* and *Seyhun* to Zonguldak. In order to obtain a clear picture of the state of the loading posts the commander of the First Destroyer Flotilla, the German Kaptl Firle, goes along on the voyage.

8 August 1915: Russian destroyers appeared off Zonguldak at 2000hrs. Both sides open fire but no damage is recorded.

9 August 1915: The Russians again appear, but take no action.

10 August 1915: The convoy sails at 0300hrs and meet up with the *Yavuz* off Kefken Ada. At noon the periscope of the Russian submarine *Tyulen,* known to be operating in the area, is sighted by *Muavent-i Milliye.* The convoy begins to zig-zag, but on the first tack *Zonguldak* is torpedoed and sinks in seven minutes. Four destroyers come out from the Bosporus to join *Yavuz,* and the convoy returns to Zonguldak, then back to İstinye.

10 August 1915: *Kagul, Pamyat Merkuriya* and five destroyers attack Zonguldak but find the port empty, sinking only the bark *Adile* and the tug *Adi Landana.*

4–5 September 1915: The steamers *Eresos, Illiria* and *Seyhun* leave Zonguldak with over 10,000 tons of coal and with *Nümune-i Hamiyet* as escort. At 0500hrs south of Kefken Ada the *Hamidiye* and *Muavent-i Milliye* join. At 0630hrs the destroyers *Bystriy* and *Pronzitel'niy* are sighted. The colliers make for the coast and *Hamidiye* closes the enemy. Shortly afterwards the 150mm suddenly fails, and when the submarine *Nerpa* is sighted the cruiser and escorts make off. At 1020hrs the Russians attack the defenceless colliers, some of which are beached near the estuary of the Sakarya. The ships are soon ablaze, and the Ottoman navy writes off 10,000 tons of coal. *Nerpa* also sinks the tug *Seyyar* by gunfire. *Yavuz* arrives too late to take any action against the retreating enemy.

13 September 1915: The Russians sink the *Kızılirmak* (1945 gt/1890) near Sakarya.

1 October 1915: The Russian battleship *Imperatritsa Mariya* patrols off the Anatolian coast while the *Evstafiy* shells Ereğli and the *Joann Zlatoust* and *Panteleimon* shell Zonguldak. *Nora Hugo Stinnes 2* (4945gt/1910) and *Rodosto,* loading coal, are only slightly damaged.

5 October 1915: *Yavuz* escorts the two steamers to İstanbul.

14 October 1915: Bulgaria declares war on Serbia.

16 October 1915: Bulgaria joins the Central Powers.

15–19 October 1915: Britain, France, Italy and Russia declare war on Bulgaria. The Russians now leave the coal ports alone and step up their operations off Bulgaria. At the same time Admiral Souchon takes over supreme command of the Ottoman Navy. Varna in Bulgaria now becomes the main support base for German U-boats.

14 November 1915: *Yavuz* narrowly escapes being torpedoed by the Russian submarine *Morz.* After this incident the battlecruiser is withdrawn from Black Sea operations, the submarine danger now too great.

9 December 1915: The Russian destroyers *Derzkiy, Gnevniy*

and *Bespokoyniy* sink the gunboats *Yozgat* and *Taşköprü* near Kefken Ada by gunfire. Three crew members are killed. The survivors reach the mainland and are rescued by the *Hamidabad* the following day.

The German U-boat UC 13 flying the Ottoman flag.

Langensiepen

By the end of 1915 the Ottoman navy had lost most of its colliers. Transport of coal was now dependent on a fleet of small sailing vessels, dhows, tugs and the Bosporus ferries. Along the Anatolian coast naval operations became increasingly half-hearted and the commanders on both sides looked more and more on the Black Sea as a secondary front.

The chronic shortage of raw material now threatened to plunge the Ottoman Empire into a state of chaos. In addition to the coal shortage, now reducing the navy to inactivity, there was a serious shortfall of grain to contend with. Reports of hunger and starvation were reaching İstanbul.

7 January 1916: A conference is held at İstanbul to discuss the crisis. Enver Paşa learns that there is now only about 13,500 tons of 'Cardiff' coal and 900 tons of Zonguldak coal available for the fleet. Although the railway lines to Germany have been reopened following the defeat of Serbia, little help can be expected from the Empire's chief ally since Germany is also suffering from a coal shortage.

After the disbanding of the Dardanelles transport fleet, additional vessels were available for collier duties in the Black Sea. This tonnage was not, however, sufficient to meet the demand, and sinkings were to reduce it even further.

In February 1916 the Coal Agency chartered the following steamers (the figures in brackets show the coal capacity per voyage in tons):

Rodosto (5500), *Nora Hugo Stinnes 2* (7600), *Dubrovnik* (7000), *Kerkyra* (4200), *Irmingard* (7200), *Lilly Rickmers* (6000), *Tevfikiye* (500), *Turan* (700), *Bitinia* (6000), *Patmos* (3200), *Arimatea* (4800), *Kızılirmak* (6800).

Yavuz and *Midilli* continued to operate as far as Zonguldak and gave the colliers some protection. *Hamidiye* was laid up, now too slow for operations in the Black Sea.

6 February 1916: Russian troops attack Ottoman positions at Trabzon and *Yavuz* and *Midilli* are used as transports to rush infantry to the threatened front. Yavuz returns immediately to İstanbul because of the danger that the Russians might bottle up the battlecruiser in one of the ports on the Anatolian coast.

6 February 1916: The Russians launch an air attack on Zonguldak with planes from the *Aleksandr* and *Nikolay*. The German steamer *Irmingard* is alone in port and slightly damaged, but is able to sail later for İstanbul.

27 February 1916: *Midilli* rushes troops from İstanbul to Trabzon and oil in drums to Sinop. A planned expedition along the Caucasus coast by *Midilli* is abandoned due to bad weather and the cruiser returns to base on 2 March.

12 March 1916: The Russian destroyers *Gromkiy* and *Bystriy* sink the *Seyyar* (3336gt/1893), sailing empty to Zonguldak, off Karasu.

17 March 1916: The steamer *Zambrak* (2570gt/1898), with a cargo of 500 tons of oil products, is torpedoed off Varna by the *Pronzitel'niy*.

24 March 1916: The Russian submarine *Morz* torpedoes the tug *Darica* off Kefken Ada.

1 April 1916: The submarine *Tyulen* torpedoes the *Dubrovnik* (4238 gt/1912) just 2,000 metres off the coast near Şile. *Gayret-i Vataniye* has just taken up position as escort when the collier, with 7,000 tons of coal on board, is hit aft. The ship is quickly abandoned and drifts on to the rocks near Galata Burnu. The destroyer picks up the survivors and returns to the Bosporus. Bad weather hampers salvage, and *Morz* returns to the site and destroys the *Dubrovnik* on 16 April.

14 April 1916: British bombers raid İstanbul, but fail to hit the gunpowder factories at Yeşilköy. As a result of the raid, the defences at the air station at İstinye are considerably improved.

18 April 1916: *Midilli* leaves İstanbul with troops for Trabzon. After landing the infantry the cruiser sail in company with U 33 to attack enemy shipping near the front line. The Russian auxiliary minesweeper *T 233* is heavily damaged in a short engagement, then U 33 returns to Trabzon. *Midilli* carried on alone to sink the sailing vessel *Nikolay* (108 tons).

19 April 1916: *Midilli* sights two large warships west of Novorossiysk. After signalling identification, the *Imperatritsa Mariya* opens fire, and *Midilli* escapes the very close salvos only by steering a zig-zag course at high speed. The cruiser reaches İstinye safely, and is docked for repairs.

24 April 1916: The *Tyulen* attacks the paddle ferry *Resanet* (230 gt/1892) near Akçakoca. The ferry, towing six coal barges, is beached on fire, but is later refloated and towed to Ereğli for repairs.

3 May 1916: *Midilli* leaves İstinye to lay a 60-mine barrage off Killia, using mines received from Germany by rail.

6 May 1916: *Midilli* returns to base, bunkers and loads another sixty mines. Sailing again at 2200hrs for the Crimea, the minelayer-cruiser lays three barrages off Cape Tarchankutand near Sebastopol before going on to shell Yevpatoriya. *Midilli* returns to İstinye on the 8th, remaining there until the end of May.

30 May 1916: *Midilli* takes troops to Sinop and Samsun and

The German U-boat U 33 (then in Austro-Hungarian service) in the Bosporus in March 1916 on the way to İstanbul.
Langensiepen

returns to base with deck cargoes of grain and tobacco.

During the early summer months the Russians again intensified their destroyer operations.

30 June 1916: The Bosporus ferry *Ruchan* (244gt/1894) is shelled and sunk at İğneada.

3 July 1916: *Yavuz* and *Midilli* depart for the Caucasus to attack Russian troop transports.

4 July 1916: *Yavuz* shells the harbour at Tuapse and sinks the steamer *Knyaz Obolenskiy* (248gt/–) and several sailing vessels. *Midilli* leaves the battlecruiser to patrol off the Crimea and sinks the *Marina Anetta N-103* (961gt) and the sailing vessel *Rezviy,* off Sochi, and finishes off the *Rockliffe N-55* (3073gt/–), which was torpedoed two days previously by U 38. Although the battleships *Imperatritsa Mariya* and *Ekaterina II* are at sea on patrol, the *Yavuz* and *Midilli* are able to slip down the Bulgarian coast and reach base safely on 6–7 July. *Yavuz* is then again docked for overdue repairs to the propeller shafts, and is out of service until September.

16 July 1916: The *Bystriy* and *Pospesniy* capture the *İttihat* (921 gt/1893) off Tuzla Burnu and the steamer is taken to Sebastopol as a prize.

17 July 1916: *Gromkiy* and *Pylkiy* attack the barge-towing ferry *İktan* (244gt/1894) off the Sakarya estuary. The ferry and two tugs are beached, but later refloated and able to make the voyage to port safely. Two of the barges are abandoned.

16–17 July 1916: The success of the German U-boats and of *Yavuz* and *Midilli* off the Crimea lead to a change of command within the Russian Navy. Vice-Admiral Kolchak replaces Admiral Ebergard as commander-in-chief of the Black Sea fleet.

17 July 1916: *Gromkiy* and *Pylkiy* sink the Bosporus ferry *Sultaniye* (591gt/1909) off Sakarya. The destroyers then attack Ereğli, but cause little damage.

21 July 1916: *Midilli* again sails from İstanbul to lay a 65-mine barrage off the approaches to Novorossiysk.

22 July 1916: At noon *Schastliviy* sights *Midilli* some 100 miles north of Sinop and opens fire, *Midilli* immediately alters course for home, but soon encounters the *Imperatritsa Mariya*, salvos from which begin to drop very close at a range of over 24 miles. Only by laying a smokescreen and dropping mines in the path of the enemy is *Midilli* able to escape. At twilight four Russian destroyers attempt another attack, but the cruiser disappears in a rain squall and is able to escape to reach the Bosporus on the 23rd.

29 July 1916: The *Tyulen* attacks the Bosporus ferry *Hale* (298 gt/1903) off Ağva. *Hale* is hit several times and beached, but later salvaged and taken to İstanbul and laid up damaged. Later *Tyulen* attacks the ferry *Neveser* (287gt/1890) near Şile, and the paddler is beached to avoid capture.

During August the Russians laid a large number of minefields off the Bosporus, and by the end of the month over 1,000 mines had been laid. On 27 August Rumania declared war on Austria and Germany. Bulgaria and the Ottoman Empire declared war on Rumania on 30 August and 1 September.

The Russian minefields soon brought all coal and food supplies to İstanbul to a complete halt and bread was further rationed. Additional minesweeper groups were formed to keep clear the large minefields off the Bosporus. The torpedo-boats *Draç, Samsun, Kütahya* and *Yunus* and the gunboat *Malatya* were quickly but inadequately fitted out for the task.

During September only a few small sailing vessels with coal cargoes managed to pass through the minefields to reach port.

12 September 1916: *Kütahya* hits a mine while working with *Musul* and *Yunus* east of Karaburnu. The damaged boat is towed into swept waters but the bulkheads give way and the boat sinks quickly with the loss of three crew members.

14 September 1916: *Patmos* (1907gt/1902), with a five- destroyer escort, leaves Zonguldak with a full cargo of coal.

15 September 1916: *Patmos* hits a mine off Karaburnu and has to be beached. *Basra* and *Samsun* rescue the crew and report the sinking.

21 September 1916: *Malatya* is sent to clear a channel to the stranded *Patmos.* While sweeping, the gunboat hits a mine, wrecking the rudder and propellers. *Malatya* is taken in tow to İstanbul and laid up in a damaged state.

2 October 1916: After lying fully loaded at Zonguldak for over a month, *Giresun* is ordered to sail for İstanbul. *Irmingard* leaves İstanbul for Zonguldak on the same day. Both ships proceed along the swept channels. Two miles east of Anadolu Karaburnu, *Irmingard* hits a mine. The steamer is beached with the bow to the bridge under water. Over the next few days salvage teams try to raise the freighter. The ship was dynamited abaft the bridge, but remained fast.

16 October 1916: The Russian submarine *Narval* torpedoes and sinks the steamer *Kesan* (156gt/–) off Şile.

17 October 1916: *Narval* destroys the stranded *Irmingard.*

21 October 1916: *Tyulen* captures the armed steamer *Rodosto* (3662 gt/1903) near Kefken Ada after an exchange of fire. The steamer is taken as a prize to Sebastopol.

21 October 1916: The tug *Arslan* is mined and sunk off Karasu.

21 October 1916: The battleship *Imperatritsa Ekaterina* appears off Ereğli and shells the town and the port, sinking the ferries *Ever-i Merhamnet* (230gt/1892), *Resan* (240gt/1894), the steamer *Talihiyaver* (114gt/–) and a number of small sailing vessels. The İntizam (244gt/1894) is damaged and later towed to İstanbul, laid up, then sold to the navy and lost in 1917.

September–November 1916: Operations of Bulgarian/German forces under Field Marshal von Mackensen in Rumania. Constanza falls on 22 October.

A photograph taken from the German Zeppelin SL 10 on 15 June 1916, showing the naval dockyard at İstinye. Yavuz, Midilli, *and the stationary* Urla *are visible, together with a German steamer and a number of torpedo-boats.*
BAM Freiburg

Malatya *in drydock at İstanbul in 1916 after hitting a mine.*
Güleryüz

The German transport Irmingard *aground after being torpedoed in the Black Sea; a photograph taken on 7 October 1916.*
Langensiepen

Gayret-i Vataniye *photographed in October 1916 at Varna. German official photograph*

28 October 1916: *Taşoz* sailed to Constanza with a group of German officers who are to supervise the setting up of a naval base.

30 October 1916: Admiral Souchon sails on *Muavent-i Milliye*, with *Nümune-i Hamiyet* as escort, for Varna where he holds talks with von Mackensen. *Gayret-i Vataniye* is detailed to act as a dispatch vessel between Varna and Constanza. While en route from İstanbul the destroyer runs on to an unchartered reef near Varna. Salvage attempts fail and the warship has to be abandoned.

21 December 1916: The *Pamyat Merkuriya* sinks the motor gunboats *No 12* and *No 16* by gunfire off Rumeli Karaburnu. Both boats have been at Burgaz since October, the presence of enemy patrols delaying their sailing for İstanbul until the day of their loss.

7 January 1917: *Nerpa* sights the ferry *Nusret* (230gt/1872) towing sailing barges off Şile. The barges are sunk by gunfire and *Nusret* beached.

12 January 1917: *Narval* attacks the salvage fleet sent to assist *Nusret,* and sinks the ferry *Neveser* (257gt/1890), the steam barge *Moda* and the brig *Dervis.* The larger vessels are later salvaged and towed to İstanbul.

6 February 1917: The *Neveser,* only just repaired, is mined off Incilli and sinks with the loss of two lives.

7 March 1917: The Russian submarine *Kashalot* attacks the ferry *Resanet* (230gt/1892) and two tugs off Sakarya. The three boats are driven ashore but easily salvaged the following day.

25 March 1917: The *Samrak* (709gt/1881) is mined off Ağva while en route from İstanbul to Varna with a cargo of aviation fuel. Ten of the crew are killed in the explosion. The steamer is beached and later salvaged.

During the early months of 1917 Russian destroyers sank a considerable number of small sailing vessels and dhows, now the sole means of transportation along the coast. Due to the weak coastal defences *Derzkiy* was even able to sail into Sinop on 29 January and destroy seven sailing ships. In March the Russians shelled Giresun and Tirebolu and a number of small craft were lost.

24 March 1917: *Nerpa* shells and sank the paddle steamer *Marmara* (250gt/1874) off Şile.

11 May 1917: A German plane based at Kefken bombs and sinks the submarine *Morz* off Ereğli.

During April and May the minefields and channels off the Bosporus were swept clear. The Russians then sent in a fleet of small motorboats to re-mine the approaches, the work being carried out without being seen by the coastal patrols. Only on 27 May, after a mine had exploded, were the defence forces made aware of what had occurred.

23 June 1917: *Midilli*, now rearmed with 150mm guns, steams from the Bosporus for the Snake Islands. Arriving there without incident, the cruiser mines the area and destroys the radio station.

25 June 1917: *Midilli* makes for home, but is sighted by the battleship *Svobodnaya Rossiya* (ex-*Imperatritsa Ekaterina*) . The destroyer *Gnevniy* is sent to investigate, but *Midilli* manages to keep a safe distance from the enemy. At 1415hrs the battleship opens fire, but the shells fell short and the cruiser is able to escape. *Midilli* and the destroyer *Basra,* sent out to meet the cruiser, reach the Bosporus safely.

14 July 1917: The minelayer *İntibah* strikes an underwater obstruction, probably a wreck, east of Anadolu Karaburnu. In use as a fast transport from Zonguldak to İstanbul with coal, the minelayer is badly damaged and beached. Salvage teams later patch up the minelayer and it is towed to İstanbul for lengthy repairs.

In August the Russian destroyers continued their raids along the

Midilli during mining operations in the Black Sea on 24 June 1917.
BAM Freiburg

coast but sinkings were limited to small sailing craft. At the end of the month landings were attempted at the coaling ports but succeeded only at Ordu. Elsewhere the alert defence forces were able to drive off the landing parties.

1 October 1917: The destroyers *Bystriy, Gromkiy* and *Fidonisi* sink the bark *Aydanik,* loaded with coal, off Kefken Ada and drive the tug *Beber* ashore.

6 October 1917: *Tyulen* captures the *Mahi* (1211gt/–) off İğneada and the prize is sent to Sebastopol. The submarine *Gagara* fires on the *Vatan* (516 tons/1862), sailing empty to İstanbul, off İğneada. The steamer is beached and not refloated until the spring of 1918. The decision is made to set up a new minesweeper base at İğneada.

29 October 1917: *Hamidabad* departs İstanbul for the new base, towing three German-built minehunters and with drums of petrol stacked on deck.

31 October 1917: As the group nears İğneada it is intercepted by the *Pylkiy* and *Bystriy,* and both destroyers open fire. The first hit sets the petrol on fire and *Hamidabad* is completely destroyed in the inferno. The destroyers then attack the hunters, the ferry *Sütlüce* (520gt/1909) and the steamer *Altay* (866gt/1893). These vessels are beached and later salvaged. *Midilli* is sent out to hunt the Russians, but returns to base the following day without sighting the enemy.

10 November 1917: *Midilli* makes a round trip to Sinop to show the flag, assuring the civilian population that their navy is still active.

13 November 1917: News is received in İstanbul that the Russian Revolution has reached the Crimea and that the war is now over for the Imperial Russian Black Sea Fleet.

4 December 1917: *İstanbul* (3569gt/1904) arrives at Zonguldak to load coal. This is the first of the large coal transports now being chartered by the Coal Agency to move urgently-needed supplies to the Bosporus.

5 December 1917: The region is hit by one of the worst winter storms ever recorded and well over twenty sailing craft are lost. *İstanbul* is driven ashore and not salvaged until January, eventually making the return voyage on 31 January 1918.

16 December 1917: An armistice is concluded by the new Russian government and Russia's former enemies. By the end of the war in the Black Sea, the Ottoman Empire has lost most of its merchant fleet and the navy is no longer a fighting force. The surviving ships are worn out and badly in need of refitting and

repairs. The morale of the ships' companies remains high, however, and the years of intensive training on land and at sea have done much to improve the fighting spirit of the Ottoman seamen.

24 February 1918: The German steamer *Minna Horn* (3415 gt/1913) carries 600 infantry to Giresun to reoccupy the area now abandoned by the Russians.

1 March 1918: *Akdeniz* (5092gt/1890) carries a further 300 infantry to Trabzon with the recommissioned *Hamidiye* and *Samsun, Nümune-i Hamiyet,* and *Muavent-i Milliye* as escorts.

17 March 1918: Vice-Admiral Albert Hofmann is appointed head of the Armistice Commission at Odessa. Germany and Austria quickly gain the main concessions from Russia, leaving little for Bulgaria and the Ottoman Empire.

20 March 1918: *Hamidiye, Nümune-i Hamiyet* and *Muavent-i Milliye* escort the German steamer *Patmos* from Constanza to Odessa with troops.

30 March 1918: *Patmos* again sails for Odessa with *Basra, Samsun* and *Taşoz* as escorts. The Germans fear that the Russian Navy may seek action again, and a combined German/Austrian force advances along the coast towards Sebastopol. *Yavuz* and *Hamidiye* cruise off the Russian forts as a precaution against a Russian attack.

The German transport General *pictured in July 1918 embarking troops at Constanza for Odessa.*
Langensiepen

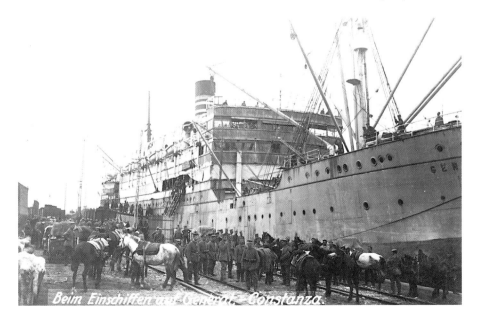

The river gunboat Hamidiye *on the Tigris with an unidentified steamer, during World War I.* Güleryüz

1 April 1918: *Burak Reis, Sakiz* and *İsa Reis* begin patrolling the eastern Black Sea on a monthly rotation basis. *Berk-i Satvet* is also recommissioned after lengthy repairs and placed at the disposal of the Army High Command to serve as a sea patrol vessel between İstanbul and Batumii. The army quickly regains control over eastern Anatolia, and *Yavuz* is no longer required for duty.

2 May 1918: *Yavuz* and *Hamidiye* enter Sebastopol to find the port already in German hands.

7–14 May 1918: *Yavuz* is drydocked for the first time in four years. The hull is scraped down and some of the many leaks are repaired.

12 May 1918: The cruiser *Prut,* the former *Mecidiye,* is recovered in a poor state. After being made seaworthy it is towed to İstanbul by the Hamidiye. After a two-day voyage both warships reach the Bosporus on 13 July.

28 June 1918: *Yavuz, Samsun, Nümune-i Hamiyet* and *Muavent-i Milliye* steam to Novorossiysk to force the internment of the Russian warships lying in the port. On arrival they discover that the Russians have scuttled their fleet. The destroyers remain in the area and *Yavuz* returns to İstanbul.

14 July 1918: *Yavuz* is laid up at İstinye till the end of the war. The fleet is reorganised with *Hamidiye* as flagship. The torpedo boats *Akhisar, Draç, Musul* and *Sultanhisar* remain on active service with *Berk-i Satvet* and *Peyk-i Şevket* being used on single voyages to the Caucasus. *Burak Reis, İsa Reis* and *Sakiz* patrol the seas between Zonguldak and Batumi. The motor gunboats *No 17* and *No 18* are stationed at the Bosporus with *Zuhaf* and the minelayer *Selanik* on reserve.

The Schichau destroyers are transferred to the Dardanelles to join a small force on patrol duties. The Germans hand over the destroyer *R 10* (ex-*Zorkiy*) and four tugs to the Ottoman Navy, all that it receives from the captured Russian fleet at Sebastopol. The navy later receives a mixed group of small naval craft and auxiliaries which are neither commissioned into the fleet nor enter naval service.

1 November 1918: Armistice signed at Mudros. The Ottoman Empire is obliged to open the Straits, repatriate Allied prisoners, demobilise its armed forces and sever relations with the Central Powers.

2 November 1918: German troops leave for Russia, and Germany formally hands over the *Yavuz* to the Ottoman Navy. The German Foreign Office arranges for the pro-German members of the government, Enver Paşa, Talat Paşa and Cemal Paşa, to sail on the *R 10* to Odessa.

Mesopotamia (Iraq), 1914 – 1918

4 August 1914: Mobilisation orders are received in Baghdad for the Sixth Army. The 13th Army Corps is in position between Baghdad and Basra and the 12th at barracks south of Mosul. On paper the four divisions have over 23,500 soldiers and thirty-two two-gun batteries of 75mm and 87mm field guns; in addition a battalion of light cavalry is stationed at Far, where any attack on Baghdad can be met.

The Ottoman naval forces in Mesopotamia consist of the gunboat *Marmaris*, the motor gunboats *No 1, No 2, No 5, No 6, No 7* and *No 8* and a number of small motor boats armed with machine guns for patrolling the Euphrates and the Tigris. A twenty-mile barrier is laid at Shat-el Arab and the old corvette *Kilidbahri,* long out of active service and now used as an accommodation ship, is scuttled off Basra to block the channel.

October 1914: The British close the Persian Gulf to all Ottoman shipping.

3 November 1914: British forces land at Far. The landings are supported by the gunboats *Odin, Espiègle* and *Lawrence* and the small Ottoman naval force was quickly overrun.

5 November 1914: Britain and France declare war on the Ottoman Empire. The motor gunboat *No 1* is shelled and sunk by British gunboats while proceeding to Abadan to attack the petroleum tanks. *No 1* is later salvaged and commissioned into the Royal Navy as HMS *Flycatcher*.

British forces advance steadily along the Shat-el Arab, the Ottoman 38th Division retreating ahead of them. Naval support is provided during the retreat by *Marmaris* and the gunboats *Nos 5, 6* and *8*.

9 November 1914: The motor gunboat *No 2* is sunk by *Odin* and *Espiègle* off Abadan.

16 November 1914: The German steamer *Ekbatania* (4573 gt/1905) and the Ottoman steamer *John O. Scott* (859gt/1874) are scuttled near the Mulammadra Islands near Shat-el Arab. *Marmaris*

The steamer Bağdat *on the Tigris during World War I.*
Güleryüz

is moved from Shat-el Arab to Basra.

19 November 1914: *Marmaris* and *Odin* exchange fire of Belcanya Ada.

21 November 1914: The gunboat *No 6* is sunk during the fighting around Basra.

24 November 1914: British forces occupy Basra. Just before the town falls, all the remaining Ottoman naval vessels are sent to Kurna (Qurna), on the junction of the Tigris and the Euphrates. In order to secure the city, the British begin to enlarge their sphere of occupation and continue the advance inland.

4–8 December 1914: Fighting takes place around Kurna, which is taken by Anglo-Indian forces on the 9th. *Marmaris* is considerably lightened, and escapes through shallow water to Amarah. The remaining motor gunboats are sent from Kurna to Nasiriye, further up the Euphrates, and a new base is set up.

From December 1914 until the spring of 1915 the front remained quiet.

11–12 April 1915: The British repulse Ottoman attacks on Basra. The British remove the mine and net barrages and began opera-

The river gunboat Doğan *photographed on the River Tigris shortly after commissioning.*
Langensiepen

tions along the Tigris at the end of May.

2 June 1915: *Marmara* shoots off all remaining ammunition at the advancing British forces, then is scuttled to avoid capture. The gunboat was damaged in action with *Espiègle* the previous day.

3 June 1915: British forces under Townshend take Amarah.

25 July 1915: British forces take Nasiriye, marking the beginning of their general advance on Baghdad. *No 5* and *No 8* are scuttled

Two detail views of the armament of the gunboat Doğan.
Langensiepen

A 105mm gun from Midilli mounted on a barge in the River Euphrates in 1917.
Güleryüz

to avoid capture.

28 September 1915: Townshend defeats the Ottoman forces at Kut-el Amara and drives them back to Azizye.

11 November 1915: Beginning of the British advance on Baghdad.

22–24 November 1915: Indecisive battle at Ctesiphon; both sides begin to retreat and the British fall back as far at Kut-el Amara, which they reach on 3 December. The German Field Marshal Colmar von der Goltz (Paşa) had taken overall command of the Ottoman army by this stage.

7 December 1915: The British forces are now trapped, and the siege begins. Three attempts are made by the British to relieve the garrison (18–21 January, 8 March, 1–9 April 1916) but the relief forces are hampered by floods and mud.

During the British retreat to Kut-el Amara a number of scuttled vessels, including the British river gunboat *Firefly,* sunk in July, were salvaged and repaired by the Germans at Baghdad. The German naval command had set up repair yards at Baghdad when they arrived in July 1915. It was here that *Firefly* was repaired and commissioned as *Selmanpak.* At about this time the Ottoman army and navy in Mesopotamia were reorganised, and the navy split into two groups. One was a fighting unit (Sat-filo) and the other a transport unit. This reorganisation proved to be of little value since the fighting unit was too small to be of any military use and the transports were plagued by a chronic shortage of coal.

29 April 1916: Capitulation of Kut-el Amara to the Ottoman army.

15 May 1916: Russian forces attack north-eastern Mesopotamia, taking Khanaqin and Ruwandiz. A detachment actually joins hands with the British on the Tigris.

13 December 1916: British advance under Sir Stanley Maude towards Kut-el Amara.

9 January–24 February 1917: After long and difficult fighting, the British forces take the city on 23 February. British forces advance along the Tigris and the Euphrates. Ottoman opposition is weak, forces detached for action against the Russians in Persia not having been returned to Mesopotamia in time.

25 February 1917: British forces capture the hospital river steamer *Basra,* the *Selmanpak, Doğan,* an ex-German river tug, and the mine barge *Maydar.*

11 March 1918: Baghdad occupied by the British. Here they find the motor gunboat *No 7* and a few small river boats, some fitted with light weapons. The British also take over the *Ganimet,* motor gunboat *No 11* and a few barges which were fitted with *Midilli*'s two discarded 105mm guns. With the capture of these few remaining units the Ottoman navy ceases to exist in Mesopotamia.

29 September 1917: British troops capture Ramadi on the Euphrates.

6 November 1917: British forces take Tikrit on the Tigris. These two points mark the furthest Allied advance in 1917.

Naval Aviation, 1913–1918

Shortly before the outbreak of the Italo-Ottoman war the Ottoman air force was founded at Yeşilköy, now İstanbul's international airport. Due to hostilities no proper training was carried out and only at the end of 1913 did French instructors begin a flying programme.

At Yeşilköy the navy established a flying boat base, and a slipway was laid on the Sea of Marmara. In the short time remaining until the outbreak of World War I only a small number of officers completed their training and purchase of aircraft from France were not completed. Nevertheless, when war broke out two spotter planes with their crew and ground staff were sent to the each of the army corps. The training school, now under the command of the German Oblt Sernos, remained at Yesilköy.

5 September 1914: Aerial reconnaissance flights begin over the Dardanelles.

October 1914: Three German planes arrive at the Dardanelles to increase patrol strength.

5 May 1915: The Ottoman air ace Üstegmen Fazil is killed near İstanbul when his plane crashes into woods. He was on an observation flight over the Russian fleet off the Bosporus at the time of the accident.

April–May 1915: Two army planes and a further naval aircraft join German aircraft over the Dardanelles during the Gallipoli landings.

June 1915: Two-seater Gotha planes are in action against British submarines in the Sea of Marmara. Successes are limited due to the lack of radio equipment and the fact that bombs have to be dropped by hand.

1916: The Ottoman forces take delivery of Fokker monoplane fighter aircraft. A naval air arm is set up under the command of the German Oblt z S Liebemann, with headquarters at Yeşilköy. A total of twenty-four Fokkers is made available, and a large force of pilots, observers and ground staff are trained for the new duties.

Two planes are sent to Kavak on the Bosporus, one to Ereğli and three to Çanakkale. The number of German officers attached to the flying corps remains small compared to the number appointed to the army.

14 April 1916: British bombers attack the munitions works at Zeytin Burnu. Steps are immediately taken to strengthen aerial defences. Further Ottoman naval pilots are sent to Wilhelmshaven for training, and these see active service with the German naval air arm.

1 January 1917: The Ottoman naval air arm now comprises a squadron of eight planes and an all-Ottoman ground crew, and is now based at İzmit. The squadron (1 Deniz Tayyare Bülu) is however placed under army control and is no longer available for naval operations. Aircraft are also stationed at Anadoluhisari on the Bosporus and at Ereğli on the Black Sea. Here the crews are joint German-Ottoman, but at Çanakkale all the crews and ground staff are German. The air training school, staff and the administration remained at Yeşilköy.

At the end of 1917 a joint base with the army was set up at Mersin for operations in Palestine.

During the war the naval air arm was confined to reconnaissance and, while the operations never made the headlines, nevertheless the pilots supplied fleet command with abundant information on enemy movements in the Narrows and the Sea of Marmara. No aircraft were lost through enemy action, any lives lost being due to material failure or pilot error.

From the Ottoman Empire to the Turkish Republic, 1918–1923

3 November 1918: The commander-in-chief Arif Paşa orders all flags to be struck on all the warships lying in the Haliç. When the ensign is lowered, the Imperial Ottoman navy ceases to exist.

At the armistice negotiations at Mudros the navy minister Rauf Paşa had been informed of the navy's future role. All warships at İstanbul and İzmir were to be interned and would be handed over to the victors at a later date. The navy would be responsible for disbanding the various staffs and the minesweepers would remain in service until the barrages had been removed and the minefields swept.

13 November 1918: The Allied fleet arrives at İstanbul; all the remaining Ottoman merchant vessels with the exception of *Akdeniz*, *Giresun* and *Resit Paşa* (which are requisitioned to transport German and Austrian military personnel home), are ordered to remain in port.

During the last weeks of 1918 the warships were disarmed in accordance with the terms of the armistice. All guns were removed, and only the torpedo boats remained armed. Torpedoes and mines were also dismantled. Relations between the Allies and the Ottoman authorities remained good throughout the period of disarmament and occupation.

26 February 1919: The British commander, Vice-Admiral Somerset Arthur Gough Calthorpe, agrees to an Ottoman request to be allowed to set up patrols to stop arms smuggling. Accordingly *Hızır Reis* at İzmit, *Aydin Reis* and *Preveze* in the Black Sea and *Akhisar* and *Draç* in the Sea of Marmara are released from internment to take up patrol duties. *Yavuz* remains in reserve.

7 March 1919: Cabinet of Damid Farid Paşa is formed, with a policy of co-operation with the Allied powers.

29 April 1919: Italian troops land at Adalia, the first step in the Allied occupation of south-west Anatolia.

14 May 1919: Greek troops land at İzmir with the approval of the Allies and under the protection of the Allied fleets. The *Hızır Reis*, *Nusret*, the motor gunboat *No 14* and the transport *Tir-i Mügan* lie in port. *Nusret* and *Tir-i Mügan* are released some weeks later but the Greeks retain the other two warships.

19 May 1919: The steamer *Bandırma* (279tons/1878) arrives at Trabzon with the hero of the Dardanelles, Mustafa Kemal Paşa, on board. He had been sent to Anatolia to arrange the disbanding of the Third Army. He immediately begins organising resistance to the further dismemberment of the Ottoman Empire.

One of Kemal Paşa's first orders concerning the navy is to arrange for coal supplies to be sent from İstanbul to bunker the gunboats *Aydin Reis* and *Preveze*. Both boats successfully combated Greek gunrunners and smugglers from February, but were then laid up through lack of fuel. Another order is for armed motor boats to combat piracy on the high seas (such piracy reached a peak with the capture of the French steamer *Pake* on a voyage from Batumi to Trabzon). The request for the motor boats is refused by the Allies, and deliveries of bunker coal considerably delayed by İstanbul.

8 July 1919: The Sultan, Mehmet VI, officially dismisses Kemal Paşa, and he is outlawed three days later.

By August it was clear to the authorities in İstanbul that gunboats had gone over to Kemal Paşa. The British investigated the matter and the boats searched but the British made no attempt to confiscate them. Adequate coal supplies were eventually delivered by *Giresun* and *Şam*.

4–9 September 1919: A Nationalist congress at Sivas affirms the unity of Turkish territory and declares against the Allied occupation.

13 September 1919: The National Pact is drawn up, its six principles guaranteeing the security of İstanbul, the opening of the Straits to all shipping and the rights of the minorities.

5 October 1919: Following the victory of the Nationalists at the election, a new cabinet under Miraly Riza Paşa is formed.

28 January 1920: The National Pact is adopted by parliament.

16 March 1920: An Allied force under General George Milne occupies İstanbul to check Nationalist agitation. The declared purpose of the occupation is to keep open the Straits.

11 April 1920: Parliament is dissolved at İstanbul.

23 April 1920: A provisional government under Kemal Paşa is set up at Ankara. A military agreement with the Soviet government to guarantee supplies is signed.

10 June 1920: The Treaty of Sèvres is presented to the Ottoman government. The Nationalists promise uncompromising opposition, and receive increasing popular support.

20 June 1920: The Greeks begin an offensive, taking Alasehir (24th), Brusa (9 July) and Edirne (25 July).

10 August 1920: The Ottoman government signs the Sèvres treaty, leading to a definitive break with the Nationalists.

16 September 1920: Negotiations with Soviet Russia are completed and *Aydin Reis* sails from Trabzon for Novorossiysk to be interned.

19 September 1920: *Aydin Reis* arrives at the Russian port. Owing to poor maintenance the gunboat can make only six knots during the voyage.

30 September 1920: *Preveze* also makes a slow voyage, using makeshift sails when the engines fail. Once both gunboats are in safety they are repaired with Soviet assistance.

After the Treaty of Sèvres had been signed, more and more warships went over to the Nationalists, including the customs steamer *Rüsumet No 4* and the naval tug *Samsun* at Ereğli on 6 September, the tug *Gazal* and the auxiliary *Mebruke* at Trabzon on the 23rd and a large number of small craft and sailing vessels.

28 January 1921: The salvage tug *Alemdar* reaches Ereğli, successfully avoiding the now regular British and French warships patrols in the area. An agreement is reached with the Soviet government for the supply of guns and ammunition for the Kemalists. All available shipping is pressed into service between Batumi and Trabzon. Over 35,000 tons of military material is shipped.

February 1921: London Conference between the Allied Powers, the government in İstanbul and Ankara representatives. Efforts to agree modifications to the Sèvres treaty fail.

13 March 1921: An agreement is reached between Kemal Paşa and the Italians. The latter agree to evacuate Anatolia in return for promises of extensive economic concessions.

16 March 1921: An agreement is reached between Kemal Paşa and Soviet Russia. Turkey is to retrocede Batumi; in return Soviet Russia recognises Turkish possession of Kars and Ardahan.

23 March 1921: Beginning of a new Greek offensive. Greek troops take Afiun-Karahisar and Eskisehir 28–30 March, but are driven back by the defence forces some three days later.

16 May 1921: *Aydin Reis* and *Preveze* return to service and are

Trabzon harbour in Summer 1922; in the foreground are the gunboat Aydin Reis *(left), the naval tug* Alemdar *and the transport* Şahin *(right), all in service as transports for the Turkish Liberation Army.*
Güleryüz

(Far right)
A cargo of aircraft from Russia being unloaded from the transport Şahin *at Trabzon in summer 1922.*
Kızıldemir

Hamidiye *in 1930 at İzmir. Damage to buildings in the city, which was virtually destroyed by Turkish troops in 1922, is visible in the background.*
Güleryüz

quickly in use as ammunition transports.

16–17 July 1921: The Greeks take Kutahia after fierce fighting and retake Afiun-Karahisar and Eskisehir.

17 July 1921: *Rüsumet No 4* is shelled by Greek destroyers while lying at anchor off Ortu. The ship is set on fire, but after the destroyer has made off the crew extinguishes the blaze and the ship reaches Trabzon on 22 July, where it is repaired.

24 August–16 September 1921: The Battle of Sahharia sees desperate defence by the Turkish forces. The Greeks fail to reach their objective, Ankara.

30 September 1921: The *Rüsumet No 4*, only recently repaired and returned to service, is again attacked by Greek warships near Gürell Burnu. Again the vessel is set on fire, and is beached and

flooded to prevent the fire from spreading.

14 October 1921: *Rüsumet No 4* is again shelled by the Greeks and totally destroyed.

During the late summer Soviet Russia handed over two motor gunboats at Novorossiysk to the Kemalists. They were commissioned as *No 1* and *No 2* on 10 October and 4 November 1921 respectively. The 35-ton boats had a sea speed of nearly twenty knots and were armed with a 47mm, a 37mm and two machine guns.

20 October 1921: An agreement is reached between Kemal Paşa and France. The French agree to evacuate Cilicia in return for economic concessions.

26 March 1922: The Allied Powers agree to some revision of the Treaty of Sèvres, and attempt to settle the Greek-Turkish conflict.

İstanbul refuses an armistice until Greek troops evacuate Anatolia.

25 April 1922: The motor gunboats *No 1* and *No 2* stop the Greek steamer *Enosis* (632gt/1891) near Novorossiysk, en route to İstanbul with general cargo. After inspecting the ship and guaranteeing the safety of the 100 passengers, the gunboats escort

the steamer was taken to Draç and then to Trabzon, arriving on 29 April. The steamer is handed over to the Kemalist navy and renamed *Trabzon*.

August 1922: Beginning of the Turkish counter-offensive. Turkish troops take Afiun-Karahisar on 30 August, Zeytin Burnu (5 September) and İzmir (9–11 September).

16 September 1922: A British force under General Harington lands at Chanak to secure the Straits against Turkish control.

3–11 October 1922: Conference and Convention of Mudanya between the Allied Powers and the Nationalists. The Allies agree to return Eastern Thrace and Edirne to Turkey, and the latter accepts the neutralisation of the Straits under international control.

7 October 1922: The Greek steamer *Urania* (1465 tons/1887) is captured by the naval tug *Gazal* on the high seas and taken to Ereğli as a prize. The steamer is handed over to the Turkish navy and renamed *Samsun*.

1 November 1922: Kemal Paşa proclaims the abolition of the Sultanate. The Sultan, Mehmet VI, departs İstanbul aboard a British warship.

End of 1922: The minelayer *İntibah,* the small steamers *Sagram, Saika, Kasim Paşa* and *Rehber*, the motorboats *Haliç, Beykoz, Darich* and the yacht *Galata* flee to İzmit from İstanbul.

20 November 1922: Opening of the Lausanne Conference, to conclude peace between the Allied Powers and Turkey. The conference breaks up temporarily at the beginning of February 1923, resumes again in April and concludes its work in July.

24 July 1923: Treaty of Lausanne. Turkey gives up all claims to non-Turkish territory lost as a result of the War, but receives Eastern Thrace. All the Aegean Islands except İmbroz and Tenedos go to Greece. Italy retains the Dodecanese and Britain Cyprus. The Straits are demilitarised: they are declared open to all nations in times of peace and in time of war if Turkey remains neutral; if Turkey is at war enemy ships, but not neutrals, may be excluded.

23 August 1923: The Allies evacuate İstanbul, the Turks taking possession on 6 October.

29 October 1923: Formal proclamation of the Turkish Republic. One of the first tasks of the Navy Ministry is to compile a list of all ships remaining. These are:

In service

Hamidiye, Peyk-i Şevket, Ertuğrul, Sagutl, Taşoz, Durak Reis, Hizir Reis, Kemal Reis, İsa Reis, Nusret, Galata, four tugs, seven motor boats.

Out of service

Yavuz, Torgud Reis, Berk-i Satvet, Mecidiye, Muavent-i Milliye, Nümune-i Hamiyet, Basra, Samsun, Sultanhisar, Yunus, Akhisar, Draç, Musul, Berkefşan, Sakiz.

Peyk-i Şevket seen in 1927 in the Sea of Marmara. Admiral Dümer

A view of the Gölçük naval yard in 1928, showing part of the torpedo cruiser Peyk-i Şevket *or* Berk-i Satvet, *the corvette* Zuhaf *being broken up, and the steamer* Trabzon, *captured by the Kemalist forces in 1921. Güleryüz*

A photograph taken in 1930 at Erdek, a small village on the Sea of Marmara. The vessels shown are (left to right) the submarine İkinci İnönü, Muin-i Zafer *(now a submarine depot ship), the submarine* Birinci İnönü, *the motor gunboat No 11 and the salvage tug* Rasit. *Erdek was a submarine base until 1938. Güleryüz*

PHOTOGRAPHIC SECTION

Mahmudiye *off the naval yard in the Haliç, about 1888.*
Turkish Navy

Aziziye *as completed in 1865, pictured off the Navy Ministry in the Haliç about 1888.*
Güleryüz

Osmaniye: *the after 240mm gun with crew, c1895/96, after rearming.*
Güleryüz

Osmaniye: *repro-duction of an artist's impression of the ship after the reconstruction of 1890–94.*
Turkish Navy

Osmaniye *at İstan-bul c1896.*
Turkish Navy

Orhaniye *as com-pleted. Illustrated in the Haliç c1888. In the background the covered slipways of the navy yard can be seen.*
Güleryüz

Orhaniye*: broad-side view at İstanbul in 1896, after rebuilding. Note the prominent gun sponsons.*
Güleryüz

(Top left)
Orhaniye anchored
off Çanakkale in the
Dardanelles in
1897. The photo-
graph shows sail
exercises.
Güleryüz

(Top right)
Hamidiye: a deck
view taken after
rebuilding, in 1894
in the Haliç. On
deck is the torpe-
doboat Şemşir-i
Hücum, carried on
board until 1896.
Güleryüz

A deck view of
Mesudiye at
İstanbul c1888,
before rebuilding.
Turkish Navy

(Below)
Mesudiye anchored
in the Haliç,
just before the
Greco-Ottoman War
in 1896.
Güleryüz

Mesudiye: the
quarterdeck
looking forward,
seen at İstanbul in
1905 after
rebuilding.
Güleryüz

Mesudiye: the
quarterdeck looking
aft, seen at İstanbul
after rebuilding.
Güleryüz

Opposite Page:

(Top left)
Mesudiye: the bat-
tery deck after
rebuilding in 1905.
Güleryüz

(Top right)
Mesudiye at anchor
off İstanbul in 1912.
Turkish Navy

(Lower)
Mesudiye laid up in
the Haliç in 1908.
In the background
left is the Navy
Ministry, now Naval
Headquarters,
Turkish Navy Nor-
thern Command.
Güleryüz

(Top left)
Mesudiye: the commanding officer, staff officers and crew, reproduced from an Ottoman Navy magazine, 1908.
Güleryüz

(Top right)
Mesudiye at the Ansaldo yard, Genoa, complete and ready for sea in 1906.
Güleryüz

(Right)
Mesudiye during the demonstration of the Ottoman Navy at Selanik, 25 May – 12 June 1911. The fleet carried members of the 'Young Turks' committee, and the demonstration was intended to humiliate the deposed Sultan Abdül Hamid II and his exiled court living at Selanik.
Güleryüz

Opposite Page:

(Top)
Mesudiye during the demonstration of the Ottoman Navy at Selanik 25 May – 12 June 1911.
Güleryüz

(Centre)
Mesudiye during the demonstration of the Ottoman Navy at Selanik 25 May – 12 June 1911.
Güleryüz

(Bottom)
Mesudiye arriving at Selanik 25 May 1911.
Güleryüz

Hamidiye *at İstanbul, 1897.*
Turkish Navy

(Centre left) Hamidiye*: reproduction from an oil painting, date unknown.*
Güleryüz

(Centre right) Asar-i Tevfik*: the midship 220mm gun and crew c1890.*
Güleryüz

Asar-i Tevfik *as completed, at İstanbul 1895.*
Güleryüz

Asar-i Tevfik *in the floating dock of the 'Germania'-Werft, Kiel, during rebuilding in 1905.*
Güleryüz

Asar-i Tevfik*: trials photograph in the Kieler Förde, 1906.*
Güleryüz

Asar-i Tevfik: *the only known photograph of an Ottoman warship taken at sea during the Balkan War, in the Sea of Marmara off Sarköy.*
Langensiepen

Asar-i Şevket *in the Haliç, laid up at anchor in 1897.*
Güleryüz

Necm-i Şevket *at anchor in the Dardanelles in 1897, during the Greco-Ottoman War.*
Güleryüz

Muin-i Zafer *at anchor in the Haliç in 1893.*
Güleryüz

Avnillah *as completed, in the Haliç in 1885.*
Güleryüz

Opposite Page:

(Top)
Muin-i Zafer *during the demonstration of the Ottoman Navy at Selanik 25 May – 12 June 1911.*
Güleryüz

(Lower)
Muin-i Zafer*: another photograph taken during the demonstration of the Ottoman Navy at Selanik 25 May – 12 June 1911.*
Güleryüz

This Page:

(Top)
Muin-i Zafer *laid up in a poor state at the naval dockyard at İstanbul, 1906.*
Güleryüz

(Centre)
Muin-i Zafer *in dry-dock at the navy yard at İstanbul in 1912.*
Langensiepen

(Lower)
Muin-i Zafer *at anchor in the Sea of Marmara in 1913.*
Musée de la Marine, Paris

(Above)
Muin-i Zafer: the quarterdeck, illustrating the ship's poor state in 1906.
Güleryüz

(Above right)
Muin-i Zafer: a view amidships, further illustrating the ship's condition in 1906.
Güleryüz

Muin-i Zafer at sea in the Bosporus in 1908.
Turkish Navy

Feth-i Bülend (left) and Avnillah (right) anchored off the naval dockyard at İstanbul in 1895.
Güleryüz

Feth-i Bülend *at anchor off the naval yard at İstanbul in 1898. The buildings in the upper background are the residences of the foreign colony in the Ottoman capital.*
Güleryüz

Feth-i Bülend *laid up out of service in the Haliç in 1907.*
Güleryüz

İclaliye *as completed, anchored in the Haliç off the naval dockyard in 1892.*
Güleryüz

İclaliye *after
rebuilding at İstan-
bul, March 1914.*
Langensiepen

(Centre left)
Feth-ül İslam *as a
guard ship at Sayir
in the Bosporus in
1906.*
Güleryüz

(Centre right)
Lütf-ü Celil: *repro-
duction of an
Ottoman engraving
showing the ship as
completed in 1870.*
Turkish Navy

Hifz-ur Rahman:
*photograph taken
during Ramadan in
the early years
of the twentieth
century.*
Güleryüz

Feth-ül İslam *as a guard ship anchored at İstaniye, in the Bosporus, in 1902.*
Güleryüz

Barbaros Hayreddin *during the demonstration of the Ottoman Navy at Selanik 25 May – 12 June 1911.*
Güleryüz

*(This page &
opposite top)*
Torgud Reis *during
the demonstration
of the Ottoman
Navy at Selanik
25 May – 12 June
1911.*
Güleryüz

Torgud Reis *laid
up, out of service, in
summer 1919 in the
Haliç.*
Güleryüz

Torgud Reis: *a view forward from the after mast c1927.*
Admiral Dümer

Barbaros Hayreddin: *the midship 280mm gun (reproduction from an Ottoman Navy magazine of 1911).*
Güleryüz

Torgud Reis *at Gölçük in 1925/26. In the foreground is the temporary slipway built to receive the guns landed from two of the turrets. These were installed in shore batteries at Erenköy and Çanakkale.*
Admiral Dümer

Torgud Reis *laid up
out of service in the
Haliç in May 1919.*
IWM

(Left)
Torgud Reis
*bunkering coal at
İstanbul in March
1915. The photo-
graph (a reproduc-
tion from a German
war newspaper
published in
Summer 1915)
shows the mixed
Ottoman-German
crew.*
Langensiepen

(Below)
Barbaros
Hayreddin*: a wash
day in 1914 or
1915.
From a German
private collection*

Crew members aboard Torgud Reis, *in a photograph dated 1930. By this time Turkish sailors wore German-style uniforms.*
Güleryüz

Barbaros Hayreddin: *the ship's officers posed before the after gun in 1911 or 1912 in the Haliç. The ship's imam is wearing the white cap. From a Turkish private collection*

Torgud Reis *in the Bosporus in 1912.*
Güleryüz

Torgud Reis *off Gölçük in 1931. From a Turkish private collection*

Yavuz *at Gölçük in 1926. The crane forward is part of the torpedo loading gear.*
Admiral Dümer

Yavuz *and*
Berk-i Satvet *at*
İstinye in September
1914. Note the
Goeben *crest still*
on the bow.
Güleryüz

Yavuz *laid up out of*
service at İstinye in
October 1918.
Güleryüz

Yavuz *at İstinye dockyard in March 1915.*
Capt Ackermann collection

Yavuz, *a* Samsun *class destroyer and the naval tug* Rasit *at Izmir in 1925/26. In the foreground, laid up out of service are (from left to right) the corvette* Muin-i Zafer, *the mine transport* Giresun *and the steamer* Trabzon, *captured in 1921 in the Black Sea.*
Langensiepen

Yavuz *at anchor off Izmir in 1925/26. In the foreground, from left to right, are two destroyers of the* Samsun *class,* Trabzon, *the corvette* İclaliye, *the mine transport* Giresun *and* Muin-i Zafer.
Langensiepen

*Ottoman ships of
the line dressed
overall in the Haliç
in 1869.*
Güleryüz

Şadiye: *reproduc-
tion of an oil paint-
ing in the İstanbul
Navy Museum,
painted by Behzad
Ahmet Bey in 1867*

(Right)
Kosova: *a photo-
graph taken before
1875 at İstanbul.*
Güleryüz

Ertuğrul *ready to leave İstanbul on a world cruise in 1889.*
Güleryüz

Rehber-i Tevfik *at anchor off İstanbul in 1892, serving as a torpedo training ship.*
Güleryüz

Ertuğrul *laid up out of service at İstanbul in 1884.*
Güleryüz

Mansure *off İstanbul in 1895 (reproduction of an Ottoman postcard incorrectly captioned 'corvette Ataid').*

(Below)
Beyrut*: reproduction of an Ottoman engraving of 1875.*
Turkish Navy

(Opposite Page – Top)
Peyk-i Şevket*: photograph taken during trials in the Kieler Förde in 1907.*
Turkish Navy

(Left)
Peyk-i Şevket: a view of the quarter-deck in May 1915. The photograph, from a German private collection, showns two German war correspondents from the Dardanelles front.
Langensiepen

(Right)
Peyk-i Şevket at İstanbul in Summer 1918. The torpedo-gunboat was employed as an escort for troop convoys to Russia at this time.
Güleryüz

(Top left)
Berk-i Satvet: *a workshop photograph taken 18 April 1907 at the 'Germania' Werft, Kiel, showing damage caused when a piston rod broke during trials.*
Langensiepen

(Top right)
Berk-i Satvet *at İstanbul in 1930.*
Güleryüz

(Centre)
Berk-i Satvet *during a visit to İzmir in 1927.*
Turkish Navy

(Lower left)
Berk-i Satvet *at sea in the Sea of Marmara c1926/27.*
Admiral Dümer

(Lower right)
Berk-i Satvet: *an official Ottoman Navy photograph from 1914.*
Turkish Navy

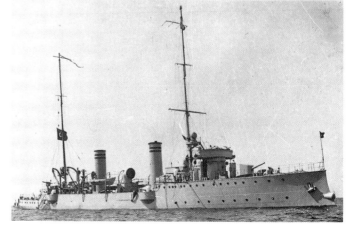

(Top left)
Mecidiye: *a quar-
terdeck view at
İstanbul in 1904,
shortly after the
cruiser arrived from
the USA.*
Güleryüz

(Top right)
Mecidiye: *quarter-
deck view looking
aft, İstanbul 1904.*
Güleryüz

Mecidiye *at anchor
in the Haliç just
after arriving from
the builders.*
Güleryüz

Mecidiye *(left) and*
Mesudiye *(right) in
the Haliç in 1908.
The prominent
building in the cen-
tre background is
the Galata tower.*
Güleryüz

Mecidiye *during the
demonstration of
the Ottoman Navy
at Selanik 25 May –
12 June 1911.*
Güleryüz

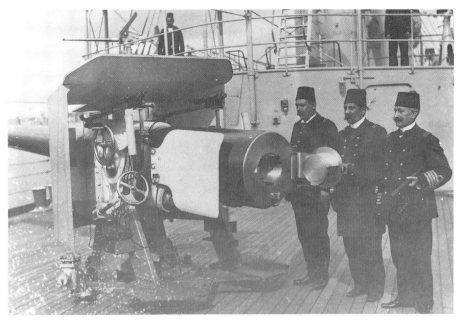

(Top left)
Mecidiye *at İstanbul navy yard in 1906.*
Güleryüz

(Above)
Mecidiye*: a detail shot taken during a visit of the commander-in-chief Hasan Rami Paşa and staff shortly after the arrvial of the cruiser from the USA.*
Güleryüz

(Left & below)
Mecidiye*: detail photographs taken on board shortly after the cruiser's arrival from the USA.*
Güleryüz

Mecidiye *at İstan-
bul in 1928.*
Güleryüz

Mecidiye *under
repair at the navy
yard at İstanbul in
1932.*
Güleryüz

Mecidiye *laid up in the Haliç in 1919, after the cruiser's return from Sevastopol in poor condition and with only one funnel.*
Güleryüz

Hamidiye *(left) and* Mecidiye *(right) at İstanbul in 1905.*
Güleryüz

Hamidiye*: a deck detail photograph taken shortly after the cruiser's arrival from the builder's yard in Britain.*
Güleryüz

Hamidiye: *the bridge being removed during refitting at the navy yard at İstanbul in January 1915.*
Langensiepen

(Left)
Hamidiye: *quarter-deck view during the Balkan War in 1912.*
Güleryüz

(Right)
Hamidiye *dry-docked at İstanbul in 1927/28.*
Admiral Dümer

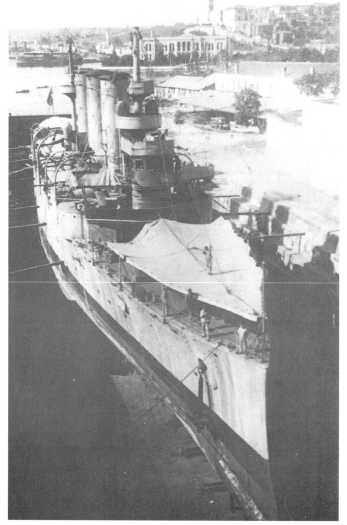

Hamidiye *visiting İstanbul during the 1930s.*
Güleryüz

Hamidiye *at the breaker's yard at Paşabahçe, in the Bosporus, in 1966. Alongside is an ex-British destroyer also being broken up. This photograph is proof that the cruiser was not scrapped shortly after World War II.*
Güleryüz

Hamidiye *in the Bosporus in 1943. The photograph shows the cruiser after the last refit, when the after mast was removed and AA guns installed, and the ship modernised. The camouflage shown was used only on* Yavuz, Hamidiye *and* Mecidiye *from 1943 to 1946.*
Güleryüz

Hamidiye *dressed overall in the Dardanelles in 1932.*
Güleryüz

Hamidiye *during the ship's first visit to İzmir in 1926.*
Güleryüz

Hamidiye *at
İstanbul in 1935.*
Güleryüz

Hamidiye*:
deck view c1932.*
Güleryüz

Hamidiye *(left) and*
Mecidiye *(right)*
with Samsun *class*
destroyers in the
background during
a visit to Zonguldak
in 1930.
Güleryüz

Hamidiye *coming*
alongside Yavuz *at*
Gölçük in 1924. The
forward 120mm
guns have still not
been installed, but
the bridge, removed
in 1915, is back in
place.
Güleryüz

Hamidiye*: official*
Ottoman Navy pho-
tograph of 1914.
Turkish Navy

Hamidiye *in 1928,
with the forward
120mm guns
reinstalled.*
Güleryüz

Hamidiye*: detail
view of one of the
150mm Armstrong
guns in 1903.*
Güleryüz

Hamidiye *lying off
the Naval Ministry
at İstanbul in 1903.*
Güleryüz

Midilli *during mining operations in the Black Sea, 24 June 1917.*
BMA-Freiburg

Midilli*: official Ottoman Navy photograph taken at İstanbul in September 1914.*
Turkish Navy

Midilli *at İstanbul
shortly after the
ship's transfer to the
Ottoman Navy in
August 1914.*
Güleryüz

Midilli: *official
Ottoman Navy pho-
tograph taken at
İstanbul in
September 1914.*
Güleryüz

Midilli: *official
Ottoman Navy pho-
tograph taken at
İstanbul in October
1914.*
Güleryüz

Şemşir-i Hücum *at
the navy dockyard
at İstanbul in 1887.*
Güleryüz

Midilli *re-arming at*
İstinye in Summer
1915.
Langensiepen

Şatvet *off İstanbul-*
Kasimpaşa in 1889.
The sailing frigate
is Ceylan-i Bahri.
Güleryüz

'Germania' *and*
Schichau *class*
torpedo-boats at
İstanbul c1890.
Güleryüz

Hamidiye *on trials
in 1902. Builder's
photograph*

Tir-i Zafer*:
a broadside view of
the torpedo-boat in
the Haliç.*
Güleryuz

Abdülmecid *on
trials in 1902.
Builder's
photograph*

Abdülmecid *at İstanbul in 1903. On the right is one of the* Osmaniye *ironclads in service as a barracks ship.*
Güleryüz

Sultanhisar *class: reproduction of a French postcard taken at the builder's yard.*
Güleryüz

Sivrihisar *class:
reproduction of a
French postcard
taken at the
builder's yard.*
Güleryüz

Draç *in the
Bosporus in 1910.*
Güleryüz

Peleng-i Derya*: a
photograph taken in
1908 in the Haliç.*
Güleryüz

Peleng-i Derya *at anchor at Southampton during her delivery voyage.*
IWM

Basra *(left),* Samsun *(centre) and* Taşoz *(right) moored at İzmir in 1926.*
Güleryüz

Samsun *(left) and* Basra *(right) in the Sea of Marmara in 1926.*
Güleryüz

Samsun *at sea in 1926. The smoke-screen is the result of burning poor-quality Ereğli coal.*
Güleryüz

Samsun *during manoeuvres in the Sea of Marmara in the 1920s.*
Güleryüz

Samsun*: a broad-side view of the destroyer in 1925.*
Güleryüz

A Samsun *class destroyer coming alongside* Yavuz *during the 1930s.*
Güleryüz

Samsun *entering İstanbul in 1932.*
Güleryüz

Opposite Page:

(Top left)
A Samsun *class destroyer taking on a torpedo while on exercise in the 1930s.*
Güleryüz

(Top right)
Samsun*: broadside view at İstanbul in the 1930s.*
Güleryüz

(Lower)
Yarhisar *pictured at Selanik during the Ottoman Navy demonstration 25 May – 12 June 1911.*
Güleryüz

This Page:

(Upper)
Samsun *dressed overall at İzmir c1928.*
Güleryüz

(Centre)
Basra *during fleet manoeuvres in the Sea of Marmara in 1911.*
Güleryüz

(Bottom)
Two from a series of rare action photographs taken when Basra *escorted the German U-boat UB8 from Çanakkale to İstanbul on 3 June 1915.*
Langensiepen

Taşoz *in heavy*
weather in the Sea
of Marmara in
Spring 1928.
Güleryüz

Muavent-i Milliye
and other Schichau
class destroyers on
exercise in the Sea
of Marmara in
1913.
Güleryüz

Muavent-i Milliye
at anchor at
İstanbul in 1912.
Güleryüz

Yadigar-i Millyet *in late 1910 or early 1911, shortly after the ship's purchase from Germany.*
Güleryüz

Yadigar-i Millyet *with extended main-mast in the Bosporus in 1915.*
Güleryüz

Destroyers and torpedo-boats at the naval base at İstinye in 1915.
Langensiepen

Muavent-i Milliye
*bunkering at
Haydarpaşa pier in
1915.*
Langensiepen

Abdülhamid *during
the submarine's first
and only sea
voyage, in the Haliç
in 1886 . The vessel
was then laid up
and subsequently
beached and left to
disintegrate.*
Güleryüz

Müstecip Onbaşı
*during a flag-show-
ing voyage round
the Bosporus in
November 1915.*
Güleryüz

(Top)
Bafra *in the Aegean in 1909.*
Güleryüz

(Above)
Malatya *at sea in the Aegean in 1909.*
Güleryüz

Kastamonu: *four photographs showing the arrival of the gunboat at İstanbul from the German builders in July 1905, together with details of the decks, guns, fittings and crew members.*
Güleryüz

Ayintab *at İzmir in 1908.*
Güleryüz

İsa Reis *at anchor off Southampton in July 1914.*
IWM

İsa Reis *undergoing builder's trails in 1912.*
Güleryüz

Sakiz *(left) and* Preveze *(right) at anchor off Southampton in July 1914.*
IWM

*The four gunboats
of the* Preveze *class
laid up at St
Nazaire early in
1914.*
Güleryüz

Preveze *in the No 1
drydock at İstanbul
in June 1914.*
Güleryüz

Preveze *at anchor in the Haliç in 1915.*
Güleryüz

Aydin Reis *at anchor off the builder's yard at St Nazaire in 1913.*
Güleryüz

Ertuğrul: *the Sultan's yacht at Selanik during the Ottoman Navy's demonstration 25 May – 12 June 1911. The presence of the deposed Sultan Abdül Hamid II's yacht was intended to heighten his humiliation.*
Güleryüz

Ertuğrul: *two photographs taken on board shortly after the vessel's arrival from the builder's yard. The large building is the the Sultan's Dolmabahçe palace. The large building above the palace is the German Embassy.*
Güleryüz

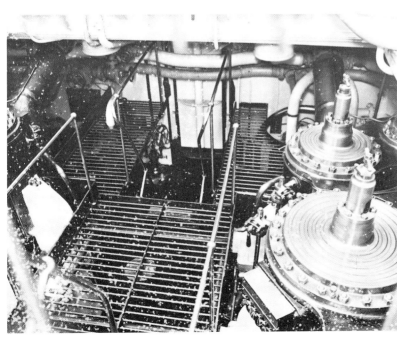

Ertuğrul: *five detail photographs of the engine room and public rooms taken shortly after the yacht arrived at İstanbul from the English builders.*
Güleryüz

Ertuğrul *under sail off İstanbul in 1908.*
Güleryüz

Ertuğrul *lying at the breaker's yard at İstanbul-Hasköy in 1959 or 1960, where the yacht had lain since 1939. The vessel on the stocks is the tanker* Asfalt II, *launched in 1960. The* Sus, *alongside the yacht, is one of the Black Sea express vessels of the state Marine Line. The yacht was slowly dismantled in the following years.*
Kizildemir

Ertuğrul *on arrival at İstanbul in 1904.*
Güleryüz

Sultaniye *at anchor in the Bosporus in 1903. From 1877 onwards the Sultan's yacht was used only as a fast naval transport.*
Güleryüz

Sultaniye*: the oldest known photograph of the yacht, taken after the Russo-Ottoman War of 1877–78.*
Güleryüz

İstanbul*: the Sultan's yacht at anchor off the Dolmabahçe palace in 1903.*
Güleryüz

İstanbul *dressed overall during a visit of the navy minister to Selanik in 1908.*
Güleryüz

Fuad *at anchor off Selanik in 1909, when the vessel was being used by the Vali of Selanik.*
Güleryüz

İsmail *lying at anchor in the Bosporus during the 1880s.*
Güleryüz

İhsaniye *in 1906 at İzmir. The vessel was built as a Bosporus ferry and later sold to the navy. The reproduction is from a badly damaged photograph.*
Güleryüz

İzzeddin*: the Sultan's yacht, also used as an aviso, photographed at anchor at İstanbul-Tophane in 1909.*
Güleryüz

Söğütlü *off the Dolmabahée palace bell tower in 1911. At the upper right a corner of the German Embassy can be seen.*
Güleryüz

Söğütlü *seen just before launching from the Armstrong, Mitchell yard at Newcastle in 1908. Builder's photograph*

Beyrut*: two deck photographs taken at İstanbul shortly after the vessel was commissioned in 1911.*
Güleryüz

Ahter *in the Bosporus in 1896. The steam launch, one of many in service in the Ottoman Navy, was used by the Khedive of Egypt. The residence of the Khevdives was situated on the hill in the centre background.*
Güleryüz

Asır: *a photograph taken during the aviso's launch at Gemlik in 1875. The wooden-hulled ship was the last vessel built at the yard before it closed. Note the army formation in the foreground.*
Güleryüz

İntibah: *the salvage tug dressed overall at İstanbul in 1914.*
Güleryüz

Nusret *undergoing builder's trials in the Kieler Förde in 1912.*
Krupp archives

An aerial view of the the naval base at Istinye, with Yavuz, Midilli *and a German steamer in dock and a number of torpedo-boats moored top right. The photograph was taken from the German airship SL 10 on 15 June 1916.*
BAM Freiburg

SHIPS' LISTING

GLOSSARY TO SHIP DATA TABLES (Dash indicates data not available)

Ship specifications
B = breadth
bm = builder's measurement
D = depth
iph = indicated horsepower
Loa = length over all
Lpp = length between perpendiculars
n = net
nhp = nominal horsepower
shp = shaft horsepower

Armament
Weapon types
BL = breech loading
ML = muzzle loading
MLR= muzzle loading rifled
QF = quick fire
RV = revolving cannon
TT = torpedo tube
Manufacturers
A = Armstrong

B = Bethlehem
C = Creusot
H = Hotchkiss
K = Krupp
N = Nordenfeldt
S = Schneider
SK = Schwartzkopf
V = Vickers
WH = Whitehead

IRONCLADS

Osmaniye Class

TYPE: Zirhli frikata (broadside iron-clad)

BUILDER: R Napier & Son, Glasgow (except *Mahmudiye* Thames Iron Works, Blackwall, London)

DISPLACEMENT: (1865) 4221t bm; 6400t normal; (1896) 6299t (*Mahmudiye* 6293t)

DIMENSIONS: Loa 91.4m, Lpp 89.3m, B 16.9m, D 7.9m

HULL: Iron

MACHINERY: Steam, 1 shaft; (1894) 2 shafts

ENGINES: (1865) 1 horizontal direct acting, _ihp, R Napier (*Mahmudiye* Ravenhill, Salkeld) (1894) 2 VTE, 3735ihp, Ansaldo

BOILERS: (1865) 6 box type, R Napier

(*Mahmudiye* Thames Iron Works) (1894) 6 cyl type, Tersane-i Amire

SPEED: (trials) 13.5kts, (1891) 6 kts, (1895) 10 kts (*Mahmudiye* 12.5kts)

BUNKERS: (1864) 750t coal

COMPLEMENT: (1865) 26 officers, 335 ratings, (1894) 250

ARMAMENT: (1865) 1–229mm MLR (A), 14–203mm MLR (A), 10–36pdr (A)
(1884) 1–229mm MLR (A), 14–203mm MLR (A), 4–47mm QF (H), 2–25.4mm (4-barrelled) (N)
(1890, planned) 2–240mm L/25 BL (K), 8–150mm L/25 BL (K), 6–105mm L/25 BL (K), 11–57mm QF (K), 2 TT 450mm (SK) (6)
(1894) 2–240mm L/35 BL (K), 8–150mm L/25 BL (K), 5–105mm L/25 BL (K), 2–47mm QF, 7–25.4mm (4-barrelled) (N)
(1897) Disarmed

Osmaniye (Yd No 255) Ordered: 1862. Laid down: 3.1863. Launched: 2.9.1864. Trials: 27.6.1865. Launched as *Gazi*

Osman. 11.1865 commissioned as *Osmaniye*. 1878 laid up at İstanbul. 1890–1894 refitted by Tersane-i Amire-Ansaldo, İstanbul. 1897 laid up at Çanakkale. 1908 towed to İstanbul. 31.7.1909 decommissioned. 1923 sold for breaking up.

Aziziye (Yd No 256) Ordered: 1862. Laid down: 5.1863. Launched: 12.1864. Trials: 1865. Launched as *Abdül Aziz*. 8.1865 commissioned as *Aziziye*. 1878 laid up at İstanbul. 1890–1894 refitted by Tersane-i Amire-Ansaldo, İstanbul. 1904 Barracks vessel at İstanbul-Kasimpaşa. 31.7.1909 decommissioned. 1923 sold for breaking up.

Orhaniye (Yd No 257) Ordered: 1862. Laid down: 1863. Launched: 26.6.1865. Trials: 1866. 1866 commissioned. 1878 laid up at İstanbul. 1892–1894 refitted by Tersane-i Amire-Ansaldo, İstanbul. 1897 laid up at Çanakkale. 1908 towed to İstanbul. 31.7.1909 decommissioned. Barracks vessel at İstanbul-Kasimpaşa. 1913 sold for breaking up.

Mahmudiye (Yd No 99e) Ordered: 1863. Laid down: 1864. Launched:

13.12.1864. Trials: 1865. 1866 commissioned. 1878 laid up at İstanbul. 1892–1894 refitted by Tersane-i Amire-Ansaldo, İstanbul. 1897 laid up at Çanakkale. 1904 towed to İstanbul. 31.7.1909 decommissioned. Barracks vessel at İstanbul-Kasimpaşa. 1913 sold for breaking up.

Fatih

TYPE: Zirhli frikata (broadside iron-clad)

BUILDER: Thames Iron Works, Blackwall, London

DISPLACEMENT: 6127t bm, 10,761t

DIMENSIONS: Loa 112.2m, B 18.3m, D 8.5m

HULL: Iron

MACHINERY: Steam, 1 shaft

ENGINES: 1 horizontal single expansion 2 cyl, 8344ihp, Maudslay

BOILERS: 8 box type, J Penn

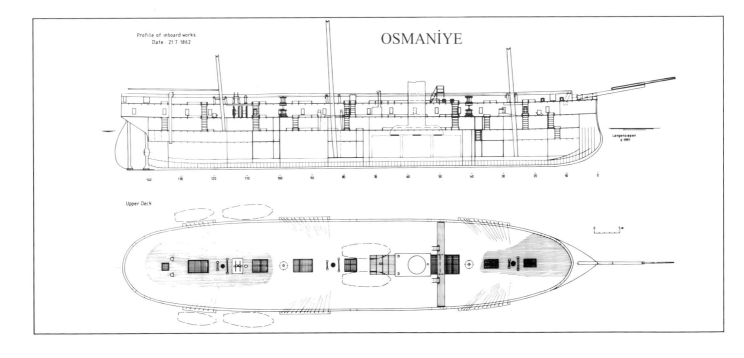

OSMANIYE

SPEED: 14kts

BUNKERS: 750t coal

COMPLEMENT: 1200

ARMAMENT: (design) 33–72 pdr (A),
1–240mm ML (A), 5–210mm ML (A)

Fatih (Yd No 30f) Ordered: 1864. Laid
down: 3.1864. Launched: 25.4.1868.
Trials: 1868. Intended name: *Fatih*
6.2.1867 purchased by Prussia
10.1.1867. *Wilhelm I* 14.12.1867. *König
Wilhelm* 20.2.1869 commissioned.
3.5.1904 harbour service. 4.1.1921 sold
for breaking up at Rönnebeck-Bremen.

Fettah

TYPE: Zirhli frikata (broadside ironclad)

BUILDER: Tersane-i Amire, İstanbul

DISPLACEMENT: 4221t bm, 6400t normal

DIMENSIONS: Loa 91.4m, Lpp 89.3m, B
16.9m, D 7.9m

HULL: Iron

MACHINERY: Steam, 1 shaft

ENGINES: 1 horizontal direct acting,
_ihp, Tersane-i Amire
BOILERS: 6 box type, Tersane-i Amire

SPEED: 12kts

BUNKERS: 750t coal

COMPLEMENT: 400

ARMAMENT: 1–229mm MLR (A),
14–203mm MLR (A), 10–36pdr (A)

Fettah Ordered: 1864. Similar to
Osmaniye class. Works not started.
Cancelled 23.4.1865. There is some evi-
dence that the name should have been

Fatih, but was wrongly transliterated
from Osmanli, the court language of the
Ottoman Empire.

Mesudiye

TYPE: (1873) Zirhli frikata (central battery ironclad)
(1903) Muharbebe gemi (armoured vessel)

BUILDER: Thames Iron Works,
Blackwall, London

DISPLACEMENT: (1873) 8938t, (1903)
9190t normal, 9710t full load

DIMENSIONS: Loa 102.4m, B 17.9m, D 7.9m

An official German ship portrait of the ironclad Mahmudiye, *taken in 1888
at İstanbul.* Güleryüz

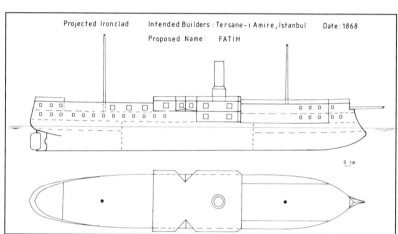

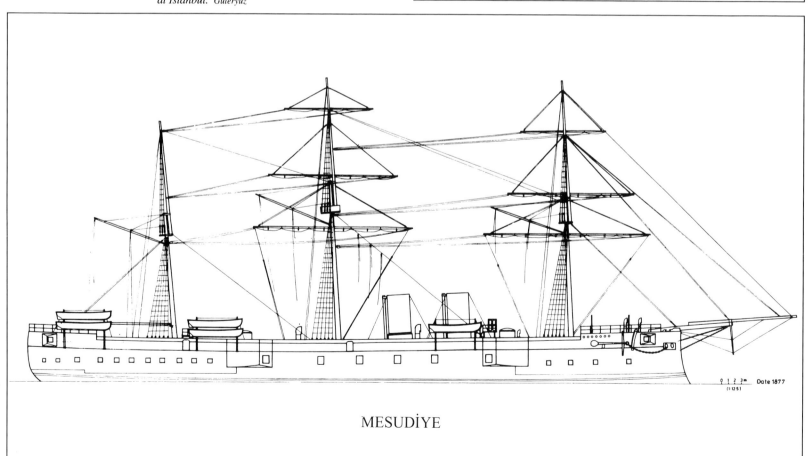

MESUDİYE

HULL: Iron

MACHINERY: Steam, 1 shaft, (1903) 2 shafts

ENGINES: (1873) 1 horizontal single expansion 2 cyl, 7431ihp, Thames IW (1903) 2 triple expansion 4 cyl, 11,135ihp, Ansaldo

BOILERS: (1873) 8 rectangular, Thames IW (1903) 16 Niclausse water-tube, Ansaldo

SPEED: (trials) 13.7kts, (1884) 10kts, (1903) 17kts

BUNKERS: 600t coal

COMPLEMENT: (1873) 1200, (1903) 800, (1914) 665

ARMAMENT: (1873) 12–254mm MLR (A), 3–178mm MLR (A)
(1891) 12–254mm MLR (A), 3–178mm (MLR (A), 6–76mm QF (K), 6–25.4mm (H)
(1903) 2–234mm L/40 BL (V), 12–152mm L/45 QF (V), 14–76mm QF (K), 2–47mm QF, 10–57mm QF
(1914) 12–152mm L/45 QF(V), 14–76mm QF(V), 2–47mm QF

Mesudiye (Yd No 80f) Ordered: 1871. Laid down: 1872. Launched: 28.10.1874. Trials: 1875. 12.1875 commissioned. 1.1891–5.1893 refitted by Tersane-i Amire, İstanbul. 1898–1903 refitted by Ansaldo, Genoa. 1910 harbour service at İzmir. 1911 active fleet. 5.9.1914 disbanded from the active fleet. 9.1914 floating battery off Çanakkale. 13.12.1914 sunk by torpedo by British submarine B 11 near Erenköy.

Mahmudiye

TYPE: (1873) Zirhli frikata (central battery ironclad)

BUILDER: Thames Iron Works, Blackwall, London

Displacement: 9120t

Dimensions: Loa 102.4m, B 17.9m, D 7.9m

HULL: Iron

MACHINERY: Steam, 1 shaft

ENGINES: 2 compound vertical, 6580ihp, Maudslay

BOILERS: 4

SPEED: 13kts

BUNKERS: 600t coal

COMPLEMENT: 1200

ARMAMENT: (design) 16–240mm ML (A)

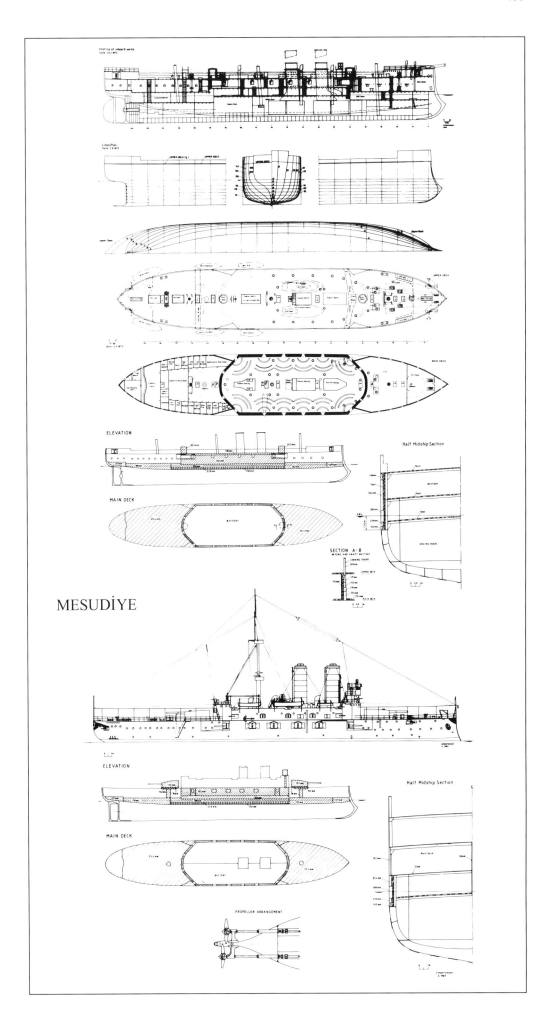

MESUDİYE

Mahmudiye (Yd No 99e) Ordered: 1871. Laid down: 1873. Launched: 16.11.1875. Trials: 15.11.1880. Intended sister for *Mesudiye*. Launched as *Mahmudiye* but 2.1876 renamed *Hamidiye*. 20.2.1878 purchased by the British Govt and entered service in the Royal Navy 1880 as *Superb*. 15.5.1906 sold for breaking up.

Hamidiye

TYPE: Zirhli frikata (central battery ironclad)

BUILDER: Tersane-i Amire, İstanbul

DISPLACEMENT: 6594t normal

DIMENSIONS: Loa 89.0m, Lpp 87.6m, B 16.9m, D 7.5m

HULL: Iron

MACHINERY: Steam, 1 shaft

ENGINES: 1 single expansion 2 cyl, 6800ihp, Maudslay

BOILERS: 4 box type, Tersane-i Amire

SPEED: (trials) 13kts

BUNKERS: 600t coal

COMPLEMENT: 350

ARMAMENT: (design) 10–240mm L/35 BL (K), 4–150mm L/35 BL (K), 2–57mm QF, 2 TT 450mm (SK) (1894) 4–238mm ML (A), 10–150mm L/35 BL (K)

Hamidiye Ordered: 1871. Laid down: 12.1874. Launched: 2.1885. Trials: 1893. Intended name *Nüsretiye*. 1893 trials without armament. 1894 commissioned, stationary training vessel for torpedo-boats. 1903 decommissioned. 11.11.1909 offered for breaking up. 1913 sold for breaking up.

Peyk-i Şeref Class

TYPE: Zirhli frikata (armoured ram)

BUILDER: Samuda & Son, London

DISPLACEMENT: 4870t

DIMENSIONS: Lpp 74.6m, B 15.8m,

D 6.4m

HULL: Iron

MACHINERY: Steam, 1 shaft

ENGINES: 1 horizontal direct acting, 4040ihp, Maudslay

BOILERS: 4

Speed: 12kts

BUNKERS: _

COMPLEMENT: 250

ARMAMENT: 4–305mm ML, 4–20pdr, 2 TT 355mm

Peyk-i Şeref Ordered: 1874. Laid down: 1874. Launched: 12.2.1876. Trials: 1878. 13.2.1878 purchased by the British Govt. 19.7.1878 became *Belleisle* in the Royal Navy. 1904 sold for breaking up.

Büruç-u Zafer Ordered: 1874. Laid down: 1875. Launched: 23.1.1878. Trials: 1881. 13.2.1878 purchased by

the British Govt. 13.7.1882 became *Orion* in the Royal Navy. 1909 renamed *Orontes*. 1913 sold for breaking up.

Asar-i Tevfik

TYPE: Zirhli korvet (barbette battery ironclad)

BUILDER: SA des Forges et Chantiers de la Mediterranée, La Seyne

DISPLACEMENT: 4687t normal

DIMENSIONS: Loa _m, Lpp 83.0m, B 16.0m, D 6.5m

HULL: Iron

MACHINERY: Steam, 1 shaft

ENGINES: 1 horizontal compound expansion, _ihp, La Seyne

BOILERS: 6 box type, La Seyne (1906) 6 Niclausse cyl, 'Germania', Kiel

SPEED: (trials) 13kts, (1895) 8kts,

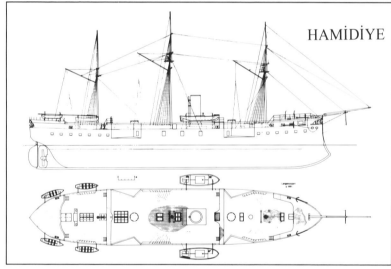

HAMİDİYE

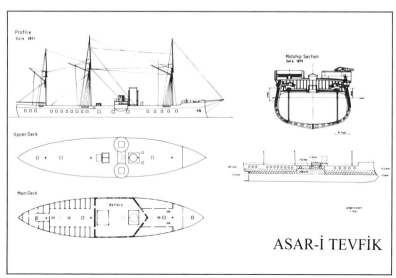

ASAR-İ TEVFİK

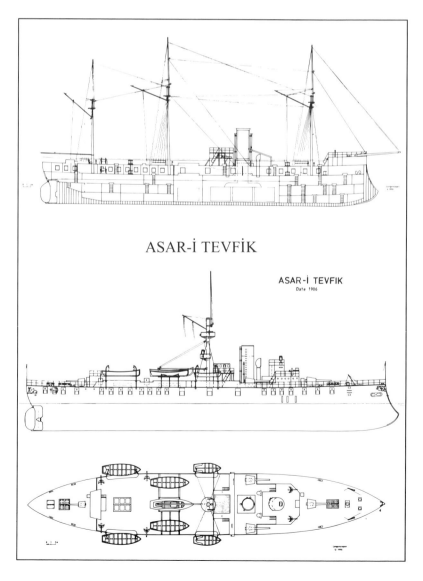

ASAR-İ TEVFİK

(1906) 15kts, (1910) 9kts

BUNKERS: 400t coal

COMPLEMENT: (1870) 450, (1907) 350

ARMAMENT: (1870) 8–220mm ML (A)
(1891) 6–220mm ML (A), 2–210mm
BK (K), 2–87mm BL (K), 2–63.5mm
BL (N)
(1906) 3–150mm L/40 QF (K),
7–120mm L/40 QF (K), 6–57mm QF
(K), 2–37mm QF (K)

Asar-i Tevfik Ordered: 1865. Laid
down: 1867. Launched: 1868. Trials:
1869. Ordered as *İbrahimiye* by the
Govt of Egypt. 29.8.1868 transferred to
Osmanli Bahriye. 1870 commissioned.
1878 laid up at İstanbul. 1890–1892
refitted and reboilered by Tersane-i
Amire, İstanbul. 1899 sent to Genoa,
laid up. 29.5.1900 arrived 'Germania',
Kiel, for refitting. 4.1.1907 returned to
İstanbul. 11.2.1913 went aground and
became total loss near Çernes
(41.25.00N, 28.29.05E)

Asar-i Şevket Class

TYPE: Zirhli korvet (central battery
ironclad)

BUILDER: SA des Forges et Chantiers
de la Mediterranée, La Seyne

DISPLACEMENT: 2047t normal, 2583t
bm

DIMENSIONS: Loa 61.9m, Lpp 66.4m, B
12.9m, D 5.0m

HULL: Iron

MACHINERY: Steam, 1 shaft

ENGINE: 1 horizontal compound expansion, 1750ihp, La Seyne

BOILERS: 4 box type, La Seyne
(1891) 4 _, Tersane-i Amire

SPEED: (trials) 12kts, (1878) 8kts

BUNKERS: 300t coal

COMPLEMENT: 170

ARMAMENT: (1870) 1–230mm ML (A),
4–180mm ML (A)
(1891) 1–230mm ML (A), 4–180mm
ML (A), 2–87mm BL (K), 2–63.5mm
BL (K), 2–37mm RV (H), 1–25.4mm (N)

Asar-i Şevket (Yd No 364) Ordered:
1866. Laid down: 1867. Ordered as
Kahira by the Govt of Egypt. 29.8.1868
transferred to Osmanli Bahriye.
3.3.1870 commissioned. 1878 laid up at
İstanbul. 1890–1892 refitted and reboilered by Tersane-i Amire, İstanbul.
12.2.1892 returned to service. 1903

An Ottoman drawing of the ironclad Necm-i Şevket. *Güleryüz*

decommissioned. 31.7.1909 offered for
breaking up.

Necm-i Şevket (Yd No 365) Ordered:
1866. Laid down: 1867. Launched:
1868. Trials: 1869. Ordered as *Muzaffer*
by the Govt of Egypt. 29.8.1868 transferred to Osmanli Bahriye. 3.3.1870
commissioned as *Necm-i Şevket*. 1878
laid up at İstanbul. 1890–1892 refitted
and reboilered by Tersane-i Amire,
İstanbul. 12.2.1892 returned to service.
1899–1909 stationary at Selanik. 1909
barracks vessel at İstanbul. 1929 decommissioned, broken up.

Lütf-ü Celil Class

TYPE: Zirhli korvet (coast defence turret ship)

BUILDER: SA des Chantiers et Ateliers
de la Gironde, Bordeaux

DISPLACEMENT: 2540t normal, 1741t
bm

DIMENSIONS: Loa 64.4m, Lpp 62.1m, B
13.6m, D 4.4m

HULL: Iron

MACHINERY: Steam, 2 shafts

ENGINE: 1 horizontal compound expansion 2 cyl, 2000ihp, SACAG

BOILERS: 2 locomotive type, SACAG

SPEED: (trials) 12kts, (1877) 10kts

BUNKERS: 300t coal

COMPLEMENT: (1870) 12 officers, 110
ratings

ARMAMENT: (1870) 2–225mm ML (A),
2–178mm ML (A)
(1875) 2–225mm ML (A), 2–178mm
ML (A), 1–120mm BL (K)
(1891 *Hifz-ur Rahman* only) 2–225mm

ML (A), 1–150mm BL (K), 1–120mm
BL (K), 4–37mm QF (H), 2–25.4mm
RV (N)

Lütf-ü Celil Ordered: 1867. Laid down:
1868. Launched: 1869. Trials: 1870.
Ordered by the Govt of Egypt.
29.8.1868 transferred to Osmanli
Bahriye. 3.1870 commissioned.
10.5.1877 sunk by Russian field guns
off İriali (Danube).

Hifz-ur Rahman Ordered: 1867. Laid
down: 1868. Launched: 1869. Trials:
1870. Ordered by the Govt of Egypt.
29.8.1868 transferred to Osmanli
Bahriye. 3.1870 commissioned. 1878
laid up at İstanbul. 1891–1894 refitted
by Tersane-i Amire, İstanbul. 1909
decommissioned. 31.7.1909 offered for
breaking up. 11.11.1909 sold for breaking up.

Avnillah Class

TYPE: Zirhli korvet (casemate ironclad)

BUILDER: Thames Iron Works,
Blackwall, London

DISPLACEMENT: 2362t normal, 1399t bm

DIMENSIONS: Loa 71.9m, Lpp 68.9m, B
10.9m, D 5.0m

HULL: Iron

MACHINERY: Steam, 1 shaft, (1906) 2
shafts

ENGINE: 1 horizontal compound expansion, 2200ihp, Maudslay

BOILERS: (1870) 4 box type, Thames
IW
(1906) 2 cyl water-tube type, Tersane-i
Amire

SPEED: (trials) 12kts, (1877) 10kts,
(1892) 8kts

BUNKERS: 220t coal

COMPLEMENT: (1870) 15 officers, 130
ratings, (1906) 200

ARMAMENT: (1870) 4–230mm ML (A)
(1882) 4–230mm ML (A), 2–87mm
BLR (K)
(1891, planned) 4–230mm ML (A),
2–87mm BLR (K), 2–63mm BL (K),
2–37mm RV (H), 2–25.4mm (H), 1 TT
450mm (SK)
(1906) 4–150mm L/40 QF (K),
6–75mm QF (K), 10–57mm QF (K),
2–47mm QF (K)
(*Avnillah* 1910) 4–57mm QF (K)
(*Muin-i Zafer* 1910) 2–75mm QF (K),
4–57mm QF (K)
(*Muin-i Zafer* 1913) Disarmed

Avnillah (Yd No 44f) Ordered: 1867.
Laid down: 1868. Launched: 21.4.1869.
Trials: 1870. 1870 commissioned. 1878
laid up at İstanbul. 1903–1906 refitted

A sail draught of the ironclad Avnillah, *from a contemporary engraving. Güleryüz*

by Ansaldo, İstanbul. 1910 stationary at Beirut. 24.2.1912 sunk by gunfire by Italian cruiser *Garibaldi* at Beirut.

Muin-i Zafer Ordered: 1867. Laid down: 1868. Launched: 6.1869. Trials: 1870. 1870 commissioned. 1878 laid up at İstanbul. 1903–1906 refitted by Ansaldo, İstanbul. 1910 Stationary at İzmir. 1913 torpedo training vessel at İstanbul. 1920 barrack vessel at İzmit. 1928 depot ship for submarines at Erdek. 1932 decommissioned. 1934 breaking up began at Erdek.

Feth-i Bülend

TYPE: Zirhli korvet (casemate ironclad)

BUILDER: Thames Iron Works, Blackwall, London

DISPLACEMENT: 2762t normal, 1601t bm

DIMENSIONS: Loa _m, Lpp 72.0m, B 11.9m, D 5.2m

HULL: Iron

MACHINERY: Steam, 1 shaft
ENGINE: 1 horizontal compound expan-

sion, 3250ihp, Humphrys, Tennant

BOILERS: (1870) 6 box type, Thames IW
(1906) 2 cyl water-tube type, Tersane-i Amire

SPEED: (trials) 13kts, (1877) 10kts, (1892) 8kts, (1906) 9kts, (1910) 7kts

BUNKERS: 300t coal

COMPLEMENT: (1870) 16 officers, 153 ratings, (1906) 220, (1911) 150

ARMAMENT: (1870) 4–222mm ML (A)
(1882) 4–222mm ML (A), 1–170mm ML (A), 2–87mm BL (K)
(1890) 4–222mm ML (A), 2–87mm BL (K), 2–63mm BL (K), 2–37mm RV (H), 1–25.4mm (H)
(1907) 4–150mm L/40 QF (K), 6–75mm QF (K), 6–57mm QF (K)
(1911) Disarmed

Feth-i Bülend (Yd No 46f) Ordered: 1867. Laid down: 5.1868. Launched: 1879. Trials: 1870. 1870 commissioned. 1878 laid up at İstanbul. 1890 refitted by Tersane-i Amire, İstanbul. 1898 all guns dismounted. 1903–1907 refitted by Ansaldo, İstanbul. 1910 stationary at

Selanik. 31.10.1913 sunk by torpedo by Greek torpedo-boat NF 11 at Selanik. 1913 wreck broken up.

Mukaddeme-i Hayir

TYPE: Zirhli korvet (casemate ironclad)

BUILDER: Tersane-i Amire, İstanbul

DISPLACEMENT: 2762t normal, 1601t bm

DIMENSIONS: Loa _m, Lpp 72.0m, B 11.9m, D 5.2m

HULL: Iron

MACHINERY: Steam, 1 shaft

ENGINE: 1 horizontal compound expan-sion, 3250ihp, Tersane-i Amire

BOILERS: 4 box type, Tersane-i Amire

SPEED: (trials) 12kts, (1892) 8kts

BUNKERS: 270t coal

COMPLEMENT: 16 officers, 153 ratings

ARMAMENT: (1874) 4–222mm ML (A)

(1882) 4–222 ML (A), 2–87mm BL (K), 2–63.5mm BL (K), 2–37mm RV(H), 2–25.4mm (N)

Mukkaddeme-i Hayir Ordered: 1868. Laid down: 1870. Launched: 28/10.1872. Trials: 1874. 1874 commissioned. Locally built version of *Feth-i Bülend* design. 1878 laid up at İstanbul. 1898 guns and boilers landed. 1911 stationary school ship at İstanbul. 1914 barrack vessel. 1920 barrack vessel at İzmit. 9.1923 decommissioned. 1923 breaking up began at İzmit.

İclaliye

TYPE: Zirhli korvet (barbette battery ironclad)

BUILDER: SA Stabilimento Tecnico Triestino, San Rocco

DISPLACEMENT: 2228t normal, 1650t bm

DIMENSIONS: Loa 66.0m, Lpp 63.6m, B 12.8m, D 4.8m

HULL: Iron

MACHINERY: Steam, 1 shaft

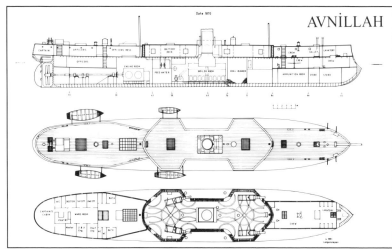

AVNİLLAH

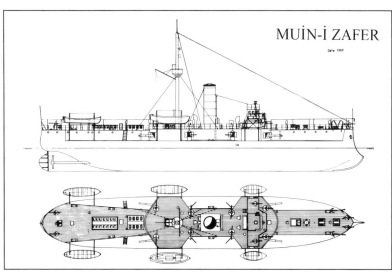

MUİN-İ ZAFER

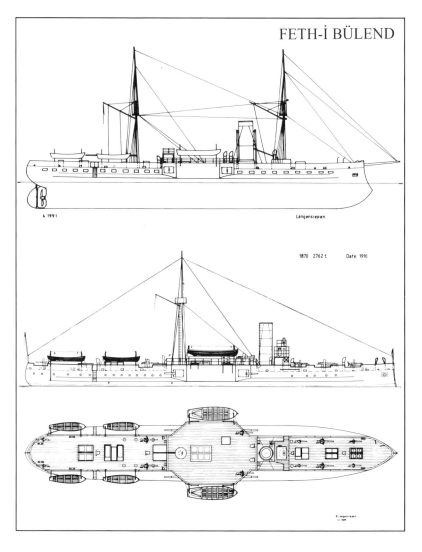

FETH-İ BÜLEND

ENGINE: 1 horizontal compound expansion, 1800ihp, Ravenhill, Salkeld

BOILERS: 2 box type, STT

SPEED: (trials) 12kts, (1877) 10kts, (1896) 6kts

BUNKERS: 250t coal

COMPLEMENT: (1871) 16 officers, 132 ratings, (1891) 180

ARMAMENT: (1871) 3–178mm ML (A), 2–228mm BL (A)
(1885) 2–278mm BL (K), 1–152mm L/22 BL (K), 2–87mm BL (K), 2–63.7mm BL (K), 2–37mm RV, 2–25.4mm (N)

(1905) 2–278mm BL (K), 2–87mm BL (K), 2–37mm RV, 2–25.4mm (N)
(1914) Disarmed

İclaliye (Yd No 51) Ordered: 5.1868. Laid down: 5.1868. Launched: 1879. Trials: 17.1.1871. Ordered by the Govt of Egypt. 29.8.1868 transferred to Osmanli Bahriye. 25.1.1871 sailed for İstanbul. 2.1871 commissioned. 1879 laid up at İstanbul. 1891 refitted by Tersane-i Amire, İstanbul. 1904 barbette removed. 1904 reserve fleet. 1913 floating battery. 2.1914 barrack vessel for navy school at Heybeliada. 2.1919 stationary cadet training ship at İstanbul - Kasimpaşa. 1923 barrack ship at Gölcük. 1928 decommissioned and sold for breaking up at Gölcük.

The ironclad Mukkaddeme-i Hayir, *seen in 1895 at the fitting-out pier of the İstanbul naval dockyard.* Güleryüz

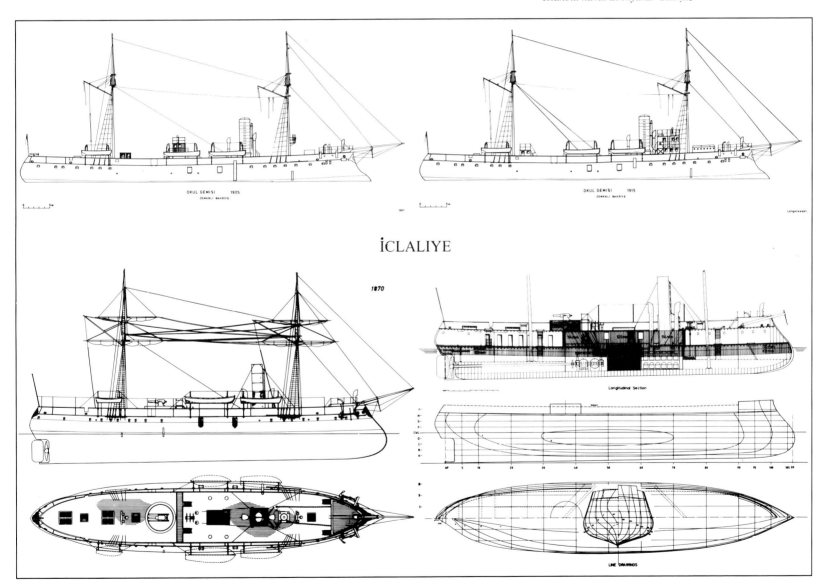

İCLALIYE

RIVER MONITORS

Feth-ül İslam Class

TYPE: Zirhli duba (river monitor)

BUILDER: SA des Forges et Chantiers de la Mediterranée, La Seyne

DISPLACEMENT: 335t

DIMENSIONS: Loa 31.5m, Lpp 30.5m, B 9.8m, D 1.7m

HULL: Iron

MACHINERY: Steam, 1 shaft, 2 screws

ENGINES: 2 high-pressure, 1 cyl, 290ihp, La Seyne

BOILERS: 2 _, La Seyne

SPEED: (trials) 8kts

BUNKERS: 20t coal

COMPLEMENT: (1865) 50

ARMAMENT: (1865) 2–150mm ML (A) (1871) 2–150mm ML (A), 6–76mm ML (A) (Semendire 1880) 2–76mm (K) (Feth-ül İslam 1884) 2–177mm (K), 2–76mm (K) (Feth-ül İslam 1901) Disarmed

Feth-ül İslam Ordered: 1863. Laid down: 1864. Launched: 1865. Trials: 1865. 1865 commissioned, based on River Danube. 1878 laid up at İstanbul. 1884 refitted by Tersane-i Amire, İstanbul. 1884 guard vessel at İstanbul. 1901 guard vessel at Istinye. 1908 decommissioned. 1909 sold for breaking up.

İşkodra Ordered: 1863. Laid down: 1864. Launched: 1865. Trials: 1865.

1865 commissioned, based on Lake İskodra. 1871 based on River Danube. 16.7.1877 captured by Russian forces at Nebula 6.10.1877 *Sistovo* Imperial Russian navy. 23.11.1889 stricken.

Böğürtlen Ordered: 1863. Laid down: 1864. Launched: 1865. 1865 commissioned, based on River Danube. 1878 laid up at İstanbul. 1880 decommissioned. 1886 sold for breaking up.

Podgoriçe Ordered: 1863. Laid down: 1864. Launched: 1865. Trials: 1865. 1865 commissioned, based on Lake İskodra. 1871 based on River Danube. 17.6.1877 captured by Russian forces at Nebula. 6.10.1877 *Nikopol* Imperial Russian Navy. 23.11.1889 stricken.

Semendire/Memduhiye Ordered: 1863. Laid down: 1864. Launched: 1865. Trials: 1865. 1865 commissioned, based on River Danube. 1878 laid up at İstanbul. 1879 renamed *Memduhiye*. 1880 guard vessel at Tarabya. 1902 decommissioned. 1909 sold for breaking up.

Hizber Class

TYPE: Zirhli duba (river monitor)

BUILDER: Tersane-i Amire, İstanbul

DISPLACEMENT: 404t, 513t bm

DIMENSIONS: Lpp 43.9m, B 9.4m, D 1.6m

HULL: Iron

MACHINERY: Steam, 1 shaft

ENGINES: 1–2 cyl, 400ihp, Tersane-i Amire

BOILERS: 1 _, Tersane-i Amire

SPEED: (trials) 8kts (1886) 6kts
BUNKERS: 18t coal

COMPLEMENT: (1876) 51, (*Hizber* 1886) 38

ARMAMENT: (1876) 2–120mm ML (K) (*Hizber* 1886) 2–120mm ML (K), 2–7mm QF (K), 2–34.5mm (N)

Hizber Ordered: 1870. Laid down: 1872. Launched: 9.1873. Trials: 1876 commissioned. 1879 laid up at İstanbul. 1886 refitted by Tersane-i Amire. 1909 decommissioned. 1991 sold for breaking up.

Seyfi Ordered: 1870. Laid down: 1872. Launched: 9.1873. Trials: 1876. 1876 commissioned. 26.5.1877 sunk by Russian torpedo cutter near Maçin.

CAPITAL SHIPS

Abdül Kadir

TYPE: Zirhli (battleship)

BUILDER: Tersane-i Amire, İstanbul

DISPLACEMENT: 8100t

DIMENSIONS: L 103.6m, B 19.8m, D 7.1m

HULL: Steel

MACHINERY: Steam, 2 shafts

ENGINES: (design) 2 VTE 3 cyl, 12,000ihp, Tersane-i Amire

BOILERS: (design) 6 _, Tersane-i Amire

SPEED: (design) 18kts

BUNKERS: 600t coal

COMPLEMENT: _
ARMAMENT: (design) 4–280mm (K), 6–150mm (K), 8–88mm QF (K),

8–37mm QF (K), 6 TT 533mm (SK)

Abdül Kadir Ordered: 1890. Laid down: 10.1892. 1895 frames set up. 1906 partly plated, work stopped officially. 1909 slipway cleared.

Torgud Reis Class

TYPE: Muharebe zirhli (battleship)

BUILDER: AG 'Vulcan', Stettin (*Barbaros Hayreddin*, Kaiserliche Werft, Wilhelmshaven)

DISPLACEMENT: 10,013t normal, 10,670t full load

DIMENSIONS: Loa 115.7m, Lpp 113.9m, B 19.5m, D 7.6m

HULL: Steel

MACHINERY: Steam, 2 shafts

ENGINES: 2 triple expansion 3 cyl, 10,110ihp, by builder

BOILERS: 12 _, by builder

SPEED: (1911) 10kts

BUNKERS: 1050t coal

COMPLEMENT: 600

ARMAMENT: (1910) 4–280mm L/40 (K), 2–280mm L/35 (K) (300), 6–105mm L/35 QF (K) (700), 8–88mm L/30 QF (K) (2450), 12 MG, 4 TT 450mm (SK) (1912) 4–280mm L/40 (K), 2–280mm L/35 (K) (300), 6–105mm L/35 QF (K), 6–88mm L/30 QF (K), 12 MG, 3 TT 450mm (SK) (9) (*Torgud Reis* 1916) 4–280mm L/40 (K), 2–280mm L/35 (K) (300), 6–88mm L/30 QF (K), 12 MG, 3 TT 450mm (SK) (*Torgud Reis* 1927) 2–280mm L/40 (K), 3–105mm L/35 QF (K), 2–88mm L/30

Feth-ül İslam, *reproduced from an Ottoman drawing of 1875.* Güleryüz

Hizber, *reproduced from an Ottoman drawing of 1875.* Güleryüz

QF (K), 2 TT 450mm (SK)

Torgud Reis (Yd No 199) Ordered: 1889. Laid down: 1890. Launched: 14.12.1891. Trials: 1893. 5.6.1894 *Weissenburg* Kaiserliche Marine. 5.8.1910 sold to the Osmanli Govt. 31.8.1910 18.30h commissioned, renamed *Torgud Reis* at Çanakkale. 30.10.1918 laid up at İstanbul. 1924–25 refitted by T C Deniz Kuvvetlari Gölcük Tersane, Gölcük. 1924–1933 stationary school ship at Gölcük. 1933 decommissioned, barrack vessel for dockyard workers. 1950 breaking up work began at Gölcük. 1953 left Dardanelles in two sections for breaking up outside Turkey.

Barbaros Hayreddin (Yd No 13) Ordered: 1889. Laid down: 1890. Launched: 30.6.1891. Trials: 1893. 24.4.1894 *Kurfürst Friedrich Wilhelm* Kaiserliche Marine. 5.8.1910 sold to the Osmanli Govt. 31.8.1910 18.30h commissioned, renamed *Barbaros Hayreddin* at Çanakkale. 8.8.1915 sunk by British submarine E 11 in the Sea of Marmara at 40.27N 26.48E. 253 lives lost.

Reşadiye Class

TYPE: Muharebe kruvazör (battlecruiser)

BUILDER: Vickers Ltd, Barrow-in-Furness

DISPLACEMENT: 23,000t normal, 25,250t full load

DIMENSIONS: Loa 170.5m, Lpp 160.8m, B 27.9m, D 8.5m

HULL: Steel

MACHINERY: Steam turbines, 4 shafts

ENGINES: 4 turbines, 26,500shp, Parsons

BOILERS: 15, Babcock & Wilcox

SPEED: (design) 21kts

BUNKERS: _

COMPLEMENT: _

ARMAMENT: (design) 10–340mm L/45 (A), 16–152mm L/50 QF (A), 4 TT 533mm

Reşadiye (Yd No 425) Ordered: 8.6.1911. Laid down: 1.8.1911. Launched: 3.8.1913. Trials: 1914. 1912 works stopped by the Balkan Wars. 5.1913 works started again. 1.8.1914 seized by the British Govt. 8.1914 became *Erin* in Royal Navy. 19.12.1922 sold for breaking up to Cox-Danks, Queenborough.

Fatih Sultan Mehmed (Yd No 460) Ordered: 29.4.1914. Laid down: 11.6.1914. 7.1914 works stopped by order of the British Govt. 8.1914 dismantled on the slipway.

Sultan Osman-i Evvel

TYPE: Muharebe zirhli (battleship)

BUILDER: Armstrong, Whitworth,

Yavuz anchored in the Sea of Marmara in October 1914. Güleryüz

Newcastle

DISPLACEMENT: 27,500t full load

DIMENSIONS: Loa 204.7m, B 27.1m, D 8.2m

HULL: Steel

MACHINERY: Steam turbines, 4 shafts

ENGINES: 4 turbines, 34,000shp, Parsons

BOILERS: 22, Babcock & Wilcox

SPEED: (design) 22kts

BUNKERS: 3200t coal, 620t oil

COMPLEMENT: _

ARMAMENT: 14–305mm L/45 (A), 20–152mm QF (A), 6–75mm QF (A), 2–75mm QF (A), 3 TT

Sultan Osman-i Evvel Ordered: 1911. Laid down: 14.9.1911. Launched: 22.1.1913. Trials: 8.1914. 1911 ordered by the Brazilian Govt as *Rio de Janeiro*. 9.1.1914 sold to Osmanli Govt. 2.8.1914 seized by the British Govt. 8.1914 became *Agincourt* in Royal Navy. 1920 decommissioned. 19.12.1922 sold for breaking up by Rosyth Ship Breaking Co.

Yavuz Sultan Selim

TYPE: Muharebe kruvazör (battlecruiser)

BUILDER: Blohm & Voss AG, Hamburg

DISPLACEMENT: 22,979t normal, 25,400t full load

DIMENSIONS: Lpp 186.5m, B 29.5m, D 8.7m

HULL: Steel

MACHINERY: Steam turbines, 4 shafts

ENGINES: 4 turbines, 85,000shp, Parsons-Blohm & Voss

BOILER: 24 Marine, Blohm & Voss

SPEED: (1914) 28kts

BUNKERS: 3100t coal

Torgud Reis during the demonstration of the Ottoman navy at Selanik 25 May to 12 June 1911 in support of the 'Young Turks'.
Güleryüz

COMPLEMENT: (1914) 1050, (1915) 1322 Germans, 24 Turks, (1930) 1280

ARMAMENT: (1914) 10–280mm L/50 (K) (810), 12–150mm L/45 (K) (1800), 10–280mm L/45 (K) (3000), 4 TT 500mm (SK) (11)
(1916) 10–280mm L/50 (K), 10–150mm L/45 (K), 16–88mm L/45 (K), 4 TT 500mm (SK) (11)
(1930) 10–280mm L/50 (K), 10–150mm L/45 (K), 6–88mm L/45 (K), 2 TT 500mm (SK)
(1941) 10–280mm L/50 (K), 12–150mm L/45 (K), 8–88mm L/45 (K), 10–40mm, 2 TT 500mm (SK),

Yavuz Sultan Selim (Yd No 200) Ordered: 1909. Laid down: 12.8.1909. Launched: 28.3.1911. Trials: 6.1912. 2.7.1912 *Goeben*. 16.8.1914 commissioned, renamed *Yavuz Sultan Selim* at İstanbul. 9.11.1918 laid up at İzmit. 1926–1930 refitted by T C Deniz Kuvetlari Gölcük Tersane, Gölcük. 1930 renamed *Yavuz Selim*. 1936 renamed *Yavuz*. 1948 laid up at Gölcük. 20.12.1950 decommissioned. 14.11.1954 deleted. 1971 sold for breaking up to M K E, Seyman. 7.6.1973 towed from Gölcük to Seyman. 7.1973–2.1976 breaking up.

SHIPS OF THE LINE

Peyk-i Zafer

TYPE: Kalyon (screw ship of the line)

BUILDER: Tersane-i Amire, Sinop

DISPLACEMENT: 3125t bm

DIMENSIONS: Lpp 66.6m, B 17.0m, D 8.8m

HULL: Wood

MACHINERY: Steam, 1 shaft

ENGINES: Horizontal direct acting 2 cyl, 2500ihp, R Napier

BOILERS: 2 tubular

SPEED: (trials) 9.5kts

BUNKERS: 315t coal

COMPLEMENT: 750

ARMAMENT: (1842) 86 guns
(1860) 32–62pdr, 30–45pdr, 16–33pdr

Peyk-i Zafer Ordered: 1840. Laid down: 1841. Launched: 1841. Trials: 1842. 1842 commissioned. 10.1856 arrived Keyham Yard, Portsmouth, to fit machinery. 1878 decommissioned. Laid up at İstanbul-Kasimpaşa as store for petroleum cans. 1894 sold for breaking up.

Kosova

TYPE: Kalyon (screw ship of the line)

BUILDER: Tersane-i Amire, İstanbul

DISPLACEMENT: 3464t bm

DIMENSIONS: Loa 93.8m, Lpp 90.3m, B 17.8m, D 7.3m

HULL: Wood

MACHINERY: Steam, 1 shaft

ENGINE: 1 set horizontal single acting, 3600ihp, Maudslay

BOILERS: 4

COMPLEMENT: 800

ARMAMENT: (1865) 32–62pdr, 34–45pdr
(1875) 1–203mm ML (A), 34–45pdr
(1878) Unarmed

Kosova Ordered: 1851. Laid down: 1855. Launched: 1858. Trials: 1864. 1864 commissioned, sailed for Portsmouth to fit engine and boilers at Southampton. 18.2.1865 sailed for Portsmouth to İstanbul. 1878 machinery removed by Tersane-i Amire, İstanbul. Stationary at İstanbul-Kasimpaşa. 1883 decommissioned. Lines taken from British *Renown/Revenge*

Fethiye Class

TYPE: Kalyon (screw ship of the line)

BUILDER: Tersane-i Amire, İstanbul (*Şadiye*, Tersane-i Amire, İzmit)

DISPLACEMENT: 3526t bm, 3380 tons

DIMENSIONS: Lpp 69.4m, B 17.2m, D 8.2m

HULL: Wood

MACHINERY: Steam, 1 shaft

ENGINE: 1 single acting 2 cyl, R Napier

BOILERS: 2

SPEED: (trials) 9kts

BUNKERS: 350t coal

COMPLEMENT: 800

ARMAMENT: (1858) 32–62pdr, 30–45pdr, 4–33pdr
(1875) 1–150pdr (A), 34–45pdr
(*Fethiye* 1889) Unarmed

Fethiye Ordered: 1853. Laid down: 1853. Launched: 30.11.1856. Trials: 1858. 1858 commissioned, sailed for Plymouth to fit machinery. 1859 sailed for İstanbul. 1877 stationary at İstanbul-Kasimpaşa. 1889 stationary cadet training ship. 1903 decommissioned. 1911 sold for breaking up.

Şadiye Ordered: 1853. Laid down: 1853. Launched: 1856. Trials: 1858. 1858 commissioned, sailed for Plymouth to fit machinery. 1859 sailed for İstanbul. 1878 decommissioned. 1879 store for petroleum cans. 1904 sold for breaking up.

FRIGATES

Mecidiye Class

TYPE: Frikata (paddle frigate)

BUILDER: Tersane-i Amire, İstanbul

DISPLACEMENT: 1443t bm (except *Mecidiye* 1448t bm)

DIMENSIONS: Loa 69.1m, B 11.7m, D 5.1m

HULL: Wood

MACHINERY: Steam, side paddle

ENGINE: 1 direct acting 2 cyl, 900ihp, Maudslay, Sons & Field

BOILERS: 2

SPEED: (trials) 9kts

BUNKERS: 150t coal

COMPLEMENT: 320

ARMAMENT: (1847) 2 long 10in iron Paixhan guns on traversing carriages on upper deck, 4–32pdr upper deck, 24–32pdr main deck.
(*Mecidiye* 1857) 4–32pdr main deck.
(rest 1857) 12–32pdr main deck
(*Feyza-i Bahri* 1867) Disarmed

Mecidiye Ordered: 1845. Laid down: 1846. Launched: 1846. Trials: 1847. 1847 commissioned. 1878 coal depot at Ereğli. 1888 towed to İstanbul, refitted by Tersane-i Amire. 1890 coal depot at Ereğli. 1896 decommissioned. 1903 breaking up at Ereğli.

Taif Ordered: 1845. Laid down: 1846. Launched: 1846. Trials: 1847. 1847 commissioned. 1857 refitted by Tersane-i Amire, İstanbul. 1867 decommissioned. 1868 broken up by Tersane-i Amire, İstanbul.

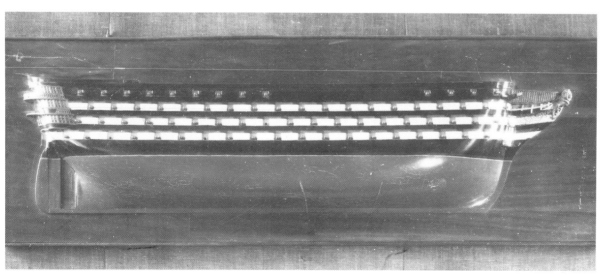

A half-hull model of the screw ship of the line Kosova *at İstanbul Navy Museum.* İstanbul Navy Museum

A contemporary British engraving of the corvette Feyza-i Bahri *at Southampton.* Langensiepen

Saik-i Şadi Ordered: 1845. Laid down: 1846. Launched: 1847. Trials: 1847. 1847 commissioned. 1867 decommissioned. 1869 broken up by Tersane-i Amire, İstanbul.

Feyza-i Bahri Ordered: 1845. Laid down: 1846. Launched: 1848. Trials: 1848. 1848 commissioned. 1867 transport. 1878 decommissioned. 1880 broken up at İstanbul.

Mubir-i Sürur

TYPE: Frikata (screw frigate)

BUILDER: Tersane-i Amire, İskenderiye

DISPLACEMENT: 1477t bm

DIMENSIONS: Loa 69.5m, Lpp 67.1m, B 12.0m, T 5.0m

HULL: Wood

MACHINERY: Steam, 1 lifting screw

ENGINE: 1 horizontal 2 cyl, 900ihp, Miller & Ravenhill

BOILERS: 2

SPEED: (trials) 10kts

BUNKERS: 200t coal

COMPLEMENT: 350

ARMAMENT: (1850) 22–60pdr (1892) 2–65mm QF (K)

Mubir-i Sürur Ordered: 1846. Laid down: 1846. Launched: 1847. Trials: 1848. 1848 commissioned as *Sarkiye* for Egyptian Navy. 1849 fitted with machinery and lifting-screw at London. 1849 presented by Abbas Paşa to Sultan Abdül Mecid. 1850 commissioned and renamed: *Mubir-i Sürur.* 1873 Sea Cadet training ship. 1885 stationary torpedo-depot vessel. 1892 refitted by Tersane-i Amire, İstanbul. 1894 laid up. 1899 decommissioned. 1904 sold for breaking up.

Kervan-i Bahri

TYPE: Frikata (steam frigate)

BUILDER: Tersane-i Amire, İstanbul

DISPLACEMENT: 1592t bm

DIMENSIONS: Lpp 63.1m, B 15.1m, D 6.9m

HULL: Wood

MACHINERY: Steam, 1 shaft

ENGINE: 1 set direct acting 2 cyl, _ihp, R Napier

BOILERS: 2 box type

SPEED: (trials) 9kts

BUNKERS: 250t coal

COMPLEMENT: 275

ARMAMENT: (1857) 42 guns (1868) 2 guns

Kervan-i Bahri Ordered: 1852. Laid down: 1852. Launched: 1853. Trials: 1857. 1856 commissioned. 1856 sailed for Liverpool for fitting engine and boilers. 22.5.1856 left Portsmouth. 1868 engine and boilers removed. Sailing

transport. 1875 decommissioned. 1878 broken up by Tersane-i Amire, İstanbul.

Ertuğrul

TYPE: Frikata (steam frigate)

BUILDER: Tersane-i Amire, İstanbul

DISPLACEMENT: 2344t bm

DIMENSIONS: Lpp 76.2m, B 15.1m, D 7.1m

HULL: Wood

MACHINERY: Steam, 1 shaft

ENGINE: 1 set direct acting 2 cyl, 2200ihp, Ravenhill, Salkeld

BOILERS: 2

SPEED: (trials) 10kts

BUNKERS: 350t coal

COMPLEMENT: 400

ARMAMENT: (1864) 30–60pdr, 10–30pdr
(1876) 1–203mm BL (A), 30–60pdr, 10–30pdr
(1888) 8–150mm BL (K), 5–150mm BL (A), 4–60mm (K), 2–24.5mm RV(H), 2–24.5mm (N), 1 TT 455mm (WH) (2)

Ertuğrul Ordered: 1854. Laid down: 1855. Launched: 1863. Trials: 1865. 1864 commissioned, sailed for London for fitting engine and boilers. 18.2.1865 left Portsmouth for İstanbul. 1885 refitted by Tersane-i Amire, İstanbul. 1888 sea cadet training ship. 13.9.1890 sunk in heavy weather off Yokohama. 584 lives lost.

The only known illustration of the steam frigate Mecidiye, *a painting by Hüsnü Cengiz in the İstanbul Navy Museum.* İstanbul Navy Museum

Hüdavendigar Class

TYPE: Frikata (screw frigate)

BUILDER: Tersane-i Amire, İzmit (*Nasr-ül Aziz* Tersane-i Amire, Gemlik)

DISPLACEMENT: 2897t bm

DIMENSIONS: Lpp 75.2m, B 15.2m, D 7.1m

HULL: Wood

MACHINERY: Steam, 1 shaft

ENGINE: 1 set direct acting 2 cyl, 2770ihp

BOILERS: 2 box type

SPEED: (trials) 10kts

BUNKERS: 325t coal

COMPLEMENT: 580

ARMAMENT: (1865) 16–60pdr upper deck, 20–32pdr main deck (*Hüdavendigar* 1882) Disarmed

Hüdavendigar Ordered: 1856. Laid down:1858. Launched: 10.1860. Trials: 1864. 1862 towed to Tersane-i Amire, İstanbul. 1864 commissioned. 1864 sailed for Southampton to fit engine and boilers. 18.2.1865 left Southampton. 1882 exercise vessel for *Fethiye*. 1890 decommissioned. 11.1909 sold for breaking up.

Nasr-ül Aziz Ordered: 1856. Laid down: 1858. Launched: 1861. Trials: 1865. 1861 towed to Tersane-i Amire, İstanbul, to fit engine and boilers. 1865 commissioned. 22.12.1876 lost in heavy weather on the way from Bar to İskenderiye at Pakus-Ada.

Selimiye

TYPE: Frikata (steam frigate)

BUILDER: Tersane-i Amire, İstanbul

DISPLACEMENT: 6442t

DIMENSIONS: Lpp 85.3m, B 17.9m, D 7.1m

HULL: Wood

MACHINERY: 1 set horizontal 2 cyl, 2600ihp, Tersane-i Amire, İstanbul

BOILERS: 2

SPEED: (trials) 10kts

BUNKERS: 350t coal

COMPLEMENT: 580

ARMAMENT: (1870) 20–30pdr upper deck, 34–30pdr main deck (1876) 1–203mm ML (A), 54–30pdr (1879) 2–203mm ML (A), 6–150mm ML (A), 3–57mm QF (H), 2–25mm (N) (1890) 2–203mm ML (A), 2–120mm ML (A), 2–150mm (K), 2–57mm QF (H), 3–24mm (N)

Selimiye Ordered: 1865. Laid down: 1866. Launched: 1869. Trials: 1870. Original machinery never fitted, but later used in the cruiser *Hamidiye*. 1870 commissioned. 1876 refitted by Tersane-i Amire, İstanbul. 1879 stationary gunnery-training ship. 1909 decommissioned. 1911 sold for breaking up.

Peyk-i Meserret Class

TYPE: Frikata (screw frigate)
BUILDER: Tersane-i Amire, Sinop (except *Mukaddeme-i Şeref* and *Rehber-i Tevfik*, Tersane-i Amire, Gemlik and Suda respectively)

DISPLACEMENT: 2132t bm

DIMENSIONS: Lpp 68.5m, B 11.2m, D 5.2m

HULL: Wood

MACHINERY: Steam, 1 shaft

ENGINE: 1–2 cyl compound, vertical, 1800ihp, Tersane-i Amire, İstanbul

BOILERS: 2 box type, Tersane-i Amire, İstanbul

SPEED: (trials) 8kts

BUNKERS: _

COMPLEMENT: 250

ARMAMENT: (design) 22 light guns (1876) 2–100mm
Disarmed: *Peyk-i Meserret* 1877, *Peyk-i Nusret* 1886, *Mukaddeme-i Şeref* 1879 (*Rehber-i Tefvik* 1892) 4–47mm QF (H)

Peyk-i Meserret Ordered: 1868. Laid

(Above)
The frigate Mehmet Selim *in 1889 at İstanbul. The other ship (background left) is one of the* Orhaniye-*class ironclads. Güleryüz*

(Opposite)
A photograph from 1869 of the launch of the screw frigate Selimiye.

(Far right)
Mukaddeme-i Şeref *pictured in about 1880 at İstanbul. Güleryüz*

down: 1872. Launched: 1874. Trials: 1876. 1874 towed to İstanbul to fit in engine and boilers. 1876 commissioned. 1877 collier. 16.9.1889 sunk near Kefken Ada (Black Sea) in heavy sea. 16 officers and 89 ratings lost.

Peyk-i Nusret Ordered: 1868. Laid down: 1872. Launched: 1875. Trials: 1877. Built under the name *Mukaddeme-i Nusret*. 1875 towed to İstanbul to fit engine and boilers. 1877 commissioned and renamed *Peyk-i Nusret*. 1877 collier. 1885 laid up at İstanbul used as stationary coal depot. 1904 decommissioned.

Mukaddeme-i Şeref Ordered: 1868. Laid down: 1873. Launched: 1875. Trials: 1876. 1875 towed to İstanbul to fit engine and boilers. 1876 commissioned. 1879 collier. 1890 laid up at İzmir used as stationary coal depot. 1904 decommissioned.

Rehber-i Tevfik Ordered: 1868. Laid down: 1873. Launched: 1879. Trials: 1880. 1879 towed to İstanbul to fit engine and boilers. 1880 commissioned. 1882 stationary torpedo training ship at İstanbul. 1895 engine and boilers removed, fitted in *Medar-i Tevfik*. 1896 floating storehouse for Tersane-i Amire, İstanbul. 1904 decommissioned.

Mehmet Selım

TYPE: Frikata (steam frigate)

BUILDER: Tersane-i Amire, İzmit

DISPLACEMENT: 120t

DIMENSIONS: Lpp 59.9m, B 10.0m, D 6.4m

HULL: Wood

MACHINERY: Steam, 1 shaft

ENGINE: 1–2 cyl compound vertical, 1800ihp, Tersane-i Amire, İstanbul

BOILERS: 2

SPEED: (trials) 12kts

BUNKERS: 250t coal

COMPLEMENT: 275

ARMAMENT: (1880) 10–150mm (K), 4–37mm QF, 4–25.4mm/4-barrelled (N) (1895) 10–150mm (K), 4–57mm QF (K), 4–37mm (1900) 1–47mm QF

Mehmet Selım Ordered: 1874. Laid down: 1877. Launched: 14.8.1879. Trials: 1880. 1879 towed to Tersane-i Amire, İstanbul, to fit engine and boilers. 1880 commissioned, stationary

training ship. 1889 laid up in poor condition. 1895 stationary training ship. 1900 stationary torpedo school ship. 1907 decommissioned. Barracks vessel at İstanbul. 1923 sold for breaking up.

CORVETTES

Eser-i Cedid

TYPE: Korvet (paddle corvette)

BUILDER: Tersane-i Amire, İstanbul

DISPLACEMENT: 1108t bm, 814t n

DIMENSIONS: Lpp 61.3m, B 11.4m, D 4.4m

HULL: Wood

MACHINERY: Steam, sidepaddle

ENGINE: 1 set single acting 1 cyl, 300nhp, R Napier

BOILER: 1

SPEED: (trials) 8kts

BUNKERS: 150t coal

COMPLEMENT: 120

ARMAMENT: (designed) 2–24pdr (1843) 2–42pdr (1855) 12 guns (1860) 6–13pdr (1884) Disarmed

Eser-i Cedid Ordered: 1840. Laid down: 1841. Launched: 19.5.1841. Trials: 1842. 1842 commissioned. 1860 transport. 1884 collier. 1889 decommissioned. 1894 sold for breaking up.

Sinop Class

TYPE: Korvet (screw corvette)

BUILDER: , J & R White, Southampton (*Bursa* and *Edirne* Money Wigram, Blackwall, London)

DISPLACEMENT: 780t bm

DIMENSIONS: Lpp 53.2m, B 9.3m, D 4.5m

HULL: Wood, copper-sheathed

MACHINERY: Steam, 1 shaft

ENGINE: 1 set 2 cyl, 640ihp, Humphreys, Tennant & Dykes (*Bursa* 650ihp, Maudslay, Sons & Field)

BOILERS: 2 box type

SPEED: (trials) 10kts

BUNKERS: 120t coal

COMPLEMENT: 150

ARMAMENT: (1859) 16–33pdr (all except *İzmir* 1885) 2–150mm BL L/25 (K), 2–120mm BL L/25 (K), 3–37mm QF, 2–25mm (N) (*Sinop* only 1889) 3–50mm L/22 (K), 3–37mm QF (K)

Sinop Ordered: 1857. Laid down: 1858. Launched: 1858. Trials: 1859. 26.11.1859 left Southampton for İstanbul. 1860 commissioned. 1889 renewed by Tersane-i Amire, İstanbul. 1901 decommissioned.

İzmir Ordered: 1857. Laid down: 1858. Launched: 1859. Trials: 1859. 1859 commissioned. 1878 laid up at İstanbul. 1879 decommissioned.

Bursa Ordered: 1857. Laid down: 1858. Launched: 1859. Trials: 1859. 24.9.1859 left London for İstanbul. 1859 commissioned. 1885–1886 renewed by Tersane-i Amire, İstanbul. 1899 decommissioned.

Edirne Ordered: 1857. Laid down: 1858. Launched: 1859. Trials: 1859. 1859 commissioned. 1887–1889 renewed by Tersane-i Amire, İstanbul. 1901 decommissioned.

(Above)
A British photograph of the corvette İskenderiye at Çanakkale in about 1895.
Güleryüz

(Left)
The corvette Muzaffer, pictured in about 1896.
Güleryüz

Beyrut Class

TYPE: Korvet (screw corvette)

BUILDER: Tersane-i Amire, İstanbul (*Seddülbahir* J & R White, Southampton; *Beyrut* Money Wigram, Thames; *Utarit* and *Meriç,* Tersane-i Amire, Gemlik)

DISPLACEMENT: 609t bm, 599 tons

DIMENSIONS: Lpp 52.8m, B 8.0m, D 3.9m

HULL: Wood, copper sheathed

MACHINERY: Steam, 1 shaft

ENGINE: 1 2 cyl, 450ihp, Humphrys, Tennant & Dyke (British-built ships, Maudslay, Sons & Field)

BOILERS: 2 box type, Tersane-i Amire, İstanbul (Turkish-built vessels)

SPEED: (trials) 10kts

BUNKERS: 120t coal

COMPLEMENT: 120

ARMAMENT: (British-built ships 1860) 12–33pdr
(Turkish-built vessels 1863) 1–45pdr, 2–11pdr (4 RV added 1869)
(Turkish-built vessels 1879) 2–120mm BL L/25 (K), 2–76mm, 2–25mm (N)
(British-built ships 1880) 2–120mm BL L/25 (K), 4–37mm QF
(*Beyrut, İskenderiye* and *Meriç* 1903) 2–120mm BL L/25 (K), 2–37mm QF, (2–25mm (N) *Beyrut* only)

Beyrut Ordered: 1857. Laid down: 1858. Launched: 1859. Trials: 1859.

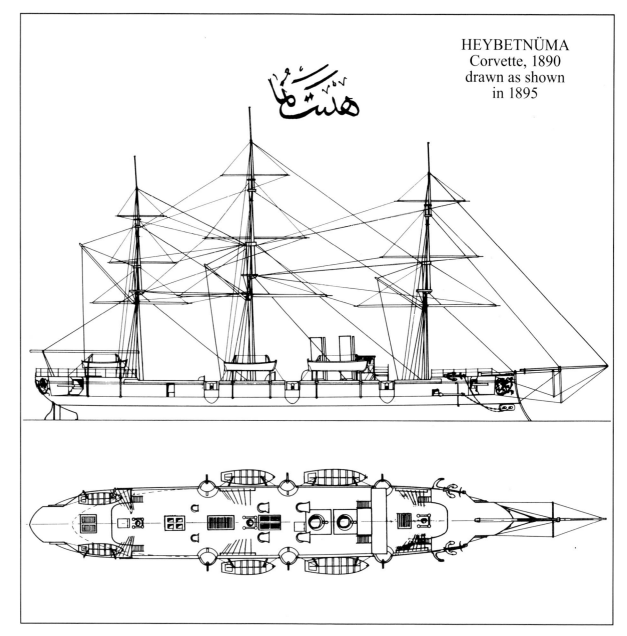

HEYBETNÜMA
Corvette, 1890
drawn as shown
in 1895

The steam corvette Sinop *in about 1890 at İstanbul. The large white building to the right is the Navy Ministry (Deryahane), and the naval dockyard (Tersane-i Amire) stretches along the waterfront.*
Güleryüz

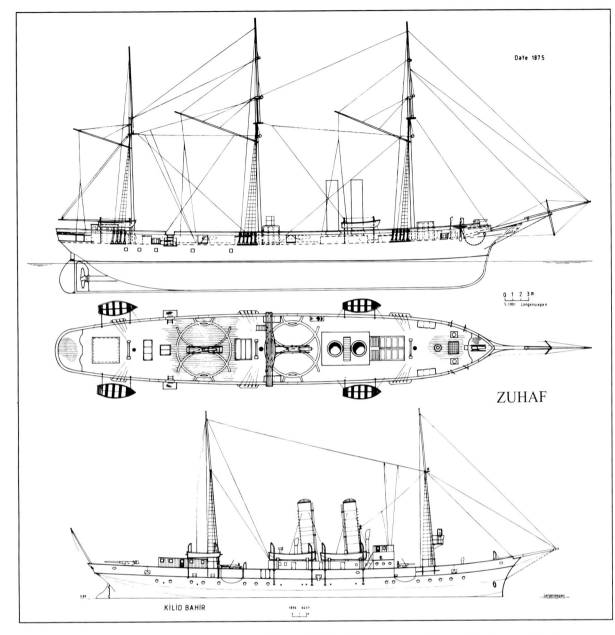

Date 1875

ZUHAF

KİLİD BAHİR

1860 commissioned. 1888 reboilered by Tersane-i Amire, İstanbul. 1907 decommissioned at Basra. 1909 breaking up.

Seddülbahir Ordered: 1857. Laid down: 1858. Launched: 1859. Trials: 1859. 1860 commissioned. 1891 decommissioned. Machinery removed, intended to be fitted in the new *Seddülbahir*, but cancelled. 1902 dismantled hull broken up.

İskenderiye Ordered: 1860. Laid down: 1860. Launched: 1862. Trials: 1863. Laid down as *Hüdavendigar*. 1863 commissioned. 1893 recoppered and reboilered by Tersane-i Amire, İstanbul. 1907 decommissioned.

Zuhaf Ordered: 1860. Laid down: 1861. Launched: 1862. Trials: 1863. 1863 commissioned. 1891 decommissioned. Machinery removed to fit in new corvette *Zuhaf*, but cancelled. 1902 broken up.

Utarit Ordered: 1860. Laid down: 1862. Launched: 1863. Trials: 1864. 1863 sailed to Tersane-i Amire, İstanbul, to fit machinery. 1864 commissioned. 1896 decommissioned. Machinery removed. 1897 stationary at Kandilli (Bosporus). 1905 broken up at Kandilli.

Meriç Ordered: 1860. Laid down: 1862. Launched: 1863. Trials: 1864. 1863 sailed to Tersane-i Amire, İstanbul, to fit machinery. 1864 commissioned. 1905 decommissioned. 1909 sold for breaking up.

Mansure Class

TYPE: Korvet (screw corvette)

BUILDER: Tersane-i Amire, İstanbul, (*Muzaffer* Tersane-i Amire, İzmit)

DISPLACEMENT: 783t bm
DIMENSIONS: Loa 55.1m, Lpp 52.6m, B 9.3m, D 4.4m

HULL: Wood, copper sheathed

MACHINERY: Steam, 1 shaft

ENGINE: 1 set 2 cyl, 650ihp, Maudslay, Sons & Field

BOILERS: 2 box type, Tersane-i Amire, İstanbul

SPEED: (trials) 10kts

BUNKER: 120t coal

COMPLEMENT: 130

ARMAMENT: (1864) 12–37pdr (*Mansure* and *Muzaffer* 1888) 2–150mm L/22 BL (K), 2–120mm BL L/25 (K), 3–37mm QF, 2–25mm (N)

Mansure Ordered: 1861. Laid down: 1863. Launched: 1864. Trials: 1864. 1864 commissioned. 1888 renewed by Tersane-i Amire, İstanbul. 1908 decom-

missioned. 13.8.1910 sunk in the Haliç in heavy weather. 1911 wreck salvaged and broken up.

Lübnan Ordered: 1861. Laid down 1862. Launched: 1864. Trials: 1864. 1864 commissioned. 4.1867 sunk off Milo Ada in heavy weather.

Muzaffer Ordered: 1861. Laid down: 1863. Launched: 1864. Trials: 1865. 1864 sailed to Tersane-i Amire, İstanbul, to fit machinery. 1864 commissioned. 1888–1895 renewed and reboilered by Tersane-i Amire, İstanbul. 1908 decommissioned. 1912 broken up at İstanbul.

Heybetnüma

TYPE: Korvet (corvette)

BUILDER: Tersane-i Amire, İstanbul

DISPLACEMENT: 1958t

DIMENSIONS: Lpp 98.9m, B 9.7m, D 4.7m

HULL: Composite; sheathed and coppered

MACHINERY: Steam, 1 shaft

ENGINE: 1 VTE, 2786ihp, Tersane-i Amire, İstanbul

BOILERS: 6 cyl Tersane-i Amire, İstanbul

SPEED: (trials) 12kts

BUNKERS: 280t coal

COMPLEMENT: (design) 190

ARMAMENT: (design) 3–170mm BL L/25 (K), 6–120mm BL L/25 (K), 6–47mm QF (K), 2 TT 450mm (SK) (1895) 1–150mm L/25 QF (K), 6–120mm L/25 (K), 6–47mm QF (K) (1898) 2–150mm BL L/25 (K) (200), 2–120mm BL L/25 (K) (150), 4–47mm QF (K)

Heybetnüma Ordered: 1879. Laid down: 1881. Launched: 30.1.1890. Trials: 1895. 1892 machinery fitted in. 1894 guns fitted in. 4.1895 commissioned. Stationary cadet training ship at Heybeliada. 1907 decommissioned. 31.7.1909 offered for breaking up and sold privately. 1911 left İstanbul for İzmit, loaded with scrap copper. Sunk near Yalova (Gulf of İzmit).

Zuhaf Class

TYPE: Korvet (corvette)

BUILDER: Tersane-i Amire, İstanbul

DISPLACEMENT: 643t

DIMENSIONS: Lpp 57.9m, B 7.3m, D 3.5m

HULL: Steel

MACHINERY: Steam, 1 shaft

ENGINE: 1 VTE, 640ihp, Tersane-i Amire, İstanbul

BOILERS: 2 cyl, Tersane-i Amire, İstanbul

SPEED: (trials) 14kts, (1904) 10kts

BUNKERS: 80t coal

COMPLEMENT: 82

ARMAMENT: (design) 2–120mm L/25 BL (K), 4–37mm QF(H), 2 TT 450mm (SK)
(1896) 1–120mm L/25 BL (K), 4–37mm QF(H)
(*Zuhaf* 1916) Disarmed

Zuhaf Ordered: 1890. Laid down: 1892. Launched: 31.8.1894. Trials: 1896. Designed by 'Germania' AG, Kiel Yard No 60. 10.1896 commissioned. 5.1915 reserve vessel. 1916 laid up. 1917 surveying vessel. 10.1918 laid up at İstanbul. 1924 sailed for Gölcük, laid up. 1932 decommissioned. 1936 broken up at Gölcük.

Kilid Bahir Ordered: 1890. Laid down: 1892. Launched: 31.8.1894. Trials: 1896. Designed by 'Germania' AG, Kiel, Yard No 61. 10.1896 commissioned. 1909 decommissioned, laid up at Basra. 8.1914 sunk as blockship off

The unprotected cruiser Lütf-ü Hümayun *about to be launched in August 1892. This is the only known illustration of this vessel.*
Güleryüz

Basra.

CRUISERS

Lütf-ü Hümayun

TYPE: Kruvazör (3rd class unprotected cruiser)

BUILDER: Tersane-i Amire, İstanbul

DISPLACEMENT: 1313t

DIMENSIONS: Lpp 64.0m, B 9.1m, D 3.9m

HULL: Composite, wood sheathed

MACHINERY: Steam, 1 shaft

ENGINE: 1 VTE, 3 cyl, 2160ihp, Tersane-i Amire

BOILERS: 2 cyl, Tersane-i Amire

SPEED: (design) 14kts (trials) 12kts

BUNKERS: 205t coal

COMPLEMENT: _

ARMAMENT: (design) 4–170mm L/25 QF (K), 6–120mm L/25 (K), 4–47mm QF (H), 6 MG, 2 TT 450mm (SK)
(1896) 3–170mm L/25 QF (K), 6–120mm L/25 (K), 6–47mm QF (H), 2 TT 450mm (SK)
(1899) 2–150mm L/40 QF (K), 2–120mm L/40 QF (K), 4–37mm QF, 2 TT 450mm (SK)
(1905) Disarmed

Lütf-ü Hümayun Ordered: 1880. Laid down: 1882. Launched: 16.8.1892. Trials: 7.1896. 10.1896 commissioned. Stationary training vessel at İstanbul. 1905 armament, machinery and masts removed. Projected to be rebuilt by Ansaldo, İstanbul. 1908 decommissioned. 11.1909 sold for breaking up. 1921 breaking-up completed.

Feyza-i Bahri Class

TYPE: Kruvazör (cruiser)

BUILDER: Tersane-i Amire, İstanbul

DISPLACEMENT: 1612t

DIMENSIONS: Lpp 68.5m, B 10.6m, D 4.2m

HULL: Steel/composite

MACHINERY: Steam, 2 shafts

ENGINES: (design) 2 VTE 3 cyl, 3500ihp, Tersane-i Amire

BOILERS: 4 cyl, Tersane-i Amire

SPEED: (design) 17kts

BUNKERS: _

COMPLEMENT: _

ARMAMENT: 6–150mm L/45 QF (K), 4–47mm QF (H), 5 TT 450mm (SK)

Feyza-i Bahri Ordered: 5.1889. Laid down: 5.1891. 1897 works stopped. In

frame and partly plated. 1906–1909 slipway cleared.

Şadiye Ordered: 5.1889. Laid down: 9.11.1891. 1897 works stopped. In frame and partly plated. 1906–1909 slipway cleared.

Hüdavendigar Class

TYPE: Kruvazör (unprotected cruiser)

BUILDER: Tersane-i Amire, İstanbul

DISPLACEMENT: 4050t

DIMENSIONS: Lpp 85.4m, B 15.2m, D 6.1m

HULL: Steel

MACHINERY: Steam, 1 shaft, (1902 2 shafts)

ENGINES: (design) 2 triple expansion 3 cyl, _ihp, Tersane-i Amire

BOILERS: (design) 4 cyl, Tersane-i Amire

SPEED: _

BUNKERS: _

COMPLEMENT: _

ARMAMENT: (design 1891) 2–210mm BL (K), 6–150mm BL (K), 4–100mm BL (K), 5 TT 450mm (SK)
(design 1902) 2–150mm L/40 QF (K), 6–105mm L/40 QF (K), 4–47mm QF (K), 4 MG, 4 TT 450mm (SK)

Hüdavendigar Ordered: 1891. Laid down: 1893. 1897 works stopped. Ship in frame and partly plated. 1902 design modified into 2-screw ship. 1905–1909 slipway cleared.

Selimiye Ordered: 1891. 7.1891 works started. 1892 order cancelled.

Peyk-i Şevket Class

TYPE: Torpido-kruvazör (torpedo cruiser)

BUILDERS: Schiffs- & Maschinenbau 'Germania' AG, Kiel

DISPLACEMENT: (1907) 775t, (1938) 850t

HULL: Steel (Krupp)

DIMENSIONS: Loa _m, Lpp 80.1m, B 8.4m, D 4.6m

MACHINERY: Steam, 2 shafts

ENGINES: 2 VTE, 5100ihp, 'Germania'

BOILERS: 4 Schulz water-tube boilers, 'Germania'

SPEED: (trials) 22kts, (1915) 18kts

BUNKERS: 244t coal

COMPLEMENT: (1907) 125, (1915) 145

ARMAMENT: (1907) 2–105mm QF L/40 (K) (691), 6–57mm SA L/40 (K) (1800), 2–37mm QF (K) 2 MG (H), 3 TT 450mm (SK) (1938) 2–88mm QF L/40 (K), 4–37mm QF (K), 2 TT 450mm (SK), (*Berk* only 25 mines)

Peyk-i Şevket (Yd No 126) Ordered: 18.1.1903. Laid down: 2.1906. Launched: 15.11.1906, Trials: 1907. 13.11.1907 arrived İstanbul from Kiel. 11.1907 commissioned. 6.8.1915 damaged by torpedo from British submarine E 11 near Silivri. 1917 returned into service. 30.10.1918 decommissioned, laid up at İstanbul-Kasimpaşa. 1924 renamed *Peyk*. 1925/1927 refurbished by T C Gölcük Tersane, Gölcük. 1927 commissioned. 1936/1938 modified by T C Gölcük Tersane, Gölcük. 1944 decommissioned, laid up at İzmit. 1953/1954 broken up at Gölcük.

Berk-i Satvet (Yd No 127) Ordered: 18.1.1903. Laid down: 2.1906. Launched: 1.12.1906. Trials: 1907. 13.11.1907 arrived İstanbul from Kiel. 11.1907 commissioned. 2.1.1915 damaged badly by Russian mine off Bosporus. 1917 returned to service. 1924 renamed Berk. 1924/1925 refurbished by T C Gölcük Tersane, Gölcük. 1925 commissioned. 1937/1938 modified by T C Gölcük Tersane, Gölcük. 1945 decommissioned. 1953–1955 broken up at İzmit.

Mecidiye

TYPE: Kruvazör (protected cruiser)

BUILDER: William Camp & Son, Philadelphia

DISPLACEMENT: 3485t normal draught, 3967t full load

HULL: Steel

DIMENSIONS: Loa 102.4m, Lpp 100.5m, B 12:8m, D 4.8m

MACHINERY: Steam, 2 shafts

ENGINES: 2 VQE, 12,500ihp, W Camp

BOILERS: 16 Niclausse water-tube boilers, W Camp, (1936) 16 Babcock & Wilcox water-tube boilers

SPEED: (trials) 22kts, (1914) 18kts, (1936) 20kts

BUNKERS: 610t coal

COMPLEMENT: (1901) 22 officers, 280 ratings, (1915) 340 Turks, 15 Germans, (1936) 25 officers, 285 ratings

ARMAMENT: (1901) 2–152mm QF L/45 (B) (300), 8–120mm QF L/45 (B) (1400), 6–47mm QF (B) (1500), 6–37mm QF(B) (3000), 2 TT 457mm (WH) (1918) 2–152mm QF L/45 (B) (300), 2–120mm QF L/45 (B) (1000), 2 TT 457mm (WH) (6) (1927) 4–130mm QF L/56 (V) (350), 4–76mm QF L/50 (S) (800), 2 TT 457mm (WH) (6)

Mecidiye (Yd No 315) Ordered: 1900. Laid down: 7.11.1901. Launched: 25.7.1903. Trials: 10.1903. Launched as *Abdül Mecidiye*. 19.12.1903 commissioned as *Mecidiye*. 3.4.1915 sunk by Russian mine 15nm off Vorokoskiy-Mayak (Odessa). 8.6.1915 salvaged by

the Russians. 29.10.1915 commissioned as *Prut* Imperial Russian Navy. 1.65.1918 seized by German armed forces at Sebastopol. 13.5.1918 returned to Osmanli Bahriye, renamed *Mecidiye*, towed to İstanbul. 31.10.1918 laid up at İstanbul-Kasimpaşa, stationary cadet training ship. 1915/1925 renewed by T C Gölcük Tersane, Gölcük. 6.1927 commissioned. 1940 stationary cadet training ship at Gölcük. 1.3.1947 decommissioned, laid up at Gölcük. 1952 sold for breaking up, towed to İstanbul-Kasimpaşa. 1952/1956 broken up.

Hamidiye

TYPE: Kruvazör (protected cruiser)

BUILDER: Sir W G Armstrong, Whitworth & Co, Newcastle

DISPLACEMENT: 3904t normal

DIMENSIONS: Loa 112.0m, Lpp 103.6m, B 14.5m, D 4.8m

HULL: Steel

MACHINERY: Steam, 3 shafts

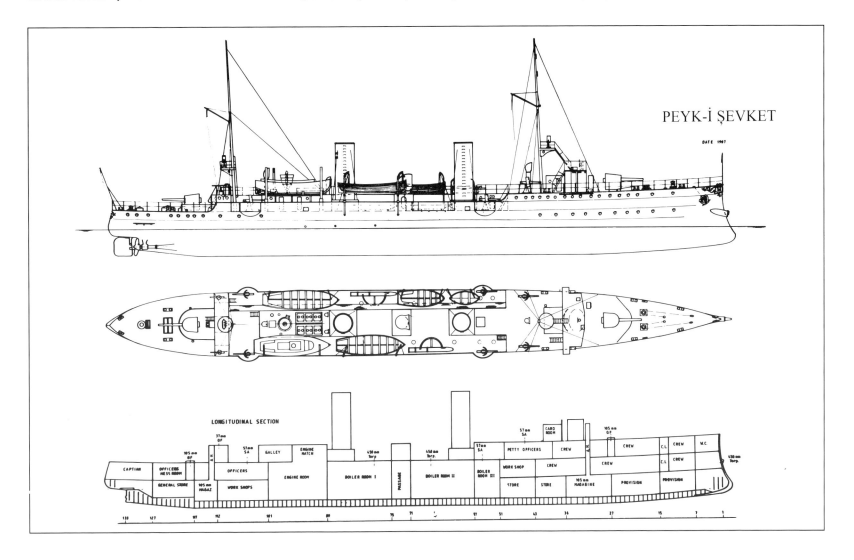

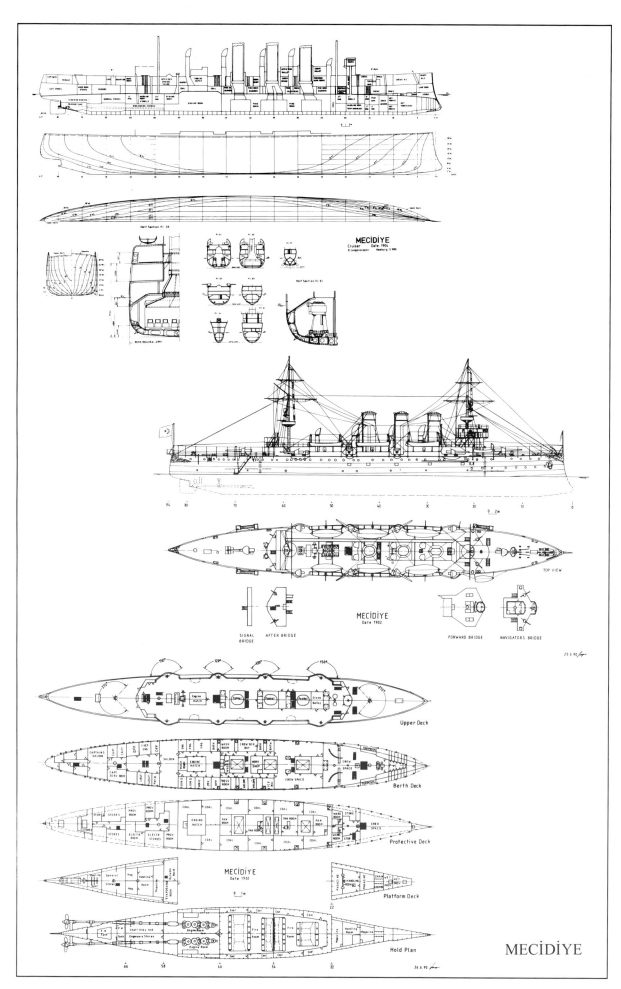

MECİDİYE
Cruiser Date 1904
B Langensiepen   Hamburg 5 mm

MECİDİYE
Date 1902

SIGNAL
BRIDGE

AFTER BRIDGE

FORWARD BRIDGE

NAVIGATORS BRIDGE

Upper Deck

Berth Deck

Protective Deck

MECİDİYE
Date 1902

Platform Deck

Hold Plan

MECİDİYE

ENGINES: 2 VTE 4 cyl, 12,000ihp, Hawthorn, Leslie

BOILERS: 16 Niclausse water-tube boilers

SPEED: (trials) 22.2kts, (1914) 16kts

BUNKERS: 600t coal

COMPLEMENT: (1904) 400, (1915) 340 Turks, 15 Germans

ARMAMENT: (1904) 2–150mm QF L/45 (A) (200), 8–120mm QF L/50 (A) (816), 6–47mm QF L/50 (A) (1500), 6–37mm QF(A) (2000), 2 TT 457mm (6) (1915) 2–150mm QF L/45 (A) (200), 6–120mm QF L/50 (A) (816), 2–46mm QF L/50 (A) (1500), 2–37mm QF(A) (2000), 2 TT 457mm (6) (1927) 2–150mm L/45 QF (K) (220), 8–75mm QF L/45 (K) (800), 2 TT 457mm, 70 mines

Hamidiye (Yd No 732) Ordered: 1900. Laid down: 4.1902. Launched: 25.9.1903. Trials: 17.12.1903. 4.1904 commissioned. 21.11.1912 damaged by Bulgarian torpedo off Varna. 12.1912 returned to service. 30.10.1918 laid up at İstanbul-Kasimpaşa. 1925–1926 refitted by T C Gölcük Tersane, Gölcük. 1940 cadet training ship. 1945 stationary cadet training ship. 3.1947 decommissioned. 1949–1951 Navy museum at İstanbul-Kabataş. 1951–1964 laid up at İstanbul-Halié. 10.9.1964 sold for scrapping, towing to İstanbul-Paşabahçe. 1966 breaking up completed.

Note: Intended name prior to launch was *Abdülhamid*

Drama

TYPE: Kruvazör (protected cruiser)

BUILDER: G Ansaldo-Armstrong & Cie, Sestri-Ponenti

DISPLACEMENT: 3760t normal, 4466t full load

DIMENSIONS: Loa 111.8m, Lpp _m, B 14.5m, D 5.5m

HULL: Steel

MACHINERY: Steam, 3 shafts

ENGINES: 2 VTE 4 cyl, 11,530ihp, Ansaldo

BOILERS: _

SPEED: (trials) 22.9kts

BUNKERS: _

COMPLEMENT: (design) 21 officers, 286 ratings

ARMAMENT: (design) 2–152mm QF(A), 8–180mm QF(A), 8–47mm QF(A), 6–37mm QF, 2 TT 457mm (6)

Drama (Yd No 156) Ordered: 4.1904. Laid down: 1907. Launched: 11.11.1912. Trials: 3.1913. Intended name: *Drama*. 9.1912 seized on stocks by Italian Govt. 25.3.1913 *Libia* Italian Navy. 11.3.1937 decommissioned.

Midilli

TYPE: Kruvazör (protected cruiser)

BUILDER: AG Vulcan, Stettin

DISPLACEMENT: 4570t, 5587t full load

DIMENSIONS: Loa 138.7m, Lpp 136.0m, B 13.5m, D 5.1m

HULL: Steel

MACHINERY: Turbine, 4 shafts

ENGINES: 2 AEG-Vulcan steam turbines, 33,740shp

BOILERS 16 marine, AG Vulcan

SPEED: (trials) 25kts

BUNKERS: 1200t coal, 106t oil

COMPLEMENT: (1914) 350, (1915) 426 Germans, 6 Turks

ARMAMENT: (1914) 12–105mm L/45 (K) (1800), 2 TT 500mm (SW), (1916) 2–150mm L/45 (K) (180), 10–105mm L/45 (K) (1500), 2 TT 500mm (5) (SH) (1917) 8–150mm L/45 (K) (741), 2 TT 500mm (6) (SW)

Midilli (Yd No 312) Ordered: 1910.

Laid down: 1911. Launched: 16.5.1911. Trials: 1912. 10.5.1912 commissioned as *Breslau* for the Kaiserliche Marine. 16.8.1914 officially transferred to Osmanli Bahriye, renamed *Midilli*. 20.1.1918 sunk after hitting four mines near Imroz, 40.05N 26.02E. 330 lives lost.

1914 Protected Cruiser Design

TYPE: Kruvazör (protected cruiser)

BUILDERS: Sir W G Armstrong, Whitworth & Co, Newcastle

DISPLACEMENT: 3600t normal

DIMENSIONS: Loa 128.0m, Lpp 121.9m, B 12.5m, D 4.1m

HULL: Steel

ARMOUR: NC nickel steel. Complete protective deck. Extending 91mm below waterline at the side. Slopes amidships in way of machinery and magazine spaces 52mm. Flat amidships and hold deck at ends 38mm. Conning tower, side 152mm, roof 38mm, floor 25mm. Protective splinter shields to 152mm and 101mm guns.

MACHINERY: Turbine, 3 shafts

ENGINES: 3 Parsons combined impulse and reaction steam turbines, 24,000ihp

BOILERS: 11 Yarrow small tube boilers/surface 4366qm

SPEED: (contract) 27kts

RANGE: 4000nm

BUNKERS: 710t coal, 255t oil

COMPLEMENT: _

ARMAMENT: (contract) 2–152mm QG L/50 (A) (200), 6–101mm QF L/50 (A) (900), 3–76mm QF L/27 (A) (450), 4–57mm QF L/50 (A) (2000), 2 TT 533mm (6)

ELECTRICAL EQUIPMENT: 2–105kW generators, 4–914mm searchlights, 1–3kW wireless set, range 230nm. '877' Ordered: 13.5.1914. 8.1914 order cancelled by builder. Works not started. '878' Ordered: 13.5.1914. 8.1914 order cancelled by builder. Works not started.

(Left)
Hamidiye *arriving at İstanbul in 1913 after her dramatic cruise in the Aegean.*
Güleryüz

(Below left)
The cruiser Drama, *seen shortly before launching after seizure by the Italian government.*
Ansaldo

(Below right)
Midilli, *seen in February 1915 off the naval dockyard at İstanbul.*
Turkish Navy

TORPEDO BOATS

Burhaneddin Class

TYPE: Torpido stimbot (2nd class torpedo boat)

BUILDER: SA des Forges & Chantiers de la Mediterranée, La Seyne

DISPLACEMENT: 38t

DIMENSIONS: Loa 31.7m, Lpp 30.8m, B 3.6m, D max 1.7m

HULL: Iron

MACHINERY: Steam, 1 shaft

ENGINE: 1 compound 2 cyl, 525ihp, La Seyne

BOILER: 1 locomotive type, La Seyne

SPEED: (trials) 17kts, (1887) 10kts

BUNKERS: 4.7t coal

COMPLEMENT: 4 officers, 20 ratings

ARMAMENT: 1–34mm RC (N), 1–25mm RC (N), 2 TT 355mm (WH) (4), 1 MacEvoy spar torpedo

Burhaneddin Ordered: 5.1883. Laid down: 1885. Launched: 8.1885. Trials: 1885. 10.1885 commissioned at İstanbul. 1902 unfit for service. 31.7.1909 auctioned for scrapping. 11.1909 towed away.

Tevfik Ordered: 5.1883. Laid down: 1885. Launched: 8.1885. Trials: 11.1885. 11.1885 commissioned at İstanbul. 1902 unfit for service. 31.7.1909 auctioned for scrapping. 11.1909 towed away.

Mecidiye Class

TYPE: Torpido stimbot (2nd class torpedo boat)

BUILDER: Tersane-i Amire, İstanbul

DISPLACEMENT: 38t

DIMENSIONS: Loa 31.7m, Lpp 30.8m, B 3.6m, D max 1.7m

HULL: Iron

MACHINERY: Steam, 1 shaft

ENGINE: 1 compound 2 cyl, 450ihp, Tersane-i Amire

BOILER: 1 locomotive type, Tersane-i

Amire

SPEED: (trials) 15kts, (service) 10kts

BUNKERS: 4.7t coal

COMPLEMENT: 4 officers, 20 ratings

ARMAMENT: 1–34mm RV (N), 1–25mm RV (N), 2 TT 355mm (WH) (4)

Mecidiye Locally built version of *Burhaneddin* class. Ordered: 5.1883. Laid down: 2.1886. Launched: 1887. Trials: 1889. 6.1889 commissioned at İstanbul. 1902 unfit for service. 31.7.1909 auctioned for scrapping. 11.1909 towed away.

Eser-i Terakki Ordered: 5.1883. Laid down: 2.1886. Launched: 1887. Trials: 1890. 8.1890 commissioned at İstanbul. 1899 based at Selanik. 1902 unfit for service. 11.1909 auctioned for scrapping.

Nımet Ordered: 5.1883. Laid down: 5.1886. Launched: 1888. Trials: 1893. 11.1893 commissioned at İstanbul. 1902 unfit for service. 11.1909 auctioned for scrapping.

Şanaver Ordered: 5.1883. Laid down:

5.1887. Launched: 6.1889. Trials: Engine and boiler not fitted. Hull laid up at builder's yard. 11.1909 auctioned for scrapping.

Timsah

TYPE: Torpido stimbot (3rd class torpedo boat)

BUILDER: Des Vignes, Chertsey, London

DISPLACEMENT: 30t

DIMENSIONS: Loa 28.6m, B 3.7m, D1.4m

HULL: Iron

MACHINERY: Steam, 1 shaft

ENGINE: 1 compound 2 cyl, 400ihp

BOILER: 1 locomotive type, Des Vignes

SPEED: (trials) 18kts, (1889) 10kts

BUNKERS: 4.8t coal

COMPLEMENT: (1887) 2 officers, 15 ratings

ARMAMENT: (1887) 2 TT 356mm (WH) (4)

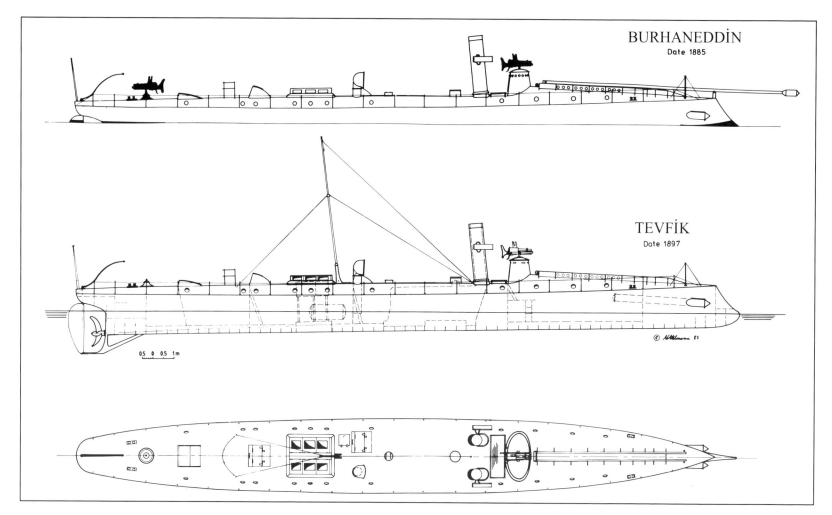

BURHANEDDİN
Date 1885

TEVFİK
Date 1897

0.5 0 0.5 1m

Timsah Ordered: 1885. Laid down: 1885. Launched: 1885. Trials: 1885. 1885 *Scirocco* British pleasure-steamer. 1887 sold to Osmanli Govt. 1887 commissioned. 1889 utility boat at Selanik. 1897 yacht for the fleet commander. 1903 decommissioned. 31.7.1909 auctioned for scrapping. 1912 broken up.

Şemşir-i Hücum

TYPE: Torpido stimbot (3rd class torpedo boat)

BUILDER: SA des Forges & Chantiers de la Mediterranée, La Seyne

DISPLACEMENT: 14t

DIMENSIONS: Loa 19.0m, Lpp _m, B 2.3m, D 0.8m

HULL: Iron

MACHINERY: Steam, 1 shaft

ENGINE: 1 compound 2 cyl, 120ihp, La Seyne

BOILER: 1 locomotive type, La Seyne

SPEED: (trials) 15kts, (1889) 9kts

BUNKERS: 0.7t coal

COMPLEMENT: 1 officer, 2 ratings

ARMAMENT: 2 TT 356mm (WH)

Şemşir-i Hücum Ordered: 5.1885. Laid down: 1885. Launched: .1885. Trials: 1886. 1886 commissioned at İstanbul. Non-autonomous craft carried in ironclad *Hamidiye*. 1896 decommissioned. 1899 cradled ashore at İstanbul. 31.7.1909 auctioned for scrapping. 1912 broken up.

Mahabet Class

TYPE: Torpido bot (torpedo boat)

BUILDER: Des Vignes, Chertsey, London

DISPLACEMENT: 83t

DIMENSIONS: Loa 38.1m, Lpp _m, B 4.6m, D 1.9m

HULL: Steel

MACHINERY: Steam, 1 shaft

ENGINE: 1 triple expansion 3 cyl, 950ihp, Maudslay

BOILER: 1 locomotive type, Maudslay

SPEED: (trials) 21kts, (1886) 12kts

BUNKERS: 22t coal

COMPLEMENT: 3 officers, 17 ratings

ARMAMENT: (1887) 2–37mm RV (H), 2 TT 356mm (WH) (6)
(1890) 2 TT 356mm (WH) (6)

Mahabet Ordered: 1886. Laid down: 1886. Launched: 12.1886. Trials: 1887. 5.1887 commissioned at İstanbul. 1892 out of service. 31.7.1909 auctioned for scrapping.

Satvet Ordered: 1886. Laid down: 1886. Launched: 12.1886. Trials: 1887. 5.1887 commissioned at İstanbul. 1892 out of service. 31.7.1909 auctioned for scrapping.

Gilyum Class

TYPE: Torpido bot (torpedo boat)

BUILDER: Fr Schichau AG, Elbing

DISPLACEMENT: 85t
DIMENSIONS: Loa 37.7m, Lpp 36.9m, B 4.8m, D 1.3m

HULL: Steel

MACHINERY: Steam, 1 shaft

ENGINE: 1 triple expansion 3 cyl, 980ihp, Fr Schichau AG

BOILER: 1 locomotive type, Fr Schichau AG

SPEED: (trials) 21kts, (1887) 18kts

BUNKERS: 18t coal

COMPLEMENT: 5 officers, 13 ratings

ARMAMENT: 2–37mm RV (K), 2 TT 428mm (SK) (4)

Gilyum (Yd No 273) Ordered: 1885. Laid down: 1885. Launched: 1886. Trials: 10–13.4.1886. 6.1886 commissioned at İstanbul. 1903 unfit for service. 31.7.1909 auctioned for scrapping. 1910 towed away.

Saiki (Yd No 274) Ordered: 1885. Laid down: 1885. Launched: 1886. Trials: 10–13.4.1886. 6.1886 commissioned at İstanbul. 1903 unfit for service. 31.7.1909 auctioned for scrapping. 1910 towed away.

Tir-i Zafer (Yd No 275) Ordered: 1885. Laid down: 1885. Launched:

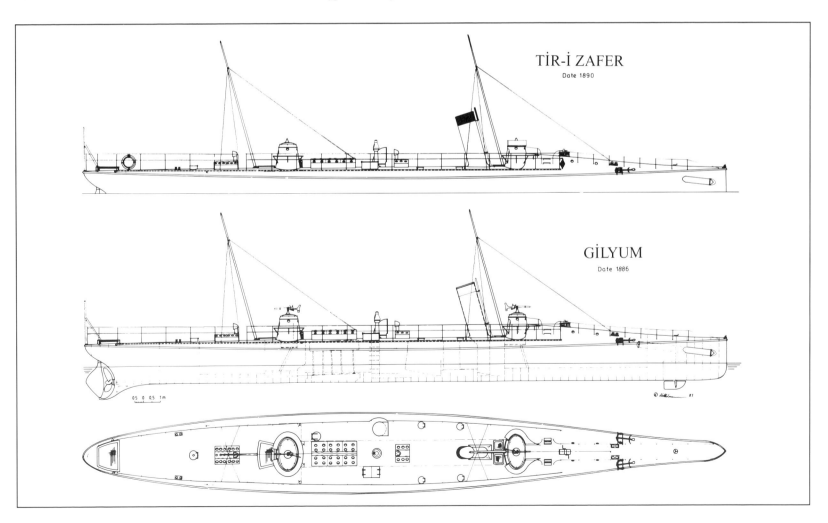

TİR-İ ZAFER
Date 1890

GİLYUM
Date 1886

1886. Trials: 10–13.4.1886. 6.1886 commissioned at İstanbul. 1905 unfit for service. 31.7.1909 auctioned for scrapping. 1910 towed away.

Seyf-i Bahri (Yd No 276) Ordered: 1885. Laid down: 1885. Launched: 1886. Trials: 10–13.4.1886. 6.1886 commissioned at İstanbul. 1909 decommissioned. 31.7.1909 auctioned for scrapping. 1910 towed away.

Vesile-i Nusret (Yd No 277) Ordered: 1885. Laid down: 1885. Launched: 1886. Trials: 10–13.4.1886. 6.1886 commissioned at İstanbul. 1906 decommissioned. 31.7.1909 auctioned for scrapping. 1910 towed away.

Nasir Class

TYPE: Torpido bot (torpedo boat)

BUILDER: Schiffs- & Maschinenbau 'Germania' AG, Kiel

DISPLACEMENT: 87t

DIMENSIONS: Loa 39.0m, Lpp _m, B 4.8m, D 1.1m

HULL: Steel
MACHINERY: Steam, 1 shaft

ENGINE: 1 triple expansion 3 cyl, 1200ihp, 'Germania'

BOILER: 1 locomotive type, 'Germania'

SPEED: (trials) 21kts, (1890) 15kts

BUNKERS: 30t coal

COMPLEMENT: 6 officers, 21 ratings

ARMAMENT: 2–37mm RV (K), 2 TT 428mm (SK) (4)

Nasir (Yd No 31) Ordered: 23.10.1886. Laid down: 1887. Launched: 1887. Trials: 17.9.1889. 12.1889 commissioned at İstanbul. 1909 decommissioned. 1922 sold for breaking up.

Fatih (Yd No 32) Ordered: 23.10.1886. Laid down: 1887. Launched: 1887. Trials: 17.9.1889. 12.1889 commissioned at İstanbul. 1911 decommissioned. 1913 sold for breaking up.

Nusret (Yd No 33) Ordered: 23.10.1886. Laid down: 1888. Launched:. 1888. Trials: 11.1889. 2.1890 commissioned at İstanbul. 1909 decommissioned. 31.7.1909 auctioned for scrapping. 1913 broken up.

Şahab (Yd No 34) Ordered: 23.10.1886. Laid down: 1888. Launched: 1888. Trials: 11.1889. 2.1890 commissioned at İstanbul. 24.3.1901 heavily damaged by a boiler explosion at Selanik. 9 lives lost. Towed to İstanbul, laid up. 31.7.1909 auctioned for scrapping. 1911 broken up.

Tarik (Yd No 35) Ordered: 23.10.1886. Laid down: 1889. Launched: 9.1889. Trials: 12.1889. 3.1890 commissioned at İstanbul. 1909 decommissioned. 31.7.1909 auctioned for scrapping. 1911 broken up.

Pervın (Yd No 36) Ordered: 23.10.1886. Laid down: 1889. Launched: 1889. Trials: 2.1890. 5.1890 commissioned at İstanbul. 1911 decommissioned. 1913 broken up.

Seham (Yd No 37) Ordered: 23.10.1886. Laid down: 1889. Launched: 1889. Trials: 2.1890. 5.1890 commissioned at İstanbul. 21.4.1901 sunk in the outer harbour at Beirut after a boiler explosion.

Ejder

TYPE: Torpido bot (torpedo boat)

BUILDER: Schiffs- & Maschinenbau 'Germania' AG, Kiel

DISPLACEMENT: 138t

DIMENSIONS: Loa 49.2m, Lpp _m, B 5.9m, D 1.3m

HULL: Steel

MACHINERY: Steam, 2 shafts

ENGINES: 2 triple expansion 3 cyl, 2200ihp, 'Germania'

BOILERS: 2 locomotive type, 'Germania'

SPEED: (trials) 24kts, (1895) 20 kts

BUNKERS: 50t coal

COMPLEMENT: 5 officers, 17 ratings

ARMAMENT: 5–37mm RV (K), 2 TT 428mm (SK) (3)

Ejder (Yd No 36) Ordered: 23.10.1886. Laid down: 1889. Launched: 1890. Trials: 1893. 1893 commissioned at İstanbul. 17.11.1897 ran aground near İzmir, towed to İstanbul, laid up. 1903 returned to service,

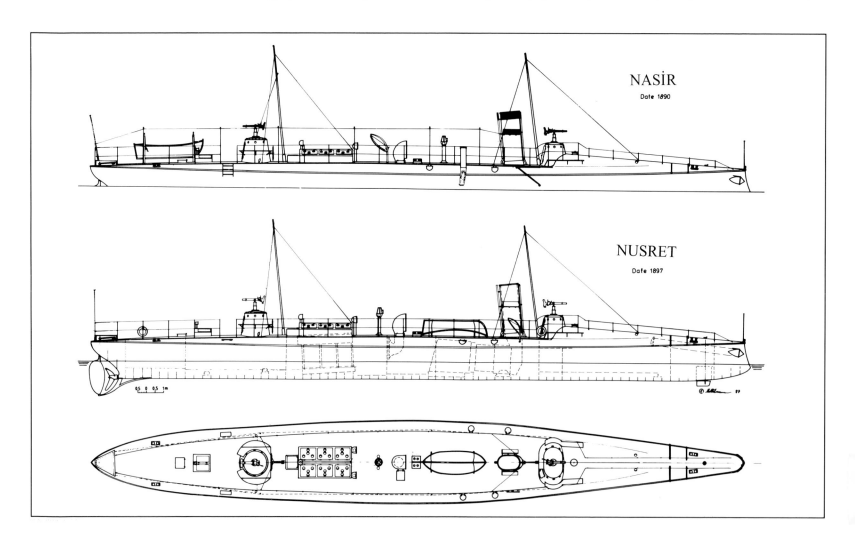

unfit for service. 1909 decommissioned. 1921 broken up.

Berk Efşan Class

TYPE: Torpido bot (torpedo boat)

BUILDER: Tersane-i Amire, İstanbul

DISPLACEMENT: 230t

DIMENSIONS: Loa 59.9m, Lpp _m, B 6.6m, D 2.4m

HULL: Steel

MACHINERY: Steam, 2 shafts

ENGINES: 2 triple expansion 3 cyl, 3500ihp, 'Germania'

BOILERS: 2 locomotive type, 'Germania'

SPEED: (trials) 21kts, (1896) 17kts

BUNKERS: 75t coal

COMPLEMENT: (1894) 8 officers, 42 ratings
(Berk Efşan 1915) 58 Turks, 4 Germans

ARMAMENT: (1886) 6–37mm RV (K), 2 TT 428mm (SK) (4)
(Berk Efşan 1912) 4–37mm RV (K), 2 TT 428mm (SK) (4)
(Berk Efşan 1915) 2–47mm L/50 QF (K) (200), 2–47mm L/30 QF (K) (200), 2 TT 428mm (SK) (4)

Berk Efşan (Yd No 41) Ordered: 23.10.1886. Laid down: 1891. Launched: 1892. Trials: 1894. Vessel ordered from 'Germania', Kiel. Sent in sections to İstanbul. 1894 commissioned. 10.1918 decommissioned. 1920 returned to service. 1924 decommis-

sioned. 1928 stricken. 1932 broken up.

Tayyar (Yd No 39) Ordered: 23.10.1886. Laid down: 1891. Launched: 1892. Trials: 1894. Vessel ordered from 'Germania', Kiel. Sent in sections to İstanbul. 1894 commissioned. 1906 unfit for service. 1909 decommissioned. 1921 broken up.

Hamidiye Class

TYPE: Torpido bot (torpedo boat)

BUILDER: Ansaldo, Armstrong & Cie, Genoa

DISPLACEMENT: 145t

DIMENSIONS: Loa 50.6m, Lpp 47.8m, B 5.6m, D 1.2m

HULL: Steel

MACHINERY: Steam, 2 shafts

ENGINES: 2 triple expansion 3 cyl, 2400ihp, Ansaldo

BOILERS: 3 Yarrow water-tube, Ansaldo

SPEED: (trials) 26kts

BUNKERS: 50t coal

COMPLEMENT: (1902) 4 officers, 26 ratings
(1915) Turks: 6 officers, 33 ratings, Germans: 1 officer, 3 NC officers

ARMAMENT: (1902) 1–37mm QF (H) (250), 2 TT 450mm (SK) (4)
(Abdülmecid 1914) 1–37mm QF (H) (250), 1 TT 450mm (SK) (4)
(Yunus 1916) 1–47mm QF (K) (170), 1 TT 450mm (SK) (4)

(Yunus 1919) 1–47mm QF (K) (170)

Hamidiye Ordered: 3.1901. Laid down: 1901. Launched: 1901. Trials: . .1902. 1902 commissioned at İstanbul. 30.9.1911 sunk by Italian destroyers at Resadiye.

Abdül Mecid/Yunus Ordered: 3.1901. Laid down: 1901. Launched: 1901. Trials: 1902. 1902 commissioned at İstanbul. 5.1908 renamed Yunus. 6.5.1915 grounded off Sarköy. 1.3.1918 collided with Draç off Tekirdağ. 10.1918 decommissioned. 2.1919 anti-smuggling duty. 1920 decommissioned. 1923/24 refitted by İstanbul Deniz Fabrikalar, İstanbul. 1926 returned to service as a dispatch boat, İstanbul-Izmit. 1929 decommissioned. 1935 broken up.

Akhisar Class

Type: Torpido bot (torpedo boat)

BUILDER: Ansaldo, Armstrong & Cie, Sestri Ponente)

DISPLACEMENT: 165t

DIMENSIONS: Loa 51.0m, B 5.7m, D 1.4m

HULL: Steel

MACHINERY: Steam, 2 shafts

ENGINES: 2 triple expansion 3 cyl, 2400ihp, Ansaldo

BOILERS: 2 locomotive type, Ansaldo

SPEED: (trials) 24kts, (1915) 14kts

BUNKERS: 60t coal

COMPLEMENT: (1904) 4 officers, 26 ratings
(Akhisar 1915) 39 Turks, 4 German

ARMAMENT: (1904) 2–37mm QF (H) (250), 2 TT 450mm (SK) (4)
(Akhisar 1915) 1–47mm QF (K) (150), 2–37mm QF (H) (250), 1 TT 450mm (SK) (4)

Akhisar (Yd No 131) Ordered: 12.1902. Laid down: 1904. Launched: 25.4.1904. Trials: 1904. 6.1904 commissioned at İstanbul. 11.12.1915 aground near Silivri, towed to İstanbul. 1916 returned to service. 10.1918 decommissioned. 2.1919 anti-smuggling duty. 1920 decommissioned. 1924/25 refitted by İstanbul Deniz Fabrikalari, İstanbul. 1925 returned to service. 1920 decommissioned. 1935 broken up.

The torpedo boat Akhisar, pictured at İstanbul shortly after arriving from the builders.
Güleryüz

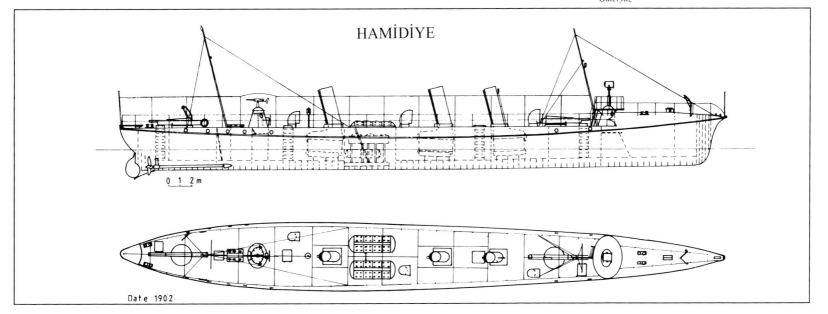

HAMİDİYE

0 1 2 m

Date 1902

Alpagot (Yd No 132) Ordered: 12.1902. Laid down: 1904. Launched: 30.4.1904. Trials: 1904. 6.1904 commissioned at İstanbul. 30.9.1912 sunk by Italian destroyers at Resadiye.

Antalya Class

TYPE: Torpido bot (torpedo boat)

BUILDER: Ansaldo, Armstrong & Cie, Sestri Ponente

DISPLACEMENT: 165t

DIMENSIONS: Loa 51.0m, Lpp _m, B 5.7m, D 1.4m

HULL: Steel

MACHINERY: Steam, 2 shafts

ENGINES: 2 triple expansion 3 cyl, 2700ihp, Ansaldo

BOILERS: 2 water-tube, Ansaldo

SPEED: (trials) 26 kts

BUNKERS: 60t coal

COMPLEMENT: 4 officers, 26 ratings (*Draç* and *Kütahya* 1915) 39 Turks, 4 Germans

ARMAMENT: 2–37mm QF (H) (250), 2 TT 450mm (SK) (4)
(*Draç* and *Kütahya* 1915) 1–57mm QF (K) (100), 2–37mm QF (H) (250), 1 TT 450mm (SK) (4)
(*Musul* 1915) 1–47mm QF (K) (150), 2–37mm WF (H) (250), 2 TT 450mm (SK) (4)
(*Draç* 1919) 2–37mm QF (H) (250)

Antalya (Yd No 134) Ordered: 1901. Laid down: 4.1904. Launched: 1904. Trials: .1905. 29.11.1906 delivered at Genoa. 12.1906 commissioned at İstanbul. 5.11.1911 scuttled by crew at Preveze. 29.11.1912 salvaged by the Greeks. 1913 *Nikopolis* Royal Greek Navy. 1916 out of service.

Urfa (Yd No 135) Ordered: 1901. Laid down: 4.1904. Launched: 1904. Trials: 1905. 29.11.1906 commissioned at İstanbul. 12.1906 commissioned at İstanbul. 11.12.1908 sunk in heavy gale off Selanik.

Ankara (Yd No 136) Ordered: 1901. Laid down: 4.1904. Launched: 1904. Trials: 1905. 29.11.1906 delivered at Genoa. 12.1906 commissioned at İstanbul. 24.2.1912 sunk by Italian warships at Beirut.

Tokad (Yd No 137) Ordered: 1901. Laid down: 4.1904. Launched: 1904.

Trials: 1905. 29.11.1906 delivered at Genoa. 12.1906 commissioned at İstanbul. 29.9.1911 deliberately beached near Preveze. 11.1912 wreck taken to Preveze. 5.11.1911 scuttled by crew at Preveze. 29.9.1912 salvaged by the Greeks. 1913 *Totoi* Royal Greek Navy. 1916 out of service.

Draç (Yd No 138) Ordered: 1901. Laid down: 4.1904. Launched: 1904. Trials: 1905. 29.11.1906 delivered at Genoa. 6.1.1907 arrived İstanbul. 8.1.1907 commissioned. 27.6.1915 aground off Sarköy. 10.1918 decommissioned. 4.1919 anti-smuggling duty. 1920 decommissioned. 1924 returned to service. 1924 decommissioned. 1926 hulk employed as work barge at Gölcük. 1936 broken up.

Kütahya (Yd No 139) Ordered: 1901. Laid down: 4.1904. Launched: 1904. Trials: 1905. 29.11.1906 delivered at Genoa. 6.1.1907 arrived İstanbul. 8.1.1907 commissioned. 14.9.1916 sunk by mine north of Karaburnu.

Musul (Yd No 140) Ordered: 1901. Laid down: 4.1904. Launched: 1904. Trials: 1905. 29.11.1906 delivered at Genoa. 6.1.1907 arrived İstanbul. 8.1.1907 commissioned. 10.1918 decommissioned. 1924 returned to service. 1929 decommissioned. 1936

broken up.

Demirhisar Class

TYPE: Torpido bot (torpedo boat)

BUILDER: Schneider & Cie, Chalons-sur-Saone

DISPLACEMENT: 97t

DIMENSIONS: Loa 40.2m, Lpp 38.0m, B 4.4m, D 1.9m

HULL: Steel

MACHINERY: Steam, 1 shaft

ENGINE: 1 triple expansion 3 cyl, 2200ihp, Schneider & Cie

BOILERS: 2 Du Temple water-tube, Schneider & Cie

SPEED: (trials) 26kts, (1915) 16kts

BUNKERS: 11.2t coal

COMPLEMENT: (1907) 3 officers, 17–20 ratings
(1915) 32 Turks, 4 Germans

ARMAMENT: 2–37mm QF (H) (200), 3 TT 450mm (SK) (5)

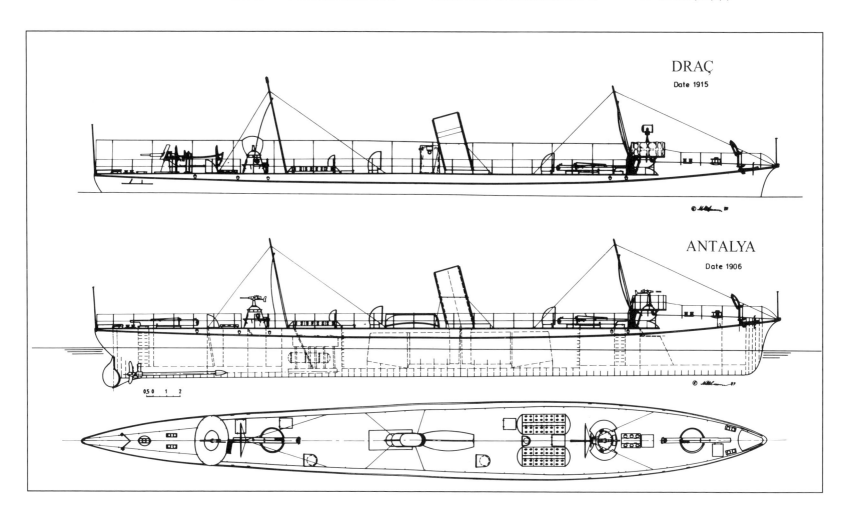

DRAÇ
Date 1915

ANTALYA
Date 1906

Demirhisar Ordered: 25.10.1906. Laid down: 1906. Launched: 1907. Trials: 1907. 1907 commissioned at İstanbul. 16.4.1915 beached and later blown up by the British at Chios.

Sultanhisar Ordered: 25.10.1906. Laid down: 1906. Launched: 1907. Trials: 1907. 1907 commissioned at İstanbul. 10.1918 decommissioned. 1924 returned to service. 1928 decommis-sioned. 1935 broken up.

Sivrihisar Ordered: 25.10.1906. Laid down: 1906. Launched: 1907. Trials: 1907. 1907 commissioned at İstanbul. 10.1918 decommissioned. 1924 returned to service. 1928 decommis-sioned. 1935 broken up.

Hamidabad Ordered: 25.10.1906. Laid down: 1906. Launched: 1907. Trials: 1907. 1907 commissioned at İstanbul.

31.10.1917 sunk by Russian destroyers at İğneada (Black Sea).

TORPEDO GUNBOATS

Peleng-i Derya Class

TYPE: Torpido gambot (torpedo gunboat)

BUILDER: Schiffswerft 'Germania' AG, Kiel

DISPLACEMENT: 755t normal, 900t full load

DIMENSIONS: Loa 75.5m, Lpp 72.0m, B 8.5m, D 2.9m

HULL: Steel

MACHINERY: Steam, 2 shafts

ENGINES: 2 triple expansion, 4700ihp, 'Germania' AG

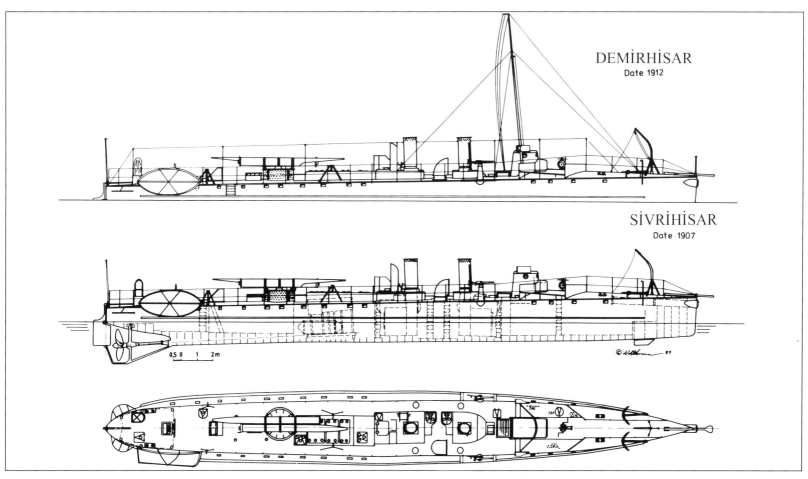

DEMİRHİSAR
Date 1912

SİVRİHİSAR
Date 1907

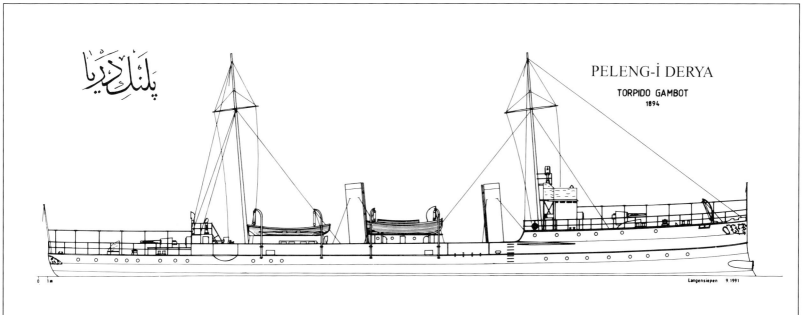

PELENG-İ DERYA
TORPIDO GAMBOT
1894

BOILERS: 4 locomotive type, 'Germania' AG

SPEED: (trials) 18kts, (1914) 14kts BUNKERS: 175t coal

COMPLEMENT: (1896) 9 officers, 11 NC officers, 60 ratings
(1914) 12 officers, 15 NC officers, 83 ratings

ARMAMENT: (1896) 2–105mm QF (K), 6–46mm QF (K), 3 TT 355mm (SK)
(1906) 2–120mm AF(K), 2–90mm QF (K), 3 TT 355mm (SK) 3 MG
(1915) 3–75mm QF (K) (300), 4–47mm QF (N) (600), 3 TT 355mm (SK)

Peleng-i Derya Ordered: 1887. Laid down: 1891. Launched: 1890. Trials: 16.5.1896. 22.5.1895 7 killed by boiler explosion at Eckernförde. Bridge, mast and forward funnel destroyed. 7.1896 left Kiel for İstanbul. 9.1896 commissioned. 1913 laid up in very poor condition. 9.1914 returned to service. 23.5.1915 torpedoed and sunk in shallow water by British submarine E 11 near Bakirköy (Bakirköy is today a district of İstanbul). 1915 wreck towed to İstanbul. 1920 broken up.

Nımet Ordered: 1887. Laid down: 1889. Launched: 30.1.1890. Trials: Delivered in sections by 'Germania' AG, Kiel, -39-. Instalments not kept up: order cancelled by 'Germania' AG in 1892. Work at İstanbul stopped 1893. Hull laid up and scrapped in 1909.

Sahın-i Derya

TYPE: Torpido gambot (torpedo gunboat)

BUILDER: Tersane-i Amire, İstanbul

DISPLACEMENT: 443t normal

DIMENSIONS: Lpp 60.9m, B 7.0m, D 2.4m

HULL: Steel

MACHINERY: Steam, 2 shafts

ENGINES: 2 triple expansion, 3500ihp, Tersane-i Amire

BOILERS: 4 locomotive type, Tersane-i Amire

BUNKERS: 100t coal

COMPLEMENT: (design) 8 officers, 75 ratings

ARMAMENT: (design 1889) 1–105mm QF (K), 6–47mm QF (H), 4 TT 355mm (SK)
(design 1895) 6–47mm QF (H), 4 TT

355mm (SK)

Sahın-i Derya Ordered: 5.1888. Laid down: 1889. Launched: 16.8.1892. Trials: 1895 engine and boiler installed. 1896 work stopped. 1909 machinery removed. 1909 sold for breaking up.

DESTROYERS

Samsun Class

TYPE: Muhrip (destroyer)

BUILDER: SA Chantiers et Ateliers de la Gironde, Bordeaux
(*Taşoz* Schneider & Cie, Nantes)

DISPLACEMENT: 284t

DIMENSIONS: Loa 58.2m, Lpp 56.3m, B 6.3m, D 2.8m

HULL: Steel

MACHINERY: Steam, 2 shafts

ENGINES: 2 triple expansion, 5950ihp, SACAG (*Taşoz* Schneider)

BOILERS: 2 Normand, SACAG (*Taşoz* Schneider)

SPEED: (1907) 28kts, (1912) 20kts, (1915) 17kts

BUNKERS: _

COMPLEMENT: (1907) 7 officers, 60 ratings
(1915) 74 Turks, 17 Germans

ARMAMENT: 1–65mm L/50 QF (C) (300), 6–47 L/50 QF (C) (1200), 2 TT 450mm (6)

Samsun Ordered: 1906. Laid down: 6.1906. Launched: 1907. Trials: 1907. 3.9.1907 commissioned at İstanbul. 10.1918 laid up at İstanbul. 1924 returned to service. 1932 decommissioned. 1949 broken up at Gölcük.

Yarhisar Ordered: 1906. Laid down: 1906. Launched: 1907. Trials: 1907.

1907 commissioned at İstanbul. 3.12.1915 torpedoed and sunk by British submarine E 11 off Yalova.

Taşoz Ordered: 1906. Laid down: 6.1906. Launched: 1907. Trials: 1907. 1907 commissioned at İstanbul. 10.1918 laid up at İstanbul. 1924–25 refitted by Deniz Fabriklari, İstanbul. 1925 returned to service. 1932 decommissioned. 1949 broken up at Gölcük.

Basra Ordered: 1906. Laid down: 6.1906. Launched: 1907. Trials: 1907. 3.9.1907 commissioned at İstanbul. 10.1918 laid up at İstanbul. 1924–25 refitted by Deniz Fabriklari, İstanbul. 1925 returned to service. 1932 decommissioned. 1949 broken up at Gölcük.

Muavenet-i Milliye Class

TYPE: Muhrip (destroyer)

BUILDER: Fr Schichau AG, Elbing

DISPLACEMENT: 765t

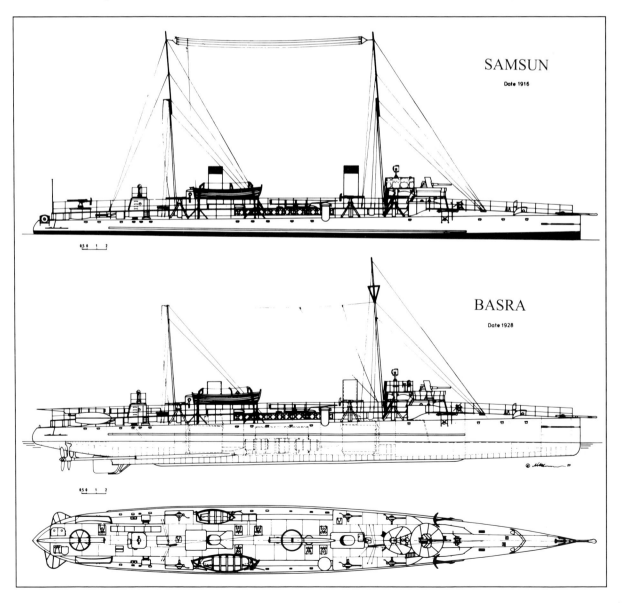

SAMSUN
Date 1916

BASRA
Date 1928

DIMENSIONS: Loa 74.0m, B 7.9m, D 3.0m

HULL: Steel

MACHINERY: Steam turbines, 2 shafts

ENGINES: 2 turbines, 17,700shp, Schichau

BOILERS: 2 marine, Schichau

SPEED: (trials) 32kts, (1912) 26kts

BUNKERS: 116t coal, 74t oil

COMPLEMENT: (1911) 6 officers, 84 ratings

(1915) 89 Turks, 23 Germans

ARMAMENT: (1910) 3 TT 450mm (SK) (8)
(1911) 2–75mm L/50 QF (150),
2–57mm L/50 QF (180), 3 TT 450mm (SK) (8)

Muavenet-i Milliye (Yd No 820)
Ordered: 1908. Laid down: 1908.
Launched: 20.3.1909. Trials: 1910.
Ordered as S 165 for German Navy.
3.1910 sold to Osmanli Govt. 17.8.1910
commissioned at Çanakkale. 10.1918
decommissioned. Storage vessel for the
Taskizak Tersane, İstanbul. 1953 breaking up commenced.

Yadigar-i Millet (Yd No 821)   Ordered:
1908. Laid down: 1908. Launched:
24.4.1909. Trials: 1910. Ordered as
S 166 for German Navy. 3.1910 sold to
Osmanli Govt. 17.8.1910 commissioned
at Çanakkale. 10.7.1917 bombed and
sunk by British aircraft at Istinye.
24.10.1917 refloated and drydocked at
Tersane-i Amire, İstanbul. 12.1918
moored in the Haliç, later sunk. 1924
raised and broken up in situ.

Nümune-Hamiyet (Yd No 822)
Ordered: 1908. Laid down: 1908.
Launched: 3.7.1909. Trials: 1910.

Ordered as S 167 for German Navy.
3.1910 sold to Osmanli Govt. 17.8.1910
commissioned at Canakkale. 10.1918
decommissioned. Storage vessel for the
Taskizak Tersane, İstanbul. 1953 breaking up commenced.

Gayret-i Vataniye (Yd No 823)
Ordered: 1908. Laid down: 1980.
Launched: 30.9.1909. Trials: 1910.
Ordered as S 168 for German Navy.
3.1910 sold to Osmanli Govt. 17.8.1910
commissioned at Çanakkale. 27.8.1916
grounded off Varna, blown up by crew
after all useful equipment had been
removed.

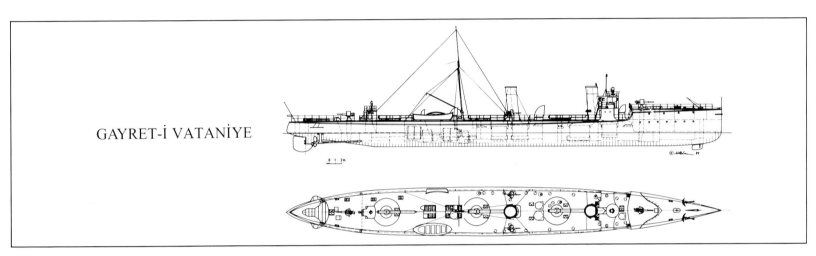

GAYRET-İ VATANİYE

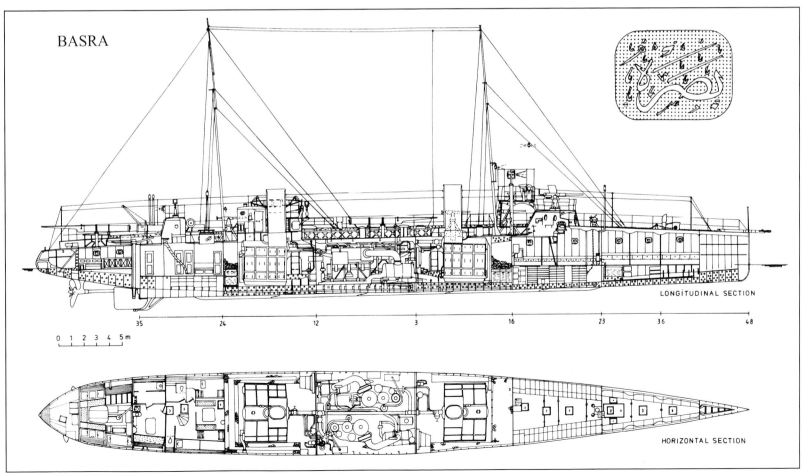

BASRA

SUBMARINES

Abdülhamid Class

TYPE: Denizalti (submarine)

BUILDER: Des Vignes, Chertsey, London

DISPLACEMENT: Surface 100t, submerged 160t

DIMENSIONS: Loa 30.5m, B 3.6m

HULL: Steel

MACHINERY: Steam, 1 shaft

ENGINE: 1- Lamm locomotive type, 250ihp

BOILER: 1 cyl.

SPEED: Surface 6kts, submerged 4kts

BUNKERS: 8t coal

COMPLEMENT: 7

ARMAMENT: 2 TT 356mm (WH) (2), 2–35mm MG (N)

Abdülhamid Ordered: 23.1.1886. Launched: 6.9.1886. Trials: 5.2.1887. Built as *Nordenfeld-2* in sections, fitted by Tersane-i Amire, İstanbul. After trials in the Haliç laid up at İstanbul-Kasimpaşa. 1889 landed at Tersane-i Amire, İstanbul. 1921 scrapped.

Abdülmecid Ordered: 23.1.1886. Launched: 4.8.1887. Built as *Nordenfeld-3* in sections, fitted by Tersane-i Amire, İstanbul. 4.8.1887 commissioned, laid up at İstanbul-Kasimpaşa. 1889 landed at Tersane-i Amire, İstanbul. 1921 scrapped.

Unnamed

TYPE: Denizalti (submarine)

BUILDER: Vickers Ltd, Newcastle-upon-Tyne

DISPLACEMENT: _

DIMENSIONS: _

HULL: Steel

MACHINERY: Motorship, 2 shafts

ENGINES: _

BOILERS: _

SPEED: _

BUNKERS: _

COMPLEMENT: _

ARMAMENT: _

Unnamed Ordered: 29.4.1914. To be delivered by 31.5.1915. Subcontracted by Vickers to Beardmore & Co, Dalmuir. Work stopped by 3.8.1914. Material was requisitioned in 8.1914 and used in the British submarines E 25 and E 26.

Unnamed Ordered: 29.4.1914. To be delivered by 30.6.1915. Subcontracted by Vickers to Beardmore & Co, Dalmuir. Work stopped by 3.8.1914. Material was requisitioned in 8.1914 and used in the British submarines E 25 and E 26.

Unnamed

TYPE: Denizalti (submarine)

BUILDER: Schneider & Cie, Chalons-sur-Saone

DISPLACEMENT: Surface 457t, submerged 670t

DIMENSIONS: Loa 56.2m, B 5.2m, D 3.0m

HULL: Steel

MACHINERY: Motorship, 2 shafts

ENGINES: 2 Schneider diesel/electric motors 2000bhp

BOILERS: _

SPEED: Surface 13.7kts, submerged 8.8kts

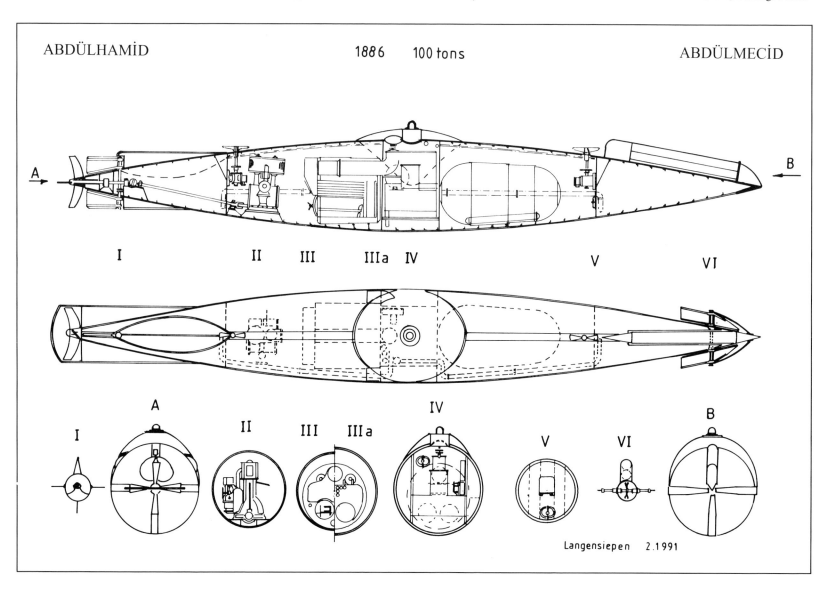

The submarine Müstecip Onbaşı (*ex* Turquoise) *in the drydock at İstanbul before being commissioned into the Ottoman navy. German official photograph*

BUNKERS: _

COMPLEMENT: (proj) 6 officers, 22 ratings

ARMAMENT: 4–450mm TT

Unnamed Ordered: 30.4.1914. To be delivered by 30.4.1916 at Toulon. Order cancelled by the French Govt by 5.11.1914.

Unnamed Ordered: 30.4.1914. To be delivered by 31.7.1916 at Toulon. Order cancelled by the French Govt by 5.11.1914.

Müstecip Onbaşı

TYPE: Denizalti (submarine)

BUILDER: Arsenal de Toulon, Toulon

DISPLACEMENT: Surface 393t, submerged 425t

DIMENSIONS: L 44.9m, B 3.9m, D 3.6m

HULL: Steel

MACHINERY: Motorship, 2 shafts

ENGINES: 2 Sautter-Harlé diesel/electric

motors 600bhp

SPEED: Surfaced 11kts, submerged 7kts

BUNKERS: _

COMPLEMENT: (11.1915) 1 officer, 5 ratings

ARMAMENT: Unarmed

Müstecip Onbaşı Ordered: 1907. Laid down: 1908. Launched: 3.8.1908. Trials: 1908. 1908 *Turquoise* Marine National (France). 30.10.1915 grounded off Akbas, captured by Ottoman forces. 31.10.1915 refloated. 5.11.1915 arrived İstanbul. 10.11.1915 commissioned, renamed *Müstecip Onbaşı*. 12.1915 stationary battery charge vessel for German U-boats. 10.1918 decommissioned. 1.7.1919 officially returned to the French Govt. 1921 broken up at İstanbul.

SEAGOING GUNBOATS

Akka Class

TYPE: Gambot (gunboat)

BUILDER: Money Wigram, Blackwall, London (*Akka* J & R White, Southampton)

DISPLACEMENT: (1860) 196t bm, (1898) 120t

DIMENSIONS: Loa 35.4m, B 6.0m, D 2.7m

HULL: (1860) wood, (1898) steel

MACHINERY: Steam, 1 shaft

ENGINE: (1860) 1 single acting 1 cyl, 225ihp, Maudslay
(1898) 1 triple expansion, 400ihp, Tersane-i Amire

BOILER: (1860) 1 _, Money Wigram (Akka White)
(1898) 1 double ended, Tersane-i Amire

SPEED: (trials) 8kts, (1898) 10kts

BUNKERS: 80t coal

COMPLEMENT: (1860) 70, (1898) 45

ARMAMENT: (1858) 4–24pdr
(1876) 4–26pdr, 1–16pdr
(1885) 3–76mm QF (K), 1–37mm QF (K)
(1898) 4–76mm QF (K), 1–37mm QF (H)
(1915) 1–57mm QF, 2–47mm QF

Akka Ordered: 1857. Laid down: 1859. Launched: 1859. Trials: 1859. 24.9.1859 left Southampton for İstanbul. 12.1859 commissioned. 1879 laid up at İstanbul. 1883 renewed by Tersane-i Amire, İstanbul. 1885 returned to service, based at Basra. 1901 decommissioned. 1903 breaking up at Basra.

Şevket Nüma Ordered: 1857. Laid down: 1859. Launched: 1859. Trials: 1859. 3.1860 commissioned. 1879 laid up at İstanbul. 1892 drydocked for

refurbishment by Tersane-i Amire, İstanbul. 31.8.1994 new steel hull launched. 1898 returned to service. 1904 Sea Cadet training ship. 1909 decommissioned. 4.1915 reactivated. 10.1918 decommissioned. 1925 sold for breaking up.

Varna/Necmifeşan Ordered: 1857. Laid down: 1858. Launched: 1859. Trials: 1859. 3.1860 commissioned as *Varna*. 1879 renamed *Necmifeşan*. 1902 engine and boiler removed. Stationary at Sayier. 8.1908 towed to İstanbul, laid up. 11.1909 sold for breaking up.

Sünne Ordered: 1857. Laid down: 1858. Launched: 1859. Trials: 1859. 8.1859 commissioned. 9.10.1877 sunk by Russian mine in the mouth of the Danube.

Musul Class

TYPE: Gambot (gunboat)

BUILDER: Tersane-i Amire, İstanbul

DISPLACEMENT: 276t bm, 125t

DIMENSIONS: Lpp 39.9m, B 6.4m, D 2.8m

HULL: Wood

MACHINERY: Steam, 1 shaft

ENGINE: 1–1 cyl

BOILER: 1 _

SPEED: (trials) 9kts

BUNKERS: 25t coal

COMPLEMENT: 35

ARMAMENT: (1866) 4–19pdr
(1881) 2–57mm QF (K), 2–37mm RC

Musul Ordered: 1863. Laid down: 1865. Launched: 1865. Trials: 1866. 1866 commissioned. 1909 decommissioned.

Seyyar Ordered: 1863. Laid down: 1865. Launched: 1865. Trials: 1866. 1866 commissioned. 1891 stationary at İstanbul-Arnutköy. 1909 decommissioned.

Sahır

TYPE: Gambot (gunboat)

BUILDER: J White, West Cowes, Isle of Wight

DISPLACEMENT: 259t bm, 163t

DIMENSIONS: Lpp 40.4m, B 6.7m, D 3.2m

HULL: Wood

MACHINERY: Steam, 1 shaft

ENGINE: 1–1 cyl

BOILER: 1 _

SPEED: (trials) 8kts

BUNKERS: 20t coal

COMPLEMENT: 35

ARMAMENT: (1866) 4–11pdr
(1880) 2–76mm QF, 2 MG

Sahır Ordered: 1864. Laid down: 1866.
Launched: 1866. Trials: 1866. 1866
commissioned. 1900 decommissioned.
11.11.1909 sold for breaking up.

İntibah Class

TYPE: Gambot (gunboat)

BUILDER: Tersane-i Amire, İstanbul

DISPLACEMENT: 163t bm

DIMENSIONS: Lpp 40.4m, B 6.7m, D 3.2m

HULL: Wood

MACHINERY: Steam, 1 shaft

ENGINE: 1–1 cyl

BOILER: 1 _

SPEED: (trials) 12kts, (1880) 8kts

BUNKERS: 20t coal

COMPLEMENT: 35

ARMAMENT: (1866) 4–18pdr
(1877) 2–100mm, 1–57mm
(1880) 4–76mm QF (K), 2 MG (H)

İntibah Ordered: 1865. Laid down:
1866. Launched: 1867. Trials: 1867.
1867 commissioned. 126.1.1878 sunk
by Russian torpedo at Batumi.

Müjderesan Ordered: 1865. Laid
down: 1865. Launched: 1866. Trials:
1866. 1866 commissioned. 1888–89
refitted by Tersane-i Amire, İstanbul.
1889 based at Basra. 1908 decommissioned, sold for breaking up at Basra.

Ziver-i Derya Ordered: 1865. Laid
down: 1865. Launched: 1866. Trials:
1866. 1866 commissioned.

1909 decommissioned.

Saheddın

TYPE: Gambot (gunboat)

BUILDER: Tersane-i Amire, İstanbul

DISPLACEMENT: 163t bm

DIMENSIONS: Lpp 40.4m, B 6.7m, D
3.2m

HULL: Wood

MACHINERY: Steam, 1 shaft

ENGINE: 1–1 cyl

BOILER: 1 _

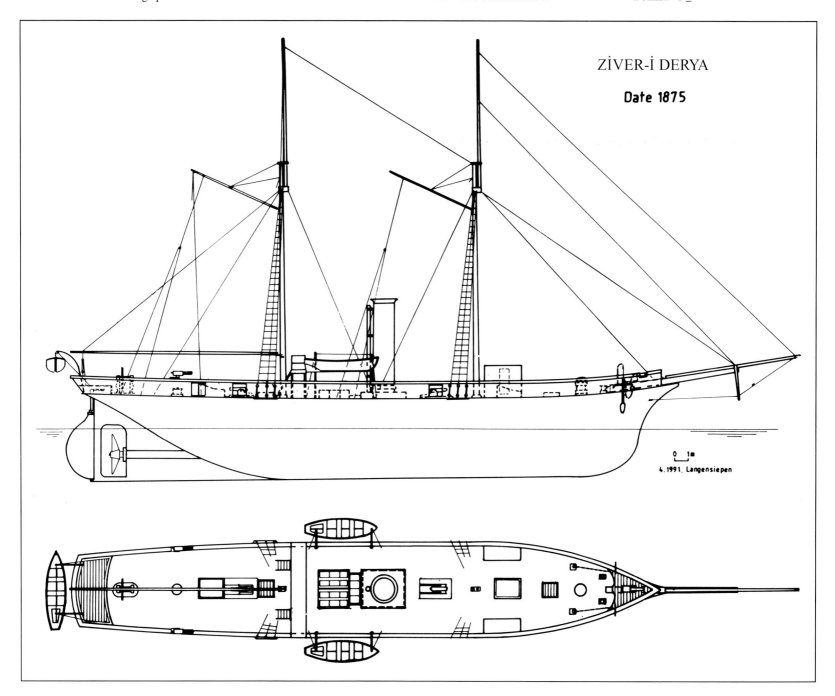

ZİVER-İ DERYA

Date 1875

0   1m

4.1991. Langensiepen

SPEED: (trials) 12 kts, (1880) 8kts

BUNKERS: 20t coal

COMPLEMENT: 35

ARMAMENT: (1866) 4–18pdr
(1877) 2–100mm
(1880) 4–76mm QF (K), 2 MG (H)

Saheddın Ordered: 1865. Laid down:
1867. Launched: 1868. Trials: 1868.
1868 commissioned. 1892–96 refurbished by Tersane-i Amire, İstanbul.
1909 stationary at Tripoli. 3.10.1911 run
on the rocks at Tripoli and scuttled.

Aynalikavak Class

TYPE: Gambot (gunboat)

BUILDER: Tersane-i Amire, İstanbul

DISPLACEMENT: 195t

DIMENSIONS: Lpp 35.9m, B 5.3m,
D 1.8m

HULL: Wood

MACHINERY: Steam, 1 shaft

ENGINE 1–1 cyl

BOILER: 1 _

SPEED: (trials) 10 kts, (1877) 7 kts

BUNKERS: 20t coal

COMPLEMENT: 35

ARMAMENT: (1868) 1–8pdr, 1–4pdr
(1874) 1–8pdr, 2–4pdr
(1888) 1–57mm QF (K), 2 MG

Aynalikavak Ordered: 1867. Laid
down: 1867. Launched: 1869. Trials:
1869. 1869 commissioned. 1888 refitted
by Tersane-i Amire, İstanbul. 1909
decommissioned.

Yalıköskü Ordered: 1867. Laid down:
1867. Launched: 1867. Trials: 1869.
1869 commissioned. 1898 service vessel
for government personnel. 1909 decommissioned.

Rodos Class

TYPE: Gambot (gunboat)

BUILDER: Tersane-i Amire, İstanbul

DISPLACEMENT: 203t bm

DIMENSIONS: Lpp 35.7m, B 5.3m,
D 1.8m

HULL: Wood

MACHINERY: Steam, 1 shaft

ENGINE: 1–1 cyl, Tersane-i Amire,
İstanbul

BOILER: 1 _

SPEED: (trials) 12kts, (1875) 8kts

BUNKERS: 20t coal

COMPLEMENT: 35

ARMAMENT: (1870) 4–11pd
(1885) 2–57mm QF, 2 MG (H)

Rodos Ordered: 1868. Laid down:
1869. Launched: 1870. Trials: 1870.
1870 commissioned. 1890 laid up at
İstanbul. 1899 decommissioned. 1903
sold for breaking up.

İstanköy Ordered: 1868. Laid down:
1869. Launched: 1871. Trials: 1874.
1874 commissioned. 1902 stationary at
Vathi (Samos). 1909 decommissioned,
towed to İstanbul. 1910 sold for breaking up.

Firat Class

TYPE: Gambot (gunboat)

BUILDER: Tersane-i Amire, İstanbul

DISPLACEMENT: 197t

DIMENSIONS: Lpp 37.0m, B 6.5m,
D 2.4m

HULL: Wood

MACHINERY: Steam, 1 shaft

ENGINE: 1 compound 2 cyl, 280ihp,
Tersane-i Amire

BOILERS: 1 cyl, Tersane-i Amire

SPEED: (trials) 10kts

BUNKERS: 80t coal

COMPLEMENT: 55

ARMAMENT: (1885) 4–76mm QF (K),
2–57mm QF (K)
(1895) 2–90mm QF (K), 1–47mm QF
(K), 1–37mm QF (H)
(1900) 2–37mm QF (H), 2 Gatling guns

Firat Ordered: 1881. Laid down: 1881.
Launched: 1883. Trials: 1885. 1885
commissioned. 2.1897 badly damaged
by gunfire of Greek gunboat *Aphroessa*
in the Gulf of Narda. 1899 returned into
service. 1912 decommissioned.

Şat Ordered: 1881. Laid down: 1881.
Launched: 1883. Trials: 1885. 1885
commissioned. 1905 engine and boiler
removed. 1906 stationary at Tarabya in
the Bosporus. 8.1908 laid up at İstanbul-

The gunboat İstanköy *in the Dardanelles in 1897.* Güleryüz

Kasimpaşa. 11.1909 sold for breaking
up.

Nasr-ü Hüda Class

TYPE: Gambot (gunboat)

BUILDER: Tersane-i Amire, İstanbul

DISPLACEMENT: 198t

DIMENSIONS: Lpp 38.6m, B 5.4m,
D 1.9m

HULL: Steel

MACHINERY: Steam, 1 shaft

ENGINE: 1 triple expansion vertical,
400ihp, Tersane-i Amire

BOILER: 1 double ended, Tersane-i
Amire

SPEED: (trials) 10kts, (1915) 8kts

BUNKERS: 80t coal

COMPLEMENT: 9 officers, 36 ratings

ARMAMENT: (design) 4–76mm QF (K),
2–37mm QF (K), 2 TT (SK)
(1904) 1–76mm QF (K), 2–47mm QF
(K), 1–37mm QF (H)
(1915) 1–57mm QF (K), 2–47mm QF
(K)

Nasr-ü Hüda Ordered: 10.1890. Laid
down: 1903. Launched: 1903. Trials:
1904. 1904 commissioned. 1914 laid up.
4.1915 reactivated. 6.1917 decommissioned. 1923 sold for breaking up.

Seyyar Ordered: 10.1890. Laid down:
1896. Launched: 1906. Trials: 1906.
1906 commissioned. 1914 laid up.
4.1915 reactivated as mine hunting boat.
10.1918 decommissioned. 1923 sold for
breaking up.

Barika-i Zafer Ordered: 10.1890. Laid
down: 1896. Launched: 1904. Trials:
1908. 1908 commissioned. 10.1918
decommissioned. 3.1922 guard vessel at

İstanbul. 1923 decommissioned. 1926
sold for breaking up.

Nur-ül Bahir

TYPE: Gambot (gunboat)

BUILDER: MacLaren & Wilson, Genoa

DISPLACEMENT: 450t

DIMENSIONS: Loa _m, Lpp 52.0m,
B 7.8m, D 4.4m

HULL: Steel

MACHINERY: Steam, 1 shaft

ENGINES: 2 compound 2 cyl, 300ihp,
MacLaren & Wilson

BOILER: 1 _

SPEED: (1906) 12kts

BUNKERS: _

COMPLEMENT: _

ARMAMENT: (1906) 2–76mm QF

Nur-ü Bahir Ordered: 1897. Laid
down; 1898. Launched: 1898. Trials:
8.1898. Ordered by the Sultan of
Morocco, intended name: *Siri ül Türk*.
Sold to Osmanli Govt while under construction. 12.1898 renamed *Nur-ül
Bahir* Osmanli Reij İdaresi, İstanbul.
1906 transferred to Osmanli Bahriye,
commissioned. 1913 decommissioned.

Kastamonu Class

TYPE: Gambot (gunboat)

BUILDER: Gebrüder Sachsenberg,
Rosslau

DISPLACEMENT: 240t full load

DIMENSIONS: Loa 42.2m, Lpp 40.4m,
B 5.8m, D 1.8m

HULL: Steel

MACHINERY: Steam, 1 shaft

ENGINE: 1 triple expansion vertical, 460ihp, Gebrüder Sachsenberg

BOILER: 1 _Gebrüder Sachsenberg

SPEED: (trials) 12kts

BUNKERS: 40t coal

COMPLEMENT: 3 officers, 9 ratings

ARMAMENT: 1–75mm QF (K) (200), 1–37mm QF (K) (1600)

Kastamonu (Yd No 544) Ordered: 15.8.1904. Laid down: 10.1904. Launched: 4.1905. Trials: 4.1905. Built and sailed to İstanbul under the name *İzmir*. 23.4.1905 left Hamburg for İstanbul under own power. 7.1905 commissioned. 7.12.1912 sunk by gunfire by Italian cruiser *Piemonte* and destroyer *Artigliere* at Konfida (Red Sea).

The gunboat Ayintab *at the builder's yard, Châlons-sur-Saone.* Güleryüz

Yozgat (Yd No 545) Ordered: 15.8.1904. Laid down: 10.1904. Launched: 4.1905. Trials: .8.1905. Built and sailed to İstanbul under the name *Beyrut*. 9.1905 left Hamburg for İstanbul under own power. 10.1905 commissioned. 10.12.1912 sunk by gunfire by Russian destroyers at Kefken Ada.

Marmaris

TYPE: Gambot (gunboat)

BUILDER: SA des Ateliers et Chantiers de la Loire, Nantes

DISPLACEMENT: 422t normal, 531t full load

DIMENSIONS: Loa 52.4m, Lpp 50.0m, B 7.5m, D 2.4m

HULL: Steel

MACHINERY: Steam, 1 shaft

ENGINE: 1 triple expansion vertical, 950ihp, Loire

BOILERS: 2-cyl, Loire

SPEED: (trials) 14.8kts, (1914) 11kts

BUNKERS: 75t coal

COMPLEMENT: 12 officers, 54 ratings

ARMAMENT: (1908) 4–65mm QF (C) (612), 2–37mm QF (C) (551), 1 TT 450mm (SK) (4) (TT removed 1908)

Marmaris Ordered: 22.1.1906. Laid down: 1906. Launched: 4.1907. Trials: 11.1907. 5.2.1908 arrived İstanbul. 2.1908 commissioned. 2.6.1915 heavily damaged by gunfire by British gunboat *Odin* south of Amara (River Tigris), beached.

Taşköprü Class

TYPE: Gambot (gunboat)

BUILDER: Schneider & Cie, Châlons-sur-Saone

DISPLACEMENT: 213t normal. 315t full load

DIMENSIONS: Loa 47.0m, Lpp 45.0m, B 6.2m, D 1.9m

HULL: Steel

MACHINERY: Steam, 1 shaft

ENGINE: 1 triple expansion vertical, 480ihp, SAAC Loire

BOILER: 1 Scotch, SAAC Loire

SPEED: (trials) 12kts

BUNKERS: 44t coal

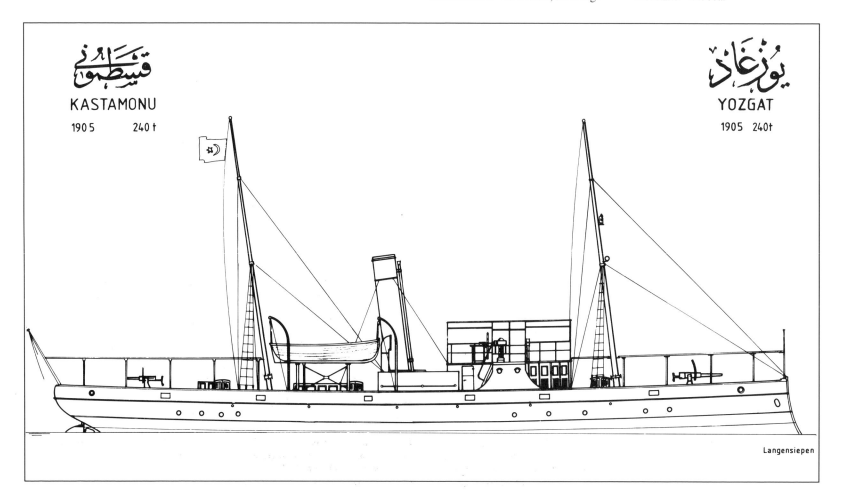

KASTAMONU 1905 240t

YOZGAT 1905 240t

Langensiepen

N

COMPLEMENT: 9 officers, 38 ratings, (1915) 10 officers (9 Turks, 1 German), 42 ratings

ARMAMENT: (1908) 2–47mm QF L/50 (C) (1200), 2–7.65mm MG (31,000), 1 TT 450mm (SK) (4) (TT removed 1908)
(1915) 1–47 mm QF L/50 (C) (1200), 2–7.65mm MG (31,000)

Taşköprü Ordered: 1906. Laid down: 1907. Launched: 1907. Trials: 1908. 1908 commissioned. 10.12.1915 sunk by gunfire from Russian destroyers at Kefken Ada.

Nevşehir Ordered: .1906. Laid down: 1907. Launched: 1908. Trials: 1908. 1908 commissioned. 30.1.1915 sunk by Turkish mine near Rumelikavagi (Bosporus).

Gökçedağ Ordered: 1906. Laid down: 1907. Launched: 1907. Trials: 1908. 1908 commissioned. 7.12.1912 sunk by Italian cruiser *Piemonte* and destroyer *Artigliere* off Konfida (Red Sea).

Refahiye Ordered: 1906. Laid down: 1907. Launched: 1907. Trials: . .1908. 1908 commissioned. 7.12.1912 sunk by Italian cruiser *Piemonte* and destroyer *Artigliere* off Konfida (Red Sea).

Ayintab Ordered: 1906. Laid down: 1907. Launched: 1907. Trials: 1907. 17.12.1907 arrived İstanbul. 1.1908 commissioned. 7.1.1912 sunk by Italian cruiser *Piemonte* and destroyer *Artigliere* off Konfida (Red Sea).

Malatya Ordered: 1906. Laid down: 1907. Launched: 1907. Trials: 1907. 17.12.1907 arrived İstanbul. 1.1908 commissioned. 17.9.1916 damaged by Russian mine east of Karaburnu (Black Sea). 19.9.1916 towed to İstanbul. Guns and equipment removed, barrack vessel. 1921 sold for breaking up.

Seddülbahir Ordered: 1906. Laid down: 1907. Launched: 1907. Trials: 1907. 5.2.1908 arrived İstanbul. 2.1908 commissioned. 9.1909 last mention in Ottoman records.

Ordu Ordered: 1906. Laid down: 1907. Launched: 1907. Trials: 1907. 5.2.1908 arrived İstanbul. 2.1908 commissioned. 7.1.1912 sunk by gunfire of Italian cruiser *Piemonte* and destroyer *Artigliere* off Konfida (Red Sea).

Bafra Ordered: 1906. Laid down: 1907. Launched: 1907. Trials: 1907. 17.12.1907 arrived İstanbul. 1.1908 commissioned. 7.1.1912 sunk by gunfire of Italian cruiser *Piemonte* and destroyer *Artigliere* off Konfida (Red Sea).

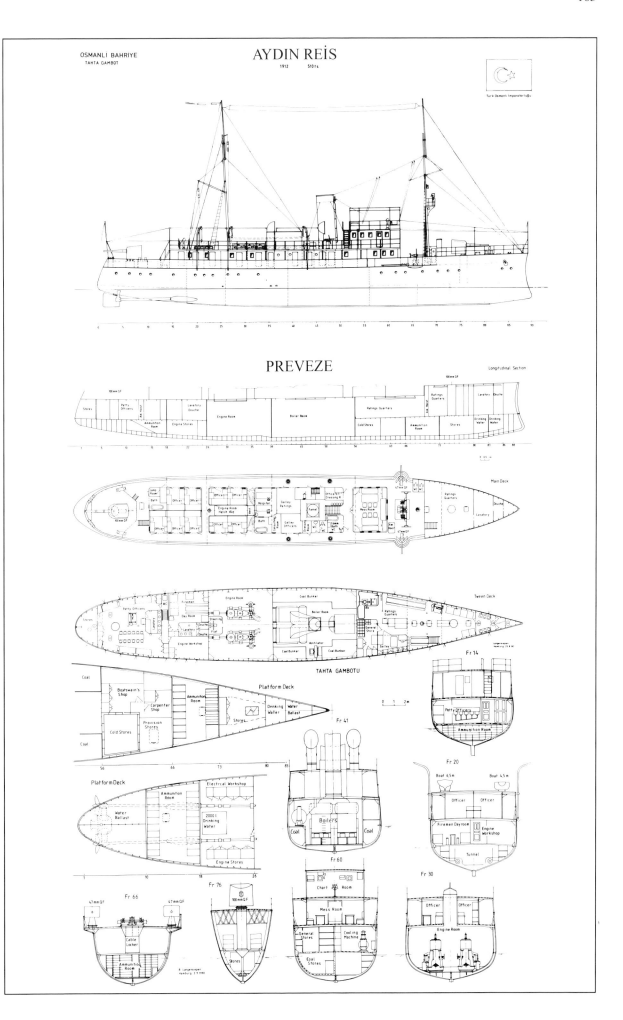

Aydin Reis Class

TYPE: Tahta gambot (gunboat)

BUILDER: SA des Chantiers & Ateliers de St Nazaire (Penhöet)

DISPLACEMENT: 503t

DIMENSIONS: Loa 54.5m, Lpp _m, B 8.2m, D 2.4m

HULL: Steel

MACHINERY: Steam, 2 shafts

ENGINES: 2 triple expansion vertical, 1025ihp, SACA St Nazaire

BOILERS: 3 Scotch, SACA St Nazaire

SPEED: (trials) 14kts, (1915) 10kts

BUNKERS: _

COMPLEMENT: 14 officers, 61 ratings

ARMAMENT: (1914) 2–100mm QF (C) (35), 2–47mm QF (C) (1500), 2–7.6mm MG (H) (35,000)
(1919) 2–76mm QF (K) (500) (Sakiz and Bürak Reis disarmed in 1919; 2–47mm AF (C) in 1924; disarmed again 1930)
(Aydin Reis 1936) 2–57mm QF

Aydin Reis Ordered: 4.1911. Laid down: 1911. Launched: 6.1912. Trials: 1912. 1912 laid up at St Nazaire.

13.6.1914 arrived İstanbul. 2.1919 anti-smuggling duty, Black Sea. 16.9.1920 left Samsun to be interned at Novorossiysk (USSR). 16.5.1921 returned to Turkish Nationalist Forces. 1925 Sea Cadet training vessel. 1926 survey vessel. 1949 decommissioned. 1954 sold for breaking up.

Preveze Ordered: 4.1911. Laid down: 1911. Launched: 1.1912. Trials: 1912. 1912 laid up at St Nazaire. 13.6.1914 arrived İstanbul. 6.1914 commissioned. 1915 Sea Cadet training vessel. 23.10.1918 interned at İstanbul. 2.1919 anti-smuggling duty, Black Sea. 30.9.1920 left Trabzon to be interned at Novorossiysk (USSR). 16.5.1921 returned to Turkish Nationalist Forces. 1926 decommissioned.

Sakiz Ordered: 4.1911. Laid down: 1911. Launched: 1912. Trials: 1912. 1912 laid up at St Nazaire. 13.6.1914 arrived İstanbul. 6.1914 commissioned. 23.10.1918 interned at İstanbul. 1924 returned to service. 1930 stationary HQ ship for submarines at Gölcük. 1935 decommissioned, sold for breaking up.

Bürak Reis Ordered: 4.1911. Laid down: 1911. Launched: 5.1912. Trials: 1912. 1912 laid up at St Nazaire. 13.6.1914 arrived İstanbul. 6.1914 commissioned. 10.1.1915 damaged by Russian mine off Bosporus. 1915 returned to service. 23.10.1918 interned at İstanbul. 1924 returned to service. 1932 survey vessel. 1953 capsized at

Heybeliada, near İstanbul, salvaged and laid up. 1955 sold for breaking up.

İsa Reis Class

TYPE: Sac gambot (gunboat)

BUILDER: SA des Forges & Chantiers de la Mediterranée, Granville

DISPLACEMENT: 413t

DIMENSIONS: Loa 47.0m, Lpp _m, B 7.9m, D 1.3m

HULL: Steel/wood

MACHINERY: Steam, 2 shafts

ENGINES: 2 triple expansion vertical, 850ihp, SAFC Granville

BOILERS: 3 Scotch, SAFC Granville

SPEED: (trials) 14kts, (1915) 11kts, (1932) 12kts

BUNKERS: _

COMPLEMENT: 12 officers, 48 ratings

ARMAMENT: (1914) 3–76mm QF (C) (100), 2–47mm QF (C) (1200), 2–7,6mm MG (H) (31,700)
(1926) 2–76mmQF (C), 2–47mm QF (C)
(1948) Unarmed

İsa Reis Ordered: 4.1911. Laid down:

1911. Launched: 11.1911. Trials: 1912. 1912 laid up at Granville. 13.6.1914 arrived İstanbul. 6.1914 commissioned. 11.7.1915 damaged by Russian mine off Bosporus. 1915–1924 laid up at İstanbul. 1924–26 refitted by D C Gölcük Tersane, Gölcük. 1926 customs vessel. 1932 minesweeper. 1948 surveying vessel. 1955 decommissioned. 1964 broken up at Seyman.

Durak Reis/Kemal Reis Ordered: 4.1911. Laid down: 1911. Launched: 2.1912. Trials: 4.1912. 1912 laid up at Granville. 13.6.1914 arrived İstanbul. 6.1914 commissioned. 16.1.1916 renamed *Kemal Reis*. 23.10.1918 interned at İstanbul. 1924–26 refitted by D C Gölcük Tersane, Gölcük. 1926 customs vessel. 1932 minesweeper. 1948 surveying vessel. 1955 decommissioned. 1964 sold to M K E, Seyman, for breaking up. 1973 broken up.

Hizir Reis Ordered: 4.1911. Laid down: 1911. Launched: 10.4.1912. Trials: 6.1912. 1912 laid up at Granville. 13.6.1914 arrived İstanbul. 6.1914 commissioned. 21.1.1915 damaged by Turkish mine near Rumelikavagi (Bosporus). 1916 returned to service. 6.7.1919 seized by Greek forces at İzmir. 1922 returned to Turkey. 1932 minesweeper. 1948 stationary pilot vessel at İzmir. 1952 decommissioned. 1958 sold, converted into a general cargo motorship. 1960 *Emin*. 1981 *Murat Ayanoglu*. 1982 *Kaptan Cavit*.

RIVER GUNBOATS

Doğan

TYPE: Nehir-gambot (river gunboat)

BUILDER: Gebr. Wiemann, Brandenburg

DISPLACEMENT: 250t, 128gt, 12nt

DIMENSIONS: Loa 35.5m, Lpp 34.8m, B 6.3m, D 1.6m

HULL: Steel

MACHINERY: Steam, 1 shaft

ENGINE: 1 triple expansion vertical, 350ihp, Wiemann

BOILER: 1 water-tube, A Borsing

SPEED: (1915) 6.5kts

BUNKERS: _

COMPLEMENT: (1915) 30 Turks, 5 Germans
(1916) 42

ARMAMENT: (7.1915) 1–60mm QF,

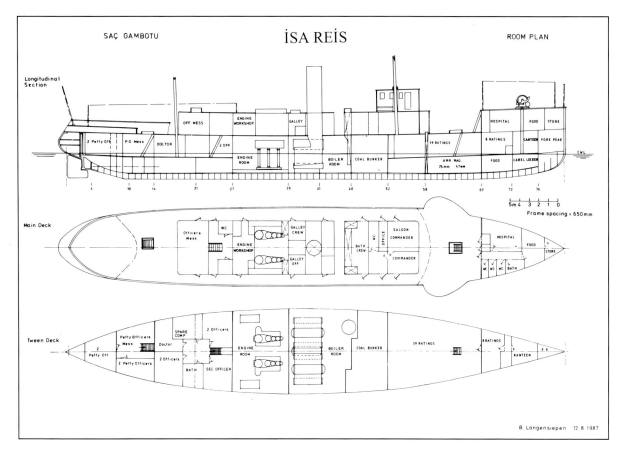

SAÇ GAMBOTU   İSA REİS   ROOM PLAN

Longitudinal Section

Main Deck

Tween Deck

5m 4 3 2 1 0
Frame spacing = 650mm

B. Langensiepen 12.8.1987

4–47mm QF, 1–37mm QF
(2.1916) 1–60mm QF, 1–57mm QF,
2–47mm QF, 1–37mm QF, 1 MG

Doğan (Yd No 140) Ordered: 10.1911.
Laid down: 4.1911. Launched: 4.1911.
Trials: 4.1911. 17.9.1912 *Pionier* R
Woenckhaus, Hamburg. 1913 based at
Baghdad as a river tug. 5.1915 chartered
by Osmanli Bahriye. 17–29.6.1915 refit-
ted by Bagdat Demiryol Insaat,
Baghdad. 2.7.1915 commissioned.
26.2.1917 heavily damaged by gunfire
by British gunboat *Mantis* near Aziziye.
Run aground.

Selmanpak

TYPE: Nehir-gambot (river gunboat)

BUILDER: Yarrow & Co, Scotstown

DISPLACEMENT: 98t

DIMENSIONS: Loa 38.4m, Lpp 31.0m,
B 6.1m, D 0.6m

HULL: Steel

MACHINERY: Steam, 1 shaft

ENGINE: 1 triple expansion, 175ihp,
Yarrow & Co

BOILER: 1, Yarrow & Co

SPEED: 10kts

BUNKERS: 5t coal, 10t oil

COMPLEMENT: (1916) 1 officer, 25 ratings

ARMAMENT: (12.1915) 1–102mm QF,
1–76mm QF, 1–57mm QF, 3 MG
(5.1916) 1–76mm QF, 1–75mm QF,
1–57mm, 3 MG

Selmanpak Ordered: 2.1915. Laid
down: 1915. Launched: 11.1915. Trials:
11.1915. 11.1915 *Firefly* Royal Navy.
1.12.1915 captured by Ottoman Army
near Elhan. 12.12.1915 commissioned.
26.2.1917 captured by British gunboat
Tarantula near Aziziye. 4.3.1917 *Firefly*
Royal Navy. 14.6.1924 sunk on the
Euphrates.

YACHTS
AND SURVEY VESSELS

Sultaniye

TYPE: Yat (yacht)

BUILDER: C J Mare, Blackwall, London

DISPLACEMENT: 2909t bm, 3095t

DIMENSIONS: Lpp 119.2m, B 12.2m, D
9.0m, D 4.8m

HULL: Wood

MACHINERY: Steam, side paddle

ENGINE: 1–2 cyl, 750ihp, Maudslay

BOILERS: 2 _

SPEED: (1870) 15kts

BUNKERS: 300t coal

COMPLEMENT: 140

ARMAMENT: (1861) 4–14pdr
(1890) 2–120mm (K), 2–37mm
(1896) 2 RV

Sultaniye Ordered: 1851. Laid down:
1852. Launched: 23.12.1852. Trials:
1853. 1853 *Feyz-i Cihat* Egyptian Navy,
frigate and yacht. 1862 rebuilt by
Forrester & Co. 1862 presented by
Ismail Paşa to Sultan Abdül Aziz. 1862
commissioned, renamed *Sultaniye*. 1905
laid up at İzmir. 10.1911 loaded with
stone and made ready to scuttle as
blockship. 20.4.1912 scuttled off
Yenikale (Bay of İzmir).

Talia

TYPE: Avizo (despatch vessel)

BUILDER: Samuda & Son, London

DISPLACEMENT: 1058t

DIMENSIONS: Lpp 76.2m, B 9.1m,
D 3.6m

HULL: Wood

MACHINERY: Steam, side paddle

ENGINES: 1–2 cyl, 200ihp, J Penn

BOILERS: 2 _

SPEED: (trials) 17.7kts

BUNKERS: 150t coal

COMPLEMENT: 130

ARMAMENT: (1864) 4–11pdr
(1880) 3–90mm (K), 2–37mm (K)
(1895) 4–57mm QF, 2–25,4mm (H)

Talia Ordered: 1863. Laid down: 1863.
Launched: 1863. Trials: 1.1864. 3.1864
commissioned. 1899 decommissioned,
laid up at İstanbul. 11.1909 sold for
breaking up.

Süreyya

TYPE: Yat (yacht)

BUILDER: Samuda Bros, London

DISPLACEMENT: 672t bm

DIMENSIONS: Lpp 56.1m, B 8.5m,
D 2.1m

HULL: Iron

MACHINERY: Steam, side paddle

ENGINES: 2–2cyl, 610ihp, J Penn

BOILERS: 4 _

SPEED: (trials) 14kts

BUNKERS: 120t coal

COMPLEMENT: 90

ARMAMENT: (1865) 2–11pdr, 2–8pdr
(1880) 2–57mm QF

Süreyya Ordered: 1864. Laid down:
1865. Launched: 1865. Trials: 1865.
1865 commissioned. 1890–92 refitted
by Tersane-i Amire, İstanbul. 1899 stationary for the Vali of İzmir. 1908
returned to İstanbul from İzmir. 1908
decommissioned. 1921 sold for breaking
up.

İzzeddin

TYPE: Avizo (despatch vessel)

BUILDER: Thames Iron Works, London

DISPLACEMENT: 1058t

DIMENSIONS: Lpp 76.2m, B 9.1m,
D 3.6m

HULL: Wood

MACHINERY: Steam, side paddle

ENGINES: 1–2 cyl, 200ihp, J Penn

BOILERS: 2 _

SPEED: (trials) 17kts

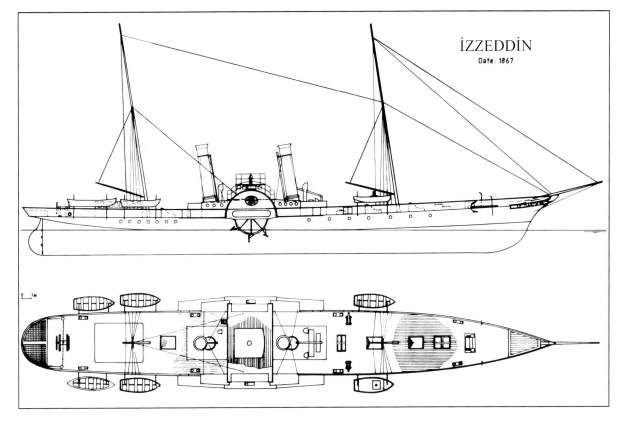

İZZEDDİN
Date: 1867

BUNKERS: 150t coal

COMPLEMENT: 130

ARMAMENT: (1865) 4–11pdr
(1874) 1–120mm (K), 3–76mm (K)
(1902) 2–76mm (K), 1–37mm QF (K)
(1908) Disarmed

Izzeddin (Yd No 3f) Ordered: 1864.
Laid down: 1864. Launched: 1865.
Trials: 1865. 1865 commissioned.
11.1885–8.1886 refitted by Tersane-i
Amire, İstanbul. 1908 stationary at İ
zmir. 14.1.1914 towed to İstanbul.
9.1914 stationary work ship at İstinye.
10.1918 decommissioned. 1929 broken
up.

Fuad

TYPE: Avizo (despatch vessel)

BUILDER: Millwall Iron Works, London

DISPLACEMENT 1075t

DIMENSIONS: Lpp 76.2m, B 9.1m,
D 3.6m

HULL: Iron

MACHINERY: Steam, side paddle

ENGINE: 1-compound 2 cyl, 200ihp,
Ravenhill

BOILERS: 2 _

SPEED: (trials) 12kts

BUNKERS: 150t coal

COMPLEMENT: 130

ARMAMENT: (1865) 4–11pdr
(1880) 2–80mm, 2–57mm
(1890) 2–75mm QF (K), 2–25.4mm (H)

Fuad Ordered: 1864. Laid down: 1864.
Launched: 27.4.1865. Trials: 1865. 1865
commissioned. 1908 stationary at
Selanik. 5.11.1912 stationary hospital
vessel at Selanik. 15.11.1912 seized by
Greek Govt. 1912 *Fuad* Royal Greek
Navy. 1919 out of service. 1921 broken
up.

İsmaıl

TYPE: Avizo (despatch vessel)

BUILDER: _, London (?)

DISPLACEMENT: 1070t

DIMENSIONS: Lpp 76.2m, B 9.1m, D
3.6m

HULL: Wood

MACHINERY: Steam, side paddle

ENGINES: 1–2 cyl, 300ihp, R Napier

BOILERS: 2 _

SPEED: (trials) 12.5kts, (1880) 10kts

BUNKERS: 250t coal

COMPLEMENT: 135

ARMAMENT: (1865) 4–11pdr
(1880) 3–90mm, 2–37mm
(1891) 4–76mm QF (K), 2–37mm

Ismaıl Ordered: 1864. Laid down:
1865. Launched: 1865. Trials: 1865.
1865 commissioned. 1898 decommissioned. 10.1909 sold for breaking up.

Hanya

TYPE: Avizo (despatch vessel)

BUILDER: J & W Dudgeson, London

DISPLACEMENT: 816t

DIMENSIONS: L 70.1m, B 8.2m, D 1.9m

HULL: Iron

MACHINERY: Steam, side paddle

ENGINE: 1 cyl

BOILERS: 2 _

SPEED: (1868) 10kts

BUNKERS: 120t coal

COMPLEMENT: 105

ARMAMENT: (1868) 1–20pdr (A)
(1880) 3–47mm (H)
(1900) Disarmed

Hanya Ordered: 1863. Laid down:
1863. Launched: 1863. Trials: 1863.
1863 *Run Her* Confederate Navy. 1863
laid up at London. 1866 sold to Osmanli
Govt. 1866 commissioned, renamed
Hanya. 1890–94 refitted by Tersane-i
Amire, İstanbul. 1904 decommissioned.
9.1909 sold for breaking up.

Kandıya

TYPE: Avizo (despatch vessel)

BUILDER: _, Great Britain

DISPLACEMENT: 820t

DIMENSIONS: L 73.0m, B 8.8m, D 2.0m

HULL: Iron

MACHINERY: Steam, side paddle

ENGINES: _

BOILERS: _

SPEED: (1867) 10kts

BUNKERS: 120t coal

COMPLEMENT: _

ARMAMENT: (1867) 6–30pdr
(1888) 3–57mm QF, 3–24.5mm
(1897) Disarmed

Kandıya Laid down: 1865. Launched:
1865. Trials: Ordered by the
Confederate Navy. 1865 laid up. 1867
bought by Osmanli Govt. 1867 commissioned. 1882 stationary at Beirut. 4.1896
returned to İstanbul, laid up. 1899
stricken.

Arkadi

TYPE: Avizo (despatch vessel)

BUILDER: W Potter & Son, London

DISPLACEMENT: 767t

DIMENSIONS: L 78.0m, B 8.0m, D 2.0m

HULL: Wood

MACHINERY: Steam, side paddle

ENGINES: _

BOILERS: _

SPEED: (1867) 13kts, (1877) 10kts

BUNKERS: 150t coal

COMPLEMENT: 120

ARMAMENT: (1867) 6–30pdr
(1884) 2–76mm QF, 1–60mm

Arkadi Ordered: 1865. Laid down:
1866. Launched: 1866. Trials: . .1866.
Ordered as Dream for Confederate
Navy. 1867 sold to Greek Govt. 1867
Arkadion Royal Greek Navy. 20.8.1867
captured by Ottoman warships north of
Elphanosia. 9.1867 commissioned,
renamed *Arkadi*. 1896 decommissioned.
1905 sold for breaking up.

Resmo

TYPE: Avizo (despatch vessel)

BUILDER: _, Great Britain

DISPLACEMENT: 765t bm

DIMENSIONS: Lpp 69.8m, B 7.9m, D
2.1m

HULL: Iron

MACHINERY: Steam, side paddle

ENGINES: 1–2 cyl, 270ihp

BOILER: 1 rectangular

SPEED: (1868) 14kts, (1877) 10kts

BUNKERS: 150t coal

COMPLEMENT: (1868) 150, (1880) 80

ARMAMENT: (1870) 1–40pdr (A),
1–20pdr (A)
(1887) 3–67mm QF
(1896) 2–37mm QF

Resmo Ordered: 1862. Laid down:
1862. Launched: 1862. Trials: 1862.
1868 sold to Osmanli Govt. 1868 commissioned, renamed *Resmo*. 1873–75,
1892–94 refitted by Tersane-i Amire,
İstanbul. 1894 laid up. 1897 returned to
service. 1905 decommissioned. 1909
sold for breaking up.

Eser-i Nusret Class

TYPE: Avizo (despatch vessel)

BUILDER: Jones Quiggin, Liverpool

DISPLACEMENT: 1343t bm

DIMENSIONS: Lpp 87.8m, B 10.8m,
D 4.5m

HULL: Iron

MACHINERY: Steam, side paddle

ENGINE: 1 _

BOILERS: 2 _

SPEED: (1869) 13kts

BUNKERS: 150t coal

COMPLEMENT: 120

ARMAMENT: (1869) 2–40pdr (A),
2–12pdr (A)
(1880) 4–47mm QF (K)

Eser-i Nusret Ordered: 1864. Laid
down: 1865. Launched: 1865. Trials:
1865. Launched as *Rosina* Confederate
Navy. 1865 laid up at Liverpool. 1869
sold to Osmanli Govt. 1869 commissioned, renamed *Eser-i Nusret*. 1890
decommissioned.

Medar-i Zafer Ordered: 1864. Laid
down: 1865. Launched: 1865. Trials:
1865. Launched as *Ruby* Confederate
Navy. 1865 laid up at Liverpool. 1869
sold to Osmanli Govt. 1869 commissioned, renamed *Medar-i Zafer*. 1890
decommissioned.

İhsaniye

TYPE: Yat (yacht)

BUILDER: Maudslay, Sons & Field, London

DISPLACEMENT: 170t bm, 90nt

DIMENSIONS: Lpp 31.7m, B 5.4m, D 2.3m

HULL: Wood

MACHINERY: Steam, side paddle

ENGINES: 1–2 cyl, Maudslay

BOILER: 1 _, Maudslay

SPEED: (1870) 8kts

BUNKERS: _

COMPLEMENT: _

ARMAMENT: (1870) 2 guns (1884) 2–37mm QF

İhsaniye Ordered: 1869. Laid down: 1869. Launched: 1869. Trials: 1869. 1870 *Rahat* Sirketi Hayriye, İstanbul. 1870 sold to Osmanli Govt. 1870 commissioned, renamed *İhsaniye*. 1906 laid up at İzmir. 1908 stationary guard vessel at Vathi (Samos). 20.4.1912 scuttled by crew after being attacked by Italian warships at Vathi.

Taif Class

TYPE: Avizo (despatch vessel)

BUILDER: Tersane-i Amire, İstanbul

DISPLACEMENT: 1609t bm

DIMENSIONS: L 71.6m, B 11.0m, D 5.1m

HULL: Wood

MACHINERY: Steam, side paddle

ENGINES: 1–2 cyl, 450ihp, Tersane-i Amire

BOILERS: 2 box, Tersane-i Amire

SPEED: (trials) 12kts, (1875) 8kts

BUNKERS: _

COMPLEMENT: 250

ARMAMENT: (1875) 4–126mm ML

Taif Ordered: 1869. Laid down: 1869. Launched: 29.1.1870. Trials: 1871. 1872 commissioned. 1894 decommissioned. 1898 sold for breaking up.

Asır Ordered: 1869. Laid down: 1871. Launched: 1875. Trials: 1876. 1875 towed to İstanbul to fit machinery. 1876

commissioned. 1894 decommissioned. 1898 sold for breaking up.

Şerıfiye/Beylerbeyi

TYPE: Yat (yacht)

BUILDER: _

DISPLACEMENT: 96t

DIMENSIONS: L 29.3m, B 4.6m, D 2.5m

HULL: Wood

MACHINERY: Screw, 1 shaft

ENGINE: 1 _

BOILER: 1 _

SPEED: (trials) 12kts

BUNKERS: 20t

COMPLEMENT: _

ARMAMENT: Unarmed

Şerıfiye/Beylerbeyi Ordered: 1873. Laid down: 1873. Launched: 1873. Trials: 1873. 1873 commissioned as *Şerıfiye*. 1893 renamed *Beylerbeyi*. 1909 decommissioned. 11.11.1910 sold for breaking up.

Şerıfiye

TYPE: Yat (yacht)

BUILDER: _, Constanza

DISPLACEMENT: 55t

DIMENSIONS: L 28.5m, B 3.2m, D 1.9m

HULL: Wood

MACHINERY: Steam, 1 shaft

ENGINE: 1 compound 2 cylinder

BOILER: 1_

SPEED: (1893) 15kts

BUNKERS: _

COMPLEMENT: _

ARMAMENT: Unarmed

Şerıfiye Ordered: 1892. Laid down: 1892. Launched: 1892. Trials: 1892. 1893 commissioned. 1909 decommissioned. 1.1909 sold for breaking up.

Ertuğrul

TYPE: Yat (yacht)

BUILDER: Armstrong, Mitchell & Co, Newcastle-upon-Tyne

DISPLACEMENT: 900t

DIMENSIONS: L 79.2m, B 8.3m, D 3.5m

HULL: Steel

MACHINERY: Steam, 2 shafts

ENGINES: 2 triple expansion 3 cyl, 2500ihp, Hawthorn, Leslie

BOILERS: 2 _, Armstrong, Mitchell

SPEED: (trials) 21kts

BUNKERS: _

COMPLEMENT: _

ARMAMENT: (1904) 8–47mm QF (A)

Ertuğrul Ordered: 1903. Laid down: 1903. Launched: 30.12.1903. Trials: 1904. 1904 commissioned. 1919 laid up at İstanbul. 1924 presidential yacht. 1937 decommissioned. 1939 sold for breaking up to İlhami Söker, İstanbul. 1960/61 broken up. One of the engines fitted in the new tanker *Asfalt II* by D B Camialti Tersane, İstanbul. The ship was laid up at the breaker's yard for more than 22 years.

Söğütlü

TYPE: Yat (yacht)

BUILDER: Armstrong, Mitchell & Co, Newcastle-upon-Tyne

DISPLACEMENT: 120gt, 8nt

DIMENSIONS: L_m, B _m, D _m

HULL: Steel

The Sultan's yacht Ertuğrul *shortly after arriving at İstanbul from Britain.* Güleryüz

MACHINERY: Steam, 1 shaft

ENGINE: 1 compound, 2 cyl, 250ihp

BOILER: 1 _

SPEED: (1908) 14kts

BUNKERS: _

COMPLEMENT: _

ARMAMENT: Unarmed

Söğütlü Ordered: 1907. Laid down: 1908. Launched: 1908. Trials: 1908. 1908 commissioned. 1923 Prime Ministerial yacht. 1933 decommissioned. 1933 despatch vessel for Ministry of Sea Transport. 1938 merchant-marine training ship. 1944 laid up at İstanbul. Not broken up before 1955.

Galata

TYPE: Avizo (despatch vessel)

BUILDER: Day, Summers & Co, Southampton

DISPLACEMENT: 120t

DIMENSIONS: Loa 40.0m, Lpp 33.7m, B 4.9m, D 2.4m

HULL: Steel

MACHINERY: Steam, 1 shaft

ENGINE: 1 triple expansion 3 cyl, Day, Summers

BOILER: 1 _

SPEED: (1911) 8kts

BUNKERS: _

COMPLEMENT: (1911) 24

ARMAMENT: (1911) 1–63mm QF, 2 MG
(1914) Disarmed

Galata (Yd No 109) Ordered: 1895. Laid down: 1896. Launched: 1896. Trials: 1896. 1896 *Lobelia*. 1900s *Amalie*. 1910 sold to Osmanli Govt. 1910 commissioned, renamed *Galata*. 1930 decommissioned.

Şipka

TYPE: Silahli yat (armed yacht)

BUILDER: Ramage & Ferguson, Leith

DISPLACEMENT: 420t

DIMENSIONS: L 57.8m, B 6.9m, D 3.7m

HULL: Steel

MACHINERY: Steam, 1 shaft

ENGINE: 1 triple expansion 3 cyl, 1150ihp, Ramage & Ferguson

BOILERS: 2

SPEED: (1911) 12kts

BUNKERS: _

COMPLEMENT: _

ARMAMENT: (1911) 1–57mm QF, 2–37mm QF

Şipka Ordered: 1891. Laid down: 1892. Launched: 5.1892. Trials: 1892. 1892 Fauvette E A Perignon, Marseille. 5.1911 sold to Osmanli Govt. 7.1911 commissioned, renamed Şipka. 7.1.1912 scuttled by crew at Konfida (Red Sea). 8.1.1912 raised by Italians. 1.1912 Cunfida Royal Italian Navy. 13.11.1924 decommissioned.

Trablus

TYPE: Silahli yat (armed yacht)

BUILDER: Murray Bros, Dumbarton

DISPLACEMENT: 629t, 705t full load

DIMENSIONS: Lpp 59.0m, B 7.7m, D 3.6m

HULL: Iron

MACHINERY: Steam, 1 shaft

ENGINE: 1 compound 2 cyl, 335ihp, Mair & Houston

BOILER: 1 _

SPEED: (1911) 10kts

BUNKERS: _

COMPLEMENT: _

ARMAMENT: (1911) 1–57mm QF, 2–37mm QF

Trablus Ordered: 1886. Laid down: 1887. Launched: 7.1887. Trials: 9.1887. 1887 *Thetis* John Donaldson, London. 5.1911 sold to Osmanli Govt. 7.1911 commissioned, renamed *Trablus*. 30.9.1911 scuttled by crew at Resadiye. 11.1911 raised by Italians. 19.11.1911 *Capitano Verri* Royal Italian Navy. 19.12.1926 decommissioned.

Beyrut

TYPE: Mesaha gemi (survey vessel)

BUILDER: Ramage & Ferguson, Leith

DISPLACEMENT: 411t

DIMENSIONS: L 51.9m, B 6.9m, D 4.4m

HULL: Steel

MACHINERY: Steam, 1 shaft

ENGINE: 1 triple expansion 3 cyl, Ramage & Ferguson

BOILER: 1 _

SPEED: _

BUNKERS: _

COMPLEMENT: _

ARMAMENT: (1911) 2–57mm QF, 2–37mm QF

Beyrut Ordered: 1898. Laid down: 1899. Launched: .1899. Trials: 1899. 1899 *Lady Gipsy* Thomas Pink, London. 5.1911 sold to Osmanli Govt. 9.1911 commissioned, renamed *Beyrut*. 1.11.1914 sunk by gunfire from British

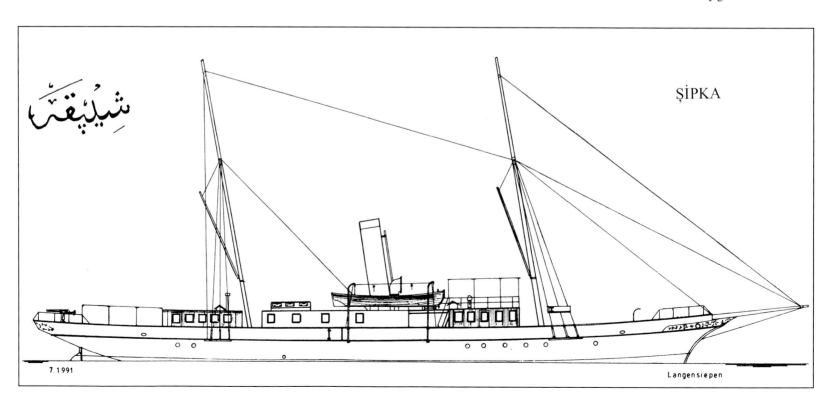

ŞİPKA

7.1991   Langensiepen

gunboats *Wolverine* and *Scorpion* at Urla (Gulf of İzmir).

ARMED STEAMERS

Sürat

TYPE: Vapur (armed steamer)

BUILDER: Nicholls Booles & William Good, Bridport

DISPLACEMENT: 139nt

DIMENSIONS: L 32.4m, B 9.8m, D 2.9m

HULL: Wood

MACHINERY: Steam, side paddle

ENGINE: 1–1 cyl (installed 1822)

BOILER: 1 _

SPEED: (1853) 5kts

BUNKERS: _

COMPLEMENT: 25

ARMAMENT: (1828) Unarmed
(1853) 2 guns

Sürat Ordered: 1801. Laid down: 1801. Launched: 1801. Trials: 1801. 1801 *Swift* London, Edinburgh & Leith Ship Co, London. 1822 lengthened, converted into a steamship. 21.8.1822 *Swift* West, Bellingham, Creasey, Hall & Others, Brighton. 23.2.1824. *Swift* Grichton, Ogilvee & Others, Leith. 15.9.1827 *Swift* H Templer, London. 20.5.1828 arrived İstanbul. 6.1828 given as a present to the Sultan, commissioned, renamed *Sürat*. 1839 Tersane-i Amire, İstanbul. 1853 Osmanli. Bahriye. 1859 decommissioned.

Sagir

TYPE: Vapur (armed steamer)

BUILDER: Scott, Greenock

DISPLACEMENT: 300t bm, 174nt

DIMENSIONS: L 38.8m, B 6.8m, D 3.9m

HULL: Wood

MACHINERY: Steam, side paddle

ENGINE: 1–1 cyl single acting, Scott & Sinclair

BOILER: 1 _

SPEED: (1839) 6kts

BUNKERS: _

COMPLEMENT: 25

ARMAMENT: (1829) 2 guns

Sagir Ordered: 1824. Laid down: 1824. Launched: 8.1.1825. Trials: 1825. 1825 *Trinacria* Scott, Greenock. 1.7.1825 *Hylton Joliffe* General Steam Navigation Co, London. 30.5.1829 sold to Osmanli Govt. 6.1829 commissioned, renamed *Sagir* 1839. *Sagir* Tersane-i Amire, İstanbul. 1843 *Sagir* Fevaid-i Osmaniye, İstanbul. 1860 decommissioned.

Peyk-i Şevket

TYPE: Vapur (armed steamer)

BUILDER: SA Chantiers Benet, La Ciotat

DISPLACEMENT: 465t bm, 339nt

DIMENSIONS: L 62.0m, B 7.4m, D 2.7m

HULL: Wood

MACHINERY: Steam, side paddle

ENGINE: 1 vertical balance, low pressure (British)

BOILER: 1 _

SPEED: _

BUNKERS: _

COMPLEMENT: 26

ARMAMENT: (1838) 2 guns

Peyk-i Şevket Ordered: 1836. Laid down: 1836. Launched: 14.4.1836. Trials: .5.1836. 1836 *La Phocéen* Toussaint, Benet, La Ciotat. 22.9.1836 *La Phocéen* T Perier, Toulon. 2. 1838 sold to Osmanli Bahriye. 2.1838 commissioned, renamed *Peyk-i Şevket*. 1839 Tersane-i Amire, İstanbul. 1853 decommissioned.

Eser-i Hayir

TYPE: Vapur (armed steamer)

BUILDER: Tersane-i Amire, İstanbul

DISPLACEMENT: 285t bm, 231nt

DIMENSIONS: L 39.6m, B 6.7m, D 2.7m

HULL: Wood

MACHINERY: Steam, side paddle

ENGINE: 1 horizontal 1 cyl, R Napier

BOILER: 1 _

SPEED: (1837) 6kts

BUNKERS: _

COMPLEMENT: 60

ARMAMENT: (1838) 2 guns
(1855) 4 guns

Eser-i Hayir Ordered: 1836. Laid down: 1837. Launched: 26.11.1837. Trials: 1838. 1838 commissioned. 1839 Tersane-i Amire, İstanbul. 1853 Osmanli. Bahriye. 1855 refitted at Malta. 1879 decommissioned.

Ereğli

TYPE: Vapur (armed steamer)

BUILDER: Greenock

DISPLACEMENT: 217t bm

DIMENSIONS: L 40.5m, B 5.9m, D 3.0m

HULL: Wood

MACHINERY: Steam, side paddle

ENGINE: 1 _, 140nhp

BOILER: 1 _

SPEED: (1853) 6kts

BUNKERS: _

COMPLEMENT: (1846) 83

ARMAMENT: (1846) 2–5 OK guns

Ereğli Ordered: 1836. Laid down: 1836. Launched: .1836. Trials: 1836. 1836 *Monarch* (British). 1840 *Monarch* Musebina, İstanbul (British). 1846 sold to Osmamli Bahriye. 1846 commissioned, renamed *Ereğli*. 30.11.1853 set on fire during the Battle of Sinop, blown up.

Pesendıre

TYPE: Vapur (armed steamer)

BUILDER: Tersane-i Amire, İstanbul

DISPLACEMENT: 193t bm

DIMENSIONS: Lpp 35.6m, B 5.4m, D 1.8m

HULL: Wood

MACHINERY: Steam, side paddle

ENGINE: 1 single acting, 350ihp, R Napier

BOILER: 1 _

SPEED: (trials) 8kts

BUNKERS: _

COMPLEMENT: (1848) 26, (1866) 34

ARMAMENT: (1848) 2–5 guns

Pesendıre Ordered: 1847. Laid down: 1847. Launched: 1848. Trials: 1848. 1848 commissioned. 1879 decommissioned. 1884 sold for breaking up.

Pursut

TYPE: Vapur (armed steamer)

BUILDER: British

DISPLACEMENT: 627t bm, 280nt

DIMENSIONS: L 54.3m, B 8.6m, D 4.1m

HULL: Wood

MACHINERY: Steam, side paddle

ENGINE: 1 single acting, 482ihp, Maudslay

BOILER: 1 _

SPEED: _

BUNKERS: _

COMPLEMENT: (1847) 45

ARMAMENT: (1846) 4–5 guns

Pursut Ordered: 1847. Laid down: 1847. Launched: 1847. Trials: 1847. 1847 commissioned. 1866 Fevaid-i Osmaniye, İstanbul. 1883 decommissioned.

Gemlık

TYPE: Vapur (armed steamer)

BUILDER: British

DISPLACEMENT: 219t bm

DIMENSIONS: L _m, B _m, D _m

HULL: Iron

MACHINERY: Steam, 1 shaft

ENGINE: 1 _

BOILER: 1 _

SPEED: _

BUNKERS: _

COMPLEMENT: _

ARMAMENT: (1848) 2 guns

Gemlık Ordered: 1848. Laid down: 1848. Launched: 1848. Trials: 1848. 1848 commissioned. 1862 Fevaid-i

Osmaniye. 1881 Osmanli Bahriye. 1904 decommissioned. 11.1909 sold for breaking up.

Peyk-i Şevket

TYPE: Vapur (armed steamer)

BUILDER: Tersane-i Amire, İstanbul

DISPLACEMENT: 465t bm

DIMENSIONS: Lpp 47.2m, B 7.6m, D 2.9m

HULL: Wood

MACHINERY: Steam, side paddle

ENGINE: 1 single acting 2 cyl

BOILER: 1 _

SPEED: (1853) 8kts

BUNKERS: _

COMPLEMENT: (1853) 44

ARMAMENT: (1853) 4–12pdr

Peyk-i Şevket Ordered: 1853. Laid down: 1853. Launched: .1853. Trials: 1853. 1853 commissioned. 1862 Fevaid-i Osmaniye, İstanbul. 1878 decommissioned.

Medar-i Ticaret

TYPE: Vapur (armed steamer)

BUILDER: Money Wigram, Blackwall, London

DISPLACEMENT: 407t bm, 317nt, 426tons

DIMENSIONS: L 41.2m, B 7.6m, D 3.0m

HULL: Wood

MACHINERY: Steam, side paddle

ENGINE: 1 single acting 2 cyl, 480ihp, Maudslay

BOILER: 1 _

SPEED: _

BUNKERS: _

COMPLEMENT: (1853)63

ARMAMENT: (1853) 4 guns

Medar-i Ticaret Ordered: 1846. Laid down: 1846. Launched: 13.8.1847. Trials: 1847. 1847 Fevaid-i Osmaniye, İstanbul. 1853 commissioned. 16.11.1853 captured by Russian steam frigate *Bessarabiya* off Kerempe. 1853

Turok Imperial Russian Navy. 11.9.1855 scuttled at Sevastopol. 1858 refloated, returned to service. 13.1.1891 stricken.

Tair-i Bahri

TYPE: Vapur (armed steamer)

BUILDER: Tersane-i Amire, İstanbul

DISPLACEMENT: 524t bm, 356nt, 506tons

DIMENSIONS: Lpp 56.9m, B 7.9m, D 3.2m

HULL: Wood

MACHINERY: Steam, side paddle

ENGINES: 2 single acting, 450ihp, R Napier

BOILER: 1 _

SPEED: _

BUNKERS: _

COMPLEMENT: (1839) 83, (1854) 137

ARMAMENT: (1854) 6 guns

Tair-i Bahri Ordered: 1838. Laid down: 1839. Launched: 1839. Trials: 1839. 1839 Tersane-i Amire, İstanbul. 1854 commissioned. 1877 decommissioned. 1892 towed to İzmir, stationary at İzmir.

Mesir-i Bahri

TYPE: Vapur (armed steamer)

BUILDER: Tersane-i Amire, İstanbul

DISPLACEMENT: 275t bm

DIMENSIONS: Lpp 48.7m, B 6.7m, D 2.4m

HULL: Wood

MACHINERY: Steam, side paddle

ENGINE: 1 single acting 2 cyl, R Napier

BOILER: 1 _

SPEED: (1853) 8kts

BUNKERS: _

COMPLEMENT: (1838) 25, (1853) 63

ARMAMENT: (1853) 4–12pdr

Mesir-i Bahri Ordered: 1838. Laid down: 1838. Launched: 1838. Trials: 1838. 1838 Tersane-i Amire, İstanbul. 1854 commissioned. 1865 laid up at İstanbul. 1877 returned to service. 1879

decommissioned.

Necım-i Şeref

TYPE: Vapur (armed steamer)

BUILDER: _

DISPLACEMENT: _

DIMENSIONS: L _m, B _m, D _m

HULL: Wood

MACHINERY: Steam, side paddle

ENGINE: 1 _

BOILER: 1 _

SPEED: _

BUNKERS: _

COMPLEMENT: _

ARMAMENT: (1854) 2 guns

Necım-i Şeref Ordered: 18 Laid down: 18 Launched: 18 Trials: 18 1854 commissioned. 1867 decommissioned.

Girit

TYPE: Vapur (armed steamer)

BUILDER: _, Great Britain

DISPLACEMENT:

DIMENSIONS:

HULL: Wood

MACHINERY: Steam, side paddle

ENGINES: _

BOILERS: _

SPEED: (1855) 8kts

BUNKERS: _

COMPLEMENT: (1847) 20, (1855) 36

ARMAMENT: (1855) 2 guns

Girit Ordered: Laid down: Launched: Trials: 1847 *Girit* Fevaidi Osmaniye, İstanbul. 1855 transferred to Osmanli Bahriye, commissioned. 1866 transferred to Fevaidi Osmaniye, İstanbul. 1873 out of service.

Vasita-i Ticaret

TYPE: Vapur (armed steamer)

BUILDER: D White, West Cowes, Isle of Wight

DISPLACEMENT: 936gt, 748nt, 1350t

DIMENSIONS: L 62.9m, B 9.5m, D 4.1m

HULL: Wood

MACHINERY: Steam, side paddle

ENGINE: 1–2 cyl, 650ihp Maudslay

BOILER: 1 _

SPEED: (1874) 15kts

BUNKERS: _

COMPLEMENT: (1847) 83

ARMAMENT: (1856) 4 guns (1871) 2 guns

Vasita-i Ticaret Ordered: 1846. Laid down: 1846. Launched: 1.3.1847. Trials: 7.1847. 1847 Fevaid-i Osmaniye, İstanbul. 1855 commissioned. 1860 Fevaid-i Osmaniye, İstanbul. 1871 Osmanli Bahriye. 1885 decommissioned. 1890 sold for breaking up.

Hüma-i Tevfik

TYPE: Vapur (armed steamer)

BUILDER: W Denny, Dumbarton

DISPLACEMENT: 699gt, 476nt

DIMENSIONS: L 68.5m, B 8.2m, D 4.8m

HULL: Iron

MACHINERY: Steam, 1 shaft

ENGINE: 1–2 cyl, MacNab & Clarke

BOILER: 1 _

SPEED: (1856) 9kts

Bunkers: _

COMPLEMENT: (1856) 76

ARMAMENT: (1856) 6 guns

Hüma-i Tevfik (Yd No 54) Ordered: 1855. Laid down: 855. Launched: 22.8.1855. Trials: 1855. Built on speculation by J & P Denny as *Baroness Tecco*. 12.10.1855 *Baroness Tecco* J Giustiani, London. 7.1856 commissioned, renamed *Hüma-i Tevfik*. 1865 Fevaid-i Osmaniye, İstanbul. 1870 stationary hospital vessel at İstanbul. 1872 laid up. 1874 sold for breaking up by Tersane-i Amire, İstanbul.

Hümayiş

TYPE: Vapur (armed steamer)

BUILDER: _, Glasgow

DISPLACEMENT: 346t bm

DIMENSIONS: L 50.6m, B 7.3m, D 1.9m

HULL: Wood

MACHINERY: Steam, side paddle

ENGINE: 1 _

BOILER: 1 _

SPEED: _

BUNKERS: _

COMPLEMENT: (1855) 86

ARMAMENT: (1855) 6 guns

Hümayiş Ordered: 1844. Laid down: 1844. Launched: 1844. Trials: 1844. 1844 home port: Genoa. 1850 *Aquila* Österreichische Lloyd, Trieste. 1855 sold to Osmanli Bahriye, commissioned, renamed *Hümayiş*. 1866 Fevaid-i Osmaniye, İstanbul. 1879 decommissioned. 1885 broken up by Tersane-i Amire, İstanbul.

Eser-i Nuzhet

TYPE: Vapur (armed steamer)

BUILDER: Tersane-i Amire, İstanbul

DISPLACEMENT: 193t bm

DIMENSIONS: L 35.6m, B 5.4m, D 1.8m

HULL: Wood

MACHINERY: Steam, side paddle

ENGINE: 1 single acting, 350ihp, R Napier

BOILER: 1 _

SPEED: (trials) 8kts

BUNKERS: _

COMPLEMENT: (1845) 41, (1856) 34

ARMAMENT: (1856) 2 guns (1887) Disarmed

Eser-i Nuzhet Ordered: 1843. Laid down: 1845. Launched: 1845. Trials: 1845. 1845 Fevaid-i Osmaniye, İstanbul. 1856 commissioned. 1887 stationary guard ship at İstanbul-Kasimpaşa. 1891 stationary collier at İstanbul-Galata. 1909 decommissioned, sold for breaking up.

Musul

TYPE: Vapur (armed steamer)

BUILDER: _, Great Britain

DISPLACEMENT: 200gt, 130nt

DIMENSIONS: L 38.6m, B 6.1m, D 3.5m

HULL: _

MACHINERY: Steam, side paddle

ENGINE: 1 _

BOILER: 1 _

SPEED: _

BUNKERS: _

COMPLEMENT: _

ARMAMENT: (1856) 2 guns

Musul Ordered: –. Laid down: –. Launched: –. Trials: –. 1856 commissioned. 1861 Fevaid-i Osmaniye, İstanbul. 1896 decommissioned. 1909 sold for breaking up.

Eser-i Ticaret

TYPE: Vapur (armed steamer)

BUILDER: B Wallis & Co, London

DISPLACEMENT: 64t bm

DIMENSIONS: L 29.8m, B 4.5m, D 3.1m

HULL: Wood

MACHINERY: Steam, side paddle

ENGINE: 1–2 cyl

BOILER: 1 _

SPEED: _

BUNKERS: _

COMPLEMENT: (1843) 3 officers, 19 ratings

ARMAMENT: (1856) 2 guns

Eser-i Ticaret Ordered: 1835. Laid down: 1835. Launched: 1835. Trials: 1835. 24.4.1835 *Levant* J Thompson & Others, London. 1839 *Levant* Donau DSG, Vienna. 1843 *Eser-i Ticaret* Tersane-i Amire, İstanbul. 1856 commissioned. 1876 decommissioned.

Vesile-i Ticaret

TYPE: Vapur (steamer)

BUILDER: Tersane-i Amire, İstanbul

DISPLACEMENT: 193t bm

DIMENSIONS: L 35.6m, B 5.4m, D 1.8m

HULL: Wood

MACHINERY: Steam, side paddle

ENGINE: 1 single acting 1 cyl, 350ihp, R Napier

BOILER: 1 _

SPEED: 8kts

BUNKERS: _

COMPLEMENT: (1841) 41, (1856) 34

ARMAMENT: (1856) 2 guns

Vesile-i Ticaret Ordered: 1843. Laid down: 1845. Launched: 1845. Trials: 1845. 1845 *Vesile-i Ticaret* Fevaid-i Osmaniye, İstanbul. 1856 transferred to Osmanli Bahriye. 1895 decommissioned.

Tuna

TYPE: Vapur (armed steamer)

BUILDER: Alexander Denny, Dumbarton

DISPLACEMENT: 156t bm, 152gt, 92nt

DIMENSIONS: L 38.1m, B 4.9m, D 2.8m

HULL: Iron

MACHINERY: Steam, side paddle

ENGINE: 1–1 cyl, Tulloch, Denny

BOILER: 1 _

SPEED: _

BUNKERS: _

COMPLEMENT: _

ARMAMENT: (1856) 2 guns

Tuna (Yd No 27) Ordered: .1853. Laid down: 1853. Launched: 6.1853. Trials: 1853. 1853 *Morecambe's Queen* Willis & Ward, Morecambe. 1.5.1855 *Nimble* Royal Navy. 8.1856 sold to Osmanli Govt at İstanbul. 11.1856 commissioned. 1864 Fevaid-i Osmaniye, İstanbul. 1871 decommissioned. 1873 broken up by Tersane-i Amire, İstanbul.

Sılıstre

TYPE: Vapur (armed steamer)

BUILDER: Alexander Denny, Dumbarton

DISPLACEMENT: 702t bm, 835ts

DIMENSIONS: L _m, B _m, D _m

HULL: Iron

MACHINERY: Steam, 1 shaft

ENGINE: 1–2 cyl, A Denny

BOILER: 1 _, A Denny

SPEED: _

BUNKERS: _

COMPLEMENT: _

ARMAMENT: (1856) 6 guns

Sılıstre (Yd No 41) Ordered: 1855. Laid down: 1856. Launched: 1856. Trials:.1856. 1856 commissioned. 9.10.1859, sunk, salvaged. 1867 decommissioned.

Sehber

TYPE: Vapur (armed steamer)

BUILDER: J White, West Cowes

DISPLACEMENT: 420gt, 116t

DIMENSIONS: L 55.4m, B 8.3m, D 3.6m

HULL: Wood

MACHINERY: Steam, side paddle

ENGINE: 1 _

BOILER: 1 _

SPEED: _

BUNKERS: _

COMPLEMENT: _

ARMAMENT: (1856) 4 guns

Sehber Ordered: 1856. Laid down: 1856. Launched: 1856. Trials: 1856. 1856 commissioned. 1866 Fevaid-i Osmaniye, İstanbul. 1883 decommissioned.

Ereğli

TYPE: Vapur (armed steamer)

BUILDER: British

DISPLACEMENT: 40t bm (?)

DIMENSIONS: L _m, B _m, D _m

HULL: Wood

MACHINERY: Steam, side paddle

ENGINE: 1 _

BOILER: 1 _

SPEED: _

BUNKERS: _

COMPLEMENT: _

ARMAMENT: (1856) 2 guns

Ereğli Ordered: – Laid down: – Launched: – Trials: 1856 commissioned. 1871 decommissioned.

Sudaver

TYPE: Vapur (armed steamer)

BUILDER: Brown & Bell, New York

DISPLACEMENT: 385t bm

DIMENSIONS: L 47.5m, B 8.5m, D 3.0m

HULL: Wood

MACHINERY: Steam, side paddle

ENGINE: 1–1 cyl crosshead, 160nhp

BOILER: 1 _

SPEED: (1856) 10kts

BUNKERS: _

COMPLEMENT: (1856) 35

ARMAMENT: (1856) 6 guns

Sudaver Ordered: 1833. Laid down: 1834. Launched: 1834. Trials 1834. 1834 Bangor Boston & Bangor SS Co, New York. 10.1842 Osmanli Govt İstanbul-Gibraltar service under US management. 1844 Yeni Dünya Fevaid-i Osmaniye, İstanbul. 1845 renamed Sudaver. 1856 commissioned. 1859 decommissioned. 1883 broken up by Tersane-i Amire, İstanbul.

Peyk-i Tıcaret

TYPE: Vapur (armed steamer)

BUILDER: Tersane-i Amire, İstanbul

DISPLACEMENT: 193t bm

DIMENSIONS: Lpp 35.6m, B 5.4m, D 1.8m

HULL: Wood

MACHINERY: Steam, side paddle

ENGINE: 1–1 cyl single acting, 280nhp

BOILER: 1 _

SPEED: (trials) 8kts

BUNKERS: _

COMPLEMENT: (1840) 26

ARMAMENT: (1857) 2 guns
(1888) Disarmed

Peyk-i Tıcaret Ordered: 1839. Laid down: 1839. Launched: 1840. Trials: 1840. 1840 Fevaid-i Osmaniye, İstanbul. 1857 commissioned. 1888 stationary guard vessel at İstanbul-Kasimpaşa. 1892 stationary office vessel at İstanbul. 1909 decommissioned, sold for breaking up.

Sulhıye

TYPE: Vapur (armed steamer)

BUILDER: _

DISPLACEMENT: _

DIMENSIONS: L _m, B _m, D _m

HULL: Wood

MACHINERY: Steam, side paddle

ENGINE: 1 _

BOILER: 1 _

SPEED: _

BUNKERS: _

COMPLEMENT: _

ARMAMENT: (1857) 2 guns

Sulhiye Ordered: – . Laid down: –. Launched: –. Trials: – .1857 commissioned. 1863 decommissioned.

Hüma-i Pervaz

TYPE: Vapur (armed steamer)

BUILDER: Glasgow, Alexandria

DISPLACEMENT: 627t bm

DIMENSIONS: L 52.4m, B 8.5m, D 3.8m

HULL: Wood

MACHINERY: Steam, side paddle

ENGINE: 1–1 cyl single acting, 280nhp

BOILER: 1 _

SPEED: _

BUNKERS: _

COMPLEMENT: (1843) 20

ARMAMENT: (1857) 6 guns

Hüma-i Pervaz Ordered: 1842. Laid down: 1842. Launched: 1843. Trials: 1843. 1843 Fevaid-i Osmaniye, İstanbul. 1857 commissioned. 1870 Fevaid-i Osmaniye, İstanbul. 1879 out of service.

Trablusgrab

TYPE: Vapur (armed steamer)

BUILDER: British

DISPLACEMENT: _

DIMENSIONS: L _m, B _m, D _m

HULL: Wood

MACHINERY: Steam, side paddle

ENGINE: 1 _

BOILER: 1 _

SPEED: _

BUNKERS: _

COMPLEMENT: _

ARMAMENT: (1858) 4 guns

Trablusgrab Ordered: – .Laid down: – .Launched: – .Trials: – .1858 commissioned. 1870 decommissioned.

Pir-i Levend

TYPE: Vapur (armed steamer)

BUILDER: British

DISPLACEMENT: _

DIMENSIONS: L _m, B _m, D _m

HULL: Wood

MACHINERY: Steam, side paddle

ENGINE: 1 _

BOILER: 1 _

SPEED: _

BUNKERS: _

COMPLEMENT: (1855) 36

ARMAMENT: (1855) 4 guns

Pir-i Levend Ordered: – . Laid down: –. Launched: –. Trials: –. 1850s commissioned. 1866 Fevaid-i Osmaniye, İstanbul. 187 out of service.

Omer Paşa

TYPE: Vapur (armed steamer)

BUILDER: _

DISPLACEMENT: _

DIMENSIONS: L _m, B _m, D _m

HULL: Iron

MACHINERY: Steam, 1 shaft

ENGINE: 1 _

BOILER: 1 _

SPEED: _

BUNKERS: _

COMPLEMENT: _

ARMAMENT: (186) 2 guns

Omer Paşa Ordered: –. Laid down: –. Launched: –. Trials: – .1860s commissioned. 1866 Fevaid-i Osmaniye, İstanbul. 1868 out of service. 1870 broken up by Tersane-i Amire, İstanbul.

Gürsur

TYPE: Vapur (armed steamer)

BUILDER: _

DISPLACEMENT: _

DIMENSIONS: L _m, B _m, D _m

HULL: Wood

MACHINERY: Steam, side paddle

ENGINE: 1 _

BOILER: 1 _

SPEED: _

BUNKERS: _

COMPLEMENT: _

ARMAMENT: (186) 2 guns

Gürsur Ordered: – . Laid down: –. Launched: –. Trials: – . 1860s commissioned. 1866 Fevaid-i Osmaniye, İstanbul. 1873 out of service.

Yıldız

TYPE: Vapur (armed steamer)

BUILDER: _

DISPLACEMENT: _

DIMENSIONS: L _m, B _m, D _m

HULL: Iron

MACHINERY: Steam, 1 shaft

ENGINE: 1 _

BOILER: 1 _

SPEED: _

BUNKERS: _

COMPLEMENT: _

ARMAMENT: (186) 2 guns

Yıldız Ordered: –. Laid down: – . Launched: –. Trials: –. 1860s commissioned. 1866 Fevaid-i Osmaniye, İstanbul. 1873 out of service. 1879 broken up by Tersane-i Amire, Istanbul.

Müverrid-i Nusret Class

TYPE: Vapur (armed steamer)

BUILDER: M Samuelson & Co, Hull

DISPLACEMENT: 3029t bm, 2913gt, 1625nt

DIMENSIONS: L 110.2m, B 12.2m, D 8.5m

HULL: Iron

MACHINERY: Steam, 1 shaft

ENGINE: 1–2 cyl

BOILERS: 2 _

SPEED: _

BUNKERS: _

COMPLEMENT: _

ARMAMENT: (1867) 2 guns
(*Müverrid-i Nusret* 1880) 4–47mm QF
(*Şiar-i Nusret* 1880) 2–47mm QF

Müverrid-i Nusret Ordered: 1860. Laid down: 1860. Launched: 1860. Trials: 1860. Launched as *Anglia*. 1861 *Munster* Atlantic Royal Mail SN., London. 11.1863 laid up at Liverpool. 1866 sold to Osmanli Govt. 1867 commissioned. 1890 decommissioned. 1901 sold for breaking up.

Şiar-i Nusret Ordered: 1860. Laid down: 1860. Launched: 1860. Trials: 1860. Launched as *Columbia*. 1861 *Ulster* Atlantic Royal Mail SN, London. 1866 sold to Osmanli Govt. 1867 commissioned. 1890 decommissioned. 1901 sold for breaking up.

Sulhıye

TYPE: Vapur (armed steamer)

BUILDER: _, Great Britain

DISPLACEMENT: 180t bm, 161ts

DIMENSIONS: L 36.5m, B 5.7m, D 2.3m

HULL: Iron

MACHINERY: Steam, side paddle

ENGINE: 1 _

BOILER: 1 _

SPEED: _

BUNKERS: _

COMPLEMENT: _

ARMAMENT: (1866) 2 guns
(1890) Disarmed

Sulhıye Ordered: 1867. Laid down: 1868. Launched: 1868. Trials: 1868. 1868 commissioned. 1900 stationary guard vessel at Büyükdere. 1909 decommissioned. 1910 broken up.

Sarıye Class

TYPE: Vapur (armed steamer)

BUILDER: _

DISPLACEMENT: 103t

DIMENSIONS: L 30.9m, B 7.5m, D 2.3m

HULL: Wood

MACHINERY: Steam, side paddle

ENGINE: 1 _

BOILER: 1 _

SPEED: _

BUNKERS: _

COMPLEMENT: _

ARMAMENT: Unarmed

Sarıye Ordered: 1867. Laid down: 1868. Launched: .1868. Trials: 1868. 1869 commissioned, based at İstanbul. 1872 based in the Red Sea. 1883 based at İstanbul. 1909 based at İstanbul. 1909 decommissioned. 1911 sold for breaking up.

Nedim Ordered: 1867. Laid down: 1868. Launched: 1868. Trials: 1868. 1869 commissioned, based at İstanbul. 1890 based at Suda. 1869 returned to İstanbul, laid up. 1907 decommissioned. 1911 sold for breaking up.

Bozcaada Ordered: 1867. Laid down: 1868. Launched: 1868. Trials: 1869. 1869 commissioned, based at İstanbul. 1890 based at Çanakkale. 1902 returned to İstanbul, laid up. 1909 decommissioned. 1911 sold for breaking up.

Babıl

TYPE: Taşit gemi (transport)

BUILDER: Millwall Shipbuilding & Engineering Company, London

DISPLACEMENT: 1733t bm

DIMENSIONS: Lpp 79.2m, B 10.6m, D 4.8m

HULL: Iron

MACHINERY: Steam, 1 shaft

ENGINE: 1 compound 2 cyl, Millwall SB

BOILERS: 2 _, Millwall SB

SPEED: (1869) 9kts

BUNKERS: 300t coal

COMPLEMENT: 70

ARMAMENT: (1871) 4 guns
(1877) Disarmed
(1884) 5–76mm QF(K)
(1906) 3–57mm QF(K)

Babıl Ordered: 1864. Laid down: 1866. Launched: 3.1866. Trials: 7.7.1866. 7.1866 *Mataura* Panama-New Zealand & Australia Royal Mail Company, London. 1868 laid up. 9.1868 sold to J Mayers (Agent). 10.1869 sold to Osmanli Govt. 10.1869 *Babil* İdare-i Umman-i Osmani, Baghdad. 1871 commissioned. 1890 Collier (İstanbul-KD Ereğli). 1906 laid up at İstanbul. 4.1912 left İstanbul for İzmir with a cargo of war equipment. 4.1912 grounded and lost near Tekirdag (Sea of Marmara). Wreck broken up 1913–20. It was intended to sink her as a blockship at Yenikale (Bay of İzmir).

Hayreddin Class

TYPE: Taşit gemi (transport)

BUILDER: J & R White, West Cowes, Isle of Wight

DISPLACEMENT: 484t bm, carried 90t of cargo

DIMENSIONS: Lpp 51.9m, B 7.56m, D 1.8m

HULL: Wood

MACHINERY: Steam, side paddle

ENGINE: 1 set single acting, 350ihp, Day & Summers

BOILER: 1 _, Day & Summers

SPEED: (trials) 11kts

BUNKERS: _

COMPLEMENT: 70

ARMAMENT: (1858) 2–32pdr on pivot
(1865) Disarmed

(1874) 2–33pdr on pivot
(1881) 2–57mm QF, 2–25.4mm RV(H)
(1892) Disarmed

Hayreddin Ordered: 1857. Laid down: 1858. Launched: 1858. Trials: 1858. Built under provisional name *Danbe*. 15.5.1858 Fevaid-i Osmaniye, İstanbul. 1874 commissioned. 1892 stationary at Beirut. 1908 decommissioned, sold for breaking up at Beirut.

Kiliç Alı Ordered: 1857. Laid down: 1858. Launched: 1858. Trials: 1858. Built under provisional name *Constantinople*. 15.5.1858 left Southampton for İstanbul. 7.1858 renamed *Kiliç Alı* Fevaid-i Osmaniye, İstanbul. 1874 commissioned. 1890 stationary at Selanik. 1908 decommissioned. 1909 sold privately, laid up at İzmir. 1924 broken up at İzmir.

Bar

TYPE: Vapur (armed steamer)

BUILDER: J White, West Cowes, Isle of Wight

DISPLACEMENT: 170gt, 45nt

DIMENSIONS: Lpp 42.6m, B 4.4m, D 2.3m

HULL: Wood

MACHINERY: Steam, side paddle

ENGINE: 1–1 cyl, 80nhp, J. Penn

BOILER: 1 _

SPEED: (1875) 6kts

BUNKERS: _

COMPLEMENT: _

ARMAMENT: (1875) 2–18pdr

Bar Ordered: 1859. Laid down: 1860. Launched: 1860. Trials: 1860. 1860 *Kabatas No.12* Sirketi Hayriye, İstanbul. 1875 sold to Osmanli Bahriye, commissioned. Renamed *Bar*, based on Lake Iskodra. 1880 decommissioned. Tender for government personnel. 1901 laid up.

Gör

TYPE: Vapur (armed steamer)

BUILDER: T White, East Cowes, Isle of Wight

DISPLACEMENT: 288gt, 122nt

DIMENSIONS: Lpp 41.1m, B 6.0m, D 3.0m

HULL: Wood

MACHINERY: Steam, side paddle

ENGINE: 1–1 cyl, 60nhp, Maudslay

BOILER: 1 _

SPEED: (1875) 6kts

BUNKERS: _

COMPLEMENT: _

ARMAMENT: (1875) 2–18pdr
(1880) 1–37mm QF
(1909) 1–76mm QF

Gör Ordered: 1856. Laid down: 1857. Launched: 1857. Trials: 1857. 1857 *Beykoz No.10* Sirketi Hayriye, İstanbul. 1875 sold to Osmanli Bahriye, commissioned. Renamed *Gör,* based on Lake Iskodra. 1880 decommissioned. Tender for government personnel. 1911 commissioned. 5.1913 transferred to the newly-founded Albanian navy.

Trabzon

TYPE: Vapur (armed steamer)

BUILDER: _

DISPLACEMENT: 70t

DIMENSIONS: L _m, B _m, D _m

HULL: Wood

MACHINERY: Steam, 1 shaft

ENGINE: 1 _

BOILER: 1 _

SPEED: (1901) 10kts

BUNKERS: _

COMPLEMENT: _

ARMAMENT: (1901) 1–70mm, 1–57mm QF

Trabzon Ordered: 1860s . Laid down: 1860s Launched: 1860s Trials: 1860s . 1901 commissioned. 9.11.1912 torpedoed and sunk by Greek torpedo boat No.14 off Mytilli.

Haliç

TYPE: Vapur (armed steamer)

BUILDER: _

DISPLACEMENT: _

DIMENSIONS: L _m, B _m, D _m

HULL: Wood

MACHINERY: Steam, 1 shaft

ENGINE: 1 _

BOILER: 1 _

SPEED: _

BUNKERS: _

COMPLEMENT: _

ARMAMENT: (1911) 2–37mm QF

Haliç Ordered: –. Laid down: –. Launched: –. Trials: –. Haliç Sirketi, İstanbul. 1911 chartered by Osmanli Bahriye, commissioned. 5.11.1911 damaged by gunfire by Italian cruiser *Puglia* off Akaba (Red Sea), wreck scuttled by crew.

Kıyoçya

TYPE: Vapur (armed steamer)

BUILDER: _

DISPLACEMENT: 100t

DIMENSIONS: L _m, B _m, D _m

HULL: Iron

MACHINERY: Steam, 1 shaft

ENGINE: 1 _

BOILER: 1 _

SPEED: _

BUNKERS: _

COMPLEMENT: (1911) 8

ARMAMENT: (1911) 1–37mm QF

Kıyoçya Ordered: –. Laid down: –. Launched: –. Trials: –. Private Osmanli steamship on Lake Iskodra. 1911 chartered by Osmanli Bahriye, commissioned. 5.1913 handed over to the newly formed Albanian navy.

Malakof Class

TYPE: Taşit gemi (transport)

BUILDER: Denny & Renkie, Glasgow

DISPLACEMENT: 1020gt, 826nt

DIMENSIONS: L 66.1m, B 8.5m, D 3.0m

HULL: Iron

MACHINERY: Steam, 1 shaft

ENGINE: 1–1 cyl

BOILER: 1 _

SPEED: _

BUNKERS: _

COMPLEMENT: 45

ARMAMENT: Unarmed

Malakof (Yd No 110) Ordered: 1855. Laid down: 1855. Launched: 3.2.1856. Trials: 1856. 1856 commissioned. 1866 Fevaid-i Osmaniye, İstanbul. 1883 decommissioned.

Kars (Yd No 111) Ordered: 1855. Laid down: 1855. Launched: 7.5.1856. Trials: 1856. 1856 commissioned. 1866 Fevaid-i Osmaniye, İstanbul. 1874 decommissioned.

Cidde

TYPE: Taşit gemi (transport)

BUILDER: SA Cockerill, Antwerp

DISPLACEMENT: 1826gt, 1190nt

DIMENSIONS: L 84.4m, B 11.7m, D 6.5m

HULL: Iron

MACHINERY: Steam, 1 shaft

ENGINE: 1 compound 2 cyl, Hawks

BOILER: 1 _

SPEED: _

BUNKERS: _

COMPLEMENT: _

ARMAMENT: (1890) 3–76mm QF(K)

Cidde Ordered: 1856. Laid down: 1856. Launched: 1856. Trials: 1856. 1856 *Scotland* A Carnegie, Liverpool. 1870 *Scotland,* The Scotland SS Co, Liverpool. 1884 *Cidde* İdare-i Mahsusa, İstanbul. 1890 commissioned, coal depot at KD-Ereğli. 1895 towed to İstanbul, decommissioned. 1903 sold for breaking up.

Note: There are two towns called Ereğli in Turkey, differentiated officially by the prefixes KD (Kara Deniz – Black Sea) and MD (Marmara Deniz – Sea of Marmara).

İzmir

TYPE: Taşit gemi (transport)

BUILDER: T Wingate & Co, Glasgow

DISPLACEMENT: 2528gt, 1420nt

DIMENSIONS: L 100.5m, B 11.2m, D 6.4m

HULL: Iron

MACHINERY: Steam, 1 shaft

ENGINE: 1 compound 2 cyl, T Wingate

BOILERS: 4_

SPEED: (1891) 7kts

BUNKERS: _

COMPLEMENT: _

ARMAMENT: Unarmed. Carried 6000 troops

İzmir (Yd No 181) Ordered: 1873. Laid down: 1874. Launched: 27.8.1874. Trials: 9.1874. Launched as *Indiana* States Line, New York. 8.1874 State of Indiana States Line, New York. 1891 *State of Indiana* C H Pile, Glasgow. 1891 *State of Indiana* Allan Line, Liverpool. 4.1891 sold to Osmanli Govt. 6.1891 commissioned renamed *İzmir.* 1909 decommissioned, laid up at İstanbul. 3.1911 sailed for İzmir. 4.1912 sunk as a blockship at Yenikale (Bay of İzmir). 1913 salvaged and broken up.

Hüdeyde

TYPE: Taşit gemi (transport)

BUILDER: C Mitchell & Co, Glasgow

DISPLACEMENT: 2057gt, 1325nt

DIMENSIONS: L 98.6m, B 10.7m, D 5.6m

HULL: Iron

MACHINERY: Steam, 1 shaft

ENGINE: 1 quart 4 cyl, Central E W

BOILERS: 2 _

SPEED: (1896) 10kts

BUNKERS: _

COMPLEMENT: _

ARMAMENT: (1896) 2–57mm QF

Hüdeyde (Yd No 298) Ordered: 1874. Laid down: 1874. Launched: 1874. Trials: 1874. 1874 *Suez* Nelson & Donkin, Glasgow. 1891 *Hüdeyde* Essanyan Sirketi, İstanbul. 1893 *Hüdeyde* İdare-i Mahusa, İstanbul. 1896 commissioned. 1897 decommissioned, returned to İdare-i Mahusa, İstanbul. 1912 out of service.

Marmara

TYPE: Depit gemi/Taşit gemi (depot ship/transport)

BUILDER: London & Glasgow Co, Glasgow

DISPLACEMENT: 2472gt, 1719nt

DIMENSIONS: L 100.9m, B 111.2m, D 6.4m

HULL: Iron

MACHINERY: Steam, 1 shaft

ENGINE: 1 compound 2 cyl, London & Glasgow Co

BOILERS: 4 _, London & Glasgow Co

SPEED (1896) 7kts

BUNKERS: _

COMPLEMENT: _

ARMAMENT: (1896) 2–57mm QF (1912) Disarmed

Marmara (Yd No 166) Ordered: 1871. Laid down: 1871. Launched: 1872. Trials: 4.1872. 1872 *Pennsylvania* States Line, New York. 12.1873 *State of Pennsylvania* States Line, New York. 1891 *State of Pennsylvania* Allan Line, Liverpool. 1893 *Mekke* Hamidiye Sirketi, İstanbul. 1894 *Mekke* İdare-i Mahsusa, İstanbul. 1896 commissioned. 1897 returned to İdare-i Mahsusa, İstanbul. 1909 out of service, laid up at İstanbul. 10.1912 commissioned, renamed *Marmara*. 1913 decommissioned. 1920 sold for breaking up.

Mekke

TYPE: Depit gemi (depot ship)

BUILDER: London & Glasgow Co, Glasgow

DISPLACEMENT: 2488gt, 171nt

DIMENSIONS: L 100.9m, B 11.2m, D 6.4m

HULL: Iron

MACHINERY: Steam, 1 shaft

ENGINE: 1 compound 2 cyl, London & Glasgow Co

BOILERS: 4 _, London & Glasgow Co

SPEED: (1896) 7kts

BUNKERS: _

COMPLEMENT: _

ARMAMENT: (1896) 2–76mm QF

Mekke (Yd No 175) Ordered: 1873. Laid down: 1874. Launched: 1874. Trials: 1874. 1874 *State of Nevada* States Line, New York. 1891 *State of Nevada* Allan Line, Liverpool. 1893 *Mekke* Hamidiye Vapur Sirketi, İstanbul. 1894 *Mekke* İdare-i Mahsusa, İstanbul. 1896 commissioned. 1897 decommissioned, returned to İdare-i Mahsusa, İstanbul. 1909 out of service, laid up at İstanbul. 1920 broken up.

Dolmabahçe

TYPE: Taşit gemi (transport)

BUILDER: _, Glasgow

DISPLACEMENT: 834gt, 522nt

DIMENSIONS: L 66.1m, B 8.5m, D 5.2m

HULL: Iron

MACHINERY: Steam, 1 shaft

ENGINE: 1 _, MacNab

BOILER: 1 _

SPEED: _

BUNKERS: _

COMPLEMENT: _

ARMAMENT: (1896) 2–57mm QF

Dolmabahçe Ordered: 1856. Laid down: 1856. Launched: 1856. Trials: 1856. 1856 Fevaid-i Osmaniye, İstanbul. 1896 commissioned. 1898 decommissioned, returned to İdare-i Mahsusa, İstanbul. 1909 out of service.

Bezm-i Alem

TYPE: Taşit gemi (transport)

BUILDER: Fairfield Shipbuilding Co, Glasgow

DISPLACEMENT: 4527gt, 2950nt, 3286tdw

DIMENSIONS: L 118.1m, B 13.4m, D 9.8m

HULL: Iron

MACHINERY: Steam, 1 shaft

ENGINE: 1 triple expansion 3 cyl, 3000ihp, Fairfield SB

BOILERS: 2 _, Fairfield SB

SPEED: (1906) 10kts

BUNKERS: _

COMPLEMENT: _

ARMAMENT: Unarmed

Bezm-i Alem (Yd No 337) Ordered: 1888. Laid down: 1888. Launched: 1.12.1888. Trials: 1.1889. 3.1898 *Dresden* Norddeutscher Lloyd, Bremen. 25.11.1903 *Helius* R P Houston & Co, Liverpool. 1904 *Helius* Union Castle Line, London. 1904 laid up at Southampton. 1906 sold to Osmanli Govt. 1906 commissioned. 6.11.1914 sunk by gunfire by Russian destroyers near Kandilli (31.32E 41.23N).

Tirimüjgan

TYPE: Depo gemi (depot ship)

BUILDER: Barrow Shipbuilding Co, Barrow

DISPLACEMENT: 4045gt, 2541nt

DIMENSIONS: L 121.8m, B 12.9m, D 6.5m

HULL: Iron

MACHINERY: Steam, 1 shaft

ENGINE: 1 compound, 2 cyl, 450ihp, Barrow SB

BOILERS: 2 _, Barrow SB

SPEED: _

BUNKERS: _

COMPLEMENT: _

ARMAMENT: Unarmed

Tirimüjgan (Yd No 105) Ordered: 1882. Laid down: 1883. Launched: 5.1883. Trials: 7.1883. 7.1883 *Pembroke Castle* Castle Mail Packet, London. 1900 *Pembroke Castle* Union Castle Line, London. 1906 sold to Osmanli Govt. 1906 *Tirimüjgan* İdare-i Mahsusa, İstanbul. 1908 commissioned as destroyer depot ship. 1910 transport. 1914 engineer school ship. 5.1915 stationary ammunition ship at Çanakkale. 2.1919 depot ship at İzmir. 4.1919 Osmanli Seyrisefain İdaresi, İstanbul. 31.3.1920 grounded and lost off Bafra Burnu (Kizilirmak River, Black Sea) on passage İstanbul-Trabzon with returning military personnel.

Eser-i Cedid

TYPE: Taşit gemi (transport)

BUILDER: T Royden & Son, Sunderland

DISPLACEMENT: 1518gt, 981nt

DIMENSIONS: L 79.1m, B 10.3m, D 5.1m

HULL: Iron

MACHINERY: Steam, 1 shaft

ENGINE: 1 compound 2 cyl, 750ihp, J Jack

BOILERS: 2 _

SPEED: (1909) 9kts

BUNKERS: _

COMPLEMENT: (1909) 45

ARMAMENT: Unarmed

Eser-i Cedid (Yd No 200) Ordered: 1879. Laid down: 1880. Launched: 3.1880. Trials: 5.1880. 5.1890 *Barnesmore* Barnesmore SS Co, Liverpool. 1898 *Eser-i Cedid* İdare-i Mahsusa, İstanbul. 1909 commissioned. 1911 Osmanli Seyrisefain İdare, İstanbul. 1912 *Julia* Fokius & Co, Piraeus. 1915 Julia, registered at Bandar Abbas, Persia (Iran). 1915 Julia Imperial Russian Navy. 1916 *N116* Imperial Russian Navy. 1919 *Artemida* White Russian Navy. 1919 *Jon Cuza* Coudougoris, Sulia. 1921 Valetta A Rizza, *Valetta*. 1922 *Marie Louise* E Countrians, İstanbul. 1924 *Mesut* Hacizade Mesut, İstanbul. 1925 *Torgud* Sofuzade Sudi Ahmet, İstanbul. 1927 *Ordu* Kirzade Sirketi, İstanbul. 22.11.1937 sunk in collision with the cruiser *Hamidiye* off Kizkulesi-İstanbul.

Kosova

TYPE: Taşit gemi (transport)

BUILDER: P Odero, Sestri Ponente

DISPLACEMENT: 1577gt, 1029nt

DIMENSIONS: L 85.1m, B 9.2m, D 5.3m

HULL: Iron

MACHINERY: Steam, 1 shaft

ENGINE: 1 compound 2 cyl, 1000ihp, Odero

BOILERS: 2 _, Odero

SPEED: (1909) 8kts

BUNKERS: _

COMPLEMENT: (1909) 36

ARMAMENT: Unarmed

Kosova Ordered: 1874. Laid down: 1874. Launched: 1874. Trials: 1874. 1874 Sco. N Odero fu Alessandro,

Genoa. 187 *Enrique Calvet* E de Calvet, Garrucha. 1885 *Principe* F Gaggino, Genoa. 1886 *Principe* Canestro & Bonino, Genoa. 1886 *Asia* L. Scorcia & Figli, Bari. 1887 *Asia* Sco. di Nav. a Vapore Adriatica, Bari. 1897 *Asia* V Granata, Bari. 28.5.1899 sold to Osmanli Govt. 7.1899 *Kosova* İdare-i Mahsusa, İstanbul. 1909 commissioned. 1911 decommissioned. 1911 Osmanli Seyrisefain İdare, İstanbul. 1911 out of service.

Mithat Paşa Class

TYPE: Taşit gemi (transport)

BUILDER: Sir Raylton Dixon & Co, Newcastle

DISPLACEMENT: 4455gt, 2482nt

DIMENSIONS: L 112.8m, B 14.1m, D 6.7m

HULL: Steel

MACHINERY: Steam, 1 shaft

ENGINE: 1 triple 3 cyl, 3500ihp, Dixon

BOILERS: 2 Scotch, Dixon

SPEED: (1911) 12kts

BUNKERS: _

COMPLEMENT: _

ARMAMENT: Unarmed

Mithat Paşa (Yd No 476) Ordered: 1900. Laid down: 1900. Launched: 18.11.1900. Trials: 23.1.1901. 2.1900 *Port Royal* Imperial Direct West India Mail Service (managed by Elder, Dempster & Co, Bristol). 1911 bought by Donanmay-i Muavenete-i Milliye Cemiyeti. 22.4.1911 arrived İstanbul. 4.1911 *Mithat Paşa* Osmanli Seyri Sefain İdare, İstanbul. 10.1912 commissioned. 9.1914 Osmanli Seyri Sefain İdare, İstanbul. 6.11.1914 sunk by Russian destroyers near Kandilli on passage İstanbul-Trabzon with troops and war equipment.

Resit Paşa (Yd No 477) Ordered: 1900. Laid down: 1900. Launched: 22.3.1901. Trials: 11.7.1901. 7.1901 *Port Antonio* Imperial Direct West India Mail Service (managed by Elder, Dempster & Co, Bristol). 1911 bought by Donanmay-i Muavenete-i Milliye Cemiyeti. 22.4.1911 arrived İstanbul. 4.1911 *Reit Paşa* Osmanli Seyri Sefain İdare, İstanbul. 9.1911 commissioned as hospital ship. 8.1914 transport. 19.1.1916 decommissioned. 5.1920 Osmanli Seyri Sefain İdare, İstanbul. 1933 T C Deniz Kuvvetlari, commissioned as stationary

depot ship at Gölcük. 1940 decommissioned. 1953 sold for breaking up.

Plevne

TYPE: Taşit gemi (transport)

BUILDER: Thompson & Co, Dundee

DISPLACEMENT: 1154gt, 480nt

DIMENSIONS: L 74.1m, B 7.0m, D 4.8m

HULL: Steel

MACHINERY: Steam, 1 shaft

ENGINE: 1 triple 3 cyl, Thompson & Co

BOILERS: 2 _, Thompson & Co

SPEED: (1911) 10kts

BUNKERS: _

COMPLEMENT: _

ARMAMENT: Unarmed

Plevne (Yd No 100) Ordered: 1892. Laid down: 1892. Launched: 1892. Trials: 1892. 1892 *Sanda* Clyde Shipping Co, Glasgow. 1912 sold to Osmanli Govt. 1912 Plevne Osmanli Seyri Sefain İdare, İstanbul. 10.1912 commissioned. 11.1913 decommissioned. 11.1913 Osmanli Seyri Sefain İdare, İstanbul. 20.10.1915 torpedoed by British submarine H 1 at Şarköy and sunk.

Urla

TYPE: Taşit gemi (transport)

BUILDER: Denny Bros, Dumbarton

DISPLACEMENT: 4179gt, 247nt

DIMENSIONS: L 113.0m, B 13.7m, D 7.7m

HULL: Steel

MACHINERY: Steam, 1 shaft

ENGINE: 1 triple 3 cyl, 2500ihp, Denny Bros

BOILERS: _, Thompson & Co

SPEED: (1914) 12kts

BUNKERS: 720t coal

COMPLEMENT: _

ARMAMENT: Unarmed

Urla (Yd No 481) Ordered: 28.3.1893. Laid down: 1893. Launched:

12.10.1893. Trials: 22.1.1893. 1.1894 *Koroleva* Olga Russkoe Obscetvo Pachodstva, Odessa. 29.10.1914 seized by Osmanli govt while laid at anchor at Büyükdere (Bosporus). Taken to Istinye. 3.11.1914 commissioned, renamed *Urla* barrack ship for Turkish/German naval and dockyard personnel. (For a short time under German flag as *Olga*). 11.1917 transport. 2.1919 decommissioned, laid up at Istinye. 1.10.1921 ownership returned to Russia. 2.1921 purchased by Turkey. 11.1921 *Cumhüriyet* Türkiye Seyri Sefain İdare, İstanbul. 15.1.1952 out of service. 13.3.1954 arrived La Spezia for breaking up.

Nara

TYPE: Taşit gemi (transport)

BUILDER: _

DISPLACEMENT: 300t (?)

DIMENSIONS: L _m, B _m, D _m

HULL: Steel

MACHINERY: Steam, 1 shaft

ENGINE: 1 _

BOILER: 1 _

SPEED: (1915) 10kts

BUNKERS: _

COMPLEMENT: _

ARMAMENT: Unarmed

Nara Ordered:–. Laid down: –. Launched:–. Trials:–. Enemy vessel, 11.1914 seized by Osmanli Govt. 4.1915 commissioned, renamed *Nara*. 4.1915 refitted by Tersane-i Amire. 24.5.1915 captured and sunk by British submarine E 11 at 40.51N 25E (off Tekirdag) on passage İstanbul-Gelibolu.

Mahmut Şevket Paşa

TYPE: Taşit gemi (transport)

BUILDER: J L Thompson & Son, Sunderland

DISPLACEMENT: 2690gt, 2403nt

DIMENSIONS: L 103.6m, B12.2m, D 7.7m

HULL: Steel

MACHINERY: Steam, 1 shaft

ENGINE: 1 triple 3 cyl, 2000ihp, Richardson

BOILERS: 2 _

SPEED: _

BUNKERS: _

COMPLEMENT: _

ARMAMENT: (1915) 2–57mm QF

Mahmut Şevket Paşa (Yd No 211) Ordered: 1886. Laid down:1886. Launched: 10.1886. Trials: 12.1886. 12.1886 *Moyune* China Mutual Steam Navigation Co, London. 1896 Shibata Maru Nippon Yusen KK., Tokyo. 1908 *Shibata Maru* C V Sale, Hong Kong. 1910 *Mahmut Şevket Paşa* Gümüciyan İ dare, İstanbul. 4.1915 seized by Osmanli Govt. 7.1915 protection ship for Osmanli battleships in the Dardanelles. 8.8.1915 torpedoed by British submarine E 14 off Doğan Aslan. Beached. 1915 towed to İstanbul for repair. 1917 returned to service as transport. 1.1.1918 decommissioned. 2.1919 *Ararat* M Gümüciyan, Trabzon. 1921 *Mahmut Şevket Paşa* Osmanli Seyri Sefain İdare, İstanbul. 6.12.1924 Türkiye Seyri Sefain İdare, İstanbul. 8.1933 out of service. 1935 broken up at İstanbul.

Trabzon

TYPE: Taşit gemi (transport)

BUILDER: Kockums MV, Malmö

DISPLACEMENT: 632gt, 369nt, 1200tdw

DIMENSIONS: L 52.3m, B 8.1m, D 3.9m

HULL: Steel

MACHINERY: Steam, 1 shaft

ENGINE: 1 triple 3 cyl, _ihp, Kockums

BOILER: 1 Scotch, Kockums

SPEED: (1922) 8kts

BUNKERS: _

COMPLEMENT: (1922) 25

ARMAMENT: Unarmed

Trabzon (Yd No 57) Ordered: 1891. Laid down: 1891. Launched: 891. Trials:1891. 1891 *Franz* Trelleborge Anf. Ny. Akt., Trelleborg. 1918 *Franz* Rederi A/B Baltic-France, Göteborg. 1920 *Enosis* G A Dracoulis, Piraeus. 26.4.1922 captured by Turkish motor gunboat No.1 in the Black Sea, taken to Trabzon. 5.1922 commissioned, renamed *Trabzon*. 1924 decommissioned, laid up at Gölcük. 1934 sold for breaking up.

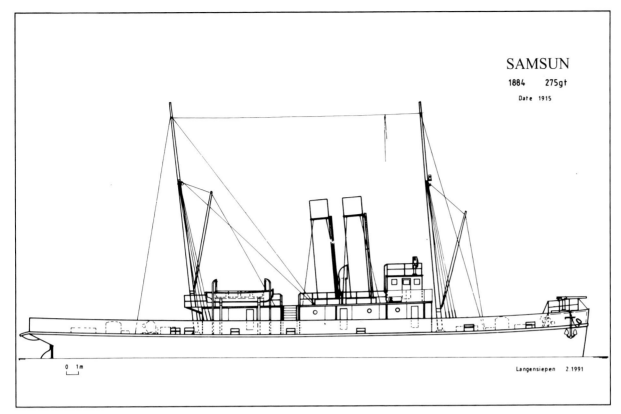

SAMSUN

1884   275gt

Date 1915

0 1m

Langensiepen 2.1991

Samsun

TYPE: Taşit gemi (transport)

BUILDER: C S Swan Hunter, Newcastle

DISPLACEMENT: 1465gt, 857nt, 2130tdw

DIMENSIONS: L 78.0m, B 10.6m, D 5.4m

HULL: Steel

MACHINERY: Steam, 1 shaft

ENGINE: 1 triple 3 cyl, 750ihp, Wallsend EW

BOILER: 1 _

SPEED: (1922) 9kts

BUNKERS: _

COMPLEMENT: (1922) 23

ARMAMENT: Unarmed

Samsun (Yd No 68)   Ordered: 1882. Laid down: 1882. Launched: 14.8.1882. Trials: 2.10.1882. 10.1822 *Klyde* Klyde SS Co, London. 1884 *Klyde* Klyde SS Co, Glasgow, 1896 *Klyde* Maclay & Macintyre, Glasgow. 1900 *Vrisida* Bank of Athens, Syra. 1903 Vissis A Nstragis, Syra. 1906 *Urania* Valsmchios, Syra. 1907 *Urania* M G Barbati, Maripol. 1921 *Urania* Nicola, Piraeus. 7.10.1922 captured by Turkish armed tug *Gazal* in the Black Sea off Bosporus. Taken to

Samsun. 10.1922 commissioned, renamed *Samsun*. 1924 Türkiye Seyri Sefain İdare, İstanbul. 1927 *Galata* Sirzade Sevki Sürekasi, İstanbul. 1938 *Galata* Sosyete Silep T A S., İstanbul. 1.1.1939 aground and sunk near KD-Ereğli.

TUGS

These vessels spent most of their careers serving as tugs for the Ottoman navy. Note that ships seized by the Ottoman government during World War I were not renamed, but some of the existing names were transliterated into Turkish: for example *Stamboul* became *İstanbul, Dauphin* became *Dofen, Stena* became *İstinye.*

Yenikapi

TYPE: Römorkör (tug)

BUILDER: Stabilimente Technico, San Rocco

DISPLACEMENT: 107t, 70gt, 30nt

DIMENSIONS: L 26.4m, B 4.8m, D 2.9m

HULL: Wood

MACHINERY: _

ENGINE: 1 cyl, 150ihp, Stabilimente Technico.

BOILER: 1, Stabilimente Technico

SPEED: (1869) 9kts

BUNKERS: _

COMPLEMENT: 15

ARMAMENT: Unarmed

Yenikapi (Yd No 39)   Ordered: 1866. Laid down: 1866. Launched: 1866. Trials: 1866. 1866 Ercole, Trieste. 8.1.1869 bought by Osmanli Govt. 5.1869 commissioned. 1880 converted into fire-fighting tug and watertanker. 1888 transferred to Idare-i Mahusa, İstanbul. 1909 out of service.

Mesut

TYPE: Römorkör (tug)

BUILDER: _

DISPLACEMENT: 162t, 116gt, 64nt

DIMENSIONS: L 32.2m, B 5.3m, D _m

HULL: Iron

MACHINERY: Steam.

ENGINE: 1 compound 2 cyl vertical, _ihp (made 1882) Tersane-i Amire

BOILER: 1

SPEED: (1896) 8kts

BUNKERS: _

COMPLEMENT: _

ARMAMENT: (1896) 2–37mm RC

Mesut Ordered: 1869. Laid down: 1869. Launched: 1869. Trials: 1869. 1869 *Hawk* (British) based at Gelibolu. 1882 sold to Osmanli Govt. 1882 *Mesut* İdare-i Mahsusa, İstanbul. 1896 transferred to Osmanli Bahriye, commissioned, based at İstanbul. 1909 decommissioned.

Samsun

TYPE: Römorkör (tug)

BUILDER: Scott & Sons, Bowling

DISPLACEMENT: 105gt, 89nt

DIMENSIONS: L 27.4m, B 5.6m, D 2.6m

HULL: Steel

MACHINERY: Screw steamer, 1 shaft

ENGINE: 1 compound 2 cyl, _ihp, Fisher, Paisley

BOILER: 1

SPEED: _

BUNKERS: _

COMPLEMENT: 12

ARMAMENT: Unarmed

Samsun (Yd No 224) Ordered: 1909. Laid down: 1910. Launched: 1910. Trials: 1910. 1910 commissioned, based at Çanakkale.

Menderes

TYPE: Römorkör (tug)

BUILDER: Scott & Sons, Bowling

DISPLACEMENT: 105gt, 89nt

DIMENSIONS: L 27.4m, B 5.6m, D 2.6m

HULL: Steel

MACHINERY: Steam, 1 shaft

ENGINE: 1 compound 2 cyl vertical, _ihp, Fisher, Paisley

BOILER: 1

SPEED: _

BUNKERS: _

COMPLEMENT: _

ARMAMENT: Unarmed

Menderes Ordered: 1909. Laid down: 1910. Launched: 1910. Trials: 1910.

Built as *Semender.* 1910 commissioned, based at Çanakkale. 1.5.1912 sunk by Turkish mine off Akbas, while clearing a minefield. 15 soldiers, 7 civilians killed.

Sürat

TYPE: Römorkör (tug)

BUILDER: _

DISPLACEMENT: _

DIMENSIONS: _

HULL: Steel

MACHINERY: Steam, 1 shaft

ENGINE: 1

BOILER: 1

SPEED: _

BUNKERS: _

COMPLEMENT: _

ARMAMENT: (1911) Unarmed (1913) 1–37mm QF

Sürat Ordered: Laid down: Launched: Trials: Private tug at Selanik. 1911 seized by Osmanli Govt, commissioned at Selanik. 1913 based at Çanakkale. 11.1918 decommissioned.

Katerin

TYPE: Römorkör (tug)

BUILDER: _

DISPLACEMENT: _

DIMENSIONS: _

HULL: _

MACHINERY: Steam, 1 shaft

ENGINE: 1

BOILER: 1

SPEED: _

BUNKERS: _

COMPLEMENT: _

ARMAMENT: (1913) 1–37mm QF

Katerin Ordered: –. Laid down:–. Launched: –. Trials: –. Private tug at Selanik. 12.1911 seized by Osmanli Govt at Selanik. 12.1911 commissioned, based at Selanik. 1913 based at Çanakkale. 12.3.1915 heavily damaged

by Turkish gunfire at Soganli (Dardanelles).

Teshıla

TYPE: Römorkör (tug)

BUILDER: _

DISPLACEMENT: _

DIMENSIONS: _

HULL: _

MACHINERY: Steam, 1 shaft

ENGINE: 1

BOILER: 1

SPEED: _

BUNKERS: _

COMPLEMENT: _

ARMAMENT: (1913) 1–37mm QF

Teshıla Ordered: – . Laid down: – . Launched: – . Trials: – . Private tug at Selanik. 12.1911 seized by the Osmanli Bahriye at Selanik. 12.1911 commissioned, based at Selanik. 1913 based at Çanakkale.

Muha

TYPE: Römorkör (tug)

BUILDER: _

DISPLACEMENT: 200t

DIMENSIONS: _

HULL: Steel

MACHINERY: Steam, 1 shaft

ENGINE: 1

BOILER: 1

SPEED: _

BUNKERS: _

COMPLEMENT: 20

ARMAMENT: 1–70mm, 1–37mm QF

Muha Ordered: Laid down: Launched: Trials: 1911 bought by the Osmanli Bahriye. 1911 commissioned. 7.1.1912 sunk by Italian cruiser *Piemonte* and destroyers off Konfida (Red Sea).

Kurt

TYPE: Römorkör (tug)

BUILDER: _

DISPLACEMENT: _

DIMENSIONS: _

HULL: Steel

MACHINERY: Steam, 1 shaft

ENGINE: 1

BOILER: 1

SPEED: _

BUNKERS: _

COMPLEMENT: _

ARMAMENT: Unarmed

Kurt Ordered: – . Laid down: – . Launched: –. Trials: –. 1911 commissioned as tug and pump vessel, based at İstanbul. 1923 decommissioned.

İgtinam

TYPE: Römorkör (tug)

BUILDER: _

DISPLACEMENT: _

DIMENSIONS: _

HULL: Steel

MACHINERY: Steam, 1 shaft

ENGINE: 1

BOILER: 1

PUMP CAPACITY: 20t/h

SPEED: _

BUNKERS: _

COMPLEMENT: _

ARMAMENT: Unarmed

İgtinam Ordered: –. Laid down: – . Launched: –. Trials: –. 1911 commissioned, based at İstanbul. 20.10.1915 based at Çanakkale. 1919 decommissioned.

Gazal

TYPE: Römorkör (tug)

BUILDER: H Vuijk & Zonen, Cappelle a/d Ysel

DISPLACEMENT: 182gt, 15nt

DIMENSIONS: L 30.1m, B 6.7m, D 3.1m

HULL: Steel

MACHINERY: Steam, 1 shaft

ENGINE: 1 compound 2 cyl vertical, 750ihp, G T Gray

BOILER: 1

SPEED: (1912) 12kts

BUNKERS:

COMPLEMENT: _

ARMAMENT: Unarmed

Gazal (Yd No 366) Ordered: 1910. Laid down: 1910. Launched: 12.1910. Trials: 1.1911. 1.1912 *Underwriter* R A Grech, İstanbul (British flag) 9.7.1912 sold for 8400 GL to Osmanli Govt. 8.1912 commissioned as Lazal. 1921 vessel went over to the Turkish Liberation Forces. 12.1923 transferred to Türkiye Seyri Sefain İdaresi, İstanbul. 1954 out of service, sold for breaking up.

Memo

TYPE: Römorkör (tug)

BUILDER: _

DISPLACEMENT: _

DIMENSIONS: _

HULL: _

MACHINERY: Steam, 1 shaft

ENGINE: 1

BOILER: 1

SPEED: _

BUNKERS: _

COMPLEMENT: 1 officer, 8 ratings

ARMAMENT: Unarmed

Memo Ordered: – . Laid down: – . Launched: – . Trials: –. Greek private tug at İstanbul. 20.10.1912 seized by Osmanli Bahriye, commissioned. 12.12.1915 sunk by gunfire by British submarine E 11 near Eskihisar.

Express

TYPE: Römorkör (tug)

BUILDER: _

DISPLACEMENT: _

DIMENSIONS: _

HULL: Steel

MACHINERY: Steam, 1 shaft

ENGINE: 1 compound 2 cyl, 160ihp

BOILER: 1

SPEED: 8kts

BUNKERS: _

COMPLEMENT: 5

ARMAMENT: Unarmed

Express Ordered: – . Laid down: – . Launched: –. Trials: –. Greek private tug at İstanbul. 20.10.1912 seized by Osmanli Govt. 12.1912 commissioned, dockyard tug at İstanbul. 5.1915–3.1917 German crew. 4.1919 decommissioned.

Fatihiye

TYPE: Römorkör (tug)

BUILDER: Scott & Sons, Bowling

DISPLACEMENT: 192gt

DIMENSIONS: L 32.2m, B 7.0m, D 3.6m

HULL: Steel

MACHINERY: Steam, 1 shaft

ENGINE: 1 compound 2 cyl vertical, _ihp, Aitchison, Blair & Co

BOILER: 1

SPEED: _

BUNKERS: _

COMPLEMENT: _

ARMAMENT: Unarmed

Fatihiye (Yd No 255) Ordered: 1914. Laid down: 1914. Launched: 6.1914. Trials: 1914. Launched as *Wrestler* Steel & Bennic, Glasgow. 6.1914 bought by Osmanli Bahriye, renamed *Fatihiye*. 11.1914 seized by British Govt at Bowling. 11.1914 *Hotspur* Royal Navy. 1920 *Muria* W Watkins, London. 8.11.1940 sunk by mine 5 miles off North Foreland.

İstanbul

TYPE: Römorkör (tug)

BUILDER: F Barachini, Sestri Ponente

DISPLACEMENT: 114gt, 32nt

DIMENSIONS: L 27.3m, B 6.0m, D 3.4m

HULL: Wood

MACHINERY: Steam, 1 shaft

ENGINE: 1 compound 2 cyl vertical, _ihp, Bow Maclachlan

BOILER: 1

SPEED: _

BUNKERS: _

COMPLEMENT: 1 officer, 8 ratings

ARMAMENT: Unarmed

İstanbul Ordered: 1895. Laid down: 1895. Launched: 1895. Trials: 1895. 1895 *Stamboul* Cie de Remorquage de Pilotage et de Sautage, Marseille. 1903 *Stamboul* Cie de Remorquage de Pilotage et de Sautage, Marseille (mgr) S Bandermaly, İstanbul (French flag). 4.11.1914 seized by the Osmanli Govt at İstanbul. 12.1915 commissioned as *İstanbul*. 5.9.1916 sunk in the Black Sea on passage KD-Ereğli to İstanbul.

France

TYPE: Römorkör (tug)

BUILDER: Cox & Co, Falmouth

DISPLACEMENT: 178gt, 25nt

DIMENSIONS: L 36.2m, B 6.4m, D 3.6m

HULL: Steel

MACHINERY: Steam, 1 shaft

ENGINE: 1 triple 3 cyl vertical, 700ihp, Cox & Co

BOILER: 1

SPEED: (1914) 10kts

BUNKERS: _

COMPLEMENT: 5 officers, 26 ratings

ARMAMENT: (1914) 2–57mm QF

France (Yd No 78) Ordered: 1900. Laid down: 1901. Launched: 1901. Trials: 1901. 1901 *Pinguin* W Rowe, Falmouth. 1905 *France* Cie de Remorquage de Pilotage et de Sautage, Marseille (mgr) S Bandermaly, İstanbul (French flag). 9.1914 seized by the Osmanli Govt at İstanbul. 10.1914 commissioned as mine-hunting boat. 4.1915 Salvage tug and pump vessel. 4.1919 returned to French owner.

Bordeaux

TYPE: Römorkör (tug)

BUILDER: S MacKnight & Co, Ayr

DISPLACEMENT: 142gt, 1nt

DIMENSIONS: L 28.0m, B 6.1m, D 3.4m

HULL: Iron

MACHINERY: Steam, 1 shaft

ENGINE: 1 triple 3 cyl vertical, _ihp, Muir & Houston

BOILER: 1

SPEED: _

BUNKERS: _

COMPLEMENT: _

ARMAMENT: Unarmed

Bordeaux Ordered: 1888. Laid down: 1888. Launched: 1888. Trials: 1888. 1888 *Alexandra* Alexandria Towing Co, Liverpool. 1906 Bordeaux Cie de Remorquage de Pilotage et de Sautage, Marseille (mgr) S Bandermaly, İstanbul (French flag). 1912 *Bordeaux* SA Ottomane de Dock et Ateliers du Haut-Bosphore, İstanbul (French flag). 8.1914 seized by Osmanli Govt. 9.1914 commissioned as tug.

Maggie Grech

TYPE: Römorkör (tug)

BUILDER: Admiralty Dockyard, Sheerness

DISPLACEMENT: 642gt, 185nt

DIMENSIONS: L 59.6m, B 8.5m, D _m

HULL: Iron

MACHINERY: Steam, 2 shafts

ENGINES: 2 triple 3 cyl vertical, _ ihp, J & G Rennie

BOILERS: 2

SPEED: _

BUNKERS: _

COMPLEMENT: _

ARMAMENT: Unarmed

Maggie Grech Ordered: 1888. Laid down: 1.5.1888. Launched: 6.4.1888. Trials: 1889. 24.6.1890 *Basilisk* Royal Navy (sloop). 1905 out of service, sold to a private owner and converted into salvage tug. 18.11.1905 *Maggie Grech* V S E Grech, Gelibolu (British flag) 14.10.1910 *Maggie Grech* R A Grech, İstanbul (French flag). 4.11.1914 seized by Osmanli Govt at Gelibolu. 11.1914 commissioned as tug. 18.4.1915 decommissioned, laid up at İstanbul. 4.1919 returned to French owner. 1924 sold for breaking up.

Bospordok

TYPE: Römorkör (tug)

BUILDER: _

DISPLACEMENT: 1gt, 16nt, 66ts

DIMENSIONS: L 18.0m, B 4.8m, D 1.8m

HULL: Steel

MACHINERY: Steam, 1 shaft

ENGINE: 1 compound 2 cyl vertical

BOILER: 1

SPEED: _

BUNKERS: _

COMPLEMENT: _

ARMAMENT: Unarmed

Bospordok Ordered: 1900s Laid down: 1900s Launched: 1900s Trials: 1900s1912 *Bospordok* SA Ottomane de Dock & Ateliers du Haut-Bosphore, İstanbul (French flag). 8.1914 seized by Osmanli Govt. 8.1914 commissioned as mine-hunting boat. 10.1914 tug. 4.1919 returned to French owner. 1924 renamed Vatan. 4.1938 *Vatan* T C Deniz Bank umum Müdürlügü, İstanbul. 1.3.1952. *Vatan-12* D B Istinye Tersanesi, İstanbul. 196? out of service, sold for breaking up at İstanbul.

Mary Louise

TYPE: Römorkör (tug)

BUILDER: J P Rennoldson, South Shields

DISPLACEMENT: 100gt, 10nt

DIMENSIONS: L 30.0m, B 5.8m, D 2.9m

HULL: Wood

MACHINERY: Steam, side paddle

ENGINE: 1-L2 cyl, _ihp, J P Rennoldson

BOILER: 1 single-ended

SPEED: _

BUNKERS: _

COMPLEMENT: _

ARMAMENT: Unarmed

Mary Louise (Yd No 60) Ordered: 1878. Laid down: 1878. Launched: 1878. Trials: 7.1878. 7.1878 *Mary*

Louise James Wardle, South Shields.
3.3.1901 *Mary Louise* V S E Grech,
London, based at Gelibolu. 14.1.1910
Mary Louise R A Grech, İstanbul
(British flag). 3.11.1914 seized by
Osmanli Govt at Gelibolu. 11.1914
commissioned. 4.1915 out of service,
laid up at Gelibolu.

Lutèce

TYPE: Römorkör (tug)

BUILDER: S MacKnight & Co, Ayr

DISPLACEMENT: 197gt, 21nt

DIMENSIONS: L 53.6m, B 6.7m, D 3.7m

HULL: Iron

MACHINERY: Steam, 2 shaft

ENGINES: 2 compound 2 cyl vertical,
_ihp, Ross & Duncan

BOILER: _

SPEED: _

BUNKERS: _

COMPLEMENT: _

ARMAMENT: Unarmed

Lutéce (Yd No 22) Ordered: 1889. Laid
down: 1889. Launched: 2.4.1890. Trials:
4.1890. 4.1890 *Hornby* Alexandra
Towing Co Ltd, Liverpool. 1906 *Lutèce*
Cie de Remorquage et de Pilotage,
Marseille (mgr) S Bandermaly, İstanbul
(French flag). 1912 *Lutèce* SA
Ottomane de Dock & Ateliers du Haut-
Bosphore, İstanbul (French flag). 8.1914
seized by the Osmanli Govt at İstanbul.
8.1914 commissioned as *Lutèce*. 4.1919
returned to French owner. 1924 *Vega* S
Serra, Genoa. 1926 Vega Quintino
Viglienzoni, Genoa. 25.11.1940 *Vega*
Royal Italian Navy. 9.9.1943 seized by
German forces at La Spezia. 10.4.1945
scuttled at La Spezia. 1946 salvaged.
1946 Vega Q Viglienzoni, Genoa. 1953
sold for breaking up at Genoa.

Eole

TYPE: Römorkör (tug)

BUILDER: F Barachini, Sestri Ponente

DISPLACEMENT: 108gt, 25nt

DIMENSIONS: L 26.1m, B 5.9m, D 3.4m

HULL: Wood

MACHINERY: Screw, 1 shaft

ENGINE: 1 triple 3 cyl vertical, _ihp,
Wilson & MacLaren

BOILER: 1

SPEED: (1914) 8kts

BUNKERS: _

COMPLEMENT: _

ARMAMENT: (1914) Unarmed
(1915) 1–47mm QF

Eole Ordered: 1895. Laid down: 1895.
Launched: 1895. Trials: 1895. 1895
Eole Cie de Remorquage de Pilotage et
de Sautage, Marseille (mgr) S
Bandermaly, Marseille. 1902 *Eole* (mgr)
S Bandermaly, İstanbul (French flag).
9.1914 seized by the Osmanli Govt. at
Zonguldak. 10.1914 commissioned as
Eole, based at Zonguldak. 4.1919
returned to French owner. 1923
Zonguldak Ereğli Sirketi, *Zonguldak.*
1939 *Zonguldak* Et Bank (mgr) Ereğli
Kömürleri İsletmesi, Zonguldak. 1961
Zonguldak Türkiye Kömür İsletmesi,
Zonguldak (mgr) Ereğli Kömür İ
sletmesi, Zonguldak. 1962 out of ser-
vice.

Paris

TYPE: Römorkör (tug)

BUILDER: D J Dunlop & Co, Port
Glasgow

DISPLACEMENT: 116gt, 33nt

DIMENSIONS: L 27.9m, B 5.7m, D 2.6m

HULL: Steel

MACHINERY: Steam, 1 shaft

ENGINE: 1 compound 2 cyl vertical,
_ihp, D J Dunlop

BOILER: 1 boiler

SPEED: (1914) 8kts

BUNKERS: _

COMPLEMENT: (1914) 1 officer, 15 ratings

ARMAMENT: (1914) Unarmed
(1915) 1–47mm QF

Paris (Yd No 231) Ordered: 1896.
Laid down: 1896. Launched: 1896.
Trials: 1896. 1896 *Paris* Towage &
Salvage Co (mgr) J Fitzgerald, London.
1896 *Paris* Cie de Remorquage et de
Pilotage, Marseille (mgr) P Bandermaly,
İstanbul (French flag). 9.1914 seized by
the Osmanli Govt at İstanbul. 11.1914
commissioned as *Paris* mine-hunting
boat. 11.1914 tug. 4.1919 returned to
French owners. 1919 sunk in the Black
Sea.

Liverpool

TYPE: Römorkör (tug)

BUILDER: D J Dunlop & Co, Port
Glasgow

DISPLACEMENT: 116gt, 33nt

DIMENSIONS: L 27.9m, B 5.7m, D 2.6m

HULL: Steel

MACHINERY: Steam, 1 shaft

ENGINE: 1 compound 2 cyl vertical,
_ihp, D J Dunlop

BOILER: 1

SPEED: (1914) 8kts

BUNKERS: _

COMPLEMENT: (1914) 1 officer, 15 ratings

ARMAMENT: (1914) Unarmed
(1915) 1–57mm QF

Liverpool Ordered: 1896. Laid down:
1896. Launched:.1896. Trials: 1896.
1896 *Liverpool* Towage & Salvage Co
(mgr) J Fitzgerald, London. 1896
Liverpool Cie de Remorquage et de
Pilotage, Marseille (mgr) P Bandermaly,
İstanbul (French flag). 9.1.14 seized by
Osmanli Govt at İstanbul. 11.1914 com-
missioned as *Liverpool* mine-hunting
boat. 11.1914 tug. 4.1919 returned to
French owners. 1919 sunk in the Black
Sea.

İstinye

TYPE: Römorkör (tug)

BUILDER: _

DISPLACEMENT: _

DIMENSIONS: _

HULL: Steel

MACHINERY: Steam, 1 shaft

ENGINE: 1 compound 2 cyl vertical

BOILER: 1

SPEED: (1914) 10kts

BUNKERS: _

COMPLEMENT: _

ARMAMENT: Unarmed

İstinye Ordered: 1900s Laid down:
1900s Launched: 1900s Trials: 1900s.
1912 *Stena* SA Ottomane de Dock et
Ateliers du Haut-Bosphore, İstanbul

(French flag). 8.1914 seized by Osmanli
Govt at İstinye. 8.1914 commissioned as
İstinye mine-hunting boat. 10.1914 tug.
2.1919 returned to French owner,
renamed *Stena,* dockyard-tug at İstinye.
4.1938 *İstinye* Deniz Bank umum
Müdürlügü, İstanbul. 1.3.1952 D B
İstanbul Liman İsletmesi, İstanbul. 1961
out of service.

Foça

TYPE: Römorkör (tug)

BUILDER: Piraeus

DISPLACEMENT: 48gt, 23nt

DIMENSIONS: L 20.3m, B 4.4m, D 1.8m

HULL: Wood

MACHINERY: Steam, 1 shaft

ENGINE: 1 compound 2 cyl vertical,
120ihp

BOILER: 1

SPEED: (1914) 10kts

BUNKERS: 6t coal

COMPLEMENT: 8

ARMAMENT: Unarmed

Foça Ordered: 1906. Laid down: 1907.
Launched: 1907. Trials: 1907. 1907
Foça Guiffray Sirketi, İzmir. 8.1914
chartered by Osmanli Govt., commissioned as tug and service boat at İzmir.
12.1918 returned to owner. 1924 İzmir
Liman İsletmesi, İzmir. 1938 D B İzmir
Liman İsletmesi, İzmir. 1953 rebuilt as
motor tug (160bhp diesel). 1962 out of
service.

Elena

TYPE: Römorkör (tug)

BUILDER: Guiffray Tersane, İzmir

DISPLACEMENT: 125gt, 18nt

DIMENSIONS: L 29.5m, B 5.8m, D 3.1m

HULL: Wood

MACHINERY: Steam, 1 shaft

ENGINE: 1 compound 2 cyl vertical,
250ihp

BOILER: 1

SPEED: (1914) 8kts

BUNKERS: _

COMPLEMENT: 5

ARMAMENT: Unarmed

Elena Ordered: 1912. Laid down:
1912. Launched: 1912. Trials: 1912.
1912 *Elena* Guiffray Sirketi, İzmir.
10.1914 chartered by Osmanli Bahriye,
commissioned, based at İzmir. 11.1918
returned to owner. 1923 *İmdat* Semplus
Kazase, İstanbul. 1926 *Asma* Ereğli
Sirketi, Zonguldak. 1939 Eti Bank (mgr)
Ereğli Kömürleri İsletmesi, Zonguldak.
1939 re-engined (450bhp diesel). 1959
out of service.

Cemıl

TYPE: Römorkör (tug)

BUILDER: _

DISPLACEMENT: _

DIMENSIONS: _

HULL: _

MACHINERY: Steam, 1 shaft

ENGINE: 1

BOILER: 1

SPEED: _

BUNKERS: _

COMPLEMENT: _

ARMAMENT: Unarmed

Cemil Ordered: –. Laid down: –.
Launched: –. Trials: –. Osmanli private
tug. 10.1914 chartered by Osmanli
Bahriye, commissioned. 2.1919 returned
to owner.

Gürçıstan

TYPE: Römorkör (tug)

BUILDER: _

DISPLACEMENT: 55t

DIMENSIONS: L 21.5m, B 4.5m, D 1.8m

HULL: Steel

MACHINERY: Steam, 1 shaft

ENGINE: 1 compound 2 cyl vertical,
120ihp

BOILER: 1

SPEED: (1914) 9kts

BUNKERS: _

COMPLEMENT: 4

ARMAMENT: Unarmed

Gürçıstan Ordered:1900s Laid down:
1900s Launched: 1900s Trials: 1900s
Greek prize of 1912 or Osmanli private
tug. 10.1914 commissioned, based at
Çanakkale. 4.1919 returned to owner.

Bayrakli

TYPE: Römorkör (tug)

BUILDER: _

DISPLACEMENT: _

DIMENSIONS: _

HULL: _

MACHINERY: Steam, 1 shaft

ENGINE: 1

BOILER: 1

SPEED: _

BUNKERS: _

COMPLEMENT: _

ARMAMENT: Unarmed

Bayrakli Ordered: 1900s. Laid down:
1900s. Launched: 1900s. Trials: 1900s
Bayrakli Guiffray Sirketi, İzmir.
10.1914 chartered by Osmanli Bahriye.
1.1915 commissioned as tug and service
boat. 4.1919 returned to owner.

Şevkiyat

TYPE: Römorkör (tug)

BUILDER: _

DISPLACEMENT: _

DIMENSIONS: _

HULL: _

MACHINERY: Steam, 1 shaft

ENGINE: 1

BOILER: 1

SPEED: _

BUNKERS: _

COMPLEMENT: _

ARMAMENT: Unarmed

Şevkiyat Ordered: 1900s. Laid down:
1900s . Launched: 1900s. Trials: 1900s.
Private tug at İzmir. 11.1914 seized by
Osmanli Bahriye at İzmir. 1.1915 com-

missioned as tug and service boat at
İzmir. 4.1919 returned to owner.

Bornova

TYPE: Römorkör (tug)

BUILDER: _

DISPLACEMENT: _

DIMENSIONS: _

HULL: _

MACHINERY: Steam, 1 shaft

ENGINE: 1

BOILER: 1

SPEED: _

BUNKERS: _

COMPLEMENT: _

ARMAMENT: Unarmed

Bornova Ordered: 1900s. Laid down:
1900s. Launched: 1900s. Trials: 1900s.
Private tug at İzmir. 11.1914 seized by
Osmanli Bahriye at İzmir. 1.1915 com-
missioned as tug and service boat at
İzmir. 4.1919 returned to owner.

Dofen

TYPE: Römorkör (tug)

BUILDER: F Barachini, Sestri Ponente

DISPLACEMENT: 125gt, 23nt

DIMENSIONS: L 26.1m, B 5.89m,
D 3.5m

HULL: Steel

MACHINERY: Steam, 1 shaft

ENGINE: 1 compound 2 cyl vertical,
ihp, Wilson & MacLaren

BOILER: 1

SPEED: _

BUNKERS: _

COMPLEMENT: 1 officer, 12 ratings

ARMAMENT: 1–37mm QF

Dofen Ordered: 1894. Laid down:
1895. Launched: 1895. Trials: 1895.
1895 *Dauphin* J Compte Calise (mgr) G
P Lecos, İstanbul (French flag).
4.11.1914 seized by Osmanli Govt at
Zonguldak. 3.1915 towed to İstanbul,

commissioned as *Dofen*. 22.8.1915 sunk
by gunfire by British submarine E 11 off
Tekirdağ.

Maltepe

TYPE: Römorkör (tug)

BUILDER: _

DISPLACEMENT: 60t

DIMENSIONS: L 20.2m, B 4.3m, D 2.3m

HULL: Steel

MACHINERY: Steam, 1 shaft

ENGINE: 1 compound 2 cyl vertical

BOILER: 1

SPEED: (1915) 6kts

BUNKERS: 12t coal

COMPLEMENT: 8

ARMAMENT: Unarmed

Maltepe Ordered: 1911. Laid down:
1912. Launched:1912. Trials: 1912.
1912 *Maltepe* Osmanli Seyri Sefain
İdaresi, İstanbul. 3.1915 transferred to
Osmanli Bahriye. 4.1915 commissioned. 12.1918 returned to owner.
6.12.1923 Türkiye Seyri Sefain İdaresi,
İstanbul. (after 1935 not in the Turkish
Ship Register.)

Sa'na

TYPE: Römorkör (tug)

BUILDER: _

DISPLACEMENT: 85t, 52nt

DIMENSIONS: L 20.4m, B 4.2m, D 2.3m

HULL: Iron

MACHINERY: Steam, 1 shaft

ENGINE: 1 compound 2 cyl vertical,
200ihp

BOILER: 1

SPEED: (1915) 6kts

BUNKERS: 10t coal

COMPLEMENT: 1 officer, 9 ratings

ARMAMENT: Unarmed

Sa'na Ordered: 1897. Laid down:
1896. Launched:1897. Trials: 1897.
1897 *Sa'na* İdare-i Mahusa. 10.8.1910
Osmanli Seyri Sefain İdares, İstanbul.
3.1915 transferred to Osmanli Bahriye.

4.1915 commissioned, based at Gelibolu. 11.1918 returned to owner. 6.12.1923 Türkiye Seyri Sefain İdaresi, İstanbul. 1.12.1933 D B İstanbul Liman İsletmesi, İstanbul. 1953 out of service.

Alemdar

TYPE: Römorkör (salvage tug)

BUILDER: Helsingörs Jernsk & Mak., Helsingör

DISPLACEMENT: 363gt, 192nt

DIMENSIONS: L 49.4m, B 7.9m, D 3.9m

HULL: Steel

MACHINERY: Steam, 1 shaft

ENGINE: 1 triple 3 cyl vertical, 580ihp, Helsingör J & M.

BOILERS: 2, Helsingör J & M

SPEED: (1915) 10kts

BUNKERS: 90t coal

COMPLEMENT: _

ARMAMENT: Unarmed

Alemdar (Yd No 62) Ordered: 1898. Laid down: 1898. Launched: 4.6.1898. Trials: 1899. 21.5.1899 *Danmark* Em Z Sviter Bjerg Enterprise, Copenhagen. 8.11.1914 seized by the Osmanli Govt at İstanbul and laid up. 1.1915 commissioned as *Danmark*. 5.1915 renamed *Alemdar*. 12.1.1916 officially bought by Osmanli Govt. 10.1918 laid up at İstanbul. 1920 joined Turkish Liberation Forces. 1924 transferred to Türkiye Seyri Sefain İdaresi, İstanbul. 1959 out of service, laid up at Büyükdere. 1960 sold to a private owner, rebuilt as a tankbarge. 1964 *Garzan* İsikurt Denizcilik Transport ve Ticaret, İstanbul. 1980 *Garzan* Aksoy Denizcilik ve Ticaret, İstanbul. 1982 broken up at İstanbul.

Abdül Kadir

TYPE: Römorkör (tug)

BUILDER: _

DISPLACEMENT: 79t

DIMENSIONS: _

HULL: Steel

MACHINERY: Steam, 1 shaft

ENGINE: 1

BOILER: 1

SPEED: _

BUNKERS: _

COMPLEMENT: _

ARMAMENT: Unarmed

Abdül Kadir Ordered: –. Laid down: –. Launched: –. Trials: –. *Abdül Kadir* Ahmet ve Süleyman Beyler, İstanbul. 4.1915 chartered by the Osmanli Bahriye, commissioned, based at Gelibolu. 4.1919 returned to owner.

Arslan

TYPE: Römorkör (tug)

BUILDER: _

DISPLACEMENT: _

DIMENSIONS: _

HULL: _

MACHINERY: Steam, 1 shaft

ENGINE: 1

BOILER: 1

SPEED: _

BUNKERS: _

COMPLEMENT: 6

ARMAMENT: Unarmed

Arslan Ordered: –. Laid down: –. Launched: –. Trials: –. Osmanli private tug. 1915 chartered by Osmanli Bahriye. 1915 commissioned. 12.10.1916 sunk by mine in the Black Sea near Karasu. Crew of 6 killed.

Süleymaniye

TYPE: Römorkör (tug)

BUILDER: _

DISPLACEMENT: 98t

DIMENSIONS: _

HULL: Steel

MACHINERY: Steam, 1 shaft

ENGINE: 1

BOILER: 1

SPEED: _

BUNKERS: _

COMPLEMENT: _

ARMAMENT: Unarmed

Süleymaniye Ordered: Laid down: Launched: Trials: 1900s. *Süleymaniye* Ahmet ve Süleyman Beyler, İstanbul. 1915 chartered by Osmanli Bahriye, commissioned, based at Gelibolu. 1919 returned to owner.

Leonida

TYPE: Römorkör (tug)

BUILDER: J Readhead & Co, South Shields

DISPLACEMENT: 377gt, 109nt

DIMENSIONS: L 49.2m, B 7.5m, D 3.7m

HULL: Iron

MACHINERY: Steam, side paddle

ENGINE: 1 L2 cyl, 1200ihp, J Readhead

BOILERS: 2 single-ended (made 1895)

SPEED: 8kts

BUNKERS: _

COMPLEMENT: _

ARMAMENT: Unarmed

Leonida Ordered: 1879. Laid down: 1879. Launched: 1879. Trials: 12.1879. 1879 *Pilot Fish* Kelsall, Hodgkinson & Waterloo, Liverpool. 187 converted from trawler to tug. 187 *Pilot Fish* St John Steam Tug Co, Liverpool. 5.1.1882 *Pathfinder*, Liverpool Steam Tug Co, Liverpool. 13.5.1910 *Pathfinder*, R A Grech, Liverpool (based at İstanbul). 6.12.1913 *Leonida*, N C Zarcalis & A P Lascarides, İstanbul. 8.1915 seized by Osmanli Bahriye, commissioned. 5.10.1915 torpedoed and sunk by British submarine E 12 off Tekirdag.

Menfaat

TYPE: Römorkör (tug)

BUILDER: _

DISPLACEMENT: 3nt

DIMENSIONS: _

HULL: Steel

MACHINERY: Steam, 1 shaft

ENGINE: 1

BOILER: 1

SPEED: _

BUNKERS: _

COMPLEMENT: _

ARMAMENT: Unarmed

Menfaat Ordered: –. Laid down: –. Launched: –. Trials: –. Osmanli private tug. 3.1915 chartered by Osmanli Bahriye, commissioned, based at Gelibolu. 12.8.1915 sunk off Tekirdag in a collision.

HARBOUR SERVICE VESSELS

The ships in the following section were classified as tugs but were used more as water tankers and fire fighting vessels than for towing duties.

Boyana

TYPE: Römorkör (tug)

BUILDER: John Thompson, Rotherhithe, London

DISPLACEMENT: 193t, 162nt, 80t bm

DIMENSIONS: Lpp 37.0m, B 5.7m, D 1.8m

HULL: Wood, diagonal planked hull

MACHINERY: Steam, side paddle

ENGINE: 1 2 cyl, Ravenhill, Salkeld & Co

BOILER: 1

SPEED: _

BUNKERS: _

COMPLEMENT: 21

ARMAMENT: (1858) 1 pivot gun forward
(1863) 2 guns
(1872) 2–115mm (K)
(1880) Unarmed

Boysms Ordered: 1857. Laid down: 1858. Launched: 24.7.1858. Trials: 1857. 1858 commissioned, based on Lake Scutari. 1880 based at İstanbul. 1906 decommissioned. 1910 sold for breaking up.

Çatalca

TYPE: Römorkör (tug)

BUILDER: J & R White, West Cowes, Isle of Wight

DISPLACEMENT: 82t bm

DIMENSIONS: Loa 24.3m, Lpp 22.4m, B 4.8m, D 0.9m

HULL: Iron

MACHINERY: Steam, 1 shaft

ENGINE: 1 single acting 1 cyl 25nhp, Day & Summers

BOILER: 1, Day & Summers

SPEED: (trials) 9.5kts

BUNKERS: _

COMPLEMENT: 15

ARMAMENT: Unarmed

Çatalca Ordered: 1857. Laid down: 1858. Launched: 1858. Trials: 1858. Built under temporary name *Sweet Waters*. 15.5.1858 commissioned. 30.5.1858 left Southampton for İstanbul. 1884 decommissioned.

Oltanıca

TYPE: Römorkör (tug)

BUILDER: J & R White, West Cowes, Isle of Wight

DISPLACEMENT: 82t bm

DIMENSIONS: Loa 24.3m, Lpp 22.4m, B 4.8m, D 0.9m

HULL: Iron

MACHINERY: Screw steamer, 1 shaft

ENGINE: 1 single-acting 1 cyl, 25nhp, Day & Summers

BOILER: 1, Day & Summers

SPEED: (trials) 9.5kts

BUNKERS: _

COMPLEMENT: 15

ARMAMENT: Unarmed

Oltanıca Ordered: 1857. Laid down: 1858. Launched: 1858. Trials: 1858. Built under temporary name *Golden Horn*. 15.5.1858 commissioned. 30.5.1858 left Southampton for İstanbul. 1884 decommissioned

Suda

TYPE: Römorkör (tug)

BUILDER: Tersane-i Amire, İstanbul

DISPLACEMENT: 186tbm, 136t

DIMENSIONS: Lpp 30.5m, B 5.8m,

D 1.8m

HULL: Wood

MACHINERY: Steam, side paddle

ENGINE: 1 1 cyl

BOILER: 1

SPEED: _

BUNKERS: _

COMPLEMENT: _

ARMAMENT: Unarmed

Suda Ordered: 1863. Laid down: 1864. Launched: 1864. Trials: 1864. 1864 commissioned, based on Lake Iskodra. 1876 based at İstanbul. 1892 decommissioned. 11.11.1909 sold for breaking up at İstanbul.

Şeref Nüma

TYPE: Römorkör (tug)

BUILDER: _

DISPLACEMENT: 104t bm

DIMENSIONS: Lpp 53.2m, B 7.9m, D _m

HULL: Wood

MACHINERY: Steam, side paddle

ENGINE: 1 1 cyl

BOILER: 1

SPEED: _

BUNKERS: _

COMPLEMENT: _

ARMAMENT: Unarmed

Şeref Nüma Ordered: –. Laid down: –. Launched: –. Trials: –. 1863 commissioned, based at İzmir. 1896 decommissioned. 1909 sold for breaking up.

Sarıye

TYPE: Vapur (steamer/tug)

BUILDER: _

DISPLACEMENT: 103t

DIMENSIONS: Lpp 30.9m, B 7.5m, D _m

HULL: Wood

MACHINERY: Steam, 1 shaft

ENGINE: 1 1 cyl

BOILER: 1

SPEED: _

BUNKERS: _

COMPLEMENT: _

ARMAMENT: Unarmed

Sarıye Ordered: 1867. Laid down: 1868. Launched: 1868. Trials: 1868. 1869 commissioned, based at İstanbul. 1872 based in the Red Sea. 1883 based at İstanbul. 1909 decommissioned. 1911 sold for breaking up.

Nedım

TYPE: Vapur (steamer and tug)

BUILDER: _

DISPLACEMENT: 103t

DIMENSIONS: Lpp 30.9m, B 7.5m, D _m

HULL: Wood

MACHINERY: Steam, 1 shaft

ENGINE: 1 1 cyl

BOILER: 1

SPEED: _

BUNKERS: _

COMPLEMENT: _

ARMAMENT: Unarmed

Nedim Ordered: 1867. Laid down: 1868. Launched: 1869. Trials: 1869. 1869 commissioned, based at İstanbul. 1890 based at Suda. 1896 returned to İstanbul, laid up. 1907 decommissioned. 1911 sold for breaking up.

Bozcaada

TYPE: Vapur (steamer & tug)

BUILDER: _

DISPLACEMENT: 103t

DIMENSIONS: Lpp 30.9m, B 7.5m, D _m

HULL: Wood

MACHINERY: Steam, 1 shaft

ENGINE: 1 1 cyl

BOILER: 1

SPEED: _

BUNKERS: _

COMPLEMENT: _

ARMAMENT: Unarmed

Bozcaada Ordered: 1867. Laid down: 1868. Launched:1869. Trials: 1869. 1869 commissioned, based at İstanbul. 1890 based at Çanakkale. 1902 returned to İstanbul, laid up. 1909 decommissioned. 1911 sold for breaking up.

Ereğli

TYPE: Römorkör (tug)

BUILDER: Tersane-i Amire, İstanbul

DISPLACEMENT: 166t bm, 125t

DIMENSIONS: Lpp 29.3m, B 6.3m, T 1.9m

HULL: Wood

MACHINERY: Steam, side paddle

ENGINE: 1 1 cyl

BOILER: 1

SPEED: _

BUNKERS: _

COMPLEMENT: 15

ARMAMENT: Unarmed

Ereğli Ordered: 1869. Laid down: 1870. Launched: 1870. Trials: 1870. 1870 commissioned, based at İstanbul. 1880 based at KD-Ereğli. 1902 based at İstanbul. 1908 decommissioned. 1910 sold for breaking up.

İslahat

TYPE: Römorkör (tug)

BUILDER: Tersane-i Amire, İstanbul

DISPLACEMENT: 166t bm, 125t

DIMENSIONS: Lpp 29.3m, B 6.3m, T 1.9m

HULL: Wood

MACHINERY: Steam, side paddle

ENGINE: 1 1 cyl

BOILER: 1

SPEED: _

BUNKERS: _

COMPLEMENT: 15

ARMAMENT: Unarmed

İslahat Ordered: 1869. Laid down: 1870. Launched: 1870. Trials: 1871. 1871 commissioned, based on the Danube. 1877 based at KD-Ereğli. 1908 decommissioned. 1910 sold for breaking up.

Marmara

TYPE: Römorkör (tug)

BUILDER: _

DISPLACEMENT: 153t bm, 136t

DIMENSIONS: Lpp 30.4m, B 5.5m, D 1.8m

HULL: Wood

MACHINERY: Steam, side paddle

ENGINE: 1 1 cyl

BOILER: 1

SPEED: _

BUNKERS: _

Complement: _

ARMAMENT: Unarmed

Marmara Ordered: 1871. Laid down: 1872. Launched: 1873. Trials: 1873. 1873 commissioned, based at İstanbul. 1885 based at Bengazi. 1908 decommissioned. 1909 sold for breaking up.

Nüzhet

TYPE: Römorkör (tug)

BUILDER: _

DISPLACEMENT: 105t

DIMENSIONS: L 52.4m, B 9.2m, D _m

HULL: Wood

MACHINERY: Steam, side paddle

ENGINE: 1 1 cyl, 150ihp

BOILER: 1

SPEED: _

BUNKERS: _

COMPLEMENT: _

ARMAMENT: Unarmed

Nüzhet Ordered: – . Laid down: – . Launched: – . Trials: –. 1873 commissioned, based at İstanbul. 1889 based at

İşkodra. 1905 based at İstanbul. 1909 decommissioned. 1910 sold for breaking up at İstanbul.

Alos

TYPE: Römorkör (tug)

BUILDER: _

DISPLACEMENT: 77t, 141t bm

DIMENSIONS: L 35.6m, B 6.5m

HULL: Wood

MACHINERY: Steam, side paddle

ENGINE: 1 1 cyl, 150ihp

BOILER: 1

SPEED: (1873) 8kts

BUNKERS: _

COMPLEMENT: _

ARMAMENT: Unarmed

Alos Ordered: –. Laid down: – . Launched: –. Trials: –. 1873 commissioned, based at İstanbul. 1890 based at İzmir. 1905 decommissioned. 1909 sold for breaking up at İzmir.

Fazılillah

TYPE: Römorkör (tug)

BUILDER: _

DISPLACEMENT: 77t, 141t bm

DIMENSIONS: L 35.6m, B 6.5m

HULL: Wood

MACHINERY: Steam, side paddle

ENGINE: 1 1 cyl, 150ihp

BOILER: 1

SPEED: (1873) 8kts

BUNKERS: _

COMPLEMENT: _

ARMAMENT: Unarmed

Fazilillah Ordered: –. Laid down: – . Launched: –. Trials: –. 1873 commissioned, based at İstanbul. 1890 based at Silivri. 1905 decommissioned. 1909 sold for breaking up at İstanbul.

Kasim Paşa

TYPE: Römorkör/Su tanker (tug/water tanker)

BUILDER: Tersane-i Amire, İstanbul

DISPLACEMENT: 78t

DIMENSIONS: Lpp 22.5m, B 4.5m, D 1.5m

HULL: Wood

MACHINERY: Steam, 1 shaft

ENGINE: 1 1 cyl

BOILER: 1

SPEED: (trials) 8kts

BUNKERS: _

COMPLEMENT: _

ARMANENT: Unarmed

Kasim Paşa Ordered: 1873. Laid down: 1873. Launched: 1873. Trials: 1873. 1873 commissioned, based at İstanbul. 1923 based at Gölcük. 1928 decommissioned. Sold for breaking up.

Fındıklı

TYPE: Römorkör/Su tanker (tug/water tanker)

BUILDER: Tersane-i Amire, İstanbul

DISPLACEMENT: 78t

DIMENSIONS: Lpp 22.5m, B 4.5m, D 1.5m

HULL: Wood

MACHINERY: Steam, 1 shaft

ENGINE: 1 1 cyl

BOILER: 1

SPEED: (trials) 8kts

BUNKERS: _

COMPLEMENT: 5

ARMAMENT: Unarmed

Fındıklı Ordered: 1873. Laid down: 1873. Launched: 1873. Trials: 1873. 1873 commissioned, based at İstanbul. 1909 decommissioned. 1910 sold for breaking up.

Kabataş

TYPE: Römorkör (tug)

BUILDER: Tersane-i Amire, İstanbul

DISPLACEMENT: 112t, 107t bm

DIMENSIONS: Lpp 24.3m, B 5.1m, D 1.5m

HULL: Wood

MACHINERY: Steam, 1 shaft

ENGINE: 1 1 cyl

BOILER: 1

SPEED: (trials) 10kts

BUNKERS: _

COMPLEMENT: 15

ARMAMENT: Unarmed

Kabataş Ordered: 1872. Laid down: 1874. Launched: 1874. Trials: 1875. 1875 commissioned, based at İstanbul. 1888 converted into water tanker/fire-fighting tug. 1909 decommissioned.

Medvet Resan

TYPE: Römorkör/Su tanker (tug/water tanker)

BUILDER: Tersane-i Amire, İstanbul

DISPLACEMENT: 78t

DIMENSIONS: Lpp 22.5m, B 4.5m, D 1.5m

HULL: Wood

MACHINERY: Steam, 1 shaft

ENGINE: 1 1 cyl

BOILER: 1

SPEED: (trials) 8kts

BUNKERS: _

COMPLEMENT: 15

ARMAMENT: Unarmed

Medvet Resan Ordered: 1873. Laid down: 1880. Launched: 1881. Trials: 1882. 1882 commissioned, based at İstanbul. 1909 decommissioned. 1911 sold for breaking up.

Cıbalı

TYPE: Römorkör (tug)

BUILDER: Tersane-i Amire, İstanbul

DISPLACEMENT: 112t, 107t bm

DIMENSIONS: Lpp 24.3m, B 5.1m, D 1.5m

HULL: Wood

MACHINERY: Steam, 1 shaft

ENGINE: 1 1 cyl

BOILER: 1
SPEED: (trials) 10kts

BUNKERS: _

COMPLEMENT: 15

ARMAMENT: Unarmed

Cıbalı Ordered: 1873. Laid down: 1874. Launched: 1874. Trials: 1874. 1875 commissioned, based at İstanbul. 1889 converted into water tanker and fire-fighting tug. 1898 transferred to İdares-i Mahsusa, İstanbul. 1909 out of service.

Rusçuk

TYPE: Römorkör (tug)

BUILDER: Tersane-i Amire, İstanbul

DISPLACEMENT: 112t, 107t bm

DIMENSIONS: Lpp 24.5m, B 5.1m, D 1.5m

HULL: Wood

MACHINERY: Steam, 1 shaft

ENGINE: 1 1 cyl

BOILER: 1

SPEED: (trials) 10kts

BUNKERS: _

COMPLEMENT: 15

ARMAMENT: Unarmed

Rusçuk Ordered: 1872. Laid down: 1873. Launched: 1874. Trials: 1874. 1875 commissioned, based at İstanbul. 1881 decommissioned.

Tophane

TYPE: Römorkör (tug)

BUILDER: Tersane-i Amire, İstanbul

DISPLACEMENT: 112t, 107t bm

DIMENSIONS: Lpp 24.3m, B 5.1m, D 1.5m

HULL: Wood

MACHINERY: Steam, 1 shaft

ENGINE: 1 1 cyl

BOILER: 1

SPEED: (trials) 10kts

BUNKERS: _

COMPLEMENT: 15
ARMAMENT: Unarmed

Tophane Ordered: 1873. Laid down: 1874. Launched: 1874. Trials: 1875. 1875 commissioned, based at İstanbul. 1889 converted into water tanker and fire-fighting tug. 1909 decommissioned.

WARTIME ACQUISITIONS AND CONVERSIONS

Dere

TYPE: Q-ship

HULL: Wood/2-mast sailing craft

MACHINERY: None

COMPLEMENT: (1915) 1 officer, 6 ratings, 4 ratings for the gun (*Hamidiye* crew)

ARMAMENT: (1915) 1–47mm QF(40)

Dere Ordered: – . Laid down: – . Launched: – . Trials: –. 23.6.1915 commissioned as *Dere*. 24.6.1915 action with a Russian submarine off Kefken: 4–5 shells fired. Later anchored at Kefken-Liman. 27.6.1915 towed by tug İstanbul to *İstanbul*. 29.6.1915 decommissioned.

Nur-ül Bahir

TYPE: Karakol gemi (guard ship)

BUILDER: Gourlay Bros & Co, Dundee

DISPLACEMENT: 295gt

DIMENSIONS: Lpp 45.7m, B 7.0m, D 3.5m

HULL: Steel

MACHINERY: Steam, 1 shaft

ENGINE: 1 triple expansion 3 cyl, 350ihp, Gourlay Bros

BOILER: 1, Gourlay Bros

SPEED: (1903) 12kts

BUNKERS: _

COMPLEMENT: _

ARMAMENT: (1894) 1 Gardner QF
(1903) 1–47mm QF, 1–37mm QF

Nur-ül Bahir (Yd No 158) Ordered:

1893. Laid down: 1893. Launched: 11.1893. Trials: 12.1893. 1.1894 *Nur-ül Bahir* Osmanli Reji İdaresi, İstanbul. 1903 transferred to Osmanli Bahriye, commissioned. 1913 decommissioned.

Rüsumet No 1

TYPE: Karakol gemi (guard vessel)

BUILDER: J T Eltringham & Co, South Shields

DISPLACEMENT: 143gt, 43nt, 200t

DIMENSIONS: L 30.5m, B 6.1m, D 3.1m

HULL: Steel

MACHINERY: Steam, 1 shaft

ENGINE: 1 triple expansion 3 cyl, ihp, G.T. Gray

BOILER: 1 Scotch, J T Eltringham

SPEED: (1914) 9kts

BUNKERS: _

COMPLEMENT: (1915) 3 officers, 16 ratings

ARMAMENT: (1914) 2–37mm QF

Rüsumet No 1. (Yd No 231) Ordered: 1901. Laid down: 1901. Launched: 1901. Trials: 1901. 1901 *New Century* J T Eltringham & Co, South Shields (trawler). 1913 *Rüsumet No 1* Gümrük Dairesi (Customs), İstanbul. 8.1914 transferred to Osmanli Bahriye, commissioned as minesweeper. 4.1915 guard ship. 2.1918 transport. 10.1918 decommissioned. 1924 returned to Turkish customs service. 1929 out of service.

Rüsumet No 2

TYPE: Karakol gemi (guard vessel)

BUILDER: _, Great Britain

DISPLACEMENT: 120t

DIMENSIONS: _

HULL: Steel

MACHINERY: Steam, 1 shaft

ENGINE: 1 triple expansion 3 cyl

BOILER: 1

SPEED: (1915) 6kts

BUNKERS: _

COMPLEMENT: (1914) 1 officer, 15 ratings

ARMAMENT: (1914) 2–47mm QF

Rüsumet No 2 Ordered: – . Laid down: –. Launched: –. Trials: –. Formerly British trawler. 1913 *Rüsumet No 2* Gümrük Dairesi, İstanbul. 8.1914 transferred to Osmanli Bahriye, commissioned. 8.1914 minesweeper. 4.1914 guard ship. 10.1918 decommissioned. 1924 sold, converted into cargo vessel. 1924 *İnayet* Haci Esref, İstanbul. 1926 burnt and lost at KD-Ereğli.

Rüsumet No 3

TYPE: Karakol gemi (guard ship)

BUILDER: J T Eltringham & Co, South Shields

DISPLACEMENT: 143gt, 43nt, 200t

DIMENSIONS: L 30.5m, B 6.1m, D 3.1m

HULL: Steel

MACHINERY: Steam, 1 shaft

ENGINE: 1 triple expansion 3 cyl, ihp, G T Gray

BOILER: 1 Scotch, J T Eltringham

SPEED: _

BUNKERS: _

COMPLEMENT: (1914) 4 officers, 16 ratings

ARMAMENT: (1914) 2–37mm QF

Rüsumet No 3 (Yd No 232) Ordered: 1901. Laid down: 1901. Launched: 1901. Trials: 1901. 1901 *New Enterprise*, R Irvin & Sons, North Shields (trawler). 1913 *Rüsumet No 3* Gümrük Dairesi, İstanbul. 8.1914 transferred to Osmanli Bahriye, commissioned. 8.1914 minesweeper. 4.1915 guard ship. 18.5.1916 collier. 10.1918 decommissioned. 1923 sold, converted into cargo vessel. 1924 *Feyyaz* Refik Bey, İstanbul. 1930 *Feyyaz* Ahmet Kemalettin, İstanbul. 1933 *Feyyaz* Sosyete Vapuréuluk T A S, İstanbul. 1935 *Feyyaz* L Ayral, İstanbul. 1958 broken up.

Rüsumet No 4

TYPE: Karakol gemi (guard vessel)

BUILDER: _

DISPLACEMENT: 310t

DIMENSIONS: Lpp 29.8m, B 8.6m, D 3.2m

HULL: Steel

MACHINERY: Steam, 1 shaft

ENGINE: 1

BOILER: 1

SPEED: _

BUNKERS: _

COMPLEMENT: (1915) 5 officers, 16 ratings

ARMAMENT: (1914) 2–37mm QF

Rüsumet No 4 Ordered: 1891. Laid down: 1891. Launched: 1891. Trials: 1891. Formerly British trawler. 1913 *Rüsumet No 4*. Gümrük Dairesi, İstanbul. 8.1914 transferred to Osmanli Bahriye, commissioned. 8.1914 minesweeper. 4.1915 guard ship. 11.1918 laid up at KD-Ereğli. 10.6.1919 joined the T B M M Armed Forces. 30.9.1921 beached on strand at Görele Burnu, after gunfire by Greek warships. 14.10.1921 wreck totally destroyed by gunfire of Greek warships.

Rüsumet No 5

TYPE: Karakol gemi (guard vessel)

BUILDER: Hall, Russell & Co, Glasgow

DISPLACEMENT: 155gt, 61nt, 200t

DIMENSIONS: L 31.8m, B 6.1m, D 3.3m

HULL: Steel

MACHINERY: Steam, 1 shaft

ENGINE: 1 triple expansion 3 cyl,_ihp, Hall, Russell

BOILER: 1 Scotch, Hall, Russell

SPEED: (1915) 4kts

BUNKERS: _

COMPLEMENT: (1915) 1 officer, 15 ratings

ARMAMENT: (1914) 2–37mm QF (1.1915) Disarmed

Rüsumet No 5 (Yd No 328) Ordered: 1900. Laid down: 1900. Launched: 1900. Trials: 1900. 1900 *Ivernia* Irvin Steam Fishing Co, North Shields. 1913 *Rüsumet No 5* Gümrük Dairesi, İstanbul. 8.1914 transferred to Osmanli Bahriye, commissioned. 9.1914 minesweeper. 1.1915 sent to KD-Ereğli, guns removed. Guard ship. 5.5.1915 sunk by Russian destroyers at KD-Ereğli.

Aydin

TYPE: Karakol gemi (guard vessel)

BUILDER: Stabilimente Technico, Trieste

DISPLACEMENT: 75gt, 35nt, 210t

DIMENSIONS: Loa 31.7m, Lpp 29.8m, B 4.2m, D 1.9m

HULL: Steel

MACHINERY: Steam, 1 shaft

ENGINE: 1 compound 2 cylinder, 200ihp, Stabilimente Technico, Trieste

BOILER: 1_, Stabilimente Technico, Trieste

SPEED (1915) 8kts

BUNKERS: 25t coal

COMPLEMENT: (1915) 3 officers, 17 ratings

ARMAMENT: (1915) 1–47mm QF

Aydin (Yd No 264) Ordered: 1890. Laid down: 1890. Launched: 1890. Trials: 1890. 1890 *Aydin* Osmanli Reij Idaresi, İstanbul. 4.1915 transferred to Osmanli Bahriye, commissioned. 10.1918 decommissioned, laid up at İstanbul.

Bahr-i Sefid

TYPE: Karakol gemi (guard vessel)

BUILDER: Tersane-i Amire, İstanbul

DISPLACEMENT: 210t

DIMENSIONS: Lpp 38.6m, B 5.4m, D 1.9m

HULL: Steel

MACHINERY: Steam, 1 shaft

ENGINE: 1 triple expansion, 400ihp, Tersane-i Amire

BOILER: 1 double-ended, Tersane-i Amire

SPEED: (1915) 6kts

BUNKERS: 80t coal

COMPLEMENT: (1915) 4 officers, 17 ratings

ARMAMENT: (1915) 1–47mm QF, 1–37mm QF

Bahr-i Sefid Ordered: 10.1890. Laid down: 1901. Launched: 1903. Trials: 1905. Ordered as gunboat *Nusr-i Hüda* class. Transferred on stocks to Osmanli Reji İdaresi. 1905 *Bahr-i Sefid* Osmanli Reji İdaresi, İstanbul. 4.1915 transferred to Osmanli Bahriye and commissioned. 10.1918 decommissioned, laid up at İstanbul.

İskenderun

TYPE: Karakol gemi (guard vessel)

BUILDER: J Fullerton & Co, Paisley

DISPLACEMENT: 142gt, 30nt

DIMENSIONS: L 35.2m, B 5.8m, D 3.4m

HULL: Steel

MACHINERY: Steam, 1 shaft

ENGINE: 1 compound 2 cyl, _ihp, Ross & Duncan

BOILER: 1 _

SPEED: (1915) 5kts

BUNKERS: _

COMPLEMENT: (1915) 2 officers, 6 ratings, 8 civilians

ARMAMENT: (4.1915) 1–37mm QF (9.1915) 2–47mm QF

İskenderun Ordered: 1894. Laid down: 1895. Launched: 1895. Trials: 1895. 5.1896 *İskenderun* Osmanli Reji İdaresi, İstanbul. 4.1915 transferred to Osmanli Bahriye, commissioned. 10.1918 decommissioned. 3.1919 returned to Osmanli Reji İdaresi. 1923 sold, converted into cargo vessel. 1923 *Mudanya* Cemal Bey, İstanbul. 1924 renamed *Mudanya Zafer.* 1927 converted into motorship. 1927 *Sürat* Kocaeli Nakliyat Sirketi, İstanbul. 1.1.1933 *Sürat* Soseyte Vapurculuk T.A.S., İstanbul. 1934 *Sürat* Bekir Aslan, Mehmet Mete, İstanbul. 1938 *Tuna* Illays Tuna, İstanbul. 1964 broken up.

Sakiz

TYPE: Karakol gemi (guard vessel)

BUILDER: J Fullerton & Co, Paisley

DISPLACEMENT: 142gt, 30nt

DIMENSIONS: L 35.2m, B 5.8m, D 3.4m

HULL: Steel

MACHINERY: Steam, 1 shaft

ENGINE: 1 compound 2 cyl, _ihp, Ross & Duncan

BOILER: 1 _

SPEED: (1915) 5kts

BUNKERS: _

COMPLEMENT: (1915) 2 officers, 6 ratings, 8 civilians

ARMAMENT: (4.1915) 1–37mm QF

Sakiz Ordered: 1894. Laid down: 1895. Launched: 1895. Trials: 1895. 5.1895 *Sakiz* Osmanli Reji İdaresi, İstanbul. 4.1915 transferred to Osmanli Bahriye, commissioned. 20.8.1915 sunk by British submarine E 2 at Erdek.

Giresun

TYPE: Mayin depo gemi (mine transport)

BUILDER: Robert Napier & Son, Glasgow

DISPLACEMENT: 4663tdw, 3065gt, 1880nt

DIMENSIONS: L 106.3m, B 11.3m, D 8.7m

HULL: Iron

MACHINERY: Steam, 1 shaft

ENGINE: 1 triple expansion 3 cyl vertical, 2400ihp (made 1892) Fairfield Co

BOILERS: 2

SPEED: (1910) 10kts, (1916) 7kts

BUNKERS: _

COMPLEMENT: (1914) 90

ARMAMENT: (1910) 1–88 QF L45 (K) (1917) Disarmed

Giresun (Yd No 362) Ordered: 1878. Laid down: 1877. Launched: 1877. Trials: 10.1877. 10.1877 *Warwick Castle* D Currie & Co, London. 1896 *Warwick Castle* Union Castle Line, London. 1897 *Jerome* Booth S.S. Co, London. 1910 sold to Osmanli Govt. 1910 commissioned as mine transport, renamed *Giresun* 1916 collier. 1917 laid up at İstanbul. 15.5.1919 released by the French Govt and transferred to Osmanli Seyri Sefain İdaresi, İstanbul. 6.12.1924 Türkiye Seyri Sefain İdaresi, İstanbul. 1926 out of service. 1927 sold for breaking up to İlhami Söker, İstanbul.

Selanik

TYPE: Mayin dökme gemi (minelayer)

BUILDER: _

DISPLACEMENT: 270t

DIMENSIONS: _

HULL: Steel

MACHINERY: Steam, 1 shaft

ENGINE: 1 triple 3 cyl

BOILER: 1 _

SPEED: (1911) 12kts

BUNKERS: _

COMPLEMENT: _

ARMAMENT: (1911) 1–37mm QF, 25 mines

Selanik Ordered: – . Laid down: –. Launched: –. Trials: –. 1900s *Selanik* Selanik Liman İslemesi, Selanik, tugboat. 9.1911 seized by Osmanli Bahriye, converted into minelayer. 9.1911 commissioned. 1927 decommissioned, laid up at Gölcük.

Samsun

TYPE: Mayin dökme gemi (minelayer)

BUILDER: W A Stevens, Birkenhead

DISPLACEMENT: 275gt, 48nt

DIMENSIONS: L 43.8m, B 6.8m, D 3.5m

HULL: Iron

MACHINERY: Steam, 2 shafts

ENGINES: 2 triple 3 cyl vertical, _ihp

BOILERS: 2

SPEED: _

BUNKERS: _

COMPLEMENT: _

ARMAMENT: (1911) Unarmed (1914) 1–76mm QF, 30 mines

Samsun Ordered: 1883. Laid down:884. Launched: 1884. Trials: 1884. 1884 *Knight of St John* Knight of St John Tug Co, Liverpool. 1894 *Knight of St John*, Knight Steamship Co, Liverpool. 1896 *Knight of St John* Empreza Insulana de Nav., Lisbon. 1897 *Knight of St John* Vincent Stephan Emanuel Grech, London (based at Gelibolu). 1897 *Samsun* İdare-i Mahusa, İstanbul. 28.8.1910 *Samsun* Osmanli Seyri Sefain İdaresi, İstanbul. 9.1911 transferred to Osmanli Bahriye, commissioned as salvage tug. 11.1913 returned to Osmanli Seyri Sefain İdaresi, İstanbul. 3.11.1914 transferred to Osmanli Bahriye. Converted into minelayer by Tersane-i Amire, İstanbul. 23.11.1914 commissioned as minelayer. Sunk by British submarine E 2 at Erdek.

İntibah

TYPE: Mayin dökme gemi (minelayer)

BUILDER: R Duncan & Co, Glasgow

DISPLACEMENT: 616gt, 82nt

DIMENSIONS: L 61.2m, B 9.1m, D 4.7m

HULL: Iron

MACHINERY: Steam, 2 shaft

ENGINES: 2 triple 3 cyl vertical, 1670ihp, Rankie & Blackmore

BOILERS: 2 _

SPEED: (1912) 12kts

BUNKERS: _

COMPLEMENT: (1915) 12 officers, 46 ratings

ARMAMENT: (1912) Unarmed (1915) 1–76mm QF(K), 2–47mm QF(A), 50 mines

İntibah (Yd No 233) Ordered: 1886. Laid down: 1886. Launched: 1886. Trials: 1886. 1886 *Warren Hastings* Patrick Keith, J H Mudie, Greenock. 21.12.1891 *Warren Hastings* J H Mudie, Greenock. 2.6.1899 *Warren Hastings* Clive Steam Tug Co Ltd, London. 20.4.1903 *Warren Hastings* Vincent Stephen Emanuel Grech, London (based at Gelibolu). 29.11.1907 receiver appointed for Grech at High Court. 14.1.1910 *Warren Hastings* Richard Anthony Grech, London (based at Gelibolu). 4.3.1912 sold to Osmanli Govt. 4.1912 commissioned *İntibah* as salvage tug. 12.1914 converted to minelayer by Tersane-i Amire, İstanbul. 10.1918–10.1923 laid up at İstanbul. 1923 renamed *Uyanik*. 1933 renamed *İntibah*. 1933–34 refitted by T C D K Gölcük Tersane, Gölcük. 1956 decommissioned, laid up at Gölcük. 1958 sold privately. 1959–64 converted to general cargo motorship. 1964 *Ararat* M Okan, İstanbul. 1994 still in service.

Muzaffer

TYPE: Mayin dökme gemi (minelayer)

BUILDER: _

DISPLACEMENT: 70t

DIMENSIONS: _

HULL: _

MACHINERY: Steam, 1 shaft

ENGINE: _

BOILER: _

SPEED: (1915) 8kts

BUNKERS: _

COMPLEMENT: _

ARMAMENT: (1914) 10 mines

Muzaffer Ordered: – . Laid down: – . Launched: –. Trials: – . 1913 commissioned as a tug. 8.1914 converted into minelayer by Tersane-i Amire, İstanbul. 1915 pilot vessel in the Bosporus. 10.1918 decommissioned.

Nusret

TYPE: Mayin dökme gemi (minelayer)

BUILDER: Schiffs- & Maschinenbau AG 'Germania', Kiel

DISPLACEMENT: 365t

DIMENSIONS: Lpp 40.2m, B 7.5m, D 3.4m

HULL: Steel

MACHINERY: Steam, 2 shafts

ENGINES: 2 triple 3 cyl vertical, 1200ihp, 'Germania'

BOILERS: 2 Schultz watertube, 'Germania'

SPEED: (trials) 15kts, (1914) 12kts

BUNKERS: _

COMPLEMENT: _

ARMAMENT: (1913) 2–47mm QF(K), 40 mines (1927) 2–57mm QF, 60 mines

Nusret Ordered: 1910. Laid down: 1911. Launched: 4.12.1911. Trials: 1912. 1913 commissioned. 10.1918–26 laid up at İstanbul. 1926–27 refitted by T C D K Gölcük Tersane, Gölcük. 1937 renamed *Yardin* diver vessel. 1939 renamed *Nusret* tender. 1955 decommissioned, laid up at Gölcük, intended as a museum ship. 1962 sold privately. 1962–6 conerted into general cargo motorship. 1966 *Kaptan Nusret* K Kalkavan ve İsmali Kaptanoglu, İstanbul. 1979 *Kaptan Nusret* A Tombul, İstanbul. 1980 *Kaptan Nusret* M Okan, İstanbul. 4.1989 sunk.

Gayret

TYPE: Mayin dökme gemi (minelayer)

BUILDER: Wigham Richardson & Co, Newcastle

DISPLACEMENT: 144gt, 37nt, 130t

DIMENSIONS: L 30.6m, B 5.8m, D 3.4m

HULL: Iron

MACHINERY: Steam, 1 shaft

ENGINE: 1 compound 2 cyl vertical, _ihp, A Shanks & Son

BOILER: 1 Scotch, _

SPEED: (1914) 9kts

BUNKERS: _

COMPLEMENT: _

ARMAMENT: (1914) 15 mines

Gayret (Yd No 86) Ordered: 1885. Laid down: 1885. Launched: 1885. Trials: 1885. 1885 *Shannon* E A Gore, Limerick. 24.4.1890 *Shannon* B Nicholson, Limerick. 3.7.1890 *Harlequin* B. Nicholson, Limerick. Converted into salvage tug. 20.7.1890 *Harlequin* G A Courtenay Schenley, Limerick. 1891 *Harlequin* R Grech, Limerick (based at Gelibolu). 27.10.1896 *Harlequin* Alfred, William & Richard Grech, Limerick. 19.11.1901 Harlequin Vincent Stephen Emanuel Grech, Limerick. 18.6.1907 sold to Osmanli Govt. 7.1907 *Gayret* İdares-i Mahusa, İstanbul. 28.8.1910 *Gayret* Osmanli Seyri Sefain İdaresi, İstanbul. 30.7.1914 transferred to Osmanli Bahriye. Convt. into minelayer by Tersane-i Amire, İstanbul. 30.7.1914 commissioned. 10.1918 returned to Osmanli Seyri Sefain İdaresi, İstanbul. 1927 out of service, sold for breaking up at İstanbul.

Nilüfer

TYPE: Mayin dökme gemi (minelayer)

BUILDER: J & G Thompson, Glasgow

DISPLACEMENT: 1088gt, 753nt, 1545ts

DIMENSIONS: Loa 80.7m, Lpp 77.1m, B 10.6m, D 3.6m

HULL: Steel

MACHINERY: Steam, 2 shafts

ENGINES: 2 triple 3 cyl vertical, 5500ihp, J & G Thompson

BOILERS: 2, J & G Thompson

SPEED: (1914) 15kts

BUNKERS: 95t coal

COMPLEMENT: 55

ARMAMENT: 1–57mm QF, 60 mines

Nilüfer (Yd No 250) Ordered: 1889. Laid down: 1890. Launched: 5.6.1890. Trials: 21.7.1890. 7.1890 *Frederica* London & South Western Railway Co, Southampton. 6.1911 sold to Osmanli Govt. 7.1911 *Nilüfer* Osmanli Seyri Sefain İdaresi, İstanbul. 7.1914 transferred to Osmanli Bayriye. 7.8.1914 conerted into minelayer by Tersane-i Amire, İstanbul. 4.9.1914 commissioned. 17.11.1914 left İstanbul for operations in the Black Sea. 19.11.1914 sunk by Russian mine about 10 miles NW of the Bosporus. 55 lives lost.

Ron

TYPE : Mayin dökme gemi (minelayer)

BUILDER: J P Rennoldson & Co, South Shields

DISPLACEMENT: 216gt, 33nt

DIMENSIONS: L 36.7m, B 6.4m, D 3.2m

HULL: Steel

MACHINERY: Steam, 2 shafts

ENGINES: 2 triple expansion 3 cyl, 600ihp, Rennoldson

BOILERS: 2 surface condenser, _

SPEED: (1914) 9kts

BUNKERS: _

COMPLEMENT: 2 officers, 12 rating

ARMAMENT: 20 mines

Ron (Yd No 154) Ordered: 1895. Laid down: 1895. Launched: 1895. Trials: 1895. 1895 *Flying Coot* Clyde Shipping Co, Glasgow. 8.9.1903 Rhône Cie de Remorquage, de Pilotage et du Sautage, Marseille. 1911 manager: S

Bandermaly, İstanbul (French flag). 9.1914 seized by Osmanli Govt. 11.9.1914 commissioned *Ron*. 30.12.1914 sunk by Russian mine off Bosporus. 3 lives lost.

Castor Class

TYPE: Mayin tamara gemi (minesweeper)

BUILDER: Stettiner AG für Schiffs- und Maschinenbau, Stettin

DISPLACEMENT: 52t

DIMENSIONS: Lpp 22.6m, B 4.7m, D 1.6m

HULL: Steel

MACHINERY: Steam, 1 shaft

ENGINE: 1 compound 2 cyl, 120ihp, Stettiner AG

BOILER: 1 locomotive-type, Stettiner AG

SPEED: (1914) 6kts

BUNKERS: _

COMPLEMENT: (1914) 1 officer, 5 ratings

ARMAMENT: (1914) 1–37mm QF (1915) Disarmed

Castor Ordered: 1889. Laid down: 1890. Launched: 1890. Trials: 1890. 1890 *Castor* Kaiserliche Marine. 8.1913 decommissioned. 1914 sold privately and sent to İstanbul. 8.1914 seized by the Osmanli Govt. 8.1914 commissioned as minesweeper. 10.1918 decommissioned.

Pollux Ordered: 1889. Laid down: 1890. Launched: 1890. Trials: 1890. 1890 *Pollux* Kaiserliche Marine. 8.1913 decommissioned. 1914 sold privately and sent to İstanbul. 8.1914 seized by the Osmanli

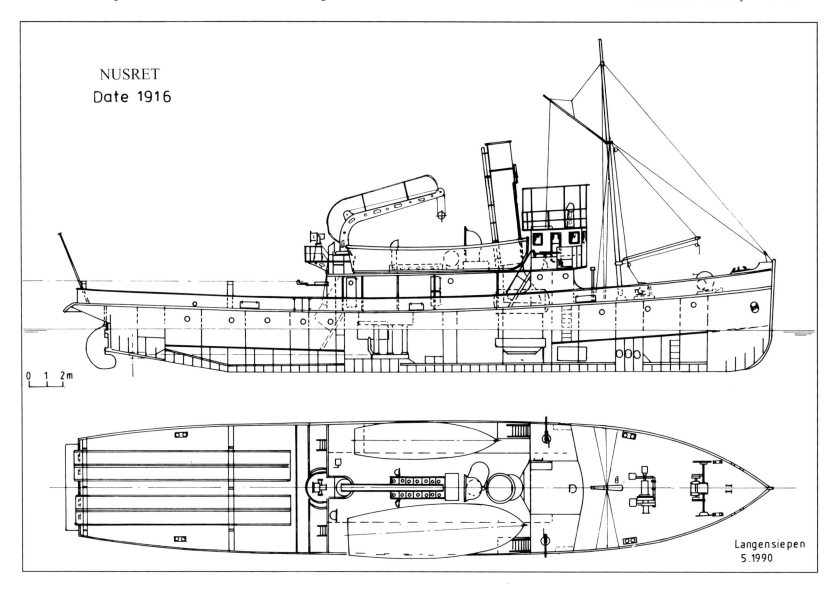

NUSRET
Date 1916

0 1 2m

Langensiepen
5.1990

Govt. 8.1914 commissioned as minesweeper. 10.1918 decommissioned.

MTB 1 – MTB 6

TYPE: Mayin tamara bot (minesweeping boat)

BUILDER: Kremer Sohn, Elmshorn

DISPLACEMENT: 10t

MACHINERY: 1 diesel, 1 shaft

ARMAMENT: Unarmed

MTB 1 – MTB 6 Ordered: 6.1915. Launched: 1915. Commissioned: 10.1916. 1919 decommissioned, laid up at İstanbul.

MTB 7 – MTB 9

TYPE: Mayin tamara bot (minesweeper)

DISPLACEMENT: 2.5t

DIMENSIONS: Lpp 8.0m, B 1.8m, D 0.7m

MACHINERY: 1 diesel, 50bhp, 1 shaft

COMPLEMENT: 4

ARMAMENT: Unarmed

MTB 7 Ordered: 1916. Launched: 1916. Commissioned: 1917. 1919 decommissioned, laid up at İstanbul.

MTB 8 Ordered: 1916. Launched: 1916. Commissioned: 1916. 1919 decommissioned, laid up at İstanbul.

MTB 9 Ordered: 1916. Launched: 1916. Commissioned: 1916. 1919 decommissioned, laid up at İstanbul.

STEAM LAUNCHES AND SERVICE BOATS

Ahter Launched: 30.8.1894. Commissioned: 1894. Builder: Tersane-i Amire, İstanbul. 70ts Engine: 1 compound 2 cyl, 1 boiler. Steam launch for the Vadi of Egypt.

Bahir Launched: 1900s . Commissioned: 1900s . Steam launch for government personnel.

Bolayır Launched: 1900. Commissioned: 1900. 1900–1919 steam launch at Çanakkale.

Fettah Launched: 1903. Commissioned: 1903. 1903–14 service

boat at İstanbul. 1914–18 tug and service boat for torpedo boats at İstinye.
Filiyo Bilanya Launched: 1909. Commissioned: 1911. 90t, 5kts, wooden hull. 1909 private motorboat on Lake İşkodra. 1911 seized by Osmanli Bahriye. (1–76mm QF (K)). 5.1913 seized by the newly founded Albanian Navy.

Gayret Launched: 1880s Commissioned: 1880s Steam boat at İstanbul.

Göksu Launched: 1880s Commissioned: 1880s Steam boat at İstanbul.

Hareket Launched: 1880s Commissioned: 1880s Steam boat at İstanbul.

Haydariye Launched: 1887. Commissioned: 1887. Steamboat at İstanbul.

İşkodra Launched: – . Commissioned: 1911. 39t, 8kts. Private steamboat on Lake İşkodra. 1911 seized by Osmanli Bahriye (2–37mm QF). 5.1913 seized by the newly founded Albanian Navy.

İstavroz Launched: 1897. Commissioned: 1897. 95t, L 33.8m, B 3.8m, D 1.5m. Engine: 1 compound, 25ihp. 1897 service boat for government personnel.

Kamer Launched: 1880s Commissioned: 1880s. 1880–1919 service boat in the Dardanelles.

Kavak Launched: 1896: Commissioned: 1896. 1896–1919 service boat at Çanakkale.

Keref Launched: 1880s Commissioned: 1880s Service boat at İstanbul.

Kilidbahir Launched: 1880s Commissioned: 1880s 1880–1919 service boat in the Dardanelles.

Lavazim Launched: 1893. Commissioned: 1893. Service boat at İstanbul.

Marika Launched: 1900s Commissioned: 1915. 14t, Engine: 1 compound, 25ihp. Steam boat owned by Kosmos-Linie, Hamburg. 1915 chartered by Osmanli Bahriye. 1919 returned to German owner.

Mesrutıye Launched: 1889. Commissioned: 1889. 56t. 1889–1915 service boat at İstanbul. 1915–19 service boat for Marmara-group. (1915 2 officers, 7 ratings.)

Meyment Launched: 1885.

Commissioned: 1885. 1885 service boat at İstanbul.

Nahıd Launched: 1885. Commissioned: 1885. Service boat at İstanbul.

Nevruz Launched: 1892. Commissioned: 1892. Service boat at İstanbul.

Pertev Launched: 1886. Commissioned: 1886. Service boat at İstanbul.

Refkat Launched: 1883. Commissioned: 1883. Service boat at İstanbul.

Rehber Launched: 30.8.1894. Commissioned: 1894. 70t, Builder: Tersane-i Amire, İstanbul. Service boat for government personnel.

Roket Launched: 1899. Commissioned: 1899. Service boat at İstanbul.

Sahın Launched: 1883. Commissioned: 1883. Service boat at İstanbul. 1909 sold.

Sana Launched: 1881. Commissioned: 1881. Service boat at İstanbul. 1909 sold.

Sark Launched: 1901. Commissioned: 1901. Service boat at İstanbul.

Semak Launched: 1883. Commissioned: 1883. Service boat at İstanbul. 1909 sold.

Servet Launched: 1887. Commissioned: 1887. Service boat at İstanbul.

Seyfı Launched: 1889. Commissioned: 1889. Service boat at İstanbul.

Seyyah Launched: 1883. Commissioned: 1883. Service boat at İstanbul. 1909 sold.

Suhulet Launched: 1884. Commissioned: 1884. Service boat at İstanbul.

Yıldız Launched: 1883. Commissioned: 1883. Service boat at İstanbul.

Zınet Launched: 1883. Commissioned: 1883. Service boat at İstanbul.

MOTORBOATS

Motor gunboat No 1 Class

TYPE: Motorgambot (motor gunboat)

BUILDER: J T Thornycroft, Southampton-Woolston

DISPLACEMENT: 12t, full load 20t

DIMENSIONS: Lpp 18.3m, B 3.3m, D 1.6m, D 0.7m

HULL: Wood, hull and wheelhouse sheeted with bulletproof nickel steel.

MACHINERY: Motorboat, 1 shaft

ENGINES: 2 paraffin 6 cyl, 70ehp, J T Thornycroft

SPEED: (trials) 11.9kts

BUNKERS: 1.9t paraffin

COMPLEMENT: 2 officers, 4 ratings

ARMAMENT: (1911) 2–37mm QF(V) (1000)
(1911) 1–37mm QF(V) (1000)

ORDERED: Yd Nos 576–585: 31.5.1911
598–610: 15.6.1911
652: 1.9.1911

No 1 (Yard No 576). Launched: 1911. 1911 commissioned at Basra. 7.11.1914 sunk by British gunboat near Abadan (Shat el Arab).

No 2 (Yard No 577). Launched: 1911. 1911 commissioned at Basra. 9.11.1914 sunk by gunfire by British gunboat *Espiègle* south of Dadda-Ada (Muhammara). 1915 salvaged by the British. 12.1915 *Flycatcher* Royal Navy.

No 3 (Yard No 578). Launched: 1911. Not commissioned by the Osmanli Bahriye.

No 4 (Yard No 579). Launched: 1911. 1911 commissioned at Hodeid (Red Sea). 2.10.1911 sunk by gunfire by Italian destroyers at Hodeid.

No 5 (Yard No 580). Launched: 1911. 1911 commissioned at Basra. 5.7.1915 scuttled by crew at Mecayise (Nasiriye, River Euphrates).

No 6 (Yard No 581). Launched: 1911. 1911 commissioned at Basra. 19.11.1914 sunk by gunfire of British gunboat *Espiègle* NW of Dabba-Ada.

No 7 (Yard No 582). Launched: 1911. 1911 commissioned at Basra. 1917 left at Baghdad.

No 8 (Yard No 583). Launched: 1911. 1911 commissioned at Basra. 24.7.1915 sunk by gunfire by British gunboat *Shushan* at Nasiriye (River Euphrates).

No 9 (Yard No 584). Launched: 1911. 1911 commissioned at Preveze. 20.10.1912 scuttled by crew at Preveze.

No 10 (Yard No 585). Launched: 1911. 1911 commissioned at Preveze. 20.10.1912 scuttled by crew at Preveze.

No 11 (Yard No 598). Launched: 1911. 1914 commissioned at Cesme. 1916 taken by train to Bandirma. 1916 based at İstanbul. 1939 decommissioned.

No 12 (Yard No 599). Launched: 1911. 1914 commissioned at İzmir. 1916 taken by train to Bandırma. 1916 based at Varna (Black Sea). 21.12.1916 sunk by Russian cruiser 30 miles off the Bosporus.

No 13 (Yard No 600). Launched: 1911. 1914 commissioned at İstanbul. 1914 based at Çanakkale. 1927 decommissioned.

No 14 (Yard No 601). Launched: 1911. 1914 commissioned at İzmir. 1932 renamed *Mülazim Hayati*. 1949 decommissioned.

No 15 (Yard No 602). Launched:; 1911. 1914 commissioned at Foça. 9.1914 based at Çanakkale. 1939 decommissioned.

No 16 (Yard No 603). Launched: 1911. 7.1914 commissioned at Ayvalik. 9.1914 based at İstanbul. 1916 based at Varna. 21.12.1916 sunk by Russian cruiser 30 miles off the Bosporus.

No 17 (Yard No 604). Launched: 1911. 7.1914 commissioned at Çanakkale. 1932 decommissioned.

No 18 (Yard No 605). Launched: 1911. 7.1914 commissioned at Marmaris. 9.1914 based at Çanakkale. 1943 decommissioned.

No 19 (Yard No 606). Launched: 1911. 7.1914 commissioned for the Osmanli Karakol (Ministry of the Interior). 2.1915 transferred to Osmanli Bahriye, based at Çanakkale.

No 20 (Yard No 607). Launched: 1911. 7.1914 commissioned at Çanakkale. 1934 decommissioned.

No 21 (Yard No 608). Launched: 1911. 7.1914 commissioned at Çanakkale. 1941 decommissioned.

No 22 (Yard No 609). Launched: 1911. 7.1914 commissioned at Çanakkale. 1934 decommissioned.

No 23 (Yard No 610). Launched: 1911. 7.1914 commissioned at Çanakkale. 1934 decommissioned.

No 24 (Yard No 652). Launched: – . Not commissioned by Osmanli Bahriye.

Motorboat No 23

TYPE: Motor bot (motorboat)

BUILDER: _

LAUNCHED:

DISPLACEMENT: 48t

DIMENSIONS: _

ENGINE: 1 petrol

COMPLEMENT: 4 officers, 7 ratings

No 23   1910s. *Lady Abondert* British Embassy, İstanbul. 3.11.1914 seized by Osmanli govt. 3.1915 Commissioned as *No 23* based at Gelibolu. 2.1919 Returned to British govt.

Motorboat No 30

TYPE: Motor bot (motorboat)

BUILDER: Fr Lürssen, Vegesack

LAUNCHED: 1912

DISPLACEMENT: 19t

DIMENSIONS: L 15.0m, B 3.1m, D 0.7m

ENGINE: 1 petrol, 40shp

No 30   1912 *Brema* J Klatte, Berlin. 11.1914 132 German Navy. 1.9.1917 based on River Danube. 10.1918 transferred to Osmanli Bahriye as No. 30. 3.1918 commissioned, Naval Air Base Çanakkale. 2.1919 Decommissioned, sold privately.

Motorboat No 31

TYPE: Motor bot (motorboat)

BUILDER: C Engelbrecht, Zeuthen

LAUNCHED: 1906

DISPLACEMENT: 17t

DIMENSIONS: L 13.5m, B 2.7m, D 0.6m

ENGINE: 1 petrol, 22shp

No 31   1906 *Putz* H Steinworth, Kassel. 11.1914 528 German Navy. 1.9.1917 based on River Danube. 10.1917 transferred to Osmanli Bahriye. 3.1918 commissioned, Naval Air Base Çanakkale as No 31. 2.1919 Decommissioned, sold privately.

MB1 Class

TYPE: Motor bot (motorboat)

BUILDER: Schlosswerft, Holtz, Harburg MB1-MB5, MB10-MB12; Kremer

Sohn, Elmshorn MB6-MB9, MB13, MB14

DISPLACEMENT: 13.5t

DIMENSIONS: Lpp 16.5m, B 3.0m, D 0.6m

MATERIAL: Wood

MACHINERY: Motorboat, 2 shafts

ENGINES: 2 petrol, 70shp, Hanomag-Lloyd

BUNKERS:

SPEED: (trials) 4.8kts

COMPLEMENT: 4

ARMAMENT: MB1-MB7, MB10, MB11 1MG
MB8, MB9, MB12   1–60mm QF (K), 1 MG

ORDERED: 13.6.1917 MB1-MB10, 8.1917 MB12-MB15

23 boats were ordered for service in the Ottoman province of Irak. The last eight boats did not leave Germany.

MB1   Launched: 1917. 6.11.1917 arrived Crablus. 17.11.1917 commissioned. 13.9.1918 decommissioned, left at Crablus.

MB2   Launched: 1917. 10.1917 arrived Mersin. 11.1917 commissioned, Naval Air Base Mersin. 2.1919 seized by French govt.

MB3   Launched: 1917. 6.11.1917 arrived Crablus. 6.12.1917 commissioned. 27.3.1918 scuttled at Ana. 8.1918 salvaged by British forces.

MB4   Launched: 1917. 6.11.1917 arrived Crablus. 28.12.1917 commissioned. 8.9.1918 decommissioned, left at Crablus.

MB5   Launched: 1917. 6.11.1917 arrived Crablus. 6.1.1918 commissioned. 13.9.1918 decommissioned, left at Crablus.

MB6   Launched: 1917. 11.1917 arrived Taberiye Göl (Palestine). 1917 commissioned.

MB7   Launched: 1917. 12.12.1917 arrived Crablus. 1917 commissioned. 3.1918 decommissioned.

MB8   Launched: 1917. 12.12.1917 arrived Crablus. 13.12.1917 commissioned. 27.3.1918 scuttled at Ana.

MB9   Launched: 1917. 11.1917 arrived Crablus. 23.11.1917 commissioned. 27.3.1918 scuttled at Ana.

MB10   Launched: 1917. 1918 arrived Crablus. 1918 commissioned. 8.9.1918 decommissioned at Crablus.

MB11   Launched: 1918. 3.1918 arrived Crablus. 8.4.1918 commissioned. Boat had radio. 8.9.1918 decommissioned at Crablus.

MB12   Launched: 1918. 3.1918 arrived Crablus. 14.4.1918 commissioned. 8.9.1918 decommissioned at Crablus.

MB13   Launched: 1918. 3.1918 arrived Crablus. 26.3.1918 commissioned. 8.9.1918 decommissioned at Crablus.

Appendices

GLOSSARY OF TERMS USED IN APPENDICES

Organisational terms

Donama	fleet
Filo	division
Filotilla	flotilla
Firka	squadron
Grup	group
Tümen	squadron
muhrip tümen	destroyer squadron
torpidobot tümen	torpedo boat squadron

Geographical terms

Akdeniz	Mediterranean Sea
Anadolu	Asiatic
Boğazi	Bosporus
Canakkale Boğazi donama	Dardanelles fleet
İstanbul Boğazi filo	Bosporus division (İstanbul based)
Karadeniz Boğazi donama	Bosporus fleet (Black Sea based)
Karadeniz	Black Sea
Karadeniz Karargah	Black Sea Fleet
Rumeli	European
Tuna	River Danube

Other terms

Ahsap	wooden-hulled
Mayin	mine
Mayin Taman Filo	Minesweeping Division
Muharebe	armoured
Zirhli	ironclad

APPENDIX 1

FLEET LIST 1839

Name	Built	No of guns
Kalyon (Ships of the Line)		
MUKADDEME-İ HAYIR	1806	74
SELİMİYE	1809	128
NEÇM-İ ŞEVKET	1815	80
BÜRUÇ-U ZAFER	1815	74
HIFZ-UR RAMAN	1826	64
FETHİYE	1827	96
MAHMUDİYE	1829	128
MEMDUHİYE	1833	96
TEŞRİFİYE	1834	96
TEŞVİKİYE	1834	96
NUSRETİYE	1835	64
TEVFİKİYE	1836	64
ŞADİYE	1836	64
FETHİYE	1836	96

Name	Built	No of guns
Frikata (Frigates)		
MUİN-İ RAHMET	1828	40
AVNULLAH	1832	50
YAVER-İ TEVFİK	1832	32
SURİYE	1833	56
TAİR-İ BAHRİ	1833	62
MİRAT-İ ZAFER	1834	44
ŞİHAB-İ BAHRİ	1837	58
PİR-İ ŞEVKET	1837	64
NAVEK-İ BAHRİ	1834	42
Korvet (Corvettes)		
NECM-İ FESAN	1824	26
FAZLULLAH	1828	22
FEYZ-İ MABUT	1828	22
CEYRAN-İ BAHRİ	1828	26
KAREM-İ BAHRİ	1828	26
NECAT-İ FER	1831	22
GÜL-İ SEFİD	1831	22
SİR-İ ZAFER	1832	26
FERAŞ	1835	22
MESİR-İ FERAH	1829	16
Brig (Brigs)		
MANSURIYE	1827	16
TİR-İ ZAFER	1837	11
AHTER	1834	20
FETH-İ BÜLEND	1833	20
NECM-İ SEFİD	1831	20
FERC-İ SEFİD	1830	16
SEYYAH	1830	12
Vapur (Steamers)		
SAĞİR	1824	2
SÜRAT	1804	2
PEYK-İ ŞEVKET	1836	4
ESER-İ HAYIR	1839	2

APPENDIX 2

FLEET ORGANISATION 1 October 1853

Topal Mahmud Paşa's fleet

Ships of the Line
MUKADDEME-İ HAYIR, TEŞRİFİYE, PEYK-İ MESİ RET, HALEP MEFTA CİHAT, BEN ZUHAF
Frigates
NUSRETİYE, RESİD, PERVAZ-İ BAHRİ

Steamer
PERVAZ-İ BAHRİ

Mustafa Paşa's fleet

Steam frigates
TAİF, MECİDİYE, SAİK-İ SADI, FEYZA-İ BAHRİ

Osman Paşa's fleet

Frigates
AVNİLLAH, DİMYAD, NİZAMIYE, NAVIK-İ BAHRİ, KAAD-İ ZAFER, FEYZ-İ MABUT, NECM-İ ZAFER

Corvettes
FAZULLAH, NECM-İ FESAN, GÜL-İ SEFİD

Steamers
EREĞLİ, GEMLİK, MEDAR-İ TİCARET

Kayserili Ahmet Paşa's fleet

Frigates
BAHRİ, ZIR-İ CİHAT, SERAFEDDİN

Corvettes
CİHAT BAKER, CENA BAHİR, SAMAN BAHRİ, MESİR-İ FERAH, BURCUŞEREF, NECAT-İ FER, ALAYIS-İ DERYA

Brigs
FERAHNUMA, TİR-İ ZAFER, TABİDAR, AHTER, BERGÜZİDE, FERY-İ SEFİD, KAVİZAFER, FETH-İ HÜNER

APPENDIX 3

AEGEAN SEA DISPOSITIONS March 1866

Base	Units
Selanik	PEYK-İ ZAFER, REHBER, AKKA, SELANİK
Galos	ŞEVKET NUMA
Pire	SİNOP
Preveze	PEYK-İ SEVKET
Bar	BEYRUT, EDIRNE
Midilli	TAİR-İ BAHRİ
Ayvalik	BOYANA
İzmir	MUBİR-İ SÜRUR
Sisam	SÜNNE
Rodos	İSKENDERİYE

APPENDIX 4

FLEET ORGANISATION April/May 1866

Rumeli Filo (Ferik Ethem Paşa)
I Tümen (Ferik Ethem Paşa)
SADİYE, FETHİYE, ERTUĞRUL, MUBİR-İ SÜRUR,
ESER-İ CEDİD, TALIA, MEDAR-İ ZAFER
II Tümen (Albay Selim)
ŞEVKET NUMA, SINOP

Anadolu Filo (Ferik İbrahim Paşa)
I Tümen (Ferik İbrahim Paşa)
PEYK-İ ZAFER, MEDAR-İ ZAFER, İSKERDERİYE,
MERİÇ
II Tümen (Albay Hasan Hüsnü)
AKKA, VARNA

APPENDIX 5

FLEET ORGANISATION 1869

Anadolu Filo (Ferik İbrahim Paşa)
I Tümen (Ferik Ibrahim Paşa)
ASAR-İ TEVFİK, NECM-İ ŞEVKET, ASAR-İ
ŞEVKET
II Tümen (Amiral Hobart Paşa)
HİFZ-ÜL RAHMAN, LÜTF-Ü CELİL, AVNİLLAH,
MUİN-İ ZAFER
III Tümen (Albay Hüseyin)
NASAR-İ AZİZ, MUBİR-İ SÜRUR, MANSURE,
MERİÇ, ZUHAF, SEDDÜLBAHİR, SÜNNE, PEYK-İ
ŞEVKET, ESER-İ HAYIR, ESER-İ CEDİD, MUSUL,
SEYYAR, GEMLİK

APPENDIX 6

FLEET DISPOSITIONS 1877

Mediterranean Fleet

I Filo (Base: Volo)
MAHMUDİYE, ASAR-İ ŞEVKET, BURSA, RETMO
II Filo (Base: Crete)
AZİZİYE, MUKADDEME-İ HAYIR, ICLALİYE,
LİBNAN, MUZAFFER, EDİRNE
III Filo (Base: Preveze)
ORHANİYE, MUİN-İ ZAFER, ASAR-İ TEVFİK,
SİNOP

Bosporus Fleet
MESUDİYE, OSMANİYE, FETH-İ BÖLEND, SURAR,
İZZEDDİN, KANDİA, TALIA, İSTANBUL

İstanbul
AVNİLLAH, NECM-İ ŞEVKET, SELİMİYE,
HÜDAVENDİĞAR

Guard vessels
FETHİYE (at Büyükdere), SADİYE (in the Haliç),
MANSURE (at İzmir)

Under repair at Tersane-i Amire, İstanbul
TAHİR-İ BAHRİ, PEYK-İ ŞEVKET, KOSOVA,
PEYK-İ ZAFER, ERTUĞRUL, HİSBER, KANDİA,
AKADİYE, ESER-İ NUSRET, İSMAİL,
İSKENDERİYE

APPENDIX 7

**FLEET ORGANISATION DURING
THE RUSSO-OTTOMAN WAR (March 1877)**

Karadeniz Filo (Ferik Bozcaadali Hasan Hüsnü Paşa)
Karadeniz Zirhli Firka (Liva Mustafa Paşa)
ASAR-İ TEVFİK, ORHANİYE, ASAR-İ ŞEVKET,
NECM-İ ŞEVKET, İCLALİYE, FETH-İ BÜLEND,
MUİN-İ ZAFER, AVNİLLAH
Karadeniz Ahsap Firka (Liva Ahmet Paşa)
HÜDAVENDİĞAR, MUBIR-İ SÜRUR, SİNOP,
MUZAFFER, İZMIR, EDİRNE, ASIR, İSMAİL,
MECİDİYE

Akdeniz Filo (Ferik Giritli Hüseyin Paşa)
Akdeniz Zirhli Firka (Miralay Faik Bey)
MESUDİYE, AZİZİYE, OSMANİYE, MAHMUDİYE,
MUKADDEME-İ HAYIR
Akdeniz Ahsap Firka (Liva Hasan Paşa)
SELİMİYE, MANSURE, UTARİT, ESER-İ CEDİD,
SEHİR, TAİF, FEVAİD, TALİA

Karadeniz Boğazi Firka
FEHTİYE, İZZEDDİN, KANDİYE, HANYA,
MEDAR-İ ZAFER, ASAR-İ NUSRET

Tuna Firka (Ferik Mehmet Arif)
LÜTF-Ü CELİL, HİFZ-ÜR RAHMAN, HİZBER,
SEYFİ, SEMENDİRE, FETH-ÜL İSLAM,
BÔĞÜRTLEN, İSKODRA, PODGORİCE, AKKA,
VARNA, ŞEVKET NUMA, SULTANIYE, MÜREVT-İ
NUSRET, MESİR-İ BAHRİ, FEYZ-İ BAHRİ,
SERAFEDDİN, MEDAR-İ TEVFİK, KAYSERİYE,
BATUM, SELANİK, MERSİN, LÜTFİYE, PURSUT,
CANİK, KİLİÇ ALİ

İdare-i Nehriye
HÜSEYİN, NÜZHET, ARKADİ, İSLAHAT, RUSÇUK,
AZİZİYE, SEYYAR, LOM, VİDİN, NİŞ, ZİŞTOVİ,
SOFİA, SEYYAR

Karadeniz Filo	= Black Sea Fleet
Karadeniz Zirhli Firka	= Black Sea Ironclad Squadron
Karadeniz Ahsap Firka	= Black Sea Wooden Hulled Squadron
Akdeniz Filo	= Mediterranean Fleet
Akdeniz Zirhli Firka	= Mediterranean Ironclad Squadron
Akdeniz Ahsap Firka	= Mediterranean Wooden Hulled Squadron
Karadeniz Bogazi Firka	= Bosporus Squadron
Tuna Firka	= Danube Squadron
Idare-i Nehriye	= Ottoman Danube Steamship Company

APPENDIX 8

DANUBE SQUADRON DISPOSITIONS 1877

Base	Units
27 April	
Vidin	VARNA, ZİŞTOVİ
Lom	RUSÇUK
Rahuva	PODGORICE
Nigbolu	ISKODRA, BÖĞÜRTLEN
Ruscuk	AZİZİYE, SEYYAR, SOFİA, İSLAHAT, LOM, VİDİN, NİS
Tutraket	HİZBER, ŞEVKET NUMA, SEMENDİRE, ARKADİ
Silistre	KİLİÇALİ, AKKA, NÜZHETİYE, ŞEHBAZ-İ BAHRİ
10 July	
Vidin	VARNA, ZIŞTOVİ
Rahuva	PODGORICE
Nigbolu	ISKODRA, BÖĞÜRTLEN
Ruscuk	HIZBER, HAYREDDIN, AZİZİYE, SEYAR, SOFİA, İSLAHAT, NİS, ŞEHBAZ-İ BAHRİ, VİDİN
Tutraket	ŞEVKET NUMA
Silistre	SEMENDİRE, FETH-ÜL İSLAM, ARKADİ, AKKA, KİLİÇ ALİ

APPENDIX 9

**FLEET ORGANISATION DURING
THE GRECO-OTTOMAN WAR OF 1897 (March)**

Fleet Commander: Müşiramiral Hasan Rami Paşa
I Firka (Ferik Hayrı)
MESUDİYE, HAMİDİYE, AZİZİYE, ORHANİYE,
EJDER, BERKEFŞAN, SEHAM, PERVİN, GİLYUM,
TARIK, TİR-İ ZAFER, ESER-İ TERAKKI (plus trans-
ports İZMİR, MEKKE)
II Firka (Ferik Mehmet Resıt)
OSMANİYE, NECM-İ ŞEVKET, HİFZ-ÜL RAHMAN,
PELENG-İ DERYA, VESİLE-İ NUSRET, FATİH,
SİHAB, MECİDİYE, BURHANEDDİN (plus transports
MARMARA, HÜDEYDE)

APPENDIX 10

**FLEET ORGANISATION DURING
THE ITALO-OTTOMAN WAR (29 October 1911)**

Filo (Albay Tahir)
BARBAROS HAYREDDİN (Binbaşı Enver Hakki),
TORGUD REİS (Binbaşı Aris), MESUDİYE (dry-
docked), ASAR-İ TEVFİK (drydocked), HAMİDİYE
(Binbaşı Arif/Binbaşı Hüseyin Rauf), MECİDİYE
(Yuzbaşı Arif Nebil)
Filotilla (Binbaşı Hakki)
MUAVENT-İ MİLLİYE (Yuzbaşı Sabri), GAYRET-İ
VATANİYE (Yuzbaşı Sabri), NÜMUNE-İ HAMİYET
(Yuzbaşı Ali Riza), YADIGAR-İ MİLLET (Yuzbaşı
Fahri Aziz), BASRA (Yuzbaşı Ali Riza), TAŞOZ
(Yuzbaşı Ali Riza), SAMSUN (Yuzbaşı Şükrü),
YARHİSAR (Yuzbaşı Osman)

İzmir detachment (Binbaşı Hikmet)
MUİN-İ ZAFER, YUNUS, SELANİK, TİMSAH,
İZZEDDİN, ROMA, ARŞİPEL, TRABZON

Selanik detachment (Binbaşı Bekir Raşit)
FETH-İ BÜLEND, FUAD, SELANİK, ŞÜRAT,
TESHİLAT, KATERİN

Trablusgrab detachment (Binbaşı Ahmet)
SEYYAD-İ DERYA

Lake Işkodra detachment (Yuzbaşı Yahya)
GÔR, İŞKODRA

Preveze detachment (Binbaşı Tevfik)
HAMİDİYE, ALPAGOT, TOKAD, ANTALYA,
TRABLUS, NO 9, NO 10

Kizildeniz group (Binbaşı Hamid)
PEYK-İ ŞEVKET, ORDU, BAFRA, AYINTAB,
MALATYA, GÖKÇEDAG, REFAHİYE, ŞİPKA,
BEYRUT, MOHA, HALİÇ, YOZGAT, KASTAMONU,
TAŞKÖPRÜ, BAHRİYE, AHMER

Beyrut detachment (no naval commander)
AVNİLLAH, ANKARA

Donama Komontan	=	Commander of the Fleet
Filo	=	Fleet
Filotilla	=	(Destroyer) Squadron

APPENDIX 11

FLEET ORGANISATION DURING THE BALKAN WAR (16 October 1912)

Karadeniz Boğazı Donanma (Albay Tahir)
BARBAROS HAYREDDİN (Yuzbaşı Enver Hakki),
TORGUD REİS (Yuzbaşı Ismail Ahmer), MUAVENET-İ
MİLLİYE (Öyzbaşı Galatali Ali), YADİGAR-İ
MİLLET (Öyzbaşı Fahri Cemal), NÜMUNE HAMİ-
YET (Binbaşı Hamdi Mahmut), SAMSUN (Öyzbaşı
Osman Izzet), BASRA (Öyzbaşı Cemal Ali), TAŞOZ
(Öyzbaşı Mehmet Emin), MUSUL, AKHISAR,
SULTANHİSAR, SİVRİHİSAR, ZUHAF, NEVŞEHIR

Çanakkale Boğazı Donanma (Binbaşı Tevfik)
MESUDİYE (Binbaşı Tevfik), ASAR-İ TEVFIK
(Binbaşı Şükrü Süleyman), HAMİDBAD

Karadeniz Kararğah (Öyzbaşı Hüseyin Rauf)
HAMİDİYE (Öyzbasi Hüseyin Rauf), MECİDİYE
(Binbaşı Arif Nebil)

Tersane-i Amire, İstanbul
BERK-İ SATVET, GAYRET-İ VATANİYE,
YARHİSAR, BERKEFŞAN, KÜTAHYA, DRAÇ,
DEMİRHİSAR

Tersane   =   Istanbul Naval Dockyard

APPENDIX 12

VESSELS CHARTERED IN SEPTEMBER 1912 AS TROOP TRANSPORTS

Name	Built	Tonnage	Owner
Sea of Marmara			
MANOSIS		1363gt	Greek prize
BEZM-İ ALEM	1888	4572gt	Osmanli SSI
HEYBELİADA	1873	927gt	Adalar Kumpanyasi
PLEVNE	1892	1154gt	Osmanli SSI
EDREMİT	1887	414gt	Osmanli SSI
NİMET	1877	310gt	Osmanli SSI
NİLÜFER	1890	1088gt	Osmanli SSI
İSKALAMANĞA	1882	1591gt	Greek prize
BASLANGIC	1852	381gt	Hüdavendigar Şirketi
Black Sea			
ON TEMMUZ	1891	2132gt	Gümçiyan

			Şirketi
SEYYAR	1893	3338gt	Gümçiyan Şirketi
GÜZEL GİRİT	1891	1232gt	Hilal Şirketi
NECAT	1870	1523gt	Trabzonlu Hasan
SELAMET	1853	1692gt	Osmanli SSI
KİYOS		540gt	Greek prize
KEŞENDERE	1902	438gt	Şirketi Hayriye-i Hamidiye
ARYOS		510gt	Greek prize
GÜLCEMAL	1874	5071gt	Osmanli SSI
MARMARA	1872	2472gt	Osmanli SSI
HALEP	1881	3684gt	Osmanli SSI
AKDENİZ	1890	5062gt	Osmanli SSI
MİTHAT PAŞA	1901	4455gt	Osmanli SSI
MAHMUT ŞEVKET PAŞA	1886	2690gt	Osmanli SSI
İNEBOLU	1888	233gt	Osmanli SSI

APPENDIX 13

GREEK MERCHANT VESSELS SEIZED 16 October 1912

Name	Built	Gross tons
Steamers		
HARILOS TRIKOPIS		1620brt
ASOS ROMANOS		1500brt
MARELLA		1500brt
PAXLI	1883	145brt
ITHAKI	1895	283brt
CAMBRIDGE	1886	1259brt
KIYOS		540brt
MANOSIS		1363brt
ARYOS		510brt
ASOS		400brt
ANNA		1131brt
ISKALAMANGA	1882	1591brt
LEON IZAVROS		1864brt
SAMI	1882	298brt
NIKOLAVUS		534brt
NIKOLAUS KOSTANTINIUS		3050brt
KATINA		500brt

Steam Tugs and Steamboats
AYAVAR VARA
ZAHALA
OSPIHI
EFTAHIYA
YANGILISTRIA
ODESIYE
IRINI
NIKOLAUS
EXPRESS
AYA ANDIRYA
ELLI
DIMITRIYOS
ANNA
BARBONITIS
KOSTANTINOS
TEOFILOS
KOSTANTINOS (paddle)
ELIAS ELENI ELPIS
MARYANI
MATILLI
MEMO
BÜYÜKDERE
OBI
ISTEFANOS

ALPIDOFOS

All these vessels were subsequently used by the Ottoman
navy later in the Balkan War as transports and for harbour duties.

APPENDIX 14

FLEET DISPOSITIONS 10 October 1912

Base	Units
İstanbul-Haydarpaşa	BARBAROS HAYREDDİN, TORGUD REİS, MECİDİYE
İstanbul-Haliç (shipyard)	GAYRET-İ VATANİYE, BERKEFŞAN, PELENG-İ DERYA, BERK-İ SATVET, DRAÇ, NÜRULBAHİR
İstanbul-Haliç	IÇLALİYE, BASRA
İstanbul-Dolmabahçe	ERTUĞRUL
İstanbul-Kabataş	İSTANBUL
İstanbul-Arnavutköy	SÖĞÜTLÜ
Bosporus-Büyükdere	YADİGAR-İ MILLET, MUAVENET-İ MILLIYE, NÜMUNE-İ HAMIYET, SAMSUN, TAŞOZ, SİVRİHİSAR, DEMİRHİSAR, SULTANHİSAR, MUSUL, KÜTAHYA, ZUHAF, NEVŞEHIR, TİRİMÜJGAN
Sinop	HAMİDİYE
Çanakkale	MESUDİYE, ASAR-İ TEVFIK, YARHİSAR, HAMIDABAD, AKHISAR
Preveze	ANTALYA, TOKAT, NO 9, NO 11
Selanik	FETH-İ BÜLEND, FUAD
İzmir	MUİN-İ ZAFER, YUNUS, TİMSAH, İZZEDDIN, TRABZON
Suez (interned)	PEYK-İ ŞEVKET, BEYRUT, MALATYA, TAŞKÔPRÜ, YOZGAT

APPENDIX 15

FLEET ORGANISATION 19 December 1912

Muharebe Division (Albay Ramiz)
BARBAROS HAYREDDİN, TORGUD REİS,
MESUDİYE, ASAR-İ TEVFIK, DEMİRHİSAR,
SULTANHİSAR, SİVRİHİSAR, HAMİDABAD

I (Destroyer) Division (Öyzbaşı Hüseyin Rauf)
BERK-İ SATVET, YADİGAR-İ MİLLET, MUAVENT-İ
MİLLİYE, TASOZ, BASRA

II (Destroyer) Division (Yarbaşı Hakki Eşref)
MECİDİYE, NÜMUNE-İ HAMIYET, GAYRET-İ
VATANİYE, YARHİSAR

III Division (Binbaşı İsmail)
TİRİMÜJGAN (Workshop ship), İNTİBAH (Salvage
tug), REŞİT PAŞA (Hospital ship), SAMSUN (Tug),
AKHİSAR (Destroyer), SAMSUN (Destroyer)

APPENDIX 16

FLEET ORGANISATION after 20 December 1912

Muharebe Division (Albay Ramiz)
BARBAROS HAYREDDİN, TORGUD REİS, MESUDİYE, DEMİRHİSAR, SİVRİHİSAR, SULTANHİSAR, HAMİDABAD, REŞİT PAŞA (Hospital ship)

I (Destroyer) Division (Öyzbaşı Hüseyin Rauf)
MECİDİYE, MUAVENT-İ MİLLİYE, GAYRET-İ VATANİYE, NÜMUNE-İ HAMİYET

II (Destroyer) Division (Yarbaşı Hakki Eşref)
BERK-İ SATVET, TASOZ, YARHİSAR, BASRA

III Division (Binbaşı İsmail)
ASAR-İ TEVFİK, SAMSUN (Destroyer), TIRİMÜJGAN (Workshop ship), İNTİBAH (Salvage tug), SAMSUN (Tug)

Muharebe Division   =   Armoured Warship Division

APPENDIX 17

CASUALTIES DURING THE BALKAN WAR

16 December 1912

	Killed	Wounded
BARBAROS HAYREDDİN	7	14
TORGUD REİS	8	20
MESUDİYE	3	7
Total	18	41

18 January 1913

	Killed		Wounded	
	Officers	Ratings	Officers	Ratings
BARBAROS HAYREDDİN	4	28	5	50
TORGUD REİS	-	9	2	47
Total	4	37	7	97

APPENDIX 18

AMMUNITION CONSUMPTION DURING THE SARKÖY LANDING 8–11 February 1913

	280 mm	150 mm	120 mm	105 mm	88 mm
BARBAROS HAYREDDİN				250	180
TORGUD REİS	22	156			
BERK-İ SATVET			84		

APPENDIX 19

FLEET ORGANISATION 27 October 1914

Donama Komutan: Amiral Souchon
Donama Kurmay Başkan: Amiral Arif

I Tümen
YAVUZ (Kapt z S Ackermann), BARBAROS HAYREDDİN (Albay Mustafa Paşali Muzaffer), TORGUD REİS (Yarbaşı Sultanselimli Namik Hasan),

MESUDİYE (Binbaşı Beşiktaşli Arif Nebi)

II Tümen
MİDİLLİ (Freg Kapt Kettner), MAMİDİYE (Yüzbaşı Kasimpaşali Vasif Muhiddin), PEYK-İ ŞEVKET (Albay Üsküdarli Ibrahim Cevat), BERK-İ SATVET (Binbaşı Küçükmustafapaşali Hamdi)

I Muhrip Tümen
NÜMUNE-İ HAMİYET (out of service in drydock), MUAVENT-İ MİLLİYE (Binbaşı Ayasofyali Ahmet Saddet), GAYRET-İ VATANİYE (Yüzbaşı Kasimpaşali Cemil Ali), YADİRĞAR-İ MİLLET (Yüzbaşı Yeniçeşmeli Raif Said)

II Muhrip Tümen
SAMSUN (Yüzbaşı Üsküdarli Nezir Abdullah), TAŞOZ (Yüzbaşı Tevfik Halit), BASRA (out of service in dry-dock), YARHİSAR (Yüzbaşı Ahmet Hulusi Hasan)

I Torpidobot Tümen
DRAÇ (Yüzbaşı Aziz Mahmut Ali), KÜTAHYA (Yüzbaşı Kasimpaşali Ibrahim Halil), MUSUL (Yüzbaşı Piyaleli Ahmet Naim Hüsnü), AKHİSAR (out of service in drydock)

II Torpidobot Tümen
SULTANHİSAR (Yüzbaşı Beşiktaş Riza Mehmet), DEMİRHİSAR (Yüzbaşı Istanbullu Ahmet Şefik Hasan), SİVRİHİSAR (Yüzbaşı Kasampaşali Mehmet Sabri), HAMİDİABAD (Yüzbaşı Ibrahim Roza Kerim)

Mayin Grup (BinbaşıKasimpaşali Nazmi Emin)
YUNUS (Yüzbaşı Kasimpaşali Ahmet Mahmut), NUS-RET (Yüzbaşı Tophaneli Hakki), İHTİBAH (Binbaşı Ahmet Halit Bekir), NİLÖFER (Yüzbaşı Cibalili Hasan Murad)

Donanma Komutan	= Fleet Commander
Donanma Kurmay Başkan	= II Fleet Commander
Mayin Grup Komutan	= Mine Group Commander

APPENDIX 20

COMPOSITION OF FLEET DETACHMENTS 1915–1917

Marmara Filo
1915–1916

Gunboats	ZUHAF
Armed steamers	RÜSUMET NO 1, RÜSUMET NO 2, RÜSUMET NO 3
Guard vessels	İSKENDERUN, AYDIN, BAHR-İ SEFID
Minelayers	İNTİBAH
Motor gunboats	NO 15
Fast transports	BOSPORUS NO 38, BOSPORUS NO 47, BOSPORUS NO 52, ERTUĞRUL, LORELEY
Tugs	FRANCE, EOLE, LIVERPOOL, PARIS, ALEMDAR, KURT, SARİN, SAMSUN, MAGGIE GRECH
Motorboats	MAKOOK

2 November 1916

Gunboats	KEMAL REİS, HIZIR REİS
Armed steamers	RÜSUMET NO 2, RÜSUMET NO 3, RÜSUMET NO 4

Guard vessels	İSKENDERUN, AYDIN, BAHRİSEFID
Minelayers	İNTIBAH
Tugs	FRANCE
Motorboats	MESSERET, NO 23

1 September 1917

Minelayers	İNTİBAH
Armed steamers	RÜSUMET NO 3
Guard vessels	İSKENDERUN
Tugs	ABDÜLKADİR, SÜLEYMANİYE

Çanakkale Boğazi Filo
1915–1916

Motor gunboats	NO 19, NO 20, NO 21
Minelayers	SELANİK
Tugs	ABDÜLKADİR, SANA, CASTOR, KÜRDİSTAN
Motorboats	ÇANAKKALE, BULAİR, TAŞOZ

1 September 1917

Motor gunboats	NO 15, NO 18, NO 20, NO 21
Minelayers	NUSRET
Tugs	KÜRDİSTAN, CASTOR, MALTEPE, SANA
Motorboats	NO 7, NO 9

İstanbul Boğazi Filo
1915–1916

Gunboats	PREVEZE, SAKİZ, MALATYA, BERİKA-İ ZAFER
Tugs	POLLUX, ZAFER, GANYMEDE, BOSFORDOK, GAYRET
Motorboats	KAMER, CEMAL, NO 23

1 September 1917

Guard vessels	AYDİN, BAHRİSAFİD
Tugs	POLLUX, GAYRET, BOSPORDOK, FRANCE, GAYRET
Motorboats	KAMER, NO 23
Transports	SELDA
Pilot vessels	ZAFER
Torpedo boats	BARİK-İ ZAFER
Service boats	HALİÇ 6, HALİÇ 7, HALİÇ 10

APPENDIX 21

COMPOSITION OF MINESWEEPING GROUPS 1914–1917

I Mayin Tamara Filo (Base: Istinye, Commissioned: September 1914)

16 September 1914	CASTOR, POLLUX, ISTINYE, BOSPORDOK
1 August 1915	TAŞKÖPRÜ, MALATYA, YOZGAT, BAHRİSAFİD
1 June 1916	PREVEZE, SAKİZ, MALATYA, BERİKA-İ ZAFER, POL-LUX, BOSFORDOK
1 September 1917	BURAK REİS, KEMAL REİS, SAKIZ, HIZIR REİS, ANNA IX, ANNA X, ELSE, ERNST WETZLEN III, GUSTAV BRÜNNER, EUGEN RÜDENBERG III

**II Mayin Tamara Filo (Base: Zonguldak,
Commissioned: 15 February 1915)**

15 February 1915	RÜSUMET NO 5 (sank May 1915, replaced by RÜSUMET NO 4), MARTHA
1 June 1916	RÜSUMET NO 4, MARTHA
1 May 1917	RÜSUMET NO 2, MARTHA, GÜNEŞ, ARMINGAN, YARDIMCI
1 July 1917	RÜSUMET NO 2, MARTHA, YORGIOS

Mayin Tamara Filo = Minesweeping Division

APPENDIX 22

CASUALTIES DURING THE LOSS OF THE MESUDİYE 13 December 1914

	Rescued	Killed
1st Division	95	7
2nd Division	110	4
3rd Division	105	2
4th Division	106	2
5th Division	147	9
NCOs	11	
Officers	53	10
Total	627	34

Of the 34 killed, 10 officers and 10 ratings were on duty in the engine and boiler rooms.

APPENDIX 23

SENIOR COMMANDERS OF THE OTTOMAN NAVY

Admirals of the Fleet (Kaptan-i Derya or Derya Kaptan) 1827–1867

Name	From	To	Notes
Topla İzzet Mehmet Paşa	9 Feb 1827	24 Oct 1828	became Grand Vizier
Pabuççoğlu Ahmet Paşa	24 Oct 1828	13 Jan 1830	died in office
Damat Halil Rifat Paşa	13 Jan 1830	16 Nov 1832	
Çengeloğlu Tahir Mehmet Paşa	16 Nov 1832	10 Nov 1836	
Firari Ahmet Fevzi Paşa	10 Nov 1836	8 Jan 1840	dismissed
Damat Mehmet Said	8 Jan 1840	29 Mar 1841	
Çengeloğlu Tahir Mehmet Paşa	29 Mar 1841	6 Feb 1843	dismissed
Damat Halil Tahir Paşa	16 Feb 1843	10 Aug 1845	dismissed
Damat Hehmet Ali Paşa	10 Aug 1845	20 July 1847	dismissed
Damat Halil Tahir Paşa	20 July 1847	27 April 1848	dismissed
Damat Mehmet Ali Paşa	27 April 1848	11 Mar 1849	
Kilari Süleyman Refet Paşa	11 Mar 1849	6 Aug 1851	dismissed
Damat Mehmet Ali Paşa	6 Aug 1851	3 Dec 1852	became Grand Vizier
Topçubaşizade Mehmet Paşa	3 Dec 1852	17 Dec 1853	dismissed
Hasan Riza Paşa	17 Dec 1853	30 Jan 1854	
Kıbrıslı Mehmet Emin Paşa	30 Jan 1854	29 May 1854	became Grand Vizier
Damat Halil Rifat Paşa	29 May 1854	30 Aug 1855	dismissed
Damat Mehmet Ali Paşa	30 Aug 1855	28 Aug 1858	dismissed
Kıbrıslı Mehmet Emin Paşa	28 Aug 1858	21 Oct 1858	dismissed
Damat Mehmet Ali Paşa	21 Oct 1858	2 Jan 1863	dismissed
İngiliz Mustafa Paşa	2 Jan 1863	17 Jan 1863	dismissed
Ateş Mehmet Salih Paşa	17 Jan 1863	20 Jan 1865	died in office
Hacı Ahmed Vesim Paşa	20 Jan 1865	29 May 1865	dismissed
Halil İbrahim Paşa	29 May 1865	15 April 1866	
Damat Mehmet Ali Paşa	15 April 1866	13 Mar 1867	

The title Damat indicates a son-in-law of the Sultan. From 13 March 1867 the position of Derya Kaptan was abolished and the two new positions of Navy Minister (Bahriye Nazir) and Fleet Commander (Donama Komutan) were instituted.

Fleet Commanders (Donama Komutan) 1877–1924

Name	From	To
Amiral Bozcaadalı Hasan Hüsnü Paşa	1877	1894
Amiral Hüseyin Paşa	1894	1897
Hasan Rami Paşa	1897	1908
Tümamiral Sir Douglas Gamble	1908	8 Feb 1910
Subay Ford	Feb 1910	Apr 1910
Tuğamiral H P Williams	Apr 1910	1910
Albay Cibaliti Tahir Mehmet Bey	20 Dec 1910	24 July 1912
Albay Sermet Fazli Bey	24 July 1912	18 Aug 1912
Albay Cibaliti Tahir Mehmet Bey	18 Aug 1912	29 Nov 1912
Albay Selanikli Ramiz Numan Bey	29 No 1912	6 Feb 1913
Albay Cibaliti Tahir Mehmet Bey	6 Feb 1913	14 Nov 1913
Tuğamiral Sir A H Limpos	14 Nov 1913	3 Aug 1914
Yarbay Arif Ahmet Bey	3 Aug 1914	3 Sept 1914
Amiral Wilhelm Souchon	3 Sept 1914	24 Aug 1917
Amiral Von Rebeur Paschwitz	24 Aug 1917	3 Nov 1918
Tuğamiral Arif Ahmet Paşa	3 Nov 1918	22 Apr 1920
Albay Hamdi Tevfik Bey	22 Dec 1922	23 Jan 1924
Yarbay Hasan Fuat Kayacan	23 Jan 1924	11 May 1924

APPENDIX 25

Translations of Ottoman Ship Names

Name Translation

Abdülhamid	Named after Sultan Abdül Hamid (1876-1909)
Abdülkadir	Named after son of Sultan Abdülhamid II
Abdülmecid	Named after Sultan Abdül Mecid (1839-1861)
Ahter	Star
Akhisar	Turkish city
Akka	Acre, Lebanon
Alemdar	Standard bearer
Ali Saib Paşa	Ottoman minister of the mid-nineteenth century
Alpagot	A former Turkish city in the Balkans
Ankara	Turkish city

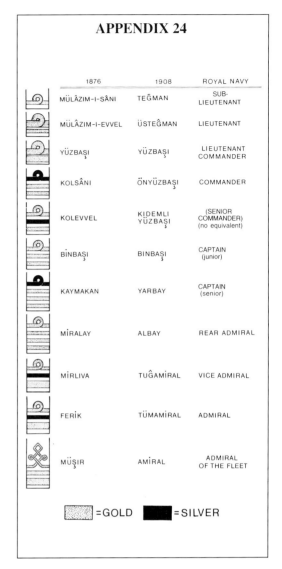

APPENDIX 24

	1876	1908	ROYAL NAVY
	MÜLÂZIM-I-SÂNI	TEĞMAN	SUB-LIEUTENANT
	MÜLÂZIM-I-EVVEL	ÜSTEĞMAN	LIEUTENANT
	YÜZBAŞI	YÜZBAŞI	LIEUTENANT COMMANDER
	KOLSÂNI	ÖNYÜZBAŞI	COMMANDER
	KOLEVVEL	KIDEMLI YÜZBAŞI	(SENIOR COMMANDER) (no equivalent)
	BINBAŞI	BINBAŞI	CAPTAIN (junior)
	KAYMAKAN	YARBAY	CAPTAIN (senior)
	MİRALAY	ALBAY	REAR ADMIRAL
	MİRLIVA	TUĞAMİRAL	VICE ADMIRAL
	FERİK	TÜMAMİRAL	ADMIRAL
	MÜŞIR	AMİRAL	ADMIRAL OF THE FLEET

⬚ = GOLD   ■ = SILVER

Antalya	Turkish city
Arkadi	Formerly Ottoman, now Greek, city on Crete
Asar-i Şevket	Work of God
Asar-i Tevfik	God's Favour
Asir	City in Saudi Arabia
Avnillah	Divine Assistance
Aydin Reis	Ottoman admiral of the sixteenth century
Ayintab	Turkish town now called Gaziantep
Aynalikavak	District of İstanbul
Azizye	Named after Sultan Abdülaziz (1861-1876)
Babıl	Babylon
Bafra	Turkish town
Bahri	The Sea
Bahr-i Ahmer	The Red Sea
Bahr-i Sefid	The Mediterranean
Bandırma	Town on the Sea of Marmara
Barbaros Hayreddin	
	Ottoman admiral of the sixteenth century
Barika-i Zafer	Flash of Triumph
Basra	City in Iraq
Berkefsan	Lightning Spreader
Berk-i Satvet	Lightning of the Almighty
Beylerbeyi	District of İstanbul
Beyrut	Beirut, Lebanon
Bezm-i Alem	Council of the Universe
Biga	Town on the Sea of Marmara
Bögurtlen	Town on the river Donau
Bolayir	Turkish town on the Dardanelles

Boyana	Turkish town in Albania	
Bozcaada	Island in the Dardanelles	
Burak Reis	Ottoman admiral of the sixteenth century	
Burhaneddin	Named after son of Sultan Abdülhamid II	
Bursa	Turkish town	
Büruç-u Zafer	Fortress of Victory	
Catalca	Town in Romania	
Cıbalı	District of İstanbul	
Demirhisar	Ottoman castle	
Derne	Town in Libya	
Doğan	Falcon	
Draç	Town in Albania	
Durak Reis	Ottoman admiral of the sixteenth century	

Edirne	Adrianople
Ejder	Dragon
Ereğli	Town on the Black Sea
Ertuğrul	Named after Sultan Ertuğrul (1231-1288)
Eser-i Cedid	Innovation
Eser-i Hayir	Charitable works
Eser-i Terakki	Progressive works
Eser-i Ticaret	Trade works

Fatih	Conqueror
Fatıh Sultan Mehmed	
	Named after Sultan Mehmed the Conqueror (1451-1481)
Fazilıllah	Holy Superiority
Fethiye	Conquest
Feth-i Bülend	Great Victory
Feth-ül İslam	Victory of Islam
Fettah	Conqueror
Feyza-i Bahri	Abundance of the Seas
Firat	Euphrates

Galata	District of İstanbul
Gayret	Endeavour
Gayret-i Vataniye	National Endeavour
Gazal	Antelope
Gemlık	Turkish town on the Sea of Marmara
Gilyum	Wilhelm (named after Kaiser Wilhelm I)
Giresun	Turkish town on the Black Sea
Girit	Crete
Gökçedağ	Turkish town
Göksu	River running into the Bosporous

Haliç	The Golden Horn
Hamidabad	Turkish town
Hamidiye	Named after Sultan Abdülhamid
Hanya	Chania, Crete
Hareket	Action
Heybetnüma	Awe-inspiring
Hiddyet	The Right Path
Hifz-ur Rahman	Merciful Protector
Hizber	Lion
Hizir Reis	Another name of Barbaros Hayreddin
Hüdavandigar	Sovereign
Hüma-i Tevfik	Holy Felicity
Hümapervaz	Felicitous
Hümayis	Felicity

İclaliye	Glorious
İntibah	Vigilance
İsa Reis	Ottoman admiral of the sixteenth century
İskenderiye	Alexandria
İşkodra	City in Albania
İslahat	Progress
İsmail	Masculine forename
İstanköy	Island of Kos
İstiniye	District of İstanbul
İzmir	Turkish city
İzzeddin	Masculine forename

Kamer	Moon
Kandıye	Candia, on Crete
Kastamonu	Turkish city
Kavak	Early name of the İstanbul district of Anadolukavaği
Kebir	Great
Kemal Reis	Ottoman admiral of the sixteenth century
Kemil Paşa	Ottoman minister of the nineteenth century
Kervan-i Bahri	Planet of the Sea (ie Saturn)
Kessaf	Explorer
Kiliç Alı	Ottoman admiral of the sixteenth century
Kilidbahri	Turkish town on thé Dardanelles
Kosova	Serbian town and sight of famous Turkish victory in the fifteenth century
Kütahya	Turkish city

Lavazım	Supplier
Lübnan	Lebanon
Lütf-ü Celil	Divine Grace
Lütf-ü Hümayun	Imperial Favour

Mahabet	Friendship
Mahmudiye	Named after Sultan Mahmud (1808-1839)
Mahmut Şevket Paşa	
	General and minister killed 1912
Malakof	City in Bulgaria
Malatya	Turkish city
Maltepe	Turkish city near İstanbul
Mansure	City in Egypt
Marmara	Sea of Marmara
Marmaris	Turkish city
Mecidiye	Named after Sultan Abdülmecid
Mehmet Selım	Named after son of Sultan Abdülaziz
Meriç	River on Greco-Ottoman border
Mersin	Turkish city
Meserret	Rejoicing
Mesrutıye	Constitution
Mesudiye	Happiness
Mesut	Happy
Meyment	Prosperity
Midilli	Greek island of Mitiline
Millet	Nation
Mithat Paşa	Reforming minister of the mid-nineteenth century
Muavent-i Milliye	Support of the Nation
Mubir-i Sürur	Informer of Happiness
Muin-i Zafer	Aid to Triumph
Müjderesan	Bearer of Good Tidings
Mukaddeme-i Hayir	
	Great Abundance
Mukaddeme-i Nusret	
	Advance of God's Help
Mukaddeme-i Şeref	
	Advance of Honour
Musul	City in Iraq (Mosul)
Müstecip Onbaşı	Named after the army officer whose field gun forced the French submarine *Turquoise* to surface and surrender
Muzaffer	Triumphant

Nasir	Aid to Victory
Nasr-ül Aziz	Holy Greatness
Necm-i İSevket	Star of Majesty
Nedim	Masculine forename
Nevruz	Old religious New Year
Nevşehir	Turkish city
Nilüfer	Water Lily
Nımet	Richness
Nımet-i Hüda	Blessed Prosperity
Nümune-i Hamiyet	
	Symbol of Patriotism
Nur-ül Bahri	Holy Light of the Sea
Nusret	Divine Victory
Nüsretiye	Divine Help
Nüzhet	Joy

Omer Paşa	Ottoman minister of the mid-nineteenth century
On Temmuz	10 July (1908) - Revolution Day
Ordu	Turkish city
Osmaniye	Named after Sultan Osman (1288-1326)

Peleng-i Derya	Tiger of the Sea
Pertev	Light
Peyk-i Meserret	Satellite of Happiness
Peyk-i Nusret	Satellite of Divine Help
Peyk-i Şeref	Satellite of Glory
Peyk-i Şevket	Satellite of Grandeur
Peyk-i Tıcaret	Satellite of Trade
Peyk-i Zafer	Satellite of Victory
Podgorice	City on the river Donau, now Podgorica
Preveze	Turkish city, now Greek Prevese

Rehber	Guide
Refkat	Escort
Rehber-i Tevfik	Divine Guidance
Reşadiye	Named after Sultan Resad (1909-1918)
Resit Paşa	Reformist Ottoman minister of the mid-nineteenth century
Rodos	Rhodes
Rusçuk	City on the River Donau, now Russe in Bulgaria

Şadiye	The Happy One
Sagir	Small
Şahab	Shooting Star
Sahın	Falcon
Sahın-i Derya	Falcon of the Sea
Sahır	Vigilant
Saik-i Sadi	Sender of Joy
Sakiz	Greek island of Chios
Samsun	Turkish city on the Black Sea
Şanaver	Messenger of Glory
Sark	East
Şat	The River Tigris
Satvet	Might
Seddülbahir	Hellespont
Seham	Arrow
Selanik	Greek city of Saloniki
Selimiye	Named after Sultan Selim (1789-1807)
Selmanpak	Village on the River Tigris
Semendire	City on the river Donau
Sems	Sun
Seref Nüma	Guide to Honour
Şerıfıye	The Honourable One
Servet	Treasure
Şevket Nüma	Guide to Majesty
Seyf	Sword
Seyfı	Swordfish
Seyf-i Bahri	Sword of the Sea
Seyyad	Wanderer
Seyyar	Travel
Sılıstre	City on the River Donau, now Silistran in Bulgaria
Sinop	Turkish city on the Black Sea
Şipka	Pass in the Balkan mountains
Sivrihisar	Old Ottoman castle
Söğütlü	Birthplace of Sultan Osman I
Suda	Bay on Crete
Suhulet	Facility/Ease
Sultaniye	Belonging to the Sultan (ie the Sultan's yacht)
Sultan Osman-i Evvel	
	Sultan Osman I (1288-1326)
Sünne	City on the River Donau, now in Romania

Taif	City in Arabia
Talia	Turkish city
Taşköpru	Turkish city
Taşoz	Greek island of Thasos
Tayyar	Flyer
Timsah	Crocodile

Tir-i Bahri	Bird of the Sea
Tir-i Zafer	Bird of Victory
Tirimüjgan	Named after the mother of Sultan Abdülhamid II
Tokad	Turkish city
Torgud Reis	Ottoman admiral of the sixteenth century
Trablusgrab/Trablus	Tripolis
Trabzon	Turkish city on the Black Sea
Tuna	River Donau
Urfa	Turkish city
Utarit	Mercury (planet)
Varna	Bulgarian city on the Black Sea
Vasita-i Ticaret	Trader
Yadigar-i Millet	Gift of the Nation
Yarhisar	Turkish city
Yavuz Sultan Selim	Named after Sultan Selim the Brave
Yenikapi	'New Gate' — one of the gates of İstanbul
Yıldız	Star
Yozgat	Turkish city
Yunus	Dolphin
Ziver-i Derya	Wolf of the Sea
Zuhaf	Zouave

Bibliography

Anderson, R C, *Naval Wars in the Levant 1559-1853* Liverpool 1952

Bleeck-Schlombach *Mit den Siegesfahnen an den Dardanellen und Gallipoli*

Bullock, D L, *Allenby's War* London 1988

Chandler, S, *A Diary of Exploits with Submarine E11* London 1919

De Nogales, R, *Vier Jahre unter dem Halbmond* Berlin 1925

Euringer, R, *Vortrupp 'Pascha'* Hamburg 1937

Fetzer, D, *Aus dem thessalischen Feldzug 1897* Leipzig 1898

Greger, R, *Die russische Flotte im ersten Weltkrieg* Munich 1976

Güleryüz, A, *Die Osmanische Marine* Hamburg 1988

Hope, S, *Gallipoli Revisited* London 1934

Hütteroth, W-D, *Türkei* Darmstadt 1982

Kannengiesser, H, *Gallipoli* Berlin 1927

Kessler, Otto, *Balkanbrand 1912–1913* Leipzig 1913

Kettner, H, *Vom Golden Tor zum Golden Horn* Berlin 1916

Levenkuehn, P, *Posten auf ewiger Wacht* Essen 1937

Lochner, R K, *Die Kaperfahrten des kl. Kreuzers* Emden Munich 1980

Löding, D, *Balkanpolitik 1912–14* Hamburg 1969

Lorey, D H, *Der Krieg in den türkischen Gewässern* Berlin 1938

Ludwig, E, *Die Fahrten der* Göben *und* Breslau Berlin 1916

Mäkela, M E, *Auf den Spuren der* Goeben Munich 1979

Malade, T, *Von Amiens bis Aleppo* Munich 1930

Melzig, H, *Kamal Atatürk* Frankfurt 1937

Neulen, H W, *Feldgrau in Jerusalem* Munich 1991

Nunn, W, *Tigris Gunboats* London 1932

Okay, K, *Enver Pasa* Berlin 1935

Plowman, H, *Diary 1915* (unpublished typescript by a crew member of AE 2)

Rüstow, W, *Der Orientalische Krieg 1877–78* Zürich 1878

Souchon, Admiral, *Auf Grosser Fahrt* Bremen 1939

Valentiner, M, *Der Schrecken der Meere* Leipzig 1931

Von Gleich, G, *Vom Balkan nach Bagdad* Berlin 1921

Von Moltke, H, *Unter dem Halbmond* Stuttgart 1984

Von Moltke, H, *Der russisch-türkische Feldzug 1828–29* Berlin 1877

Von Sanders, L, *Fünf Jahre Türkei* Berlin 1920

Von Sarauw, C, *Der russisch-türkische Krieg 1877* Leipzig 1879

Von Schoen, W, *Die Hölle von Gallipoli* Berlin 1937

Von Westarp, E J, *Unter Halbmond und Sonne* Berlin 1913

Wheat, J, *Diary 1914-1918* (unpublished typescript by a crew member of E11)

Wilson, M, *Destination Dardanelles* London 1988

Witthöft, H J, *Kurs Levante* Herford 1989

A large number of official and semi-official publications by the Historical Branch of the Turkish General Staff and by the Turkish Navy and Army represent the basic source material for all studies of the Ottoman Navy.

Index

Note: Ships are Ottoman unless other nationalities are indicated.

Page numbers in italics refer to illustrations.

Abbreviations: F/M=Field Marshal; s/m=submarine; V/A=Vice Admiral.